Portraits of Labor Market Exclusion

DIRECTIONS IN DEVELOPMENT
Human Development

Portraits of Labor Market Exclusion

Ramya Sundaram, Ulrich Hoerning, Natasha de Andrade Falcão,
Natalia Millán, Carla Tokman, and Michele Zini

WORLD BANK GROUP

Contents

Boxes

Figures

Tables

Portraits of Labor Market Exclusion • http://dx.doi.org/10.1596/978-1-4648-0539-4

Acknowledgments

This report was produced by a World Bank team co-led by Ramya Sundaram (Senior Economist) and Ulrich Hoerning (Senior Social Protection Economist), and included Natasha de Andrade Falcão (Consultant), Natalia Millán (Consultant), Carla Tokman (Consultant), and Michele Zini (Social Protection Economist). The team thanks Romain Falloux, Aylin Isik-Dikmelik, Sandor Karacsony, Matteo Morgandi, Gady Saiovici, Victoria Strokova, and Frieda Vandeninden for their contributions and advice. Carmen Laurente and Sreypov Tep provided excellent assistance to the team.

This report is a joint World Bank and European Commission product and would not have been possible without the financial and technical support of the European Commission's Directorate General of Employment, Social Affairs, and Inclusion. Lieve Fransen (Director for Social Policy and Europe 2020), Bérengère Steppé (Policy Officer, Social Services and Active Inclusion), and Istvan Vanyolos (Policy Officer, Active Inclusion of Disadvantaged Groups, Fight Against Poverty) led the efforts from the Directorate for Employment, Social Affairs, and Inclusion's side. From the European Social Funds Country Units, the team thanks Marcia Kammitsi (F.3—Greece), Ventsislav Petrov (F.5—Bulgaria), Laurent Sens (E.5—Lithuania), Ina Sesciliene (E.5—Lithuania), Sirje Sepp (E.5—Estonia), Katalin Szatmari (E.5—Hungary), George Taskoudis (F.3—Greece), and Dana Verbal (F.5—Romania) for comments and guidance. From the Horizontal Units, the authors thank Nicholas Costello (D.1), Isabel Engsted-Maquet (A.2), Kornelia Kozovska (D.1), Panagiota Stamatiou (D.2), Céline Thevenot (A.2), and Valdis Zagorskis (D.3) for comments and guidance. From the European Commission Representative Office, the authors thank Ms. Katrin Hoovelson (European Union Representative Office, Talinn), and Ms. Liliána Zúgó (European Union Representative Office, Budapest).

Overall guidance on the World Bank side was provided by Omar Arias (Human Development Economics Sector Manager, Europe and Central Asia), Elisabetta Campanelli (Country Manager for Hungary and Romania, World Bank), Xavier Devictor (Country Manager for Poland, Latvia, Lithuania, and Estonia), Kathy Lindert (former Social Protection Sector Manager, Europe and Central Asia, and currently Sector Leader, Latin American and Caribbean Region), Andrew Mason (Social Protection Sector Manager, Europe and Central Asia), Mamta Murthi (Country Director for Central Europe and the

Baltic Countries), Ana Revenga (former Director of Human Development, Europe and Central Asia), Dirk Reinermann (Program Manager for Southern Europe Countries), Markus Repnik (Country Manager for Bulgaria, Czech Republic, and Slovak Republic, World Bank), and Alberto Rodriguez (Acting Director, Europe and Central Asia).

Peer-review comments were received at different stages from Zeljko Bogetic (Lead Economist and Country Sector Coordinator for Western Balkans, World Bank); Maria Davalos (Economist, World Bank), Doerte Doemeland (Senior Economist, World Bank); Richard Florescu (Senior Operations Officer, World Bank); Corina Grigore (Analyst, World Bank); Herwig Immervoll (Senior Economist, Head of Employment-Oriented Social Policies, Organisation for Economic Co-operation and Development); Roumeen Islam (Economic Advisor, World Bank); Arvo Kuddo (Senior Labor Economist, World Bank); Kathy Lindert; Edmundo Murrugarra (Senior Social Protection Economist, World Bank); Dena Ringold (Lead Economist, World Bank); Francis Rowe (Senior Economist, World Bank); and Bérengère Steppé. The editor was Elizabeth Schwinn.

The team benefitted from extensive interaction and guidance from officials representing the governments of the countries covered in this study. In particular, the team thanks the following counterparts:

- **Government of Bulgaria.** From the Ministry of Labour and Social Policy: Elka Dimitrova (Director of Labour Market Policy and Labour Migration Directorate), Natalia Efremova (Director General of the Managing Authority of the Operational Program, Human Resources Development), Emil Miroslavov (Director of Labour Law, Social Security, and Working Conditions), and Eleonora Pachedzieva (Director of Policy for People with Disabilities, Equal Opportunities and Social Assistance). From the National Employment Agency, Asen Angelov (Executive Director). From the Ministry of Finance, Marinela Petrova (Director of Economic and Financial Policy Directorate).

- **Government of Estonia.** Nele Gerberson (Ministry of Social Affairs); Karin Kuum (Ministry of Social Affairs); Pille Liimal (Estonian Unemployment Insurance Fund—Töötukassa); Ülle Marksoo (Ministry of Social Affairs); Mariliis Niidla (Estonian Unemployment Insurance Fund—Töötukassa); Elo Piksarv (Ministry of Finance); Merlin Tatrik (Ministry of Social Affairs); and Kristi Villsaar (Estonian Unemployment Insurance Fund—Töötukassa).

- **Government of Greece.** Kostas Geormas (Deputy Head of Department of Social Protection—Registry of Social Economy, Ministry of Labour, Social Security and Welfare), Katerina Giantsiou (European Social Coordination and Monitoring Authority, Ministry of Labour, Social Security and Welfare), Stella Graikioti (Department of Social Protection—Registry of Social Economy), Kalliopi Kastani (Head of the Social Protection and Social Cohesion Directorate, Ministry of Labour, Social Security and Welfare), Meropi Komninou (Head of Special Unit Planning and Management,

Operational Programme Human Resources Development, Ministry of Labour, Social Security and Welfare), Georgios Nerantzis (Deputy Head of the Migrant's Employment Unit—Employment Directorate, Ministry of Labour, Social Security and Welfare), Panagiotis Oikonomakos (Head of the Managing Authority of Operational Programme, Human Resources Development, Ministry of Labour, Social Security and Welfare).

- **Government of Hungary.** Irén Busch (National Labour Office), Noémi Danajka (Ministry for National Economy, Head of Department, Department for Employment Programmes), Gábor Horváth (Ministry for National Economy), Csilla Lajosné Sárközi (Ministry of Human Resources), Anna Marosi (Ministry for National Economy), Zsolt Ruszkai (Ministry for National Economy), Norbert Takács (Ministry of Human Resources), and Zsófia Tóth (Ministry of Human Resources).

- **Government of Lithuania.** Evaldas Bacevičius (Head of European Union Division, Ministry of Social Security and Labour), Lina Charašauskaite (Senior Specialist, Equal Opportunity Division, Ministry of Social Security and Labour), Inga Liubertė (Head of Labour Resources Division, Lithuanian Labour Exchange), Alvydas Puodžiukas (Deputy Director, Lithuanian Labour Exchange), Egle Radišauskienė (Deputy Director Labour Department, Ministry of Social Security and Labour), Kristina Ščerbickaitė (Senior Specialist, Labour Market Division, Ministry of Social Security and Labour), and Daiva Zabarauskienė (Deputy Head, Equal Opportunity Division, Ministry of Social Security and Labour).

- **Government of Romania.** Lăcrămioara Corcheş (Ministry of Labour, Family, Social Protection, and the Elderly) and team, as well as several representatives of the National Agency for Employment (Agentia Nationala pentru Ocuparé Fortei de Munca).

About the Authors

Ramya Sundaram is a senior economist in the Social Protection and Labor Global Practice of the World Bank. She currently leads a project in Greece, assisting the government in setting up a last-resort social assistance program; and co-leads a review of Greece's social welfare system. During previous engagements with the World Bank, Ms. Sundaram has advised governments on labor market and activation systems, including profiling of those excluded from the labor market. She has also advised governments on how to measure and alleviate poverty; on policy options to tackle in-work poverty; on inequality and inclusion; and on skill mismatches and tackling unemployment. She was previously an assistant professor of economics at the University of Arizona and has also worked on supply chain management at Procter & Gamble. She has a bachelor of science in industrial engineering and a master's in business administration. Ms. Sundaram also holds a PhD in economics from the University of Pennsylvania.

Ulrich Hoerning is a senior social protection economist in the Europe and Central Asia team of the Social Protection and Labor Global Practice of the World Bank. In his work, he focuses on conceptual and operational issues of labor market and activation systems as well as on profiling of labor market exclusion. Additional project work has focused on the buildup of a social assistance pilot program in a Eurozone program country. During previous work engagements with the World Bank, Mr. Hoerning worked on the Bolsa Familia program in large Brazilian municipalities. Before joining the World Bank full time in 2013, Mr. Hoerning acted as head of administrative reform in Mannheim, Germany; as a strategy and planning officer in the minister's staff at the Federal Ministry of Finance of Germany; and as a senior project manager at an international strategy consulting firm. Mr. Hoerning holds a diploma in international economics from the University of Tuebingen in Germany and a master's in public administration from Harvard Kennedy School of Government.

Natasha de Andrade Falcão works for the Education Division at the Inter-American Development Bank, where she supports research activities on educational quality in Chile, Colombia, and Peru. Previously, she worked as a consultant in the Human Development Unit for the Europe and Central Asia Region of the World Bank. Her research interests include returns to education, human capital externalities, poverty, and inequality. She holds a PhD and a master's in economics from Universidade Federal de Pernambuco in Brazil.

Natalia Millán is a consultant in the Social Protection and Labor Global Practice of the World Bank, where her work has focused on the design and assessment of social safety nets and analysis of labor markets, skills, and tertiary education. In the past, she has been a senior adviser to the Minister of Planning in Chile, a researcher at Fedesarrollo—Colombia's leading think tank—and an adviser at the National Planning Department in Colombia. She holds a master's in public affairs from the Woodrow Wilson School at Princeton University and a bachelor of arts in economics from Wesleyan University in Middletown, Connecticut.

Carla Tokman is an economist who has worked as a consultant in the World Bank's Social Protection and Labor Global Practice. She currently also works for the Harvard Kennedy School's Center for International Development Growth Lab. She holds a master's in economic policy from Boston University and a bachelor's in economics from the University of Chile. Between 2004 and 2008, she worked in Chile at the Budget Office in the Ministry of Finance, focusing on fiscal budget expenditure, structural balance rules, and education.

Michele Zini is an economist with the World Bank's Social Protection and Labor Global Practice, working on European and Central Asian countries. Previously, he worked in the Social Protection and Labor Unit of the World Bank's East Asia Region. He is a graduate of Harvard's Kennedy School of Government with a master of public administration in international development. He also holds a master of science from the London School of Economics and a bachelor's degree in economics from the University of Bologna. Between 2007 and 2009, he worked in South Africa at the World Bank's country office, focusing on public services delivery reforms, labor market issues, and macroeconomic analysis. Before that, he worked as an economic consultant for London Economics, an economic consultancy firm in London that carries out economic studies for the European Commission and the British government.

Abbreviations

ALMP	active labor market policy
BIC	Bayesian indicator criterion
EC	European Commission
EC DG EMPL	European Commission, Directorate General Employment, Social Affairs and Inclusion
EEAG	European Economic Advisory Group
ESF	European Social Fund
ESF OP	European Social Fund Operational Programme
ESSPROS	European System of integrated Social PROtection Statistics
EU	European Union
EU-LFS	European Union Labor Force Survey
EU-SILC	European Union Statistics of Income and Living Conditions
GMI	guaranteed minimum income
ILO	International Labour Organization
ISCED	International Standard Classification of Education
LCA	latent class analysis
LFPR	labor force participation rate
LLE	Lithuanian Labor Exchange
LMP	labor market policy
MLFSPE	Ministry of Labor, Family, Social Protection, and the Elderly (Romania)
NEA	National Employment Agency (Romania)
NEET	not in employment, education, or training
OAED	Organismou Apascholisis Ergatikou Dynamikou (Greek Public Employment Services)
OECD	Organisation for Economic Co-operation and Development
PES	public employment service
RAS	reimbursable advisory service
TVET	technical and vocational education and training
UIF	Unemployment Insurance Fund
UNESCO	United Nations Educational, Scientific and Cultural Organization

CHAPTER 1

Introduction

Why and What

The financial crisis that hit the global market in the middle of 2008 gave way to the sharpest contraction of the European economies since the Great Depression. Since then, the economies have slowly recovered, but unemployment has continued to rise, reaching 11 percent in 2013, up from 7.1 percent in 2008.

The economy of the European Union shrank 4.5 percent in 2009, the largest reduction in its GDP since the Union's creation. Furthermore, for the European Union as a whole, long-term unemployment among 15- to 64-year-olds increased from 37.2 percent in 2008 to 47.5 percent of total unemployment in 2013. In several countries more than half of those unemployed are long-term unemployed, that is, they have been looking for jobs for more than 12 months. In Greece and Bulgaria the share of long-term unemployed in 2013 was 67.5 percent and 57.3 percent, respectively. Youth unemployment, on the other hand, has increased almost 8 percentage points since 2008, reaching 23.3 percent in 2013 in the EU-28 countries. In Bulgaria, Romania, and Hungary, around a fourth of 15- to 24-year-olds are unemployed; in Greece close to 60 percent of youth were unemployed in 2013.

Long spells of unemployment expose individuals to impoverishment. They can also lead to deterioration of skills and detachment from the labor market. Youth unemployment is particularly concerning as it risks damaging longer-term employment prospects for young people, leading them to face higher risks of exclusion and poverty. Youth unemployment also has growth implications as a generation of educated and productive people are not working at their potential. Finally, very high levels of youth unemployment for long periods of time can become a threat to social stability.

Another issue of concern is the demographic change in Europe. As the baby boomers' cohort approaches retirement, the younger cohorts entering the labor market are smaller due to the low birth rate of the past decades. The results are a population that is older, and an active labor force that is shrinking over time.

This demographic change, coupled with high youth unemployment, will have significant effects on Europe's fiscal balances at a time when the size of the older generations in need of adequate pensions and health care continues to increase.

With government budgets under stress and an environment marked by demographic changes, using the labor force to its full potential is key. Knowing what the out-of-work population looks like is fundamental to a holistic approach to policy making with respect to the inactive and the unemployed. To this end, this report presents "profiles" or "portraits" of individuals who have no or limited labor market attachment. The profiles are derived using the latest available European Union Statistics of Income and Living Conditions (EU-SILC) surveys and focus on those who defined themselves as unemployed, retired, or inactive at the time of the survey.

The portraits attach stories to statistics. They identify distinct groups of individuals who are the potential clients of income—and employment—support policies by examining detailed labor market, demographic, and social circumstances. The analysis is a pragmatic way of looking at individuals through the lenses of both poverty/welfare status and labor market indicators. In a sense it combines labor market analysis and poverty profiling.

Portraits of Labor Market Exclusion analysis takes a comprehensive view of policy making, focusing on both the labor market attachment of a country's out-of-work population and the social assistance package and poverty profile of the same segment of the population. Through this examination of the characteristics of different subgroups, this analysis aims to contribute policy-relevant information about the social and economic risks these subgroups are facing, and on the barriers that hold back their labor market integration. In doing so, it can facilitate effective formulation and targeting of policies that seek to alleviate these barriers. In this sense, the portraits help move the dialogue on activation from a labor market-centric view to a broader dialogue that includes social policy as a whole. Figure 1.1 provides a pictorial view of the different government agencies and activities that address labor market and social exclusion issues. This is an important shift; for instance, social protection programs, such as family benefits and maternity benefits, and broader social policy issues such as retirement ages, often have a great impact on who remains inactive. By creating a space for dialogue between citizens and between different public organizations (social, labor, health, child care, and so on) who normally do not speak to each other, analyses such as *Portraits of Labor Market Exclusion* take additional steps toward more successful labor market inclusion of citizens.

Specifically, the report presents portraits of the out-of-work population of six countries (Bulgaria, Estonia, Greece, Hungary, Lithuania, and Romania) in terms of distance from the labor market, human capital, and labor supply conditions, as well as demographic conditions. The analysis relies on the EU-SILC surveys for the years 2007–11.[1] Latent class analysis methodology allows multidimensional profiling of the out-of-work population, and identifies classes or groups of out-of-work individuals that are as homogeneous as possible within each class according to a set of observable characteristics, and as distant as possible between

Figure 1.1 Labor Market and Social Exclusion, Government Activities

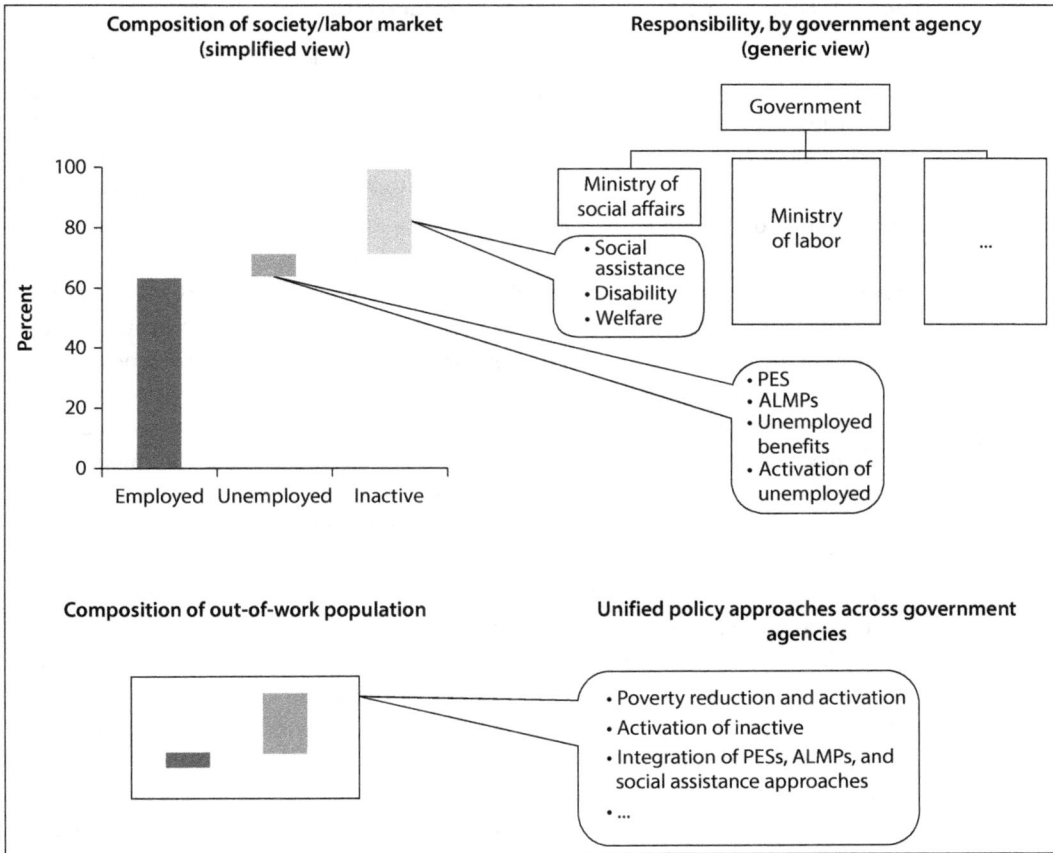

Source: World Bank staff assessment 2014.

classes. In so doing, this analysis provides a much richer glimpse of the very different barriers to labor market integration that these various groups experience, considerably augmenting the limited amount of information contained in traditional descriptive statistics.

Box 1.1 tries to provide an intuitive understanding of latent class methodology, while box 1.2 explains the statistical underpinning behind this methodology. The emerging profiles can then be contrasted with the design and targeting of current activation policies, to identify potential gaps and to enhance their design features.

The identification of latent classes relies on a number of "indicator variables" to capture different "symptoms" of an overall latent condition (in this case, joblessness). The challenge in such models is to identify a discrete number of variables that can best depict the heterogeneity among individuals. In this report, two or three sets of categorical variables were selected to show the extent

Box 1.1 Latent Class Analysis (LCA): A Sweet and Intuitive Example

LCA is used in several fields, including the medical profession and behavioral sciences, to identify hidden and underlying subgroups of individuals that share observable characteristics within a population of interest. To intuitively understand how this statistical methodology works, a simple example may help. WeMakeTheWorldHappier Ltd., a producer of "all things sweet," is interested in better understanding patterns behind the consumption of its products (ice cream, chocolate, and so on) among children and early teenagers so that it can more efficiently target marketing campaigns. Also, for prevention purposes, policy makers are trying to identify specific groups at risk of obesity or diabetes that are not noticeable to the naked eye. Now assume that individual surveys were conducted among a diverse group of children that included data on ice cream and chocolate consumption. Think of these data as "indicators," the noticeable symptoms of an underlying vulnerability or disease. For simplicity, let's say that individuals were asked about the frequency of their chocolate and ice cream (ab)use; each activity could be categorized as frequent/regular (I sneak to the fridge once dad and mom are asleep), occasional (unfortunately the fridge is usually locked at night), or nonexistent (we have actually never seen such a child but we are told they exist).

Furthermore, the survey collected information on certain main demographic characteristics (such as gender—we are told women enjoy chocolate more than men—age, and having siblings), and early-stage behaviors that are typically associated with high consumption of sweets (regular attendance at friends' parties, spending lots of time at grandparents' house(s), and regularly playing sports or not). Think of these as the main correlates of a given condition (for example, chocolate addiction); in LCA jargon, these are the active covariates. Finally, the survey includes other demographic information such as economic and social background, race, nationality, and so forth; in LCA terminology, these are the inactive covariates that will simply help describe the unobservable groups.

By running LCA on the dataset, each child surveyed will be placed in a specific group (or latent cluster), based on his or her probability of answering the sweets-consumption questions in a certain way given his/her active covariates (which, in this example, are the main demographic and behavioral characteristics). The number of groups obtained is not predetermined and will vary based on how well a certain model fits the available data; however, the groups are such that every individual can be assigned to one group only (the groups are mutually exclusive) and all observations will be assigned to a group (collectively exhaustive). Each group can then be further analyzed along additional demographic lines (the inactive covariates) that do not affect the fit of the model but allow us to get a more detailed profile of candy-devourers.

For illustrative purposes, LCA methodology applied to the described dataset will construct unobservable clusters of children that, given certain features, have the same probability of a certain pattern of consumption. For instance, LCA might detect the existence of a cluster of "will-eat-ice-cream-in-my-sleep" young children of both genders, who are very active, mostly started binge-eating ice-cream at their grandparents', and attend the birthday parties of every child in town (even if they are not invited). LCA might also

box continues next page

Box 1.1 Latent Class Analysis (LCA): A Sweet and Intuitive Example *(continued)*

define a smaller group of young chocolate-addicted girls who do well in school and have one or two older brothers who are often mean to them. It might identify a group of "candy monsters" (undiscriminating candy eaters), who consume as much chocolate and ice cream as they can, often stash goodies under their beds, live in open defiance of their desperate parents, are not very active in sports, and so on. The analysis could identify more clusters, each of which would differ from the others in at least one dimension. Knowledge of these groups would allow for the identification of early–warning signs of candy addiction, and would allow parents to take preventive measures. Note to kids: you may want to hide this research.

Source: Adapted from LCA Applied Example, The Methodology Center, Penn State University.

Box 1.2 The Statistical Basis behind Latent Class Analysis (LCA)

Descriptive statistics enable the illustration of the heterogeneity of a particular population in a limited number of dimensions. Without other measures, it is challenging to synthetically describe individuals in the population according to their prevailing characteristics.

The main purpose of LCA is to identify an organizing principle for a complex array of variables. This latent variable model uses "categorical observed variables, representing characteristics, behaviors, symptoms, or the like as the basis for organizing people into two or more meaningful homogeneous subgroups" (Collins and Lanza 2010). Formally, LCA enables a characterization of a categorical latent (unobserved) variable, starting from an analysis of the relationships among several observed variables (named "indicators"), using a maximum likelihood estimation method. The estimation model used in this study also includes covariates, which are "variables that may be used to describe or predict (rather than to define or measure) the latent classes and if active, to reduce classification error" (Vermunt and Magidson 2005).

Through LCA, individuals are scored according to the likelihood of belonging to each of the computed latent classes, and then assigned to the class to which they have the highest posterior probability of belonging (modal assignment) given their observed characteristics. Statistics such as the Bayesian Indicator Criterion (BIC) are used to identify the most appropriate number of classes, that is, the model that has on average the highest likelihood of predicting class membership for all individuals in the given sample.

A fundamental assumption underlying LCA is that of local independence, which implies that each of the chosen indicator variables is related to the others uniquely through the latent class membership, and a random error. Advanced computational techniques allow detecting and, in part, controlling for the correlation between the residuals of selected indicators, thus enabling the use of the available information to construct categories.

Source: Adapted from Collins and Lanza 2010; Vermunt and Magidson 2005.

of labor market distance and to capture some of the main factors that can affect employment on the supply side: labor supply conditions (household-level incentives to work and physical ability to take part in daily activities (or work)), prior work experience, and human capital (box 1.3 explains the definitions of labor market status and education levels used in this report).

In addition to indicators, the model includes active covariates, which are used to improve the classification of individuals into each class. Demographic variables that are normally used to disaggregate labor market outcomes, like age, gender, highest educational level achieved, and degree of urbanization, are typically active covariates.

Once the latent classes have been defined, inactive covariates that were not included in the model can be used to characterize the individuals in each class

---

Box 1.3 Definition of Labor Market Status and Educational Levels Used in This Report

In order to categorize the out-of-work population according to labor market status, we first use the European Union Statistics of Income and Living Conditions (EU-SILC) household register variable corresponding to the self-defined current activity at the time of the household interview. This variable allows for the classification of individuals as employed, unemployed, retired, or "other inactive." Next, the variable from the personal questionnaire, in which individuals again self-define their labor market status, is used to further classify the inactive into disabled or "other inactive."[a] The EU-SILC self-defined employed status differs from the standard ILO (International Labor Organization) definition used in European Union Labor Force Surveys (EU-LFS), which classifies as employed anyone who has worked for at least one hour or had a job from which they were temporarily absent during the reference period. Self-reporting of employment may lead to a larger out-of-work population, to the extent that individuals working very few hours may not perceive themselves as employed. In the same vein, the EU-SILC definition of unemployment also differs from the standard ILO definition, which restricts the unemployed to those who have actively searched for work during the reference period (usually two to four weeks) and who are also available for work in the near future.[b] Moreover, it is worth noting that because disability status (that is, permanently disabled or unfit for work) is also based on self-perception, individuals who self-report as disabled do not necessarily also report limitations on their activities due to health problems, and vice versa. Finally, in this report, individuals who self-define as unemployed are further classified as (short-term) unemployed and long-term unemployed. Specifically, individuals who report having been unemployed for the calendar year prior to the survey year are considered to be long-term unemployed.

As regards the education variable used as an active covariate, this variable is divided into three main categories: primary, secondary, and tertiary. Primary education refers to individuals who have completed at most International Standard Classification of Education (ISCED[c]) level 1; secondary refers to individuals who have completed at most ISCED level 3

box continues next page

Box 1.3 **Definition of Labor Market Status and Educational Levels Used in this Report** *(continued)*

(upper secondary school) and tertiary refers to individuals who have completed ISCED levels 5 or 6 (the first or second stages of tertiary education).[d] In order to provide greater detail on educational attainment, education levels are further disaggregated in the list of covariates, this time among the six ISCED levels: distinguishing between no education or some primary education; primary; lower secondary; upper secondary; postsecondary; and tertiary (levels 5 and 6 are combined into one level due to a very low number of out-of-work individuals with level 6 education, that is, doctoral degrees). Unfortunately, EU-SILC data do not provide further detail regarding the qualification status of individuals, such as vocational versus general education, or any training or certificates received.

Source: World Bank staff analysis 2014.

a. Individuals ages 16–24 years who self-classified as students were excluded from the sample.

b. This explains why a variable indicating whether or not the individual has been engaged in an active job search is also included as part of the inactive covariates that describe the clusters.

c. ISCED refers to the International Standard Classification of Education, developed by UNESCO (United Nations Educational, Scientific and Cultural Organization) in order to facilitate the comparison of education statistics and indicators across countries.

d. The educational classification used in EU-SILC data is the International Standard Classification of Education (ISCED1997), coded according to the seven ISCED-97 categories.

and the households in which they live in great detail. Examples of these covariates are variables that indicate household welfare conditions, such as income quintile, labor market status of a partner and home ownership, and variables for household demographics, such as household size and whether the household has children younger than six years old, among others.

The resulting groups are then labeled according to their main distinguishing characteristics. Given that a large number of characteristics describe each group, often a few salient ones are used to name the group. In short, the labeling of groups can be considered more of an art than a science. However, the names do represent an important starting point in the design of social policies and in the prioritization of activation policies.

The overarching objective of the portraits analysis is to help reduce the risk of poverty and/or labor market exclusion by strengthening the evidence base for designing and targeting income support, activation, and employment support policies. In this sense, LCA is not an operational tool, but one that can guide policy making.

Nevertheless, "without demand, everything is nothing in the labor market." In economies where there is little or no growth, it is difficult to create demand for workers in an open labor market, even with the most sophisticated profiling and targeting of activation policies. This is not to say that labor supply side interventions like training, activation, or payment of benefits (linked to activation) would be useless, but they can only do so much to "grease the wheels" of the labor market. Linkage of activation with job creation and local economic development policies, enterprise growth policies, and overall market conditions is critical.

A second caveat arises from the use of survey data from 2011. The suggestions for future policy discussions have been derived from the analysis of the EU-SILC data from 2007 to 2011. Since that time, general economic development and country-level policy reforms might have improved the labor market integration and activation of some of the groups data sets. The World Bank team remains willing to use national EU-SILC data sets to update analysis and provide more up-to-date results (provided additional reimbursement advisory services (RAS) or trust funds are available).

The report presents the analysis for six countries: Bulgaria, Estonia, Greece, Lithuania, Hungary and Romania. The current set of countries represents a pilot group for this first-time analysis. The priority for analysis in these countries was decided by the European Commission, Directorate General of Employment, Social Affairs and Inclusion (EC DG EMPL), in light of recent economic and labor market developments. The World Bank team contributed advice on the selection of countries. The country-specific reports provide a starting point to the discussion and the enrichment of the country-specific recommendation process of the European Semester. Table 1.1 presents some key statistics for the selected countries.

The *Portraits of Labor Market Exclusion* country analysis reports were written based on EU-SILC/Eurostat data according to a common methodology. See box 1.4 for a discussion of EU-SILC/Eurostat data limitations. After a first draft was submitted by the World Bank team, a first review with the respective EC DG EMPL Country Desk was conducted in Brussels. Following feedback, changes, and additions received from these meetings, a second draft of the report was presented and discussed during joint country missions of EC DG EMPL and the World Bank with the respective Member States. Joint country missions occurred on the following dates (all 2014): Bulgaria (January 23), Lithuania (March 13), Estonia (March 14), Romania (April 7), Greece (April 10), Hungary (April 25). During and after the joint country missions, Member States provided feedback and additional material for the reports.

Table 1.1 Key Statistics of Selected Countries, 2013

Country	Flag	Population (annual average, thousands)	Inactive Population (% of population ages 15–64 years)	GDP (millions of euro)	GDP per capita (euro)	GDP 2013/ GDP 2008
Bulgaria		7,242	31.6	39,940	5,500	0.98
Estonia		1,316	24.9	18,435	13,800	1.01
Greece		10,999	32.0	182,054	16,466*	0.77
Hungary		9,779	34.9	98,071	9,900	0.95
Lithuania		2,960	27.6	36,601	11,700	0.98
Romania		21,286	35.4	142,245	7,100	0.98

Source: Eurostat, except * WEO—World Economic Outlook.

**Box 1.4 Limitations of European Union Statistics of Income and Living
Conditions (EU-SILC) Data**

This report relies on 2011 harmonized EU-SILC data (published in 2013) in order to present
profiles of the out-of-work population according to their socioeconomic and labor market
characteristics. EU-SILC data, as opposed to European Union Labor Force Surveys (EU-LFS)
data, were chosen for this analysis because they provide more detailed information regarding
income; EU-LFS income data, on the other hand, are limited to labor earnings and do not provide information on income from benefits[a] or other sources. Having this more comprehensive
income information is useful for prioritizing interventions among the identified clusters
according to their risk of poverty, an important welfare dimension. Furthermore, EU-SILC data
allow for the identification of broad categories of benefits received, as well the percentage of
household income that can be attributable to benefits. Again, this type of information can be
instrumental in analyzing the current welfare situation of the out-of-work, as well as in formu-
lating active inclusion policies. Despite this comparative advantage of EU-SILC data, there are
some limitations to the data that are worth mentioning.

One limitation of EU-SILC data is that it does not result in the same official labor market
statistics that are reported by Eurostat using the EU-LFS surveys. There are several reasons
for this. First, the anonymized EU-SILC data provided by Eurostat relies on self-reported labor
market status, rather than the standard ILO definitions used by EU-LFS. Self-definition of
employment may overestimate the out-of-work population if individuals who work few hours
self-identify as inactive, and unemployment may be overestimated if individuals self-identify
as unemployed because of their willingness to work rather than their engagement in an active
job search and availability for work in the near future. While the individual EU-SILC country
questionnaires could allow for the calculation of official ILO labor market status, the May 2011
description of target variables provided by Eurostat suggests that only out-of-work individuals
below the official retirement age should be asked if they have been actively searching for a job.
Thus, unemployment may be underestimated among the population under 64 years of age
that has already reached retirement age. Another important difference between the two data
sources is the time horizon: The EU-SILC survey is conducted only at one point during the year,
whereas the EU-LFS survey is conducted continuously throughout the year. Lastly, the EU-LFS
survey includes individuals as young as 15, while EU-SILC only surveys individuals 16 years of
age and older in its personal questionnaire.

Unlike EU-LFS data, EU-SILC survey data also provide relatively little detail concerning the
educational status of individuals. In particular, the EU-SILC survey only allows for differentiation by highest ISCED level achieved. In contrast with the EU-LFS survey, no information
regarding vocational versus general education, field of study, or additional training or certifi-
cations is provided. More detailed knowledge regarding the qualifications of the out-of-work
would be useful for tailoring active labor market policies, especially those related to training.
Nonetheless, it is worth noting that even with a more detailed survey, sample limitations may
still generally preclude the labeling of clusters according to their educational status. In this
report, education was used in a cluster's label only if a clear pattern emerged, with the education status of its members visibly differentiated from that of other groups.

box continues next page

Box 1.4 Limitations of European Union Statistics of Income and Living Conditions (EU-SILC) Data *(continued)*

Another limitation of EU-SILC data concerns benefit data. The anonymized EU-SILC databases provided by Eurostat aggregate social benefits according to nine categories: old-age, survivor, family/child, unemployment, sickness, disability, social exclusion, housing, and education. While this categorization can be useful, it is nonetheless limited. On the one hand, "unemployment" and "old-age" benefits do not distinguish between social insurance and social assistance. This distinction would be helpful for evaluating the targeting of social benefits toward more socially disadvantaged groups. What is more, family/child benefits are not differentiated, for example, between child benefits and maternity leave. These two types of benefits can have profoundly different effects on female labor force participation. Differentiating between the two could also aid in further research on how benefits affect women's decisions to participate in the labor market. Perhaps in the future Eurostat could categorize individual EU-SILC country data regarding benefits in such a way that at least the contributory or social assistance nature of benefits can be identified.

Some of the profiles of the out-of-work, especially those that are most vulnerable due to low education levels, unemployment, and at-risk-of-poverty status, may comprise a significant portion of the Roma population. However, we can only arrive at this conclusion because of what is known about Roma from other sources. EU-SILC survey data do not include information regarding ethnicity.[b] Knowledge of which groups include Roma, and to what extent, can aid in prioritizing policies that aim toward Roma inclusion, including reaching out to their often isolated communities and addressing discrimination in the workforce. Information regarding ethnicity could aid in making the vulnerable situation of out-of-work Roma more visible, and even perhaps in eliminating stereotypes of Roma as not being interested in participating in the labor market and actively seeking work. As mentioned in this report, the integration of Roma in the labor market is not only a moral imperative but also smart economics in light of the aging populations and shrinking working-age populations among EU countries with significant Roma populations.

Finally, it is worth pointing out that latent class analysis benefits greatly from large sample sizes, as they allow for a larger number of clusters to be identified that can be differentiated from each other with a certain degree of statistical significance. A larger number of identified clusters can result in identified clusters that are more homogenous within themselves and more heterogeneous among each other. It is possible that with a significantly larger sample size, similar to that of the EU-LFS surveys,[c] a greater number of, and more importantly, more homogenous clusters of out-of-work population could be identified, allowing for the formulation of policies that are even more specifically tailored toward the activation potential and need faced by each group.

Source: World Bank staff analysis 2014.
a. The EU-LFS survey only includes information regarding whether or not unemployment benefits are received.
b. EU-LFS surveys also do not inquire about ethnicity.
c. Depending on the country, EU-LFS surveys can include 10 times more observations than EU-SILC surveys.

The report proceeds as follows: chapter 2 starts by presenting an overview of the general economic background and unemployment situation of the countries, followed by the main facts. The following chapters present *Portraits of Labor Market Exclusion* reports for each country separately.

Note

1. Years the survey is available differ among countries analyzed.

Portraits of Labor Market Exclusion

General Economic Background

After years of moderate growth, Europe was adversely impacted by the global financial crisis and has yet to fully recover. For the countries presented in this study, the period leading to the global financial crisis was one of high output growth. Bulgaria, Estonia, Lithuania, and Romania all grew at more than 6 percent on average from 2003 to 2007 (figure 2.1), more than twice the average rate of the region as a whole.

The timing and magnitude of the contraction that followed the crisis varied among the countries in the region. On average, the economies of the six countries analyzed contracted 8.5 percent during 2009. While Lithuania and Estonia recovered from the shock more quickly and have since experienced positive growth rates, postcrisis growth in Bulgaria, Hungary, and Romania has been more anemic, and has not reached pre-crisis growth levels. Greece, meanwhile, continued to contract through 2013, with GDP declining by almost 25 percent since the onset of the crisis.

As the crisis unraveled, unemployment rates deteriorated sharply. As unemployment rose, young workers were among the worst affected—an adverse situation that was observed in all six countries. Youth unemployment in Greece was a staggering 58 percent in 2012, and one-fourth of the 15-to-24 cohort remained without a job in Bulgaria and Hungary at the end of 2013.

A look at the unemployment rates disaggregated by gender shows that there is no common pattern among all the countries. For the average EU-28 member country prior to the crisis there was a difference of less than 1 percentage point between the unemployment rates of men and women, a difference that disappeared after 2009 (see figure 2.2). Greece is the only country where women had higher unemployment rates throughout the period, with gaps ranging from 6.3 to 9.5 percentage points.

One of the most worrying developments of the crisis is the significant increase in the share of long-term unemployed. In 2013, as shown in figure 2.3, more than

Figure 2.1 Annual Real GDP Growth, 2003–13
percent

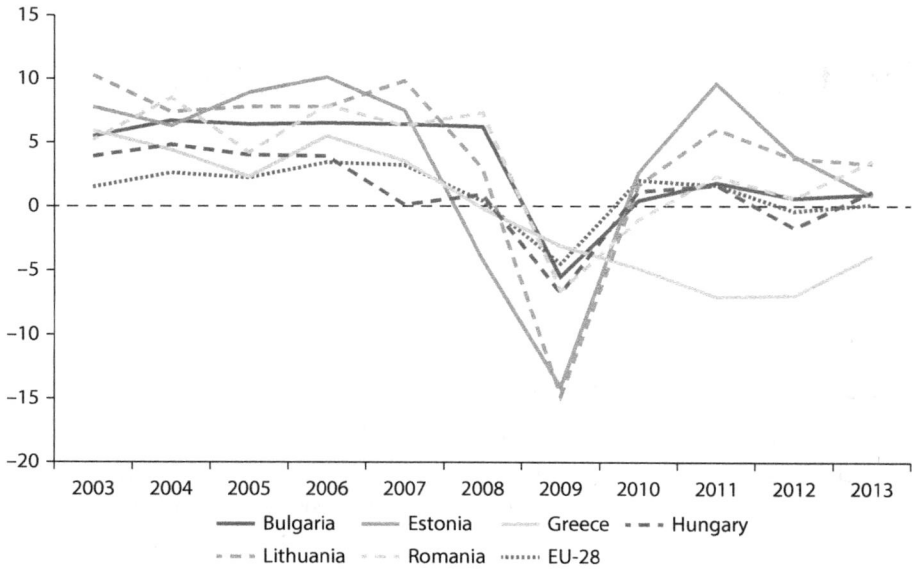

Source: Eurostat.

Figure 2.2 Gender Gap in Unemployment Rates, 2003–13
percent

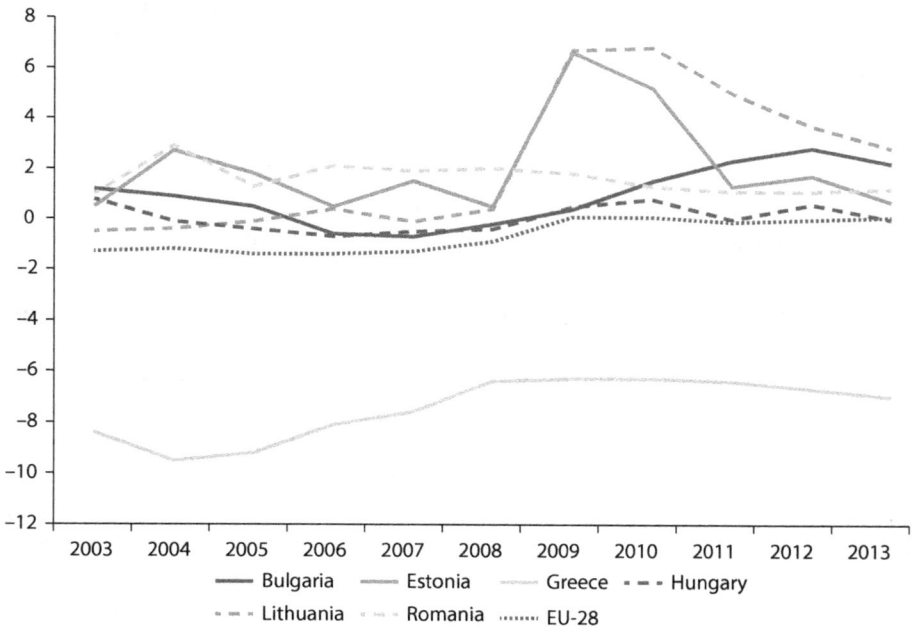

Source: Eurostat, EU-LFS.
Note: Gap is calculated by subtracting the female unemployment rate from the unemployment rate of males.

Figure 2.3 Long-Term Unemployment as a Share of Total Unemployment, 2003–13
percent

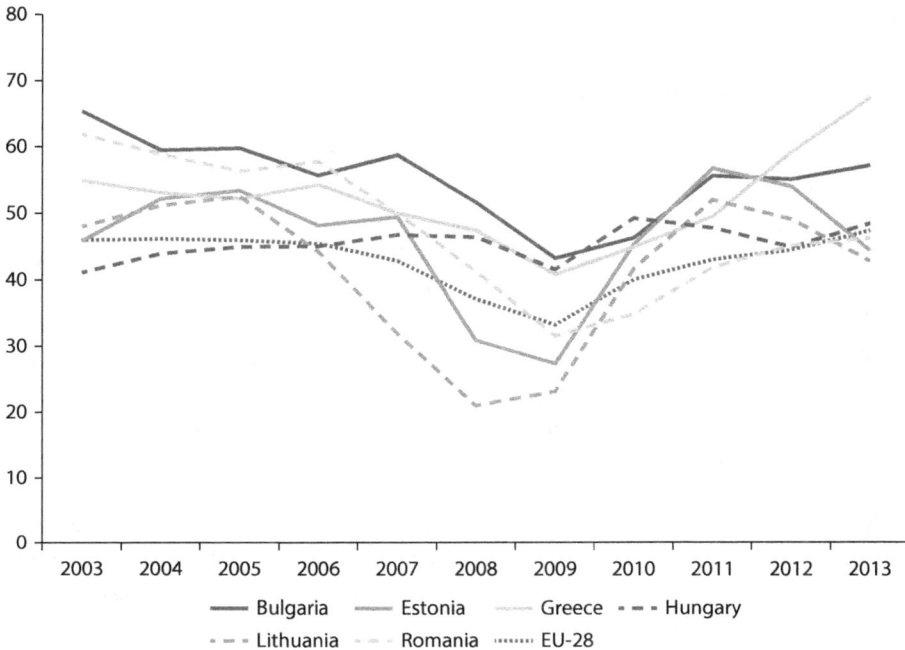

Source: Eurostat, EU-LFS.

47.5 percent of the unemployed had been looking for work for more than
12 months in the average EU-28 country. For Bulgaria and Greece, more than
half of the unemployed are long-term: 57.3 percent in Bulgaria and 67.5 percent
in Greece.

Employment levels also deteriorated following the crisis. The average employment rate for the EU-28 had been slowly rising and peaked at 65.7 percent in
2009; it had fallen to 64.1 by 2013. The fall in employment in some of the
countries studied was more pronounced. After six years of recession, employment in Greece had fallen more than ten percentage points, from 61.9 to
49.3 percent, from 2008 to 2013.

In summary, the global financial crisis impacted both output and employment outcomes in the EU region. While the magnitude and timing of the
crisis and subsequent recovery have varied in the countries studied, unemployment levels are still above pre-crisis levels. Of particular concern are the
increase in the share of long-term unemployment and the adverse labor situation that youth face. These, along with other key structural issues that have
emerged from the analysis of the European Union Statistics of Income and
Living Conditions (EU-SILC) data of the countries, are discussed in the
following section.

Stylized Issues Emerging from the Analysis

The analysis of the EU-SILC data using latent class methodology in this report focuses on the out-of-work among the working-age population (16- to 64-year-olds).[1] Only the working-age population is analyzed because labor activation options—the main policy focus of this note—are only viable for that segment of the population.

The total out-of-work population analyzed in this document has increased in five of the six countries studied (see figure 2.4). Estonia and Lithuania had the greatest increase in the out-of-work population, both increasing 33 percent from 2007 to 2011, but they had the smallest increase in terms of absolute number of individuals (55,000 and 152,000, respectively). In Greece this group increased almost 26 percent, by more than 550,000 people. Hungary had a small increase in the out-of-work population (25,000), but had the highest share of out-of-work in 2008 and second highest in 2011 (37 and 38 percent, respectively). Only in Romania did the out-of-work population decrease (2.5 percent or 106,000), but it remains a large share of the total working-age population (31.2 percent).

Such increases in the out-of-work population are of great concern, particularly given the rapidly aging populations in these countries. As expenditures on pension and disability benefits are expected to continue to grow, increasing labor force participation rates and addressing the barriers to employment of the various groups emerge as priorities to sustain the economic recovery and overall standards of living.

Addressing barriers to employment effectively requires first understanding the distinct groups that make up the out-of-work population. This report determines

Figure 2.4 Out-of-Work Population and Share of Total Working-Age Population, 2007/2008 and 2011

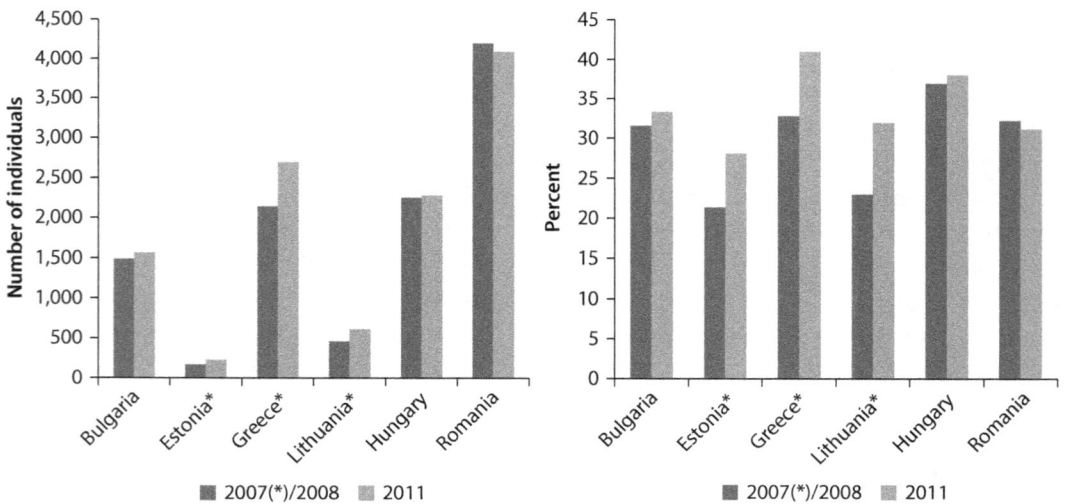

Source: World Bank staff analysis based on EU-SILC.

such groups using latent class methodology. Integration of distinct groups into the labor market may involve a variety of solutions—such as increasing the transport options for rural populations, providing young mothers with child-care options, back-to-work bonuses, and so on. Developing comprehensive solutions to the barriers faced by the distinct groups identified is outside the scope of this report. Rather, this report focuses on the first step in this process: developing distinct "portraits" of the out-of-work.

The characteristics of the groups of out-of-work population vary from country to country. Based on the EU-SILC survey for 2011, Estonia, Bulgaria, and Greece have seven groups of out-of-work individuals, while Lithuania and Romania have eight groups, and Hungary has 10. Nevertheless, there are some general groups that can be identified in all six countries. Clusters of middle-aged unemployed, long-term unemployed, retirees, disabled, inactive women or mothers, and NEETs (young people not in employment, education, or training) are present in every country. The size, share, and profile characteristics of these groups differ, reflecting the demographics and labor market of a particular country.

Detailed findings for the groups in each country are presented in their respective country chapters. In this section, we draw the main stylized facts that emerge in common across these countries. Against the backdrop of the economic crisis and recovery in the European Union, the analysis yields a number of insights across countries.

Middle-Aged Job Losers

In most countries, the number of *middle-aged job losers* has grown in absolute and relative terms. This issue is observed in Greece, Bulgaria, and Lithuania, where clusters of middle-aged unemployed account for around 20 percent of the out-of-work population. In Lithuania, there are two middle-aged unemployed groups, the *middle-aged poor rural long-term unemployed* and the *middle-aged educated unemployed family men*. Together they represent 37 percent of the out-of-work population of 2011. Most concerning is that the *middle-aged poor rural long-term unemployed* cluster more than tripled in number between 2007 and 2011, and the share that have been unemployed for more than 12 months grew from 49 to 71 percent. Although part of the increase may be ascribed to the global downturn, this group of low-income unemployed adults is now a structural feature of the Lithuanian labor market.

In Estonia, the largest cluster identified in 2011 is also composed mainly of middle-aged individuals, but unlike the aforementioned groups, 92 percent declare their labor market status as disabled (and thus not unemployed, but rather, inactive). This group represents 21 percent of the out-of-work population in 2011, has grown significantly since 2007 (24 percent) and is at high poverty risk,[2] as more than half of it is in the poorest income quintile and only 35 percent living in households with at least one working adult. Although a large majority declare themselves to be disabled, and 93 percent say they receive disability benefits, only 43 percent report that they have strong limitations in performing their usual activities because of health problems.

Individuals confronted with job losses face increased poverty risk, owing partly to limited benefit receipts (a low level of social inclusion benefits or the short duration of unemployment insurance benefits) and to large household sizes. (See box 2.1 for an explanation of the at-risk-of-poverty rate in the EU and the rate used in this report.) Some households were able to counter such job losses, possibly with the labor market entry of another household member.

Box 2.1 At-Risk-of-Poverty Rate in the EU and in This Report

According to Eurostat, "the at-risk-of-poverty rate is the share of people with an equivalized disposable income (after social transfers) below the at-risk-of-poverty threshold, which is set at 60 percent of the national median equivalized disposable income after social transfers. This indicator does not measure wealth or poverty, but low income in comparison to other residents in that country, which does not necessarily imply a low standard of living." Table B2.1.1 shows the "at-risk-of-poverty rate" in the six countries covered in this report, as reported in the Eurostat database and based on EU-SILC 2011 data.

Table B2.1.1 Percentage of Population Below 60 Percent of Median Income, by Country

Country	Percent
Bulgaria	22.2
Estonia	17.4
Greece	21.3
Lithuania	19.2
Hungary	13.8
Romania	22.2

Source: Eurostat, EU-SILC.

However, for this report's purposes, we define the at-risk-of-poverty rate as the relative risk of being in the *first* quintile of the income distribution. This enables us to provide more detail on the analyzed population. Instead of simply presenting clusters along the "at risk of poverty" or "not at risk of poverty" dimension, we present income information for all clusters divided by quintiles, and we refer to the first quintile as "at risk of poverty." Furthermore, as shown in the table above, in five of the six countries analyzed in this report the at-risk-of-poverty rate in 2011 as defined by Eurostat was very close to 20 percent (that is, it was very similar to the probability of falling in the bottom quintile of a country's income distribution). In other words, by looking at the first quintile of the income distribution in all countries except Hungary, one can get a good sense of what the at-risk-of-poverty rate would look like if defined following Eurostat's guidelines. Granted, it is worth noting that these measures of poverty refer to relative poverty, as opposed to absolute poverty. As such, they do not reflect deprivations in actual living conditions and are largely dependent on the income distribution of each respective country.

Source: http://epp.Eurostat.ec.europa.eu/statistics_explained/index.php/Glossary:At-risk-of-poverty_rate.

Youth Not in Employment, Education, or Training (NEETs)

An increase in the size of the *NEET* population was also observed in many countries, with young adults continuing to live in multigenerational households and struggling to enter the labor market. Labor force participation was low among youth in many of the countries studied to begin with (see figure 2.5). Furthermore, the percentage of young individuals ages 15–24 years who are not in employment, or education, or training (NEET rate) was high and increased in all countries following the crisis (figure 2.6). For the region as a whole, the NEET rate, which had fallen to 10.9 percent in 2008, in 2013 was back at 2003 levels (13 percent).

The adverse labor situation faced by youth is also captured in the latent class analysis of the EU-SILC data. In all six countries analyzed, it is possible to identify a cluster of youth or NEETs that make up an important share of the out-of-work population. In Estonia, this cluster almost doubled in size from 2007 to 2011 (from 11,000 to 20,000 individuals). The NEET cluster in Greece grew more than 25 percent from 2007 to 2011 and accounted for almost half a million individuals in 2011. In Bulgaria, on the other hand, this cluster grew from 197,000 individuals in 2008 to 233,000 in 2011. About 80 percent of the Estonians, 60 percent of the Bulgarians, and 46 percent of the Greeks in these clusters have no prior work experience, and around 40 percent of the Estonians and Bulgarians belong to the first income quintile (27 percent of the Greeks do). The activation of these individuals should be a priority for policy makers, to avoid the further depreciation of the stock of human capital among these young individuals and to promote their long-term well-being.

Quite importantly, some of the NEET clusters in the portraits include individuals above the age of 24 years (the usual age limit of NEET categorization).[3]

Figure 2.5 Labor Force Participation among Youth Ages 15–24 Years, European Countries, 2013
percent

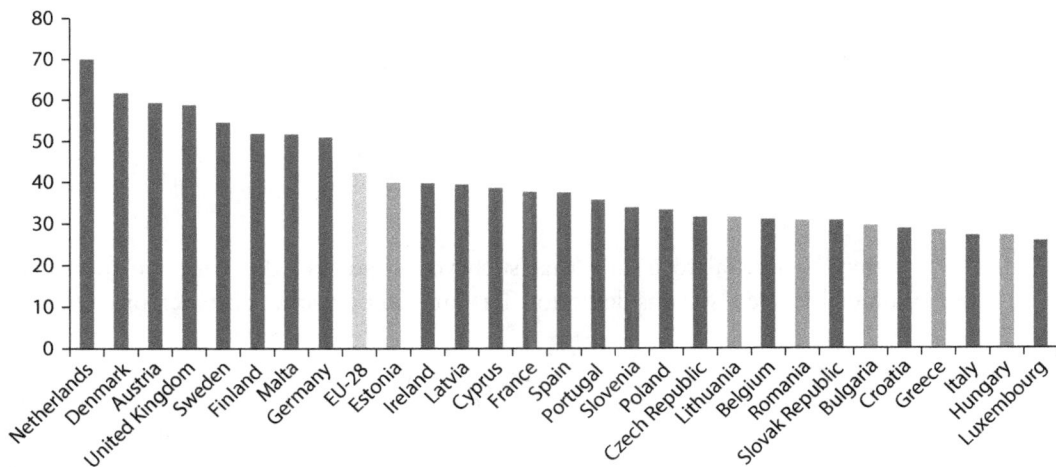

Source: Eurostat, EU-LFS.

Figure 2.6 NEET Rates, European Countries, 2008 and 2013
percent

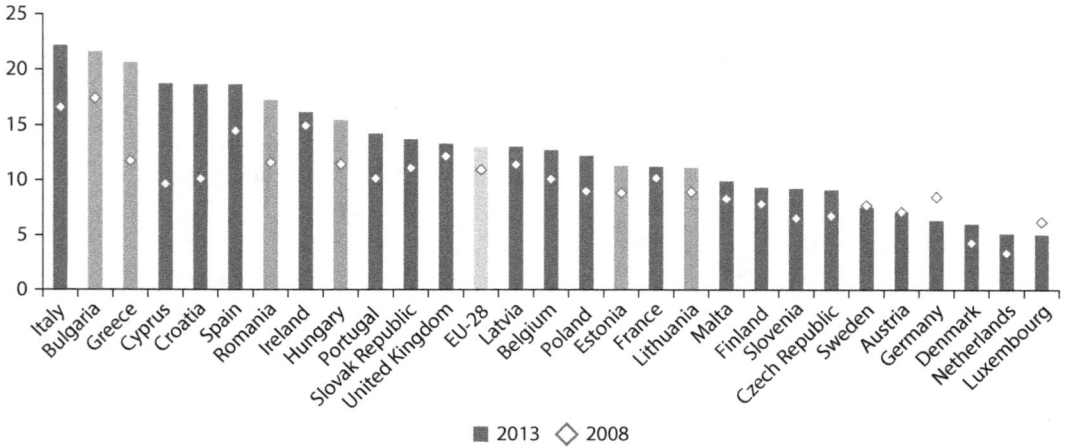

■ 2013   ◇ 2008

Source: Eurostat, EU-LFS.
Note: NEET rate is calculated as the percentage of the population between 15 and 24 years of age that is not in employment, education, or training.

Figure 2.7 Labor Force Participation as Share of Age Group, European Countries, 2013
percent

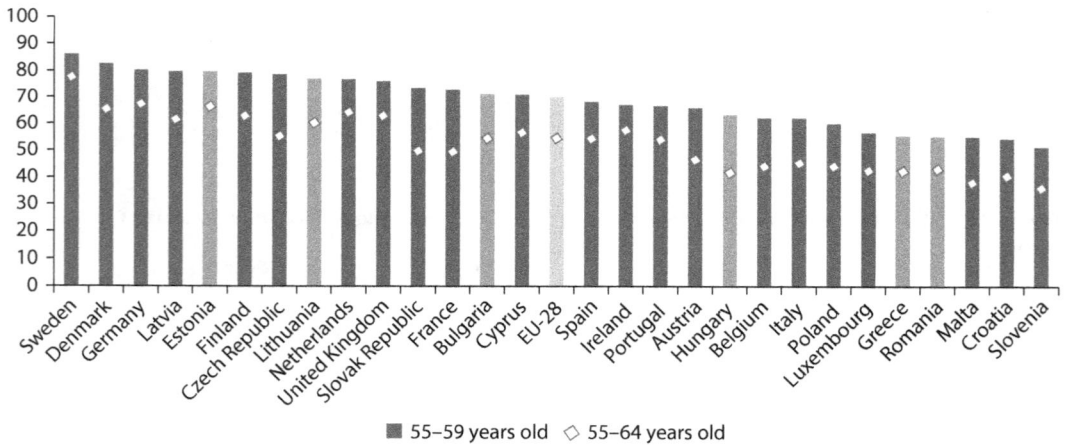

■ 55–59 years old   ◇ 55–64 years old

Source: Eurostat, EU-LFS.

It may be crucial to ensure that such young adults, who continue to remain vulnerable, are also considered for first-time labor market entrants' programs.

Early Retirees

The labor force participation rate for older people in the countries under study is, in general, among the lowest in Europe. As figure 2.7 shows, this is especially true for Romania, Greece, and Hungary, whose labor force participation rate for both the 55- to 59-year-old and 55- to 64-year-old cohort is much lower than the

EU-28 average of 70.3 and 54.3 percent, respectively. The low labor participation for the 55- to 64-year-old cohort may reflect in part that a relatively high percentage of the population between 60 and 64 years old have reached retirement age in all these countries, particularly among females.

Early retirees (in this report, under 60 years of age) and retirees (between 60 and 64 years) are a noteworthy phenomenon in most of the countries under study. Many of the members in these profiles also declare themselves to be limited in their activities because of health problems. In many countries, the welfare position (risk of poverty) of the retirees and early retirees is rather favorable in comparison to the other out-of-work population groups (due to low but stable retirement income, small household sizes, and so forth).

Retirement and disability are the main reasons for the population in these age groups to be out of the labor market. Indeed, it is possible to identify clusters of retired or disabled individuals in all the countries analyzed, and in some cases they make up an important portion of the out-of-work population. Disabled individuals, on the other hand, identified either because they declare their labor market status as disabled or otherwise declare strong limitations on daily activities due to health conditions, make up more than 20 percent of the out-of-work population in Estonia, Lithuania, and Hungary. The combination of rising numbers of disabled individuals and an aging population will likely increase expenditures on disability benefits and old-age pensions that governments will have to pay in the coming decades. As the working-age population shrinks and life expectancy grows, raising the retirement age and increasing labor force participation among older individuals may prove important to counteract a shrinking workforce and the increasing fiscal costs related to aging.

Early retirees account for around half of the out-of-work population in Romania and 30 percent in Hungary. In Romania, half of these people, almost one million individuals, have not reached retirement age; in Hungary, almost 40 percent of the *mostly male early retirees and retirees* cluster are between 45 and 59 years old.[4] In Bulgaria, two clusters contain a large number of early retirees: *retired and early retired men* and *low-educated early retired and disabled*; together they represented 16 percent of the out-of-work population in 2011. In the first cluster, almost half are between 45 and 59 years old,[5] while in the second one, all of them are under 60 years old, and half of them are retired (another 40 percent are disabled).

A cluster of early retirees also emerged in Greece after the crisis, accounting for 6.7 percent of the out-of-work population. A striking difference is that almost 70 percent have tertiary education, unlike the early retiree clusters in the other countries, whose members mostly had only secondary educations. Also, more than half of the early retirees in Greece are in the richest income quintile; 77 percent are in the top two income quintiles. Given the dire economic situation in Greece since 2009, early retirement may be an attractive alternative in times of high unemployment.

On the other hand, clusters of mainly retired women appear in Lithuania and Hungary throughout the years analyzed, but their shares have been reduced over time. In Lithuania, the *married rural women with old-age pension* cluster's share decreased from 25 percent in 2007 to 18 percent in 2011. Similarly, in Hungary, the *urban retired women* cluster's share decreased from 20 percent in 2008 to 15 percent in 2011. Unlike the other two countries, the *retired women* cluster in Bulgaria emerged in 2010, separating from the *retirees* cluster identified the previous years. It represented a share of 20 percent of the out-of-work population in 2011.

Inactive Women and Stay-At-Home Mothers

Inactive women and stay-at-home mothers can be identified as distinct categories in some countries.

The high rates of inactivity in the working-age population, particularly among women, are an issue of concern in most of the countries analyzed. Around a third of the population between 15–64 years of age in Hungary, Romania, Bulgaria, and Greece does not participate in the labor market. On the other hand, the share of inactive women is over 40 percent for Romania, Hungary, and Greece, while this share is, on average, 34.1 percent in the EU-28 countries in 2013. On average, these three countries had a gap of more than 15 percentage points between female and male participation rates (figure 2.8).

When looking at the EU-SILC data, clusters of inactive women are clearly identified in all of the countries. In Greece, the top group of the out-of-work population is made up largely of inactive women. In Hungary, the group of inactive women accounts for 17 percent of the out-of-work population, while in Romania the clusters containing inactive women make up more than 30 percent

Figure 2.8 Labor Force Participation as a Percentage of the Total Population Ages 15–64 Years by Gender, European Countries, 2013

percent

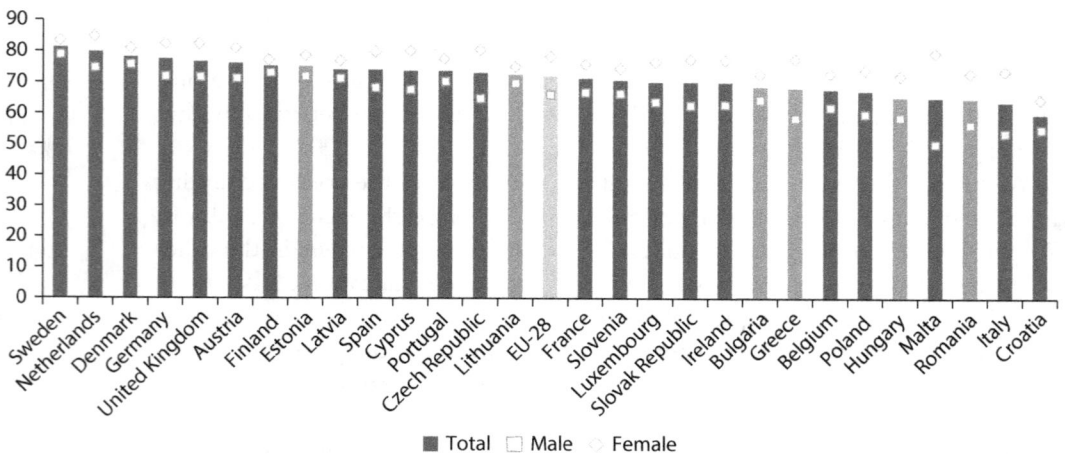

■ Total □ Male ◇ Female

Source: Eurostat, EU-LFS.

of the out-of-work population. Similarly, a stay-at-home female cluster is found in Bulgaria, Estonia, and Lithuania, accounting for 12, 17, and 5 percent of the out-of-work population in 2011, respectively.

The large groups of inactive women can be explained in part by cultural and social reasons or by the limited availability of formal child care and elder care facilities. Figure 2.9 shows that access to formal child care in all six countries is well below the 29 percent average of the EU-28. Lithuania, Hungary, Bulgaria, and Romania all have less than 10 percent of children younger than three years of age in formal child care. For Hungary and Estonia, the percentage of women 25–49 years old who reported being inactive in 2013 because they were looking after children or incapacitated adults was 56.5 and 73 percent, respectively. This is much higher than the 38.5 percent average for the EU-28. Increasing the availability of affordable child-care and elder-care facilities may help address one of the main labor market barriers that the female population faces.

A reduction in the inactivity of women after the crisis can also be identified when looking at the clusters of inactive stay-at-home mothers, possibly reflecting a fall in this option's affordability. This decline is prevalent in all the countries in terms of the stay-at-home mother clusters' share of the out-of-work population. Lithuania, Romania, and Greece had the largest decrease, all falling between 8–9 percentage points from 2007 to 2011. Romania had the largest decrease in absolute numbers, with its *low educated rural mothers without work experience* cluster decreasing by almost 332,000 individuals. It is interesting to see that the number of women within the Greek *stay-at-home mothers* cluster that declared themselves unemployed or long-term unemployed (versus inactive) increased from 12 to 23 percent; similarly, in Estonia 7 percent of the *young inactive educated mothers with working partner* declared themselves unemployed in 2011 (versus 0 percent in 2007). Notwithstanding this reduction in the inactivity of women,

Figure 2.9 Formal Child Care as a Percentage of All Children Younger than 3 Years Old, European Countries, 2011

percent

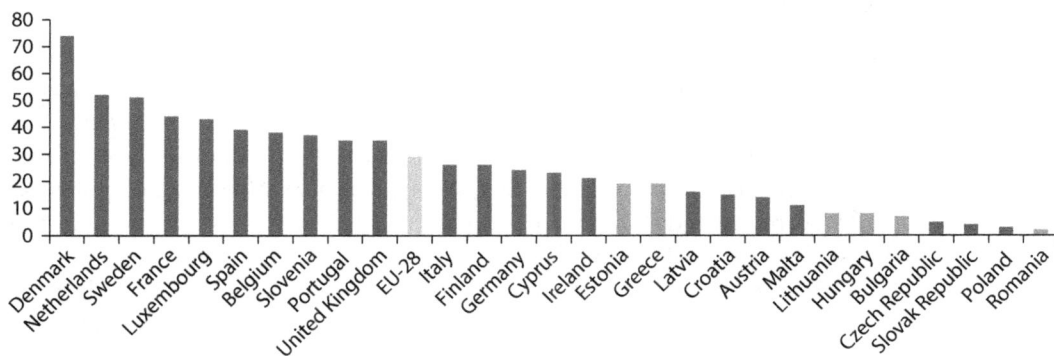

Source: Eurostat.

the clusters of stay-at-home mothers continue to represent an important share of the out-of-work population, ranging from 12 percent in Lithuania and Bulgaria to 23 percent in Greece.

Long-Term Unemployed

The high share and number of long-term unemployed is another worrisome issue in all the countries analyzed. The EU-SILC data shows that across the clusters of unemployed, the share of individuals in long-term unemployment in all countries has grown. In addition, in Lithuania, Estonia, Hungary, and Romania it is possible to identify clusters of long-term unemployed that account for 12–28 percent of the out-of-work population. Long-term unemployment not only imposes a significant financial burden on households, but affects the long-term health status of jobseekers, negatively impacts government finances, and results in a lower overall long-term level of skills among a country's workforce, with permanent negative effects on productivity (Katz 2010). Equally worrisome, many individuals who have been unemployed for extended periods become discouraged and drop out of the labor market altogether. Addressing the plea of the long-term unemployed should be among the policy priorities.

Rural Unemployed

Labor market participation differences and access to services between urban and rural living contexts can be distinguished as a defining feature in some countries. There is an important share of the out-of-work population that lives in rural areas, particularly in Lithuania and Romania. Although in all countries, except Greece, more than half of the out-of-work population live in rural areas, this share is 62 percent in Romania and 69 percent in Lithuania. In addition, the number of individuals of the out-of-work population living in a rural areas grew 40 percent from 2007 to 2011 in Lithuania. In Romania half of the clusters have more than 60 percent of their members living in rural areas. Taking into account the urban/rural divide of the out-of-work population in the design of activation policies may prove critical in order to reach the desired population.

Selected Issues for Further Policy Dialogue

The current general labor market situation, along with institutional and resource limitations, make the activation and integration of many of the identified out-of-work groups a demanding challenge. Prioritization of intervention is therefore of great importance. This section starts by presenting those groups identified in the country analysis that, given their activation need or potential, should be prioritized. We later discuss the type of activation that might best address the social or labor market barriers each prioritized group needs to overcome barriers to employment and outline the main implications for policy discussion. For this, this section draws on the recent study by the World Bank, *Back to Work* (Arias et al. 2014), which explores more deeply policies that can lead people to jobs (box 2.2).

The following should be considered as a starting point for further policy dialogue between the EC, the World Bank, and country authorities, bearing in mind that the groups identified are heterogeneous in ways that may affect the type of support required. Accordingly, these suggestions are not meant to be an exhaustive set of possible activation measures. It should also be kept in mind that the groups have been derived from the 2011 EU-SILC data. Since then, general economic development, policy actions by each government, and the EC's country-specific recommendations might have reflected some of these policy suggestions or rendered them obsolete.

A first step for prioritization ("activation priority") is assessing the activation need and potential of a group. Activation need refers to a group's need

---

Box 2.2 *Back to Work: Growing with Jobs in Europe and Central Asia*

In early 2014, the World Bank published *Back to Work: Growing with Jobs in Europe and Central Asia*, a report that studies the labor markets and enterprise dynamics in the region to address how economies in Europe create more jobs, and what specific policies help workers access those jobs. The findings of *Back to Work* intersect with those of this report, as the policy areas that bring workers into productive jobs are the same as those that will promote inclusion in the labor market of the inactive and unemployed individuals identified by the "Portraits" analysis.

The main findings of *Back to Work* are: (a) market reforms pay off in terms of jobs and productivity growth, although with a time lag; (b) a small fraction of superstar high-growth firms, largely young but not necessarily small, account for most new jobs created in the region; thus, countries need to unleash the potentially high levels of latent entrepreneurship to start up new firms; (c) skill gaps hinder employment prospects, especially of youth and older workers, due to the inadequate response of the education and training systems to changes in the demand for skills; (d) employment is hindered by high implicit taxes on work for those transitioning to formal jobs from inactivity or unemployment and by barriers that especially affect women, minorities, youth, and older workers; and (e) low internal labor mobility prevents labor relocation to places with greater job creation potential.

The report emphasizes that in order for more people to access jobs countries must carry out institutional reforms to establish the fundamentals to create jobs for all workers. A first step is taken by instituting reforms to create an auspicious environment for firms, allowing existing firms to either grow and become more productive, or exit the market and make way for new firms to emerge and succeed or fail, quickly and cheaply. A second set of policies that should be implemented are those that support workers and prepare them, in terms of skills and incentives, for the new jobs being created. These policies need to address those additional barriers to productive employability that disproportionately affect younger and older workers, women, and ethnic minorities, including lack of adequate skills, low mobility, lack of child- and elder-care options, limited flexible work arrangements, imperfect access to productive inputs, networks

box continues next page

---

and information, and adverse attitudes and social norms (figure B2.2.1). These barriers not only interact with other disincentives from labor tax and social protection systems, but also reinforce each other in aggravating exclusion from labor markets. Activation policies that help overcome these employability barriers will be fundamental for the region's future prospects.

Figure B2.2.1 Mutually Reinforcing Barriers to Employment for Younger and Older Workers, Women, and Ethnic Minorities

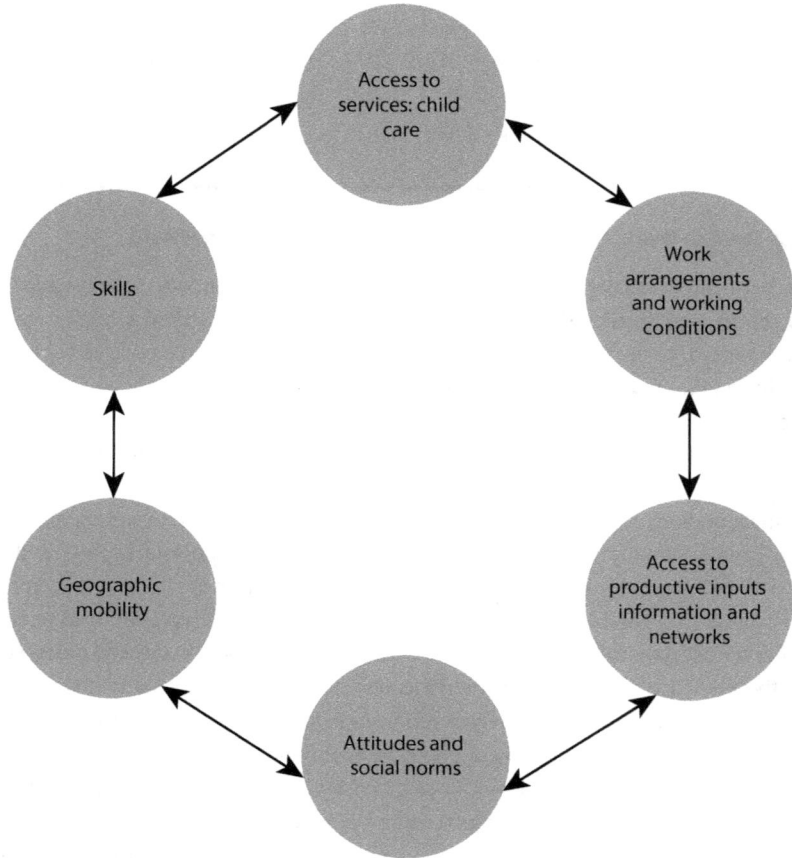

Source: Arias et al. 2014.

for inclusion in the labor market in order to achieve income and reduce or end poverty. Activation potential, on the other hand, describes the group's ability or motivation to be included in the labor market. A high activation need could be driven by high poverty risk, whereas a high activation potential could be driven by previous work experience or a relatively good educational base. Overall priority for action can also be supported by the size of the group. Table 2.1 shows the groups with high and medium priority for action.

Table 2.1 Activation Priority: Overview of Inactive Clusters with High and Medium Priority for Action

Country	Share % (2011)	Cluster	Activation need	Activation potential
High priority for action				
Bulgaria	23	Middle-aged unemployed	Medium	High
	15	Single male NEETs	High	Medium
	12	Low-educated rural long-term unemployed	High	Medium
Estonia	19	Prime-aged low income long-term unemployed	High	High
	13	Prime-aged educated unemployed	High	High
	9	Single NEETs without work experience	High	Medium
Greece	18	Highly educated single NEETs	High	Medium
	18	Middle-aged unemployed heads of households	High	High
Hungary	14	Prime-aged unemployed	High	Medium
	12	Prime-aged long-term unemployed	High	Medium
	4	Unemployed youth	High	Medium
Lithuania	28	Middle-aged poor rural long-term unemployed	High	Medium
	11	Young educated rural unemployed	High	High
	9	Middle-aged educated unemployed family men	High	High
	7	Single poor rural unemployed women	High	Medium
Romania	7	Long-term unemployed educated single youth	High	High
	5	Working-age long-term unemployed	High	Medium
Medium priority for action				
Bulgaria	15	Stay-at-home young mothers	Medium	Medium
Estonia	21	Middle-aged educated disabled with previous work experience	Medium	Medium
	17	Young inactive educated mothers with working partner	Medium	High
Greece	23	Stay-at-home mothers	Medium	Medium
Hungary	19	Disabled with previous work experience	Medium	Medium
	13	Prime-aged inactive mothers with work experience	Medium	High
	4	Low-educated rural inactive mothers without work experience	High	Low
	2	Educated single students	Low	High
Lithuania	5	Stay-at-home poor rural women	High	Medium
Romania	19	Low-educated rural mothers without work experience	High	Low
	15	Inactive middle-aged wives	High	Medium
	3	Working-age newly unemployed	Medium	High

Source: World Bank staff analysis and assessment 2014.
Note: NEET = not in employment, education, or training.

In general, clusters of unemployed have high priority owing to their activation need in terms of poverty risks and their potential through labor market proximity and/or education level. Clusters of youth, on the other hand, form prioritized groups because of the potential scarring effects of labor market detachment for young people at an early age.

The groups classified with medium priority for the most part have medium activation need in that they have comparatively lower poverty risk due to having other working adults in the household or receiving social welfare benefits. Three clusters of inactive women with high activation need, driven by their high poverty risk (in Hungary, Lithuania, and Romania), are considered of medium priority due to their distance from their labor market and therefore lower potential for activation. The Hungarian cluster of *educated single students*, although it has low activation need, is prioritized (like the other clusters of young individuals) because of the potential effects of labor market detachment on this group. The clusters of retirees, retirees' wives, and disabled are not prioritized for action owing to their lower activation need (many have reached the official retirement age or receive old-age benefits) or extreme distance (via very low educational attainment or self-declared disability) from the labor market.

The relative severity of labor market or social obstacles to be overcome for labor market integration can also be used as an orientation for activation approaches. By mapping the respective barriers for labor market integration faced by the prioritized groups, it is possible to discern the respective types of activation that could be undertaken for each group (figure 2.10).

The clusters mapped near the bottom left corner have relatively lower labor market barriers and are considered "market ready" (see each one of the six country charts in figure 2.10). *In this category of activation type are the clusters of unemployed with work experience and/or education* such as the prime-aged unemployed clusters found in Estonia, Hungary, and Lithuania, the *young educated rural unemployed* in Lithuania, and the *middle-aged unemployed heads of households* in Greece. Two groups of youth without work experience are also considered for this activation type: the Hungarian *educated single students* and the *single male NEETs* in Bulgaria. *Given that these clusters are still quite close to the labor market, activation measures should focus on market-based types of interventions, such as providing information on job openings and assisting in job search, application, and job-matching intermediation—services that could be provided through public employment services (PESs) or private employment agencies.*

The upper left quadrant clusters are individuals who will require more *intensified activation*. Clusters whose individuals have been detached from the labor market for a longer time, such as the *working-age long-term unemployed* and the *long-term unemployed single youth* in Romania, the *middle-aged unemployed* in Bulgaria, and both the *middle-aged poor rural long-term unemployed* and *middle-aged educated family men* in Lithuania, are considered to need this type of intensified activation. The Hungarian *unemployed youth* cluster and the single NEET groups in Greece and Estonia are also mapped in this quadrant as they could probably benefit from adding practical skills to their education.

Among the measures to be considered in such "intensified activation" are those that help with job market reentry, training, and mobility. Taking into account the years of work experience and potential industry and trade knowledge of the individuals in these groups, reconnecting them to their previous field

Figure 2.10 Activation Types of Prioritized Clusters

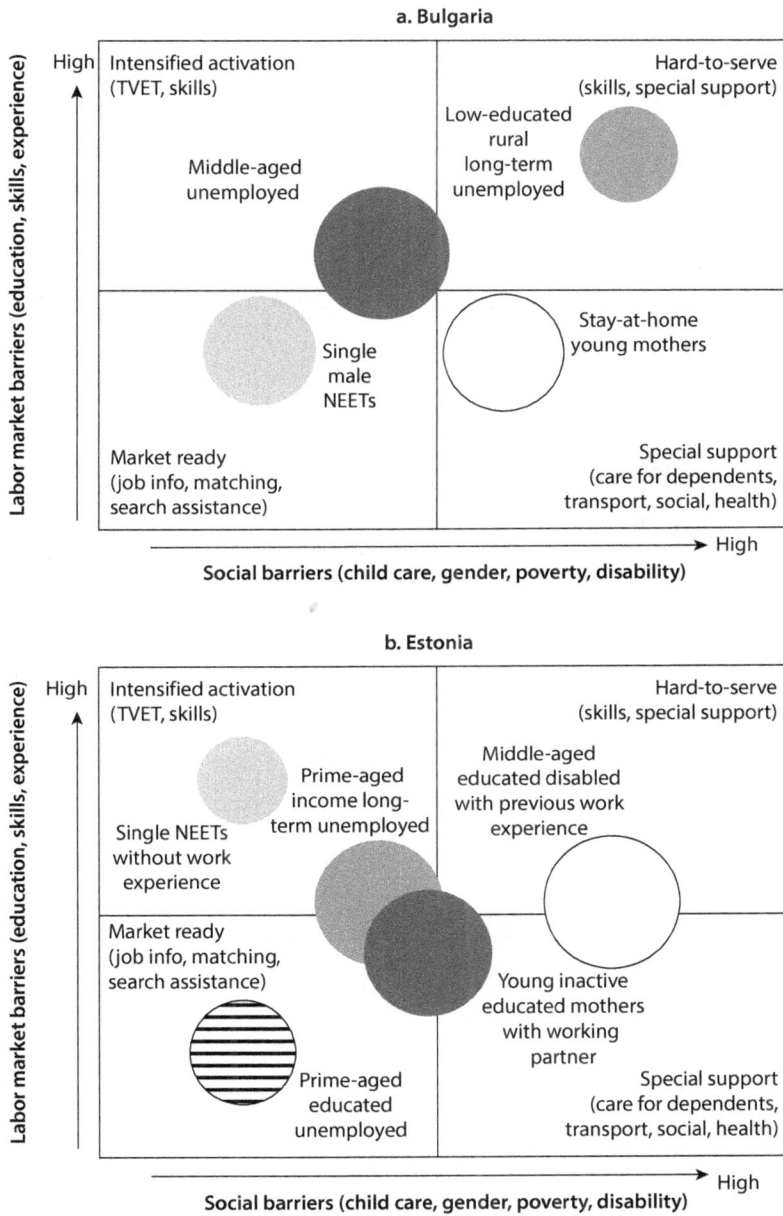

a. Bulgaria

b. Estonia

figure continues next page

Figure 2.10 Activation Types of Prioritized Clusters *(continued)*

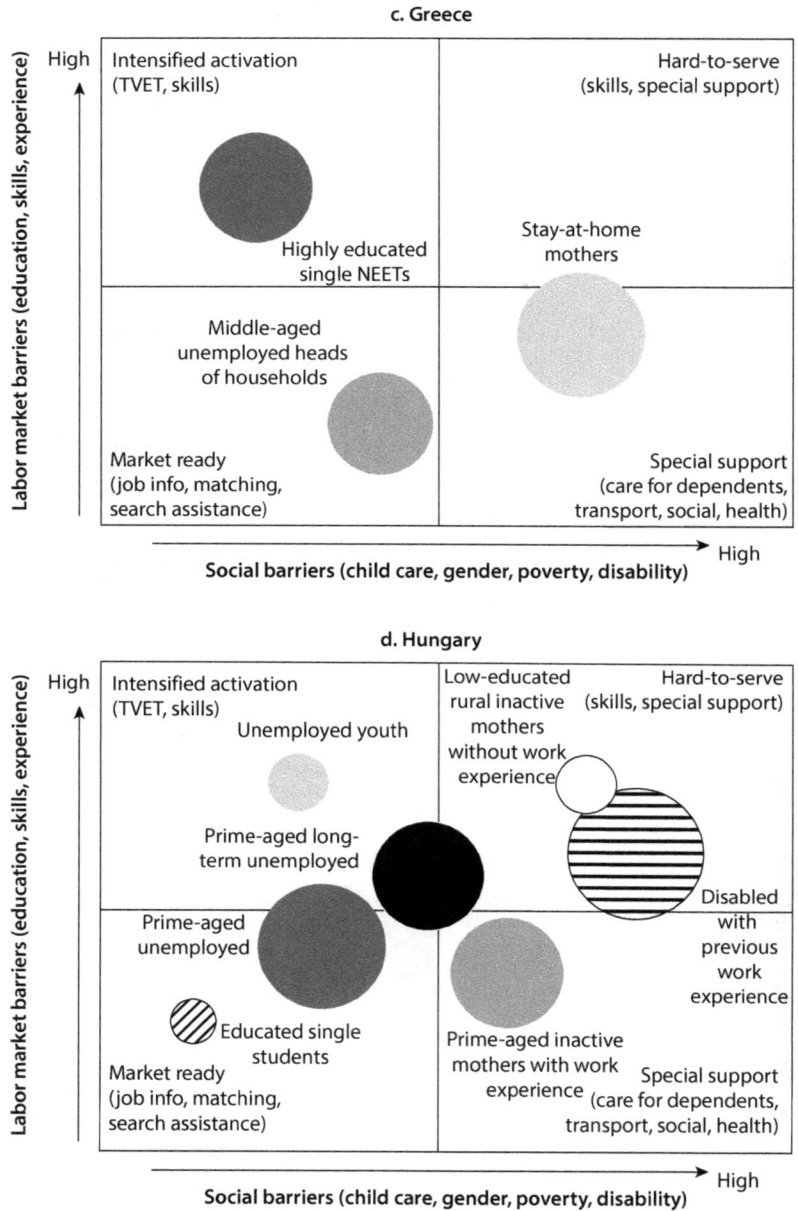

c. Greece

d. Hungary

figure continues next page

Figure 2.10 Activation Types of Prioritized Clusters (*continued*)

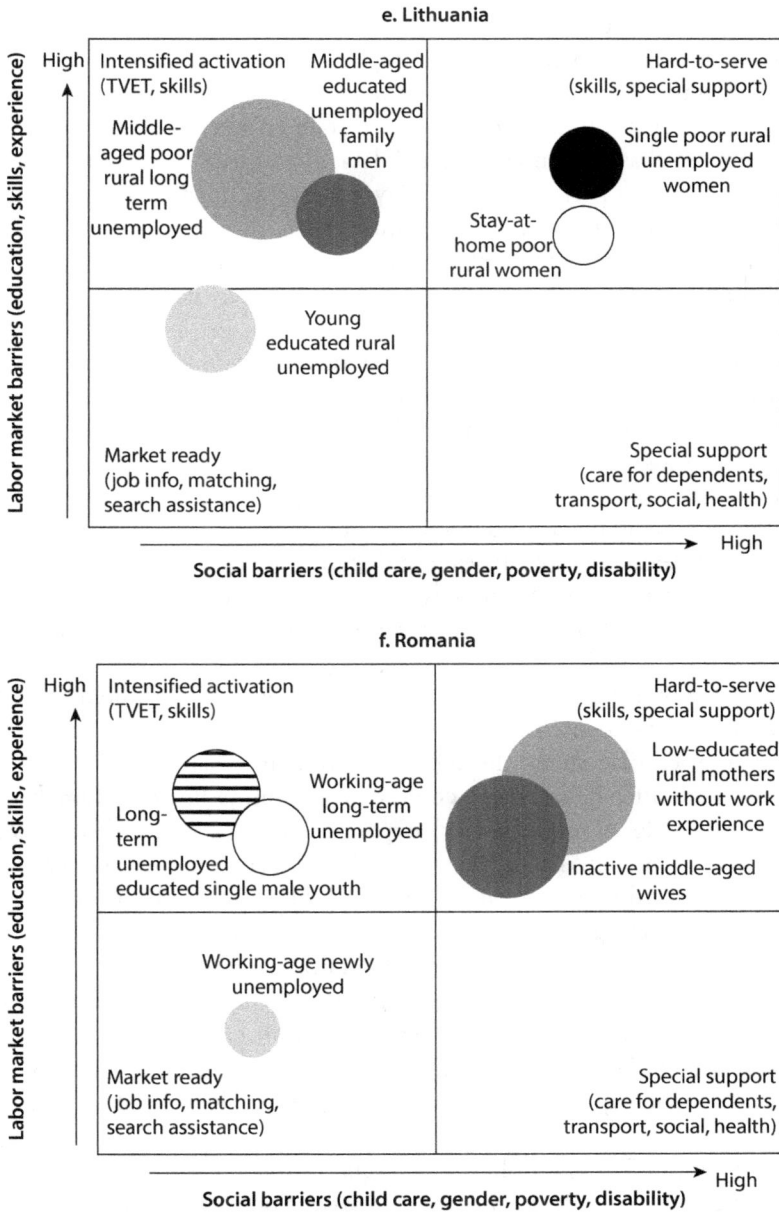

e. Lithuania

f. Romania

Source: World Bank staff analysis and assessment 2014.
Note: NEET = young people not in employment, education, or training; TVET = technical and vocational education and training.

of employment, building on their acquired skills, and upgrading missing functional or technical skills may strengthen their case with new employers. The older out-of-work population in these groups is particularly at risk of skills obsolescence as the skills demanded by employers change. Activation policies should promote effective, age-sensitive training and create the conditions for the development of a market for adult education and training services. Moreover, in order to combat any behavioral and attitudinal detachment from the labor market that may result after long periods of unemployment, programs that subject individuals to a (time-limited) public works requirement, combined with training, job search, and skills support could also be implemented. Finally, mobility measures should also be taken into account, particularly when considering long-term unemployed in rural areas.

In addition, linkage with regional economic development activities, self-employment, and entrepreneurship support could help some of these unemployed individuals attain self-sufficient lives and improve their welfare. Broader structural reforms that improve the business climate, such as those that lower the cost of starting and closing a business, improve access to financing, and promote more favorable attitudes and social norms toward risk taking can go a long way in fostering new ventures. Tapping into the latent entrepreneurship of the out-of-work population not only helps them enter the labor market, but also has the potential of playing an essential role in creating new jobs for the economy.

Given the potential scarring effects of labor market detachment at an early age, *special consideration should be taken to the clusters of youth*. Job-start programs that offer placement through subsidized internships accompanied by professional and life skills training could be a promising line of action, breaking the common barrier of required work experience for many entry-level positions. Another line of action is larger labor market policies that encourage flexible work schedules and part-time work. These would allow youth to combine work and study, help them gain the necessary experience, and facilitate full entry into the labor market. Job-search offerings by PESs should consider virtual platforms, since the use of mobile technology will be taken for granted by many members of these groups. Mobility support within each country and the EU (including foreign language training) could also be considered, particularly for those with higher qualifications, considering their low level of caregiving responsibility.

As Arias et al. (2014) emphasize, *for younger cohorts, having the wrong set of skills (both generic and technical) is often an issue*. Some educational systems still track students into vocational streams too early, neglecting generic skills that are valuable in today's workplace. Postponing this early tracking and promoting a diversified supply of courses (from traditional apprenticeships to IT skills), as well as providers that have strong linkages with employers and labor markets, would be steps forward in closing the skill gap. On the other hand, while tertiary schooling has expanded quickly among youth, quality and relevance vary. Broader reforms that manage the expansion of tertiary education through quality assurance systems and which make information available about the labor prospects of various careers will also be key for new entrants to the labor market.

Clusters in the two right quadrants of the figures above have relatively higher social barriers and therefore will require additional activation support. Most of the clusters of inactive women are mapped in these two quadrants, depending on years of work experience, education level, and/or poverty. For instance, the low education and lack of work experience of the Romanian *low-educated rural mothers without work experience* and the *inactive middle-aged wives* limit their activation potential; these groups are therefore considered hard to serve. Similarly, the *low-educated rural inactive mothers without work experience* in Hungary and *single poor rural unemployed women* in Lithuania are also mapped in the upper right quadrant. On the other hand, the clusters of stay-at-home mothers in Greece, Hungary, and Bulgaria are younger, more educated, and may have work experience, and therefore face fewer labor market barriers. Given the lower poverty risk, age, and work experience of the Estonian cluster of inactive mothers, this group mapped in the border between "market-ready" and "special support" activation type.

In general, women face important disincentives and barriers to work, which are reflected in the appearance of female out-of-work clusters in all the countries analyzed. Labor taxes and social protection systems create strong deterrents for second earners (generally women) to seek formal jobs. Along with these disincentives, women also face labor market barriers such as lack of services (child or elder care), limited flexibility in work schedules, and imperfect access to productive inputs, networks, and information. Adverse attitudes and social norms may also limit women's access to jobs and in many cases reinforce each other (Arias et al. 2014).

Potential activation measures for all the clusters of inactive women are similar in nature, ideally with options that enable women to sort into the measure that would correspond best to their needs. In general, these groups could benefit from greater access to social and public services near their home (such as child care) as well as from job-search assistance and professional training. Those with previous work experience could build on it to gain labor market entry. Opening a "window" for mothers with children in public works programs that include child care and training opportunities might help some of these women get initial work experience and address their poverty situation. Short "second chance" schooling with a focus on professional skills tailored to the needs and skills of individuals could be offered. Another possible line of action would be offering community-based social work and entrepreneurship education to help in labor market integration. In addition to training in job hunting and basic functional skills, (temporary) mobility support for transportation and housing should also be considered to help women in these groups find employment in regional or larger cities. Improving access to child-care and school after-care offerings would on their own enable many women in these clusters to better participate in the labor market or to take part in professional training or entrepreneurship offerings. Moreover, improving flexibility in work schedules, including part-time and home-based work in order to facilitate combining work with other responsibilities, would make it easier for women to hold jobs.

Finally, clusters that contain a large of share of *individuals who declare their work capacity to be strongly limited* because of health problems (in Estonia and Hungary) and *clusters of low-educated, long-term unemployed* (in Estonia and Bulgaria) are also mapped to the upper right quadrant, and will require policies that address strong social and labor market barriers. Standard PES job search assistance and placement support, while also reassessing the labor market status of those who declare themselves disabled, could be a potential activation measure. For those considered fit to work, a set of support measures and continuing benefits (potentially with a phase-out period) ought to be provided to cushion the transition to labor market integration. By reconnecting individuals in these groups with previous employment experiences, they could be equipped with missing functional or technical skills, second-chance apprenticeship programs, and upper secondary school certificates. Mobility support could be an important service. Finally, improving social inclusion benefits and linking them to activation could improve the welfare of those in low-educated, long-term unemployed clusters.

Looking at *household income composition* allows assessing potential cross-dependencies of the benefit system with labor market status. In general, only disability and old-age benefits contribute an important share to household income, and only in those groups where these benefit receipts correspond to the social-demographic situation of the cluster. *This highlights the fact that social protection in most of these countries is largely centered upon pensions, providing little protection in terms of unemployment insurance or social assistance.*

Nevertheless, in Estonia, Romania, and Hungary, the high percentage of individuals receiving disability receipts in the *middle-aged educated disabled with previous work experience, early retirees*, and *disabled with previous experience* clusters, respectively, attract attention when considering that only a small percentage in each group report strong limitations on daily activity. *These countries could potentially profit from a review of the disability benefit allocation.* At any rate, this significant group of out-of-work citizens needs to be followed closely and any new applications for disability benefits closely monitored and controlled. Limiting the inflow into this group (via more stringent disability benefit criteria) will be easier than forcing the activated exit of members from these groups. Prevention of long-term disability benefit dependency should also be addressed through a review of work capacity, together with early identification of people with disabilities who can work and their integration into the workforce through financial incentives for disabled workers and their employers.

Although social protection systems seem to have little impact on the household incomes of most of the out-of-work clusters in the countries studied, it is important to keep in mind that labor taxation in conjunction with these protection systems may play a role in deterring entry into the labor market, particularly for second earners (generally women) and lower wage earners (such as youth).

Redesigning these systems by reducing or eliminating the abrupt withdrawal of social benefits when a person starts formal work, and eliminating filters that make a household ineligible for a benefit if one of its members is employed, should be considered part of the policy agenda. The challenge for these countries lies in expanding social protection systems without creating disincentives to work.

Retirees and early retirees, on the other hand, represent a large (and growing) share of the out-of-work population, which has important implications for fiscal expenditures. Given their overall low need and activation potential these groups are not further considered for activation policies during times of low labor demand and high unemployment. As with disability recipients, stemming the outflow of new retirees may be more effective than attempting to increase the inflows back into activity. In times of high unemployment, early retirement may become more attractive for the long-term unemployed. Policies can and should be implemented to delay early retirement, including reforms to pension systems and the promotion of skill maintenance and lifelong learning, along with flexible work schedules, adaptable work environments (for example, to health requirements), and working from home.

Broader Policy Issues

In general, further policy dialogue with the authorities ought to focus as much on the general level and setup of resources devoted to labor market integration and activation of the inactive and out-of-work as on the ongoing improvement of services on the national and local levels.

From the potential activation policies mentioned in the previous section, there are a few areas that may transversely benefit different groups within the out-of-work population and could constitute a starting point for further policy dialogue. As stated before, the policies outlined are by no means an exhaustive set of possibilities, and their relevance will depend on the particular institutional framework of each country and the characteristics of its out-of-work population.

For many out-of-work individuals, particularly youth, the older population, and those who have been out-of-work for longer periods, skill deterioration or not having the adequate set for the employer's needs are important employability barriers. Policies should tackle this skill gap by prioritizing the development of a strong foundation of generic skills, ensuring quality and relevance in expanding the tertiary education system, and making the training system responsive to market needs and age-sensitive to enable lifelong learning.

In parallel to broader education and training policies, activation services should build on previous work experience for training and work placement. Considering that a large share of the out-of-work population have years of work experience, training measures combined with temporary work placement in companies, nonprofits, or social enterprises could help to strengthen labor market attachment. Reconnecting individuals with their previous industry or profession can build on existing ties and professional knowledge, improving reentry into the labor market after unemployment or maternity leaves.

Meanwhile, greater coordination between social protection policies and labor market measures will allow for more effective provision and better targeting of governmental programs, particularly for individuals with disabilities or greater poverty risk. For some inactive and unemployed clusters, labor taxes, social protection systems, and labor regulation can pose strong disincentives to work. This can be particularly true in the case of second earners (generally women), older workers (nearing retirement), and those who will access low-paying or part-time jobs. Overall pension reform and improvement to the design of social assistance and unemployment benefits, particularly by removing explicit bans or penalties to (formal) work, would reduce disincentives to work. Social programs should not only provide adequate protection to the poor and vulnerable, but also be compatible with work and linked to job search and activation. In addition, reforms that make labor taxation more progressive and take into account hours worked and family structure may also pay off in weakening the disincentives to work, particularly for those inactive women who are "market-ready" and youth who wish to balance work and study.

Women, youth, older population members, and minorities face additional barriers that should also be considered in the policy agenda. Lack of services, such as child or elder care; limited flexible work schedules; imperfect access to productive inputs, networks, and information; or adverse attitudes and social norms, limits their access to jobs. Extending child-care and early childhood development offerings as well as alternatives for elder care will play an important role in enabling earlier labor market integration of women. Broader labor market reforms that consider more flexible work schedules and encourage age-sensitive work environments may be relevant in bringing women, youth, and the older population closer to the labor market. Finally, the policy agenda should also consider influencing changes in culture and social norms in favor of greater labor market participation by women, and a more positive perception of older workers and minorities.

Geographic mobility is another policy area that is relevant for many of the clusters identified. For those living in rural areas, improving regional transportation and other policies to support mobility may prove necessary for access to more dynamic labor markets and employment matching. In addition, linking mobility to training offerings may enable some jobseekers to participate in higher-quality training in central places. Promoting labor migration within the EU, coupled with foreign language training, can be an important measure to prevent the deterioration of human capital, particularly in the younger population with higher qualifications and fewer caregiving responsibilities.

Policies that foster mobility (both internal and international) should look to remove barriers when people want to move in search of better opportunities, and make their investments and benefits portable. Arias et al. (2014) highlights several factors or barriers that can affect internal mobility. Among others, barriers, such as skill and lack of information networks, underdeveloped housing and credit markets increase the cost of migration, especially for those with liquidity constraints. Moreover, social benefits, insurance, and regional development policies can either help or hinder mobility. Inasmuch as these policies help people overcome financial constraints, they will allow people to connect with better jobs in more productive regions. On the other hand, if poorly designed, social benefits (like some housing benefits) and territorial policies (such as agricultural subsidies) can end up limiting internal mobility, tying people to economically lagging regions and decreasing incentives to work.

Finally, while active labor market policies, activation, and job-matching support can help smooth frictions in the labor market, they will not lead to stable, sustainable employment. Demand for jobs comes from the economic activity of firms and the social sector; therefore, the integration of labor market policy with regional economic development policy is especially important. Broad economic reforms to the business climate that strengthen job creation and entrepreneurship will likely be effective in fostering the attachment to the labor market of the out-of-work population. In addition, any mix of activation and enabling measures that help inactive or unemployed citizens reconnect to the labor market will need to take a wide-ranging approach (from training to self-employment), ensuring at all times linkage with firms (through work placements and so on), integration with efforts at regional economic development, and building on the activity and experience base of the jobseekers concerned. In this sense, all efforts need to be embedded into activities for economic growth and job demand creation.

Notes

1. Specifically, only individuals ages 25–64 years who are not employed, and individuals ages 16–24 years who were not employed, in education, or in training are considered. Individuals ages 16–24 years who are out of work and enrolled in education are excluded from the sample; they are considered to be investing in their final stages of human capital formation and therefore are not a particular target group for activation policies. Individuals ages 25 and 64 years enrolled in school are, however, included in the latent class analysis and will be grouped under "other inactive." It is important to note that this group of students, those older than 24 years, accounts for only 1 percent of total population of working age in each of the countries studied.

2. See box 2.1 for a definition of "at-risk-of-poverty."

3. Thirty-five percent of the individuals in the NEET cluster in Bulgaria are between 25–34 years old. This share is 18 percent in Estonia, while in Greece 60 percent are in this age group.

4. Another 4 percent are 35–44 years old.

5. Another 6 percent are 35–44 years old.

References

Arias, O. S., C. Sánchez-Páramo, M. E. Dávalos, I. Santos, E. R. Tiongson, C. Gruen, N. de Andrade Falcão, G. Saiovici, and C. A. Cancho. 2014. *Back to Work: Growing with Jobs in Europe and Central Asia*. Washington, DC: World Bank.

Katz, L. 2010. "Long-Term Unemployment in the Great Recession," Testimony for the Joint Economic Committee, U.S. Congress Hearing on "Long-Term Unemployment: Causes, Consequences and Solutions," April 29.

CHAPTER 3

Latent Class Analysis of the Out-of-Work Population in Bulgaria, 2007–11

Background

After years of economic expansion, Bulgaria was strongly affected by the global financial crisis and has yet to recover pre-crisis growth rates. Between 2003 and 2008, the country grew at an average rate of 6.3 percent, well above the 2.2 percent average among the EU-28 Member States during the same period. Like most countries in the region, Bulgaria was hit in 2009 by the crisis, causing the economy to contract 5.5 percent. Though this contraction was larger than the EU-28 member state average (4.5 percent), it was considerably smaller than countries like Latvia and Lithuania that contracted 17.7 and 14.8 percent that year, respectively. Nevertheless, Bulgaria's recovery has been less dynamic: gross domestic product grew 1 percent on average over 2010–13.

Following the economic downturn in 2009, and given the anemic recovery that followed, unemployment rates in Bulgaria have failed to recover to pre-crisis levels. The joblessness rate for the population ages 15–64 years in Bulgaria had declined steadily earlier in the decade, reaching 5.7 in 2008. However, as the effects of the global financial crisis unraveled, the country suffered a large and extremely rapid increase in unemployment; by the end of 2009, joblessness had risen to 6.9 percent. Although the economy has been growing since 2009, the unemployment rate has continued to grow and has doubled since the onset of the crisis, reaching 13 percent in 2013. While the growth in unemployment is significant, such an increase is only slightly larger than those observed in the EU-28 (11 percent) or the euro area as a whole (12 percent).

As unemployment rates continue to rise, youth are among the worst affected. Unemployment for individuals ages 15–24 years old, independent of gender, has grown dramatically since 2009, increasing from 12.7 percent in 2008 to 28.4 percent in 2013. High youth unemployment is also reflected in very low employment rates for youth: in 2013, this rate was astonishingly low at 21.2 percent, compared to an average of 32.3 percent for the EU.

The percentage of youth not in education, employment, or training (the NEET rate) increased. The NEET rate, which measures the share of youth ages 15–24 years not engaged in education, training, or employment, rose from 17.4 percent in 2008 to 21.6 percent in 2013. However, it is noteworthy that the NEET rate has been decreasing (falling almost 9 percentage points in the last ten years), perhaps reflecting the fact that many youth, facing a tight labor market in which their lack of work experience puts them at a disadvantage, have chosen to stay longer in school and/or training.

In Bulgaria, long-term unemployment as a share of total unemployment has been usually higher than the average for the EU-28 countries. In 2013, according to Eurostat and as shown in figure 3.1, in the average EU-28 country almost 48 percent of the unemployed have been looking for work for more than 12 months, up from 33 percent in 2009. Long-term unemployment in Bulgaria has been considerably higher than the EU-28 average during the last 10 years. In 2009, it had declined to 43.3 percent—still 10 percentage points higher than the average EU-28 country. By 2013, 57.3 percent of the unemployed were long-term unemployed.

Following the crisis, low-educated individuals were especially affected by the rise in unemployment. Unemployment rates were already considerably higher for the group of less educated individuals. After the crisis hit in 2009 the gap was accentuated, reflecting structural changes that increased the demand for more-skilled workers (figure 3.2). In fact, the difference in unemployment rates for low- and higher-educated workers grew from 12.6 percentage points

Figure 3.1 Long-Term Unemployment as a Share of Total Unemployment, 2003–13

percent

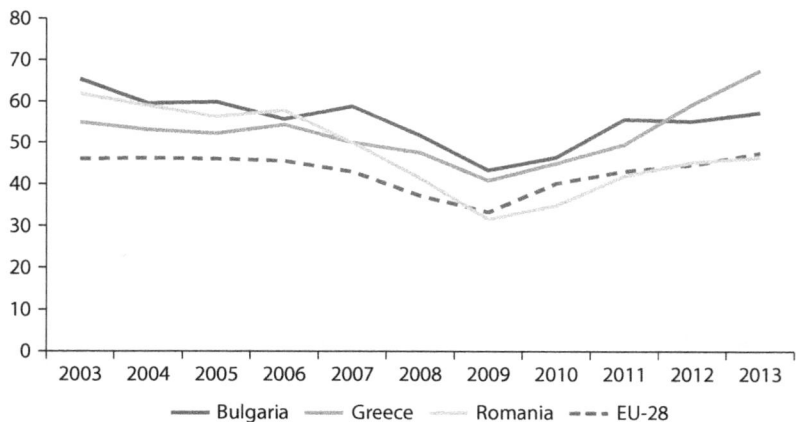

Source: Eurostat, EU-LFS.

Figure 3.2 Unemployment among 15- to 64-Year-Olds by Educational Level in Bulgaria, 2003–13

percent

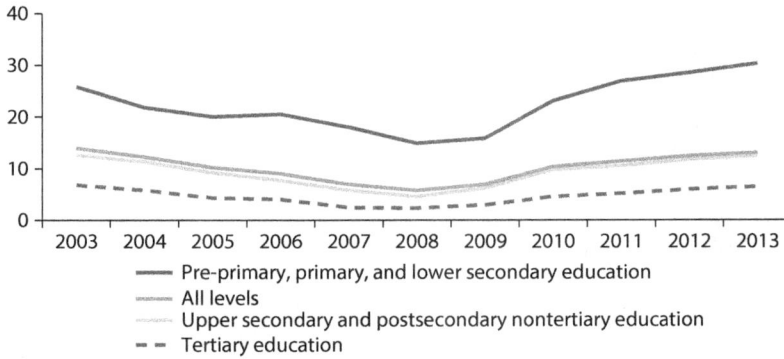

- —— Pre-primary, primary, and lower secondary education
- ---- All levels
- ········ Upper secondary and postsecondary nontertiary education
- – – Tertiary education

Source: Eurostat, EU-LFS.

in 2008 to 23.9 percentage points in 2013. However, all educational groups saw an increase in their unemployment rates from 2008 to 2013. For those with tertiary education and upper secondary and postsecondary nontertiary education, unemployment rates more than doubled, from 2.3 to 5.9 percent and from 4.5 to 11.7 percent, respectively.

Employment levels have fallen since the onset of the crisis, but less drastically than for the highly educated. The employment rate for the population ages 15–64 years peaked in 2008 at 64 percent; it was significantly lower in 2013 at 59.5. Employment rates have fallen across all education groups, but this fall is more pronounced for individuals with an upper secondary education. Individuals with lower levels of education are more susceptible to seasonal volatility. Such seasonality has also affected individuals with an upper secondary degree since the crisis.

During the period from 2008 to 2011, *the sample of out-of-work population considered in this note increased, from 1.49 to 1.56 million individuals.* The analysis of the out-of-work population in this note focuses on the working-age population (16–64 years old). Specifically, only individuals ages 25–64 years who are not employed, and individuals ages 16–24 years who were neither employed nor in education nor training were considered.[1] Only the working-age population (16- to 64- year-olds) is analyzed, as labor activation options—the main policy focus of this note—are only viable for that segment of the population. In 2011, 1.56 million out of the 4.7 million individuals in our sample, or 33.3 percent, were out of work. There have also been significant increases in the number of long-term unemployed and inactive among the out-of-work population (see figure 3.3). Moreover, the group of disabled has more than doubled, from 13,000 in 2008 to 29,000 in 2011 (table 3.1).

Figure 3.3 Distribution of Out-of-Work Population in Bulgaria, 2008 and 2011
percent

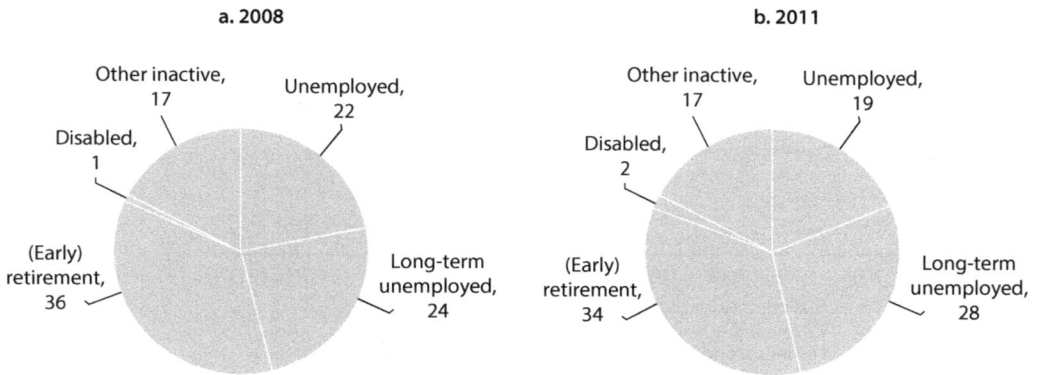

a. 2008

Other inactive, 17
Unemployed, 22
Disabled, 1
(Early) retirement, 36
Long-term unemployed, 24

b. 2011

Other inactive, 17
Unemployed, 19
Disabled, 2
(Early) retirement, 34
Long-term unemployed, 28

Source: World Bank staff analysis based on EU-SILC.

Table 3.1 Number and Percentage of Working-Age Individuals (Ages 16–64 Years) by Labor Market Attachment in Bulgaria, 2008 and 2011

	2008	2011	Change 2008–11 (%)
At work	3,221	3,130	−2.8
	68.4%	66.7%	
Unemployed	325	293	−9.9
	6.9%	6.2%	
Long-term unemployed	358	433	20.7
	7.6%	9.2%	
(Early) retirement	530	539	1.8
	11.3%	11.5%	
Disabled	13	29	115.4
	0.3%	0.6%	
Other inactive	259	271	4.9
	5.5%	5.8%	
Total	4,706	4,695	−0.2
	100%	100%	

Source: World Bank staff analysis based on EU-SILC.

Methodology: Latent Class Analysis

In chapter 1 a general overview of the latent class analysis methodology was presented. This section explains in detail the variables and covariates used to identify classes or groups of out-of-work individuals that are as homogeneous as possible within each class according to a set of observable characteristics, and as distant as possible between classes. The emerging profiles can then be contrasted with the design and targeting of current activation policies, in order to identify the potential gaps and to enhance their design features.[2]

Variable Selection

The definition of latent classes relies on a number of indicator variables to capture different "symptoms" of an overall latent condition (in this case, the typology of joblessness). The challenge in such models is to identify a discrete number of variables that can best explain the heterogeneity of individual out-comes. In this case, two sets of categorical variables were selected: the first set to show the extent of labor market distance and the other to capture some of the main factors that can affect employment on the supply side, such as labor supply conditions (household-level incentives to work and physical ability to work).

- *Distance from labor market*: short-term unemployment, long-term unemployment, (early) retirement, disability, and other inactivity (largely unpaid domestic work).[3]
- *Labor supply conditions:* whether the individual's household has at least one working adult,[4] and perceived limitations on activities due to health problems.[5]

In addition to indicators, the model includes active covariates, which are used to improve the classification of individuals in each class. In this case the active covariates are the demographic variables that are normally used to disaggregate labor market outcomes:

- Age-group category (four groups)
- Gender
- Human capital: the highest educational level achieved (three groups)
- Urban/rural location

Once the latent classes have been defined, inactive covariates that were not included in the model can be used to characterize the individuals in each class and the households in which they live. The inactive covariates chosen describe those characteristics that may provide valuable information for the design of tailored policies that address barriers to employment, including income level. They include:

- Household welfare conditions:
  - Income quintile (defined by equivalized disposable household income[6,7])
  - Labor, benefit, and other income as share of total gross household income[8]
  - Binary variable denoting whether at least one working adult (age 25 years and older) is present in the household
  - Household ownership
  - Household able to keep dwelling warm
  - Partner's labor income
  - Quintile of partner's labor income
  - Binary variables denoting whether individuals or their households are beneficiaries of any of eight social protection benefits[9]

- Household demographics:
  - Household size
  - Household composition
  - Binary variable showing whether there are children younger than 6 years of age in the household
  - Binary variable denoting whether there are three or more under-16 children in the household
  - Children younger than 13 years of age in the household receiving child care: all, some, or none of the children
  - Older person (65 years of age and older) in the household
- Other individual-level demographics:
  - More refined age groups (seven groups)
  - Marital status
- Individual human capital:
  - More refined highest educational level achieved (six groups)
  - Work experience in years
  - Binary variable for previous work experience
- Household location:
  - Degree of urbanization[10]: densely populated, intermediate area, sparsely populated
  - Regional breakdown: northern and eastern, southwestern and south-central

Group Labeling

The resulting groups are then labeled according to the greatest proportional characteristics within groups that also aid in distinguishing among groups. Granted, a large number of characteristics describe these groups, and only a few are taken into account for the purpose of labeling. In part, some of these characteristics may exhibit a large degree of heterogeneity and may thus not be relevant for defining a group. In addition, some characteristics may be more relevant for the purposes of policy design than others. In short, though the labeling of groups can be considered more an art than a science, when taken together with detailed descriptions of a group's most prominent characteristics, labeling can serve as an important starting point in the design and prioritization of activation policies.

The analysis relies on cross-sectional as well as panel data from the European Union Statistics of Income and Living Conditions (EU-SILC) surveys for 2008–11, which combine individual-level information with household characteristics. The first part of the note presents a cross-sectional analysis for the years 2008, 2009, 2010, and 2011. In particular, the latent class analysis on 2008 data shows the main characteristics of the out-of-work before the global economic crisis hit the Bulgarian economy, and thus highlight what could be considered more structural issues of the country's labor market. The 2011 latent class analysis will contrast this initial assessment with more recent developments. The second part of the note exploits longitudinal data between 2008 and 2010[11] to trace the prior labor market status of individuals observed last in 2010 in various classes, and will shed light on the relative persistence in the out-of-work status among different classes of individuals. The set of variables chosen for the cross-section and the longitudinal analysis are slightly different, due to minor differences in the set of variables recorded in each of the two types of data sets.

Main Findings

Out-of-Work Population: Group Profiles from Cross-Section Analysis
The latent class analysis categorizes the out-of-work population into six major groups prior to the crisis and into seven groups in 2010 and 2011. The groups are named according to their most salient characteristics. Figure 3.4 shows the share of each of the seven classes identified in 2011, while table 3.2 presents their summary characteristics.

The seven major clusters emerging from the LCA can be characterized as follows for the year 2011 (for more detail, see Appendix A for a link to the online-only annexes):

- Cluster 1: *Middle-aged unemployed.* This group represents 23 percent of the out-of-work sample of 2011. They are mostly of prime age—35 to 59 years old. A total of 33 percent of males in this age bracket were unemployed; more worrisome, an additional 50 percent were long-term unemployed.

Figure 3.4 Classes of Out-of-Work Individuals in Bulgaria, 2011
percent

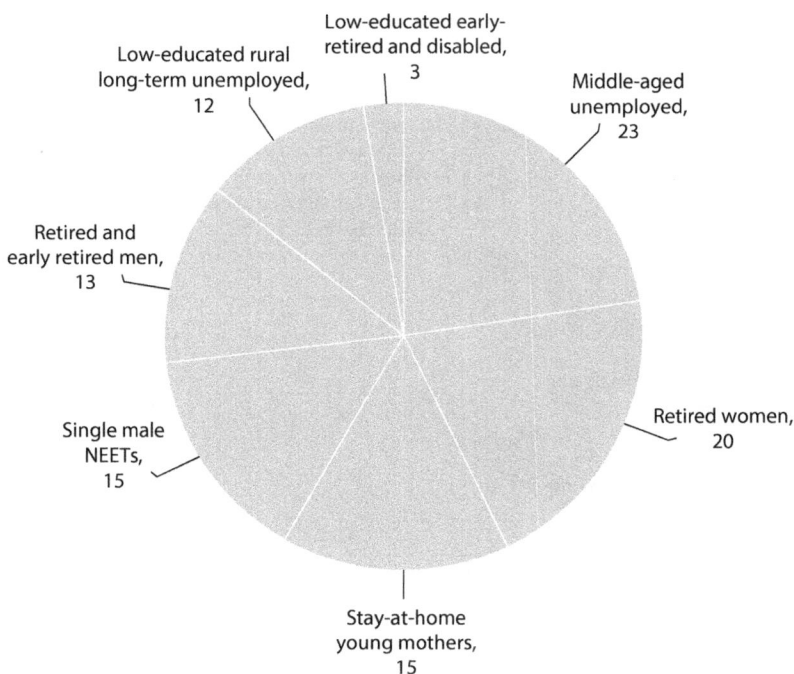

Low-educated early-retired and disabled, 3

Low-educated rural long-term unemployed, 12

Middle-aged unemployed, 23

Retired and early retired men, 13

Retired women, 20

Single male NEETs, 15

Stay-at-home young mothers, 15

Source: World Bank staff analysis based on EU-SILC.

Table 3.2 Summary Characteristics of Latent Classes of Out-of-Work Population in Bulgaria, 2011

1: Middle-aged unemployed (23%)

- 50% are long-term unemployed; 33% unemployed
- 63% are married
- 66% have at least one working adult in the household
- 66% are 35–54 years old
- Mid-skilled: 67% have completed upper secondary school
- 85% have worked before; 18 years of experience on average
- 64% live in rural areas
- High poverty risk: 37% live in poorest income quintile

2: Retired women (19%)

- 97% are retired
- 56% have a partner who is not working; 36% do not have a partner
- 86% are 60–64 years old
- 83% are female
- 94% worked before; 33 years of experience on average
- Low poverty risk: 22% live in poorest income quintile
- 82% receive old-age benefits

3: Stay-at-home young mothers (15%)

- 67% are inactive; 33% are unemployed
- 58% have a partner who is working
- 79% have at least one working adult in household
- 75% are 16–34 years old
- 99% are female
- 83% live with dependent children; 54% live with children younger than 6 years old
- High poverty risk: 37% live in poorest income quintile
- 61% receive family child benefits

4: Single male NEETs (15%)

- 43% are long-term unemployed; 25% are unemployed; 31% are inactive
- 92% have never married; 95% are without a partner
- 69% have at least one working adult in the household
- 96% are 16–34 years old; 61% are 16–24 years old
- 73% are male
- 61% have never worked before; 5 years of work experience on average
- High poverty risk: 38% live in poorest income quintile

5: Retired and early-retired men (13%)

- 86% are retired
- 65% have at least one working adult in household
- 83% are married
- 73% are 55–64 years old
- 88% male
- 93% have worked before; 29 years of experience on average
- Low poverty risk: 20% live in poorest income quintile
- 63% receive old-age benefits

6: Low-educated rural long-term unemployed (12%)

- 61% are long-term unemployed; 31% are unemployed
- 87% have a partner who is not working; 61% have an unemployed partner
- 67% have no working adults in the household
- Low skilled: 82% have below upper secondary education
- 69% are 25–54 years old
- 68% have worked before; 15 years of experience on average
- 70% live with dependent children; 39% live with children younger than 6 years old
- 70% live in rural areas
- Very high poverty risk: 69% live in poorest income quintile
- 53% receive family/child benefits; 23% receive social exclusion benefits

7: Low-educated early-retired and disabled (3%)

- 50% are retired; 40% are disabled
- 77% report having a strongly limited capacity to work
- 81% are without a partner
- 89% are 25–59 years old; 11% are 16–24 years old
- 60% are male
- Low-skilled: 40% below upper secondary school; 37% have completed upper secondary
- Moderate poverty risk: 33% live in poorest income quintile
- 80% receive disability benefits

Source: World Bank staff analysis based on EU-SILC.

Note: Percentages in parentheses following the group names refer to the share of the total out-of-work population. "Years of work experience" refer only to those individuals who have worked before. "Dependent children" include children younger than 18 years of age and household members ages 18–24 years who are economically inactive and living with at least one parent. "Working adult" refers to adults ages 25 years and older. For this report's purposes, we define the at-risk-of-poverty rate as the relative risk of being in the first quintile of the income distribution. The reference period for income reported in EU-SILC surveys is the year preceding the survey year.

This group is relatively educated: although only 7 percent have a tertiary degree, a significant majority (67 percent) have completed upper secondary school. In terms of the economic status of their partners, this group is fairly mixed: 52 percent have a working partner earning a relatively high income, whereas 48 percent either have an inactive partner or are without a partner altogether. In part, this explains why 37 percent of this class is in the poorest 20 percent of the income distribution. A little more than 50 percent live in households with at least one child, and 65 percent are receiving at least one type of social protection benefit.

- Cluster 2: *Retired women.* This group made up 19 percent of the out-of-work population in 2011. It is composed of retired women between the ages of 60 and 64 years, 53 percent of whom have no more than an upper secondary education, and 12 percent of whom have a tertiary education degree. They report an average of 33 years of work experience, are likely to live in relatively small households, and do not have a working partner: they are for the most part widowed (23 percent) or have a retired partner (about 50 percent). In addition, 82 percent receive old-age benefits and 17 percent receive disability benefits. In part, the old-age benefit receipt, along with the fact that their households are relatively small (three members, on average), may explain their relatively low risk of poverty; 22 percent of this class is in the bottom-income quintile.

- Cluster 3: *Stay-at-home young mothers.* This group, whose share of the out-of-work population for 2011 was 15 percent, comprises young women between 16 and 34 years old. A slight majority of them report having children younger than 6 years of age, and about 70 percent live in households with two or more children. This group consists of mostly inactive women (67 percent), although it is noteworthy that one-third are also unemployed. They are low skilled: 47 percent have not completed upper secondary education. Another characteristic is that 58 percent report a working partner whose average income is the highest among all the clusters in this analysis, while 79 percent report at least one working adult within the household. However, as this group's households are relatively large (5.1 members, on average) it is not surprising that despite available labor income, more than 36 percent are in the bottom 20 percent of the income distribution. A little more than 50 percent of the women in this group have no work experience and a majority (61 percent) receive family benefits at the household level (10 percent also report receiving social exclusion benefits).

- Cluster 4: *Single male NEETs.* Members of this class are predominantly male (73 percent), largely younger than 35 years of age, and concentrated among those between 16 and 24 years old.[12] They resemble the unemployed youth who have been particularly hit by the economic crisis across Europe, as 43 percent are long-term unemployed and 25 percent are short-term unemployed, although almost one-third are also inactive. They have never been married and most (61 percent) report having never worked before.

Around 17 percent have a tertiary education while another 48 percent have completed upper secondary school, making them relatively educated among the out-of-work population. Most may live at home with their parents, since despite being single, 69 percent report living with at least one working adult and in households with an average size of more than four members. Their income situation is nonetheless precarious, as 38 percent live in the bottom income quintile. Like the *stay-at-home young mothers*, this group represented 15 percent of the out-of-work population in 2011.

- Cluster 5: *Retired and early-retired men*. This group represented 13 percent of the out-of-work population in 2011. The group is composed of early-retired men between 45 and 59 years old (about 47 percent) and retired men between 60 and 64 years old (about 47 percent). Although 87 percent have a partner who is not working, 65 percent do live in households where at least one adult works. They belong to households with relatively high incomes in comparison to the rest of the out-of-work groups identified, with only 20 percent living in the bottom-income quintile. Their relatively favorable economic situation is partially explained by the fact that they live in relatively small households without children (65 percent report no children in the household, the highest percentage among the groups identified). They have on average 30 years of work experience. Some 63 percent receive old-age benefits and 31 percent receive disability benefits (14 percent report being strongly limited in their activities because of health conditions).

- Cluster 6: *Low-educated rural long-term unemployed*. This group, representing 12 percent of the population out of work in 2011, consists of individuals of prime age (25–54 years) who are largely long-term unemployed (61 percent), although almost one third are short-term unemployed. They have very low levels of education (82 percent have at most completed lower secondary school) and predominantly live in rural areas (70 percent). The majority of this group (68 percent) have previous work experience, an average of 15 years. They live in households with high dependency rates, as their partners tend to also be unemployed. Only one-third report living with at least one adult who is working, and 65 percent live in households with two or more children. The majority (71 percent) receive at least one social benefit; just over half have access to family benefits and 23 percent to social exclusion benefits at the household level, but only 13 percent receive unemployment benefits. Nonetheless, the benefits received are not sufficient to take them out of poverty, as a startling 69 percent are in the poorest quintile of the income distribution.

- Cluster 7: *Low-educated early-retired and disabled*. This group represented 3 percent of the out-of-work population in 2011, with 80 percent receiving disability benefits and 77 percent reporting a strong limitation in their daily activities due to a health condition. They are mostly of prime age (25–59 years old), mostly male (60 percent), and without a partner. Fifty percent report their labor market status as retired and another 40 percent as disabled. They are relatively low-educated: 40 percent received at most a lower secondary education, while 37 percent completed upper secondary school. A third of this group is in the bottom quintile of the income distribution, putting them at a moderate risk for poverty.

The following tables present the main characteristics of each group in 2011. For the complete table, including inactive covariates, see Appendix A for a link to the online-only annexes.

Although most of the identified out-of-work population classes have been quite stable over the last few years, they have experienced some changes in composition and in their share of the total out of work. Table 3.5 shows the evolution of the classes identified from 2008 to 2011 as a share of the total out-of-work population, while figure 3.5 graphs the absolute numbers. From the graph, the first important observation is that the size of the out-of-work population has increased only slightly, by 5 percent, between 2008 and 2011. However, some classes have changed across time; for example, classes identified in 2011 that were present in previous years changed in relative size and also in composition. The fact that the

Table 3.3 Latent Classes of Out-of-Work Population in Bulgaria: Indicators, 2011

	All out-of-work	1. Middle-aged unemployed	2. Retired women	3. Stay-at-home young mothers	4. Single male NEETs	5. Retired and early-retired men	6. Low-educated rural long-term unemployed	7. Low-educated early-retired and disabled
Cluster size (%)	100	23	20	15	15	13	12	3
Population	1,564,723	353,940	315,918	241,906	232,674	197,937	180,100	42,248
Indicators (%)								
Labor market attachment								
Unemployed	19	32	0	23	25	4	31	0
Long-term unemployed	28	50	1	10	43	8	61	8
Retired	34	11	97	0	1	86	0	50
Disabled	2	2	0	0	0	2	0	40
Other inactive	17	5	2	67	31	0	8	2
Working spouse								
Yes	28	52	8	57	0	44	1	5
No	34	17	56	15	5	41	87	14
NA*	38	32	36	28	95	15	12	81
Self-assessed physical capacity								
Strongly limited	94	1	8	1	1	14	2	77
None/limited	6	99	93	99	99	86	98	23

Source: World Bank staff analysis based on EU-SILC.
*NA = not applicable.

Table 3.4 Latent Classes of Out-of-Work Population in Bulgaria: Active Covariates, 2011

	All out-of-work	1. Middle-aged unemployed	2. Retired women	3. Stay-at-home young mothers	4. Single male NEETs	5. Retired and early-retired men	6. Low-educated rural long-term unemployed	7. Low-educated early-retired and disabled
Cluster size (%)	**100**	**23**	**20**	**15**	**15**	**13**	**12**	**3**
Population	**1,564,723**	**353,940**	**315,918**	**241,906**	**232,674**	**197,937**	**180,100**	**42,248**
Active covariates (%)								
Age groups (years)								
16–24	15	1	0	25	61	0	10	11
25–34	20	13	0	50	35	0	27	31
35–59	41	85	14	24	4	53	56	58
60–64	24	2	86	1	0	47	6	0
Gender								
Male	45	51	17	1	73	88	53	60
Female	55	49	83	99	27	12	47	40
Education								
Primary	39	25	33	48	31	34	82	40
Secondary	48	67	54	38	48	49	11	37
Tertiary	11	7	12	12	17	16	4	6
Not applicable	3	2	1	3	3	2	3	16
Urban	44	36	48	53	45	53	30	47
Rural	56	64	52	47	55	47	70	53

Source: World Bank staff analysis based on EU-SILC
Note: NEET = not in employment, education, or training.

Table 3.5 Classes of Out-of-Work Population in Bulgaria as a Percentage of Total Out-of-Work Population, 2008–11

percent

	2008	2009	2010	2011
Middle-aged unemployed (2010 and 2011)	n.a.	n.a.	31	23
Retired women (2010 and 2011)	n.a.	n.a.	25	19
Stay-at-home young mothers	16	15	12	15
Single male NEETs	13	17	17	15
Retired and early-retired men (2010 and 2011)	n.a.	n.a.	10	13
Low-educated rural long-term unemployed (not in 2010)	15	17	n.a.	12
Low-educated early-retired and disabled	5	3	4	3
Retirees (2008 and 2009)	25	30	n.a.	n.a.
Unemployed and early retirees (2008 and 2009)	26	19	n.a.	n.a.

Source: World Bank staff analysis based on EU-SILC.
Note: n.a. = not applicable; NEET = not in employment, education, or training.

Figure 3.5 Classes of Out-of-Work Population in Bulgaria, 2008–11, Thousands of Individuals

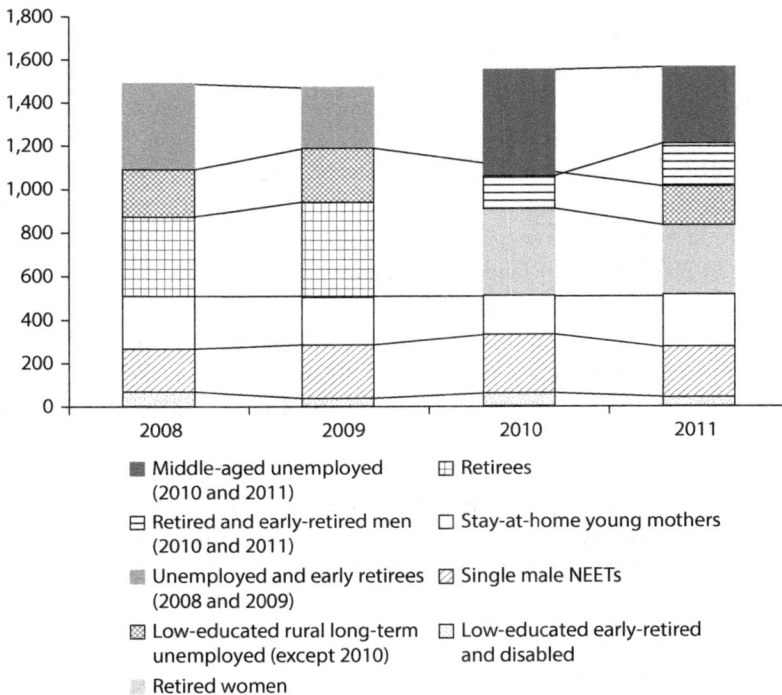

Legend:
- ■ Middle-aged unemployed (2010 and 2011)
- ⊟ Retired and early-retired men (2010 and 2011)
- ▤ Unemployed and early retirees (2008 and 2009)
- ⊠ Low-educated rural long-term unemployed (except 2010)
- ▨ Retired women
- ⊞ Retirees
- ☐ Stay-at-home young mothers
- ⊠ Single male NEETs
- ☐ Low-educated early-retired and disabled

Source: World Bank staff analysis based on EU-SILC.
Note: NEET = not in employment, education, or training.

composition of the classes changes over time is particularly important to keep in mind when interpreting changes in class size. For instance, significant increases (or decreases) in class size are sometimes due to reassignments of individuals across classes, resulting in changes in class composition. Thus, although some classes may retain similar names across years due to their most salient characteristics, their composition may nonetheless vary. The evolution of particular classes' size and composition over 2008–11 can be summarized as follows:

- Across time, one of the most significant changes is the increase in size of the group of *single male NEETs*, which grew by 18 percent from 197,000 to 233,000. The composition of this group also changed. While 76 percent of this cluster was between 16 and 24 years old in 2007, by 2011 this share had fallen to 60 percent of the group. The proportion of males also increased, from 61 to 73 percent. Moreover, the group became more skilled as the share of individuals who had tertiary education increased from 7 to 18 percent. Although the share of this group that belonged to the lowest 20 percent of the income distribution decreased, it is worrisome that the number of long-term unemployed increased in this group, from 38 to 43 percent.

- Most importantly, the previous class labeled as *unemployed and early retirees* split into two groups starting in 2010: a smaller group of *retired and early-retired men* and a relatively large group of *middle-aged unemployed*, which now accounts for 23 percent of the out-of-work. The emergence of this new group of unemployed results from the increase in joblessness following the crisis.

- On the other hand, although the total number of retirees also grew during the period,[13] many of the individuals in the newly emerged group of *retired and early-retired men* may have in earlier years been grouped in the *retirees* cluster. Starting in 2010, these individuals are now grouped together with early retired men in the newly emerged *retired and early-retired men* cluster. The *retirees* group identified in 2008 and 2009 was only 65 percent female; by 2011, it had evolved to become 83 percent female and had also diminished in size. Because of its changed composition in terms of gender, it is labeled as *retired women* starting in 2010.

- The *stay-at-home young mothers* cluster remained fairly stable in terms of its share of the out-of-work population during the period, although its composition varied slightly. In 2007 this cluster's population was younger: 40 percent were between 16–24 years old, compared to 25 percent in 2011. Another important difference is in the young mothers' partners. Although in 2009 the percentage of this group that had a working partner increased to 82 percent (from 77 the previous year), the figure decreased rapidly following the crisis to 58 percent in 2011. This loss of income in the household meant an increased risk of poverty in this cluster; the share of those in the poorest income quintile increased 9 points from 2007 to 2011.

- The *low-educated early-retired disabled* group maintained the same relative share of the out-of-work population, between 3 and 5 percent, during the period. In terms of composition, a larger share of the individuals in this group became disabled—from 15 to 40 percent—and a larger share also became long-term unemployed, 8 percent in 2011 compared to 0.1 percent in 2007.

- Finally, the cluster of *low-educated rural long-term unemployed* was a decreasing share of the out-of-work population, falling from 15 to 12 percent from 2007 to 2011. (Note, however, that in 2009 this share went up to 17 percent before falling sharply.)

Structural Aspects and Emerging Trends in the Profiles of the Out-of-Work

The clusters identified in the out-of-work population for the 2008–11 period reflect both structural aspects of the Bulgarian labor market. This section uses cross-sectional and longitudinal analysis of clusters of the out-of-work population to further examine the effects of the crisis on the Bulgarian labor market.

Figure 3.6 Labor Force Participation among Youth Ages 15–24 Years, European Countries, 2013
percent

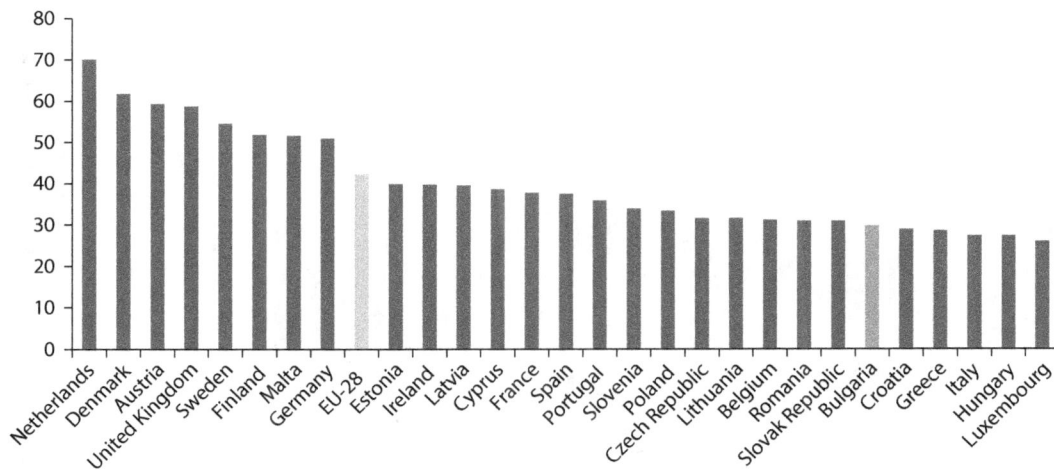

Source: Eurostat, EU-LFS.

Not only is unemployment high among youth and employment low, but youth labor force participation rates (LFPRs) in Bulgaria are among the lowest in the EU. In recent years, Bulgaria's NEET rate has consistently been among the highest among the EU, while youth LFPRs, at only 29.6 percent in 2013, are well below the EU average of 42.2 percent (figure 3.6). In part, low labor force participation and employment rates among youth reflect a full-time work tradition in Bulgaria. In many EU countries, youth have higher LFPRs because they are able to combine their studies with part-time work. For example, as many as 75 percent and 40 percent, respectively, of youth in the Netherlands and Slovenia report working part time (Dimitrov and Duell 2013). In contrast, only about 4 percent of youth in Bulgaria work part time, and this figure has remained steady in recent years (ibid).

Disabled individuals face significant barriers to employment, with important consequences for spending on disability benefits. In 2011, 53 percent of individuals of working age with at least one permanent difficulty in their daily activities were inactive, and only 31 percent were employed (Dimitrov and Duell 2013). In this analysis, the *low-educated early-retired disabled* cluster represented, on average, 4 percent of the out-of-work population (around 50,000 individuals), and 80 percent of this group received disability benefits. Although the percentage of expenditures on disability benefits as a share of GDP in Bulgaria is among the lowest in the European Union, this proportion has been increasing (see figure 3.7) and will likely continue to rise significantly in coming years, as the Bulgarian population continues to age at rapid rates. Moreover, the identified cluster is not only heavily reliant on benefits but is also relatively young,[14] implying that benefit payments are likely to continue for decades to come. Low levels of education and lack of work experience, as well as an inaccessible physical

Figure 3.7 Expenditures on Disability Benefits as a Share of GDP in Europe, 2008 and 2010
percent

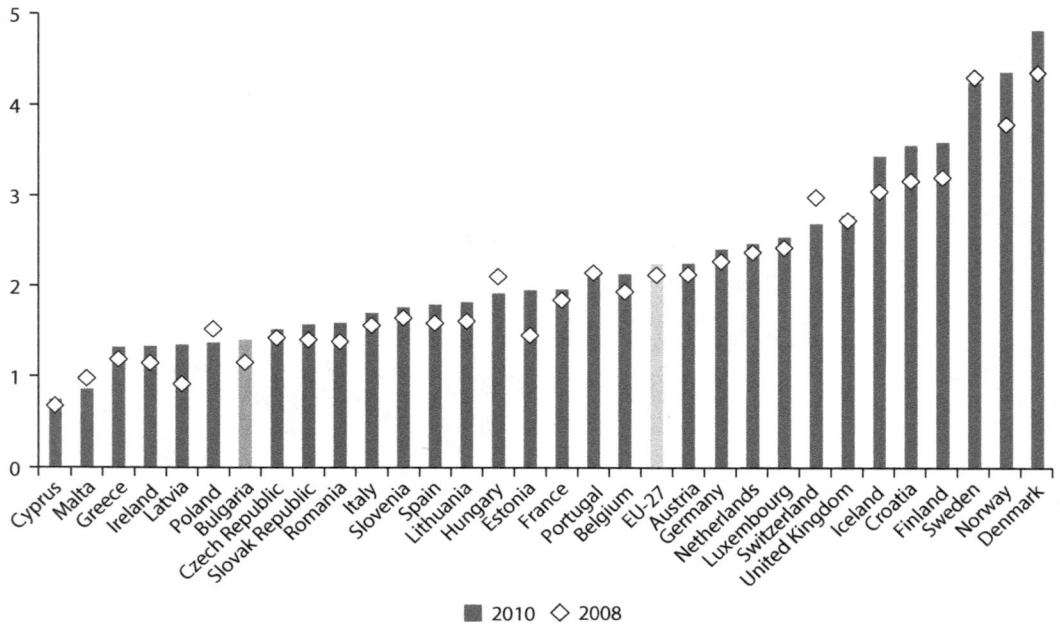

■ 2010   ◇ 2008

Source: Eurostat.

environment and employer reluctance to hire individuals with disabilities, represent some of the structural barriers faced by this population.

A relatively large percentage of the working-age population is already retired. In the working-age sample used in this analysis, two main clusters of retirees emerge, representing around a third of the out-of-work population. This may partly reflect the fact that a relatively high percentage of the population between 15 and 64 years old has reached retirement age.[15] As shown in figure 3.8, Bulgaria's population is expected to age dramatically in the coming years. The median age has already increased from 30.3 in 1960 to 42.7 in 2012. This presently represents the third highest median age in the EU, surpassed only by Germany and Italy. In addition, LFPRs for both men and women close to retirement are lower than the EU-27 average.[16] Delaying retirement and increasing labor force participation among older individuals and the general working-age population thus emerge as important policy priorities.

Not only has the number of unemployed grown with the crisis, unemployment has also changed in nature. A new distinct class of unemployed (the *middle-aged unemployed*) has emerged, representing 354,000 mostly unemployed individuals, many of whom were affected by the financial crisis. The length of unemployment spells also increased following the crisis, with a resulting rise in the number of long-term unemployed individuals. It is also evident that youth—who as a group are already at a disadvantage in the labor market for

Figure 3.8 Demographic Change in Bulgaria

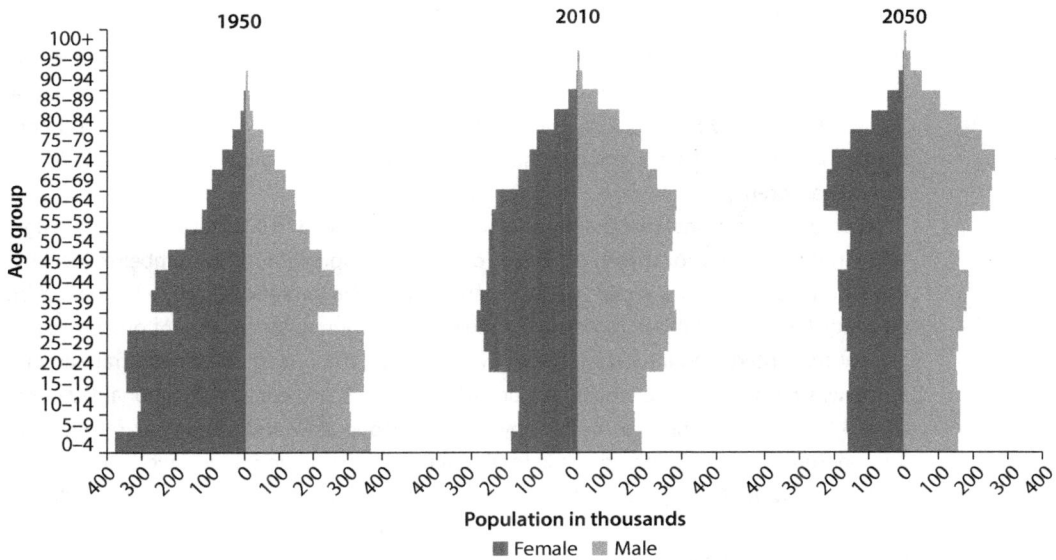

Source: World Bank 2013b, based on data from the United Nations Population Division.

structural reasons—were also affected by the crisis, as can be seen by the increasing number of *single male NEETs*.

Despite their high reliance on benefits, many of the unemployed and stay-at-home mothers identified in this study remain at risk for poverty. The key transmission channel of income shocks during the crisis was the labor market, with less-educated individuals, including most Roma (see box 3.1 for a discussion of Roma population and labor market exclusion in Bulgaria), being the most likely to have been affected by labor market shocks. The public response, which included an increase in pensions and other social protection spending, prevented a sharp increase in poverty (World Bank 2012). However, the stimulus underutilized Bulgaria's battery of well-targeted programs, including child allowances and especially the guaranteed minimum income (GMI) program, which covers a very small part of the population and of the poor. As such, inefficient targeting and low generosity have thwarted poverty reduction, even though on average more than 60 percent of the *middle-aged unemployed, stay-at-home young mothers,* and *low-educated rural long-term unemployed* identified in this study receive at least one form of social benefit. This is especially the case for the *low-educated rural long-term unemployed*, 69 percent of whom are in the poorest income quintile. The groups of retired individuals, on the other hand, are well protected from poverty, in part because of a generous old-age benefit.

Out-of-Work Population: Group Profiles from Longitudinal Analysis

Finally, by looking at longitudinal EU-SILC data for the 2008–10 period, one can better understand the dynamics within clusters and notice other movements in

---

Box 3.1 Roma Population and Labor Market Exclusion in Bulgaria

Labor market exclusion in Bulgaria cannot be discussed without giving special consideration to the situation of the country's Roma population, a population that faces significant structural barriers. Because EU-SILC data do not include a differentiating indicator for Roma and non-Roma, the out-of-work population classes identified in this exercise cannot directly be linked to a Roma/non-Roma pattern.

According to national census information, there are about 370,000 citizens of Roma origin living in Bulgaria (approximately 5 percent of the total population). This number reflects the lower bound of estimates, in part because many Roma in Bulgaria also identify with the Turkish ethnicity. Members of the Roma minority achieve lower human development outcomes and are not fully integrated into economic activity. In 2011, the poverty headcount rate among Roma was 68 percent, in contrast to a poverty rate of 23 percent at the national level (see table B3.1.1). In the same year the employment rate stood at 57 and 52 percent, respectively, for non-Roma men and women, while for Roma the corresponding figures were only 42 and 26 percent (World Bank 2013a). Willingness to work, as measured in the labor force participation rate (LFPR), has been shown to be relatively high among Roma, exceeding the LFPR in the majority population in the case of men: According to data from the 2007 World Bank Bulgaria Multi-Topic Survey, LFPR among non-Roma stood at 79 percent and 68 percent for men and women, respectively; in contrast, among Roma, the corresponding results were 85 and 59 percent. Unemployment rates are also disproportionately high among Roma, having reached as high as 53 percent among Roma women before the crisis (data are for 2007). Unfavorable labor market outcomes among Roma population can be in part explained by a significant education gap between Roma and non-Roma population that is even higher among women. A World Bank study (2010) finds large gaps in the share of Roma and non-Roma population with a secondary education: Among Roma, only 16 and 10 percent of men and women, respectively, had completed secondary education; the corresponding figures for non-Roma men and women stood at around 87 percent. Only in recent years have educational outcomes for Roma children started to improve. Lastly, discrimination appears to be the cause of about a third of the Roma/non-Roma wage gap (World Bank 2010), and may be a further contributor to low employment rates.

As World Bank (2010) outlined, the underperformance and exclusion of Roma carries a significant economic and fiscal cost for countries in the region. For Bulgaria, the economic and fiscal costs of Roma exclusion were estimated at EUR 0.56 billion and 0.37 billion in 2010, respectively. In light of the projected decline of the working-age population in Bulgaria, active inclusion of minority populations in education, labor markets, and other areas of society is a key development challenge for the country.

box continues next page

Box 3.1 Roma Population and Labor Market Exclusion in Bulgaria *(continued)*

Table B3.1.1 Poverty Headcount Rate and Distribution

	Poverty headcount rate			Distribution of the poor			Distribution of population		
	Feb-10	Oct-10	Feb-11	Feb-10	Oct-10	Feb-11	Feb-10	Oct-10	Feb-11
Total	21.1	21.2	23	100	100	100	100	100	100
Ethnicity									
Bulgarian	14.1	15.5	16.4	55.5	61.4	59.1	82.5	82.9	83.1
Turkish	41.4	43.4	50.9	18.7	21.1	22	9.5	10.2	9.9
Roma	72.5	64.4	68.4	23.1	15.1	15.4	6.7	4.9	5.2

Source: Crisis monitoring survey OSI-WB, 2010–11.

Sources: World Bank 2010, 2012, 2013a.

the labor market. The latent class analysis of the out-of-work in the 2010 longitudinal data set (which comprises a subsample of around 500 observations), yielded similar results in terms of latent classes, though in light of the reduced sample size it became necessary to combine some categories of out-of-work individuals, producing only four distinct clusters. Since there are some similarities in the size and characteristics of these four clusters compared to the cross-section analysis, the findings from the panel data can be used to understand further the dynamics of the previously described sample. The four identified classes, in order of magnitude, are:

- *Married or widowed retirees* (30 percent)
- *Low-educated rural unemployed* (30 percent)
- *Single NEETs* (26 percent)
- *Stay-at-home mothers* (14 percent)

Annex 3 (see Appendix A for a link to the online-only annexes) shows the statistical description of the latent classes in full, while table 3.6 summarizes the most salient characteristics of the four classes.

An advantage of the dynamic panel analysis is that the labor market status of individuals in these four classes can be observed across time, providing information on the flows in and out of jobs two years later (tables 3.7 and 3.8).

The longitudinal analysis indicates that the reduction in employment between 2008 and 2010 is predominantly explained by job losses and movement into unemployment. Table 3.7 shows the flows of the 2008 working-age population,[17] according to their labor market status in 2008 into any of the four latent out-of-work classes or into employment. The table shows that 11 percent of the individuals who were employed in 2008 moved into one of the four out-of-work classes in 2010, whereas the remaining 89 percent continued in employment. The group of *low-educated rural unemployed* absorbed almost half of the job losses—around 5 percent of the previously employed, versus only 2 percent in the case of *married or widowed retirees, single NEETs,* and

Table 3.6 Longitudinal Analysis: Summary Characteristics of Latent Classes of Out-of-Work Population in Bulgaria, 2010

1: Married or widowed retirees (30%)

- 96% are retired
- 43% have a partner who is not working; 38% are without a partner
- 60% are married; 19% are widowed
- 79% are 55–64 years old
- 68% are female
- 48% have upper secondary education; 30% have lower secondary
- 29 years of work experience on average
- 57% live in rural areas
- 11% report strongly limited capacity to work
- Low poverty risk: 20% in poorest income quintile
- 55% receive old-age benefits; 46% disability benefits

2: Low-educated rural unemployed (30%)

- 98% are unemployed
- 49% have a partner who is not working; 26% are without a partner
- 61% have no working adults in household
- 63% are between 35–54 years old
- Low-skilled: 60% have lower secondary education or below
- 17 years of work experience on average
- 60% live with children
- 70% live in rural areas
- Very high poverty risk: 54% in poorest income quintile
- 56% receive family child benefits

3: Single NEETs (26%)

- 67% are unemployed; 33% are inactive
- 93% are without a partner or never married
- 69% have at least one working adult in household
- 99% are between 16–34 years old
- 55% are male
- 3 years of work experience on average
- 63% live in rural areas
- High poverty risk: 43% in poorest income quintile
- 6 household members on average

4: Stay-at-home mothers (14%)

- 59% are inactive, 39% unemployed
- 96% have a working partner
- 81% are between 25–54 years old
- 99% are female
- 12 years of work experience on average
- 73% live with children
- Moderate poverty risk: 26% in poorest income quintile
- 57% receive family child benefits

Source: World Bank staff analysis based on EU-SILC.
Note: "Years of work experience" refers only to those individuals who have worked before. "Dependent children" include children younger than 18 years of age and household members ages 18–24 years who are economically inactive and living with at least one parent. "Working adult" refers to adults ages 24 years and older.

Table 3.7 Bulgaria: Composition of 2010 Clusters based on 2008 Labor Market Status (Column Percentages)

		Labor market status in 2008				
Cluster	Working-age population in 2010	Unemployed	Retired	Disabled	Other inactive	Employed
1	Married or widowed retirees	4	95	52	5	2
2	Low-educated rural unemployed	39	4	0	6	5
3	Single NEETs	21	0	48	44	2
4	Stay-at-home mothers	12	0	0	18	2
NC	Employed	25	1	0	28	89
Total		100	100	100	100	100

Source: World Bank staff analysis based on EU-SILC.
Note: For 2010, students 16–24 years old who are inactive are excluded from the sample. Numbers referred to in the text appear shaded in gray; NEET = not in employment, education, or training.

stay-at-home mothers, respectively. Given that *single NEETs* are predominantly unemployed (68 percent), it can also be inferred that roughly 7 percent of those who were employed in 2008 moved into a largely unemployed cluster in 2010, while the remaining 4 percent predominantly moved into an inactive class.

A significant proportion of all of the out-of work groups identified in 2010 were hit by job losses, meaning that they were employed in 2008; this is

Table 3.8 Bulgaria: Composition of 2010 Clusters Based on 2008 Labor Market Status (Row Percentages)

| Cluster | Working-age population in 2010 | Labor market status in 2008 | | | | | |
		Unemployed	Retired	Disabled	Other inactive	Employed	Total
1	Married or widowed retirees	5	77	1	4	12	100
2	Low-educated rural unemployed	58	3	0	5	34	100
3	Single NEETs	38	0	1	48	13	100
4	Stay-at-home mothers	39	0	0	34	27	100
NC	Employed	6	0	0	4	90	100

Source: World Bank staff analysis based on EU-SILC.
Note: For 2010, students 16–24 years old who are inactive are excluded from the sample. Numbers referred to in the text appear shaded in gray; NEET = not in employment, education, or training.

especially so among the *low-educated rural unemployed* and *stay-at-home mothers*. Table 3.8 allows for the identification of the groups in the 2010 population that were most affected by job losses. The group of *low-educated rural unemployed* is the hardest hit, with 34 percent of its members formerly employed in 2008. The second group to be affected by job losses is the class of *stay-at-home mothers*, 27 percent of whom lost their jobs. Comparatively, only 13 percent of *single NEETs* lost their jobs. However, this may explain the fact that many *single NEETs* who are unemployed are first-time jobseekers, so few were likely to have been employed in 2008 in the first place. During economic downturns, youth are generally more likely to lose their jobs, since they tend to work in cyclically sensitive industries such as construction or hold temporary contracts (Eurofound 2012).

Longitudinal analysis suggests a lack of flow into employment. Table 3.8 also shows that 90 percent of those employed in 2010 were already employed in 2008. In addition, from the previous table, it is clear that only 25 percent of the unemployed and 28 percent of the "other inactive" (that is, not retired or disabled) in 2008 moved into employment in 2010. This pattern might then reinforce the divide between the employed and the unemployed.

From Profiling to Activation

The current general labor market situation, along with institutional and resource deficiencies, make the activation and integration of many of the identified out-of-work groups a demanding challenge. Low labor demand and sluggish growth are exacerbated by deficiencies in the institutional setup and resources of the public employment service, active labor market policies (ALMPs), and related social services in Bulgaria. Spending on ALMPs has been drastically reduced in recent years, while the GMI scheme provides low coverage and is generally not associated with activation measures. Prioritizing interventions is therefore of great importance. This section will (a) give an overview of activation and inclusion policies in Bulgaria; (b) gauge the activation need and activation potential of each group of out-of-work persons; and (c) propose a focused set of interventions for the prioritized groups. It is important to keep in mind that the proposed interventions are meant only as a starting point in a discussion with country authorities on general activation policies and their respective priorities. While the latent classes identified in this exercise points generally toward certain effectively tailored policies, it would be beneficial to conduct a more detailed profiling exercise at the individual level. Latent class analysis allows for the classification of a vast population into broad meaningful categories, but variation within groups still has implications for the level of appropriate support for the purposes of activation.

Activation and Inclusion Policies in Bulgaria

After the financial crisis started to have economic and employment effects in 2009, Bulgaria responded with a further cutback of ALMP spending from 2009 onward. In contrast to the average OECD spending on labor market policies (LMPs) of 1.44 percent of GDP in 2011, Bulgaria spent only 0.59 percent of GDP on public employment service administration, ALMPs, unemployment, and early retirement benefits combined (see figure 3.9). Some of the spending from the national budget on ALMPs has since been replaced with funding from the European Social Fund (ESF), allowing for more program flexibility, but also incurring additional administrative burdens on public employment services.

The great majority (71 percent) of LMP spending in Bulgaria goes to "passive" benefits, namely unemployment benefits and early retirement. Though, on average, OECD countries also allocate most LMP spending to these types of benefits, the proportion is considerably lower, at 60 percent (see figure 3.10).

Even though a large proportion of LMP spending goes to passive policies, coverage of the unemployed by unemployment benefits or the GMI program is low. Of the registered unemployed (comprising short- and long-term unemployed workers), only 14 percent received unemployment benefits and only 6 percent received GMI. Activity in the informal economy is high, estimated at 19.5 percent for men and 12.9 percent for women in 2008, which exacerbates the lack of access to unemployment insurance (Packard, Koettl, and Montenegro 2012, 31).

Participation in the GMI program is not well linked to activation or work incentives. Recent findings from a World Bank study on the activation of vulnerable groups in Bulgaria (Dimitrov and Duell 2013) confirmed that the participation in the GMI program is generally handled in a traditional "social assistance" type way, with social workers more concerned about enforcing asset and income tests than providing activation and linkage to social services. The attractiveness of the GMI and any work incentives are further reduced by a six-month waiting period, mandatory community work (without activation, employment linkage, or skill development), and the absence of earnings disregards for benefit recipients. Absence of part-time employment legislation further increases the barriers to entry-level employment for young people, parents, and labor market outsiders (EC 2013b, 24).

Figure 3.9 Labor Market Policy (LMP) Spending in Bulgaria as a Share of GDP
percent

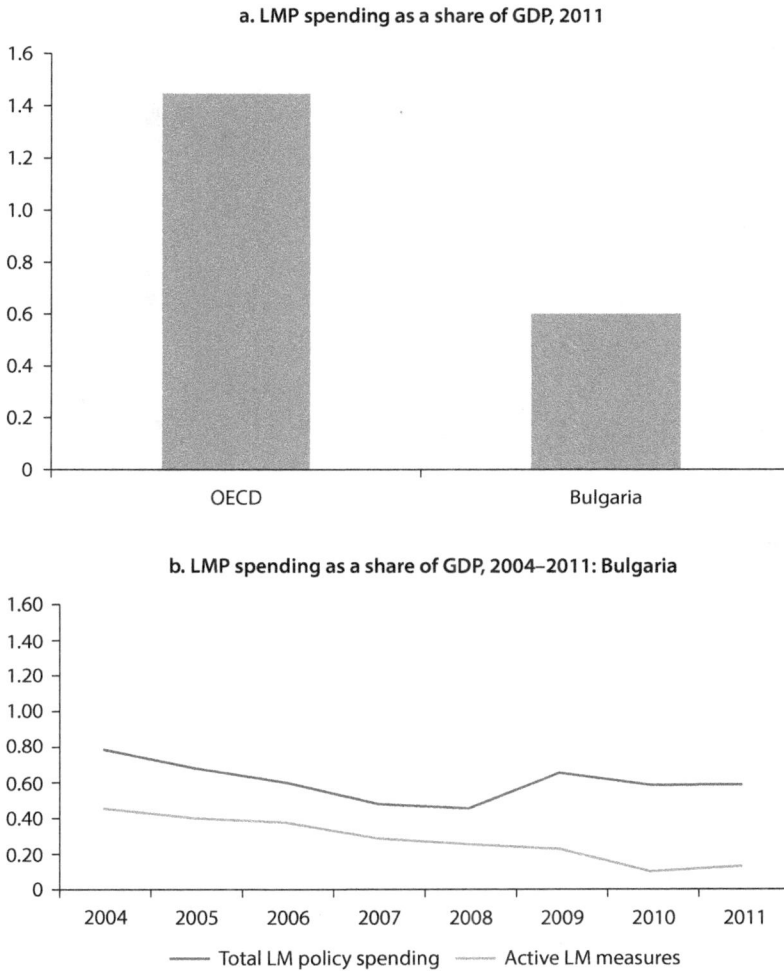

a. LMP spending as a share of GDP, 2011

b. LMP spending as a share of GDP, 2004–2011: Bulgaria

Total LM policy spending ——— Active LM measures

Sources: OECD, Eurostat.
Note: 2005 is estimate.

The institutional setup of active labor markets and services is highly fragmented. The institutional delivery structure for activating policies and services is divided between the Public Employment Service, the Social Assistance Agency, the National Security Institute, and other agencies, including the Ministry of Education (literacy) and Medical Commissions (disability). Current collaboration between these agencies is limited, focused on rule enforcement and program crosschecks rather than on activation and job linkage. Strict, regular enforcement of asset and income tests among the GMI population further reduces the incentive for (formal) work.

Figure 3.10 Composition of Spending on Labor Market Policies (LMPs) in Bulgaria, 2011

percent

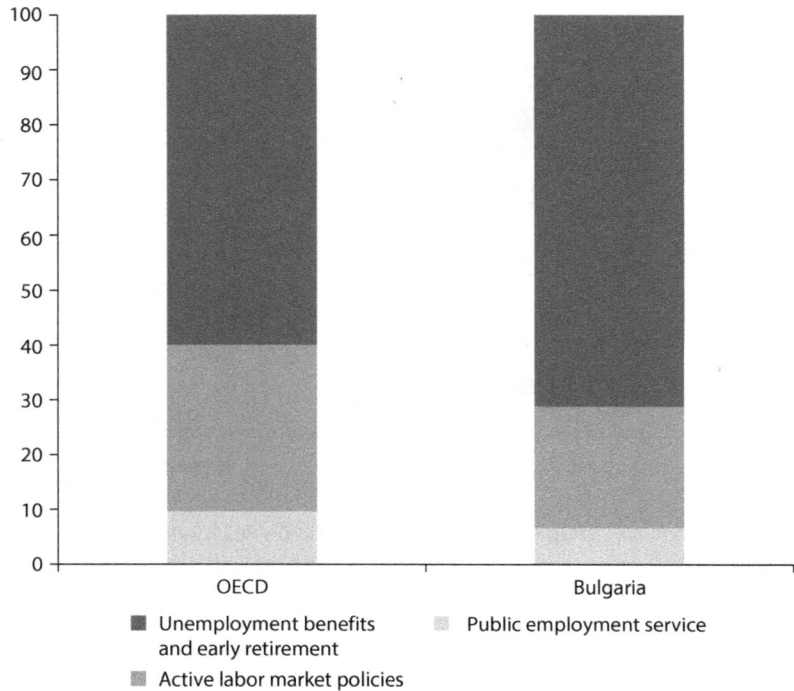

Unemployment benefits and early retirement   Public employment service

Active labor market policies

Source: OECD, Eurostat.

Labor force participation and maternity leave. Potential concerns for female labor force participants in many countries are regulations and labor market arrangements for (paid) maternity leave and extended absences from the workplace. Bulgaria grants an OECD record of 68 weeks of maternity leave, most of it with paid benefits, for formal nonagricultural workers. While the intuitive conclusion would be to assume a lower female employment rate, the opposite is true among the active population. Female unemployment (9.8 percent) for 15- to 64-year-olds is actually lower than the male unemployment rate (12.4 percent in 2011). LFPR for young women is lower (24.9 percent compared to 33.9 percent for men), but this could be explained by women's greater participation in higher education. Once women hit prime age, their labor force participation is actually quite high in Bulgaria compared to EU-27: 79.3 percent for women vs. 84.5 percent for men. The gender gap in LFPR is thus 5.2 percentage points in Bulgaria, compared to a 13 percentage point gap in the EU-27. Overall, Bulgaria could benefit from a more employment-friendly and human-capital preserving approach to maternity leave, since the overall LFPR is quite low. Women's caregiving responsibilities, combined with a lack of child-care options, play a part in this.

Finally, some programs for the inclusion of inactive and marginalized groups deserve special mention. These are the program for Roma mediators in employment offices ("Activating inactive people in the labor market") and the national literacy program for adults, which help to overcome severe under qualification and barriers to entry.

Activation Priority, Activation Type, and Benefit Receipt by Group

In further considering the approach toward labor market integration, an assessment of the priorities and potentials of the identified groups is needed. Given the limited resources for programs and the low availability and difficulty coordinating staff in the Bulgarian social assistance and public employment departments, prioritization of interventions is all the more important. After the first step ("activation priority") of prioritizing interventions along activation need and activation potential, a second step ("activation type") will classify the groups according to the kind of activation intervention needed, depending on the social or labor market barriers to be overcome. Lastly, as a third step, information on *household income composition* of the different groups will be used to assess potential cross-dependencies of the benefit system with the labor market status and activation approaches.

Activation Priority

Table 3.9 gives an overview of the identified inactive classes, their respective activation need, and activation potential. The total number of persons estimated in these clusters is 1.56 million, representing about 21 percent of the total population and 33 percent of the working-age (16–64) population of Bulgaria in 2011.

In the table, "activation need" refers to a group's level of need for inclusion in the labor market in order to gain income and reduce or end poverty. "Activation potential" describes that group's ability or motivation to be in the labor market. High activation need might be driven by high poverty risk (as in the case of the *low-educated rural long-term unemployed*), whereas high activation potential could be driven by previous work experience or a relatively good educational base (for example, the *middle-aged unemployed*).

Table 3.9 Activation Need and Potential of Different Clusters in Bulgaria

Share % (2011)	Cluster	Activation need	Activation potential	Priority for action
23	Middle-aged unemployed	Medium	High	High
19	Retired women	Low	Low	Low
15	Stay-at-home young mothers	Medium	Medium	Medium
15	Single male NEETs	High	Medium	High
13	Retired and early-retired men	Low	Medium	Low
12	Low-educated rural long-term unemployed	High	Medium	High
3	Low-educated early-retired and disabled	Low	Low	Low

Source: World Bank staff analysis and assessment 2014.

From this overview, an initial set of priorities arises: the *middle-aged unemployed, single male NEETs*, and *low-educated rural long-term unemployed* are the *highest priority for activation*. Their high priority stems from their relatively large cohort sizes, high or medium activation need due to high poverty risks, and activation potential through labor market proximity given their work histories and education. *Stay-at-home young mothers* follow closely behind these classes as a priority, but are classified as slightly lower priority owing to their nondeclared unemployment and to the significant share who have at least one working adult in their households. *Retired women* (86 percent of whom are over the current retirement age of 60 years),[18] *retired and early-retired men* (who have comparatively low poverty risk, in part due to old-age benefit income), and the *low-educated early-retired and disabled* are not prioritized for activation measures or policies due to their lower activation need and potential (almost 80 percent of the *low-educated early-retired and disabled* report a strongly limited capacity to work).

In a less constrained environment, with more established activation and labor market integration policies for younger and middle-aged jobseekers, additional consideration could be given to reprioritizing the group of *retired and early-retired men*. Nearly half, 47 percent, are between ages 45 and 59 years, and could thus be considered to be in early retirement[19] and potentially amenable to reintegration into the labor market. Given the extreme demographic pressures in Bulgaria, special attention needs to be paid to limiting inflow into this group of unemployed and avoiding further increases in the number of early retirees. Given the fact that 52 percent of this group's total household income still derives from labor and 46 percent from transfers (specifically, old-age and disability benefits for this class represent 29 percent and 11 percent, respectively, of the total spent on such benefits), all three levers need to be considered: (1) continuing labor income, (2) reducing retirements and pension payments, and (3) managing entry into disability benefits.

Activation Type

As a second step, the relative severity of labor market or social obstacles to labor market integration will serve as an orientation for activation approaches. Figure 3.11 depicts the prioritized clusters along the labor market and social barrier dimensions; the size of the bubbles correspond to their relative group size.

As a result of mapping the barriers to labor market integration faced by the four prioritized groups, we can quickly discern the respective types of activation that could be undertaken for them. Whereas the *low-educated rural long-term unemployed* will require activation across the labor market proximity and social inclusion axes, the *single male NEETs* or the *stay-at-home young mothers* will mainly require job-search and professional training assistance on the labor market dimension. For the *stay-at-home young mothers* group, local social services (especially child care) will have the greatest effect on activation. The *middle-aged unemployed* will mainly require employability-enhancing measures.

Figure 3.11 Activation Types of Prioritized Clusters, Bulgaria

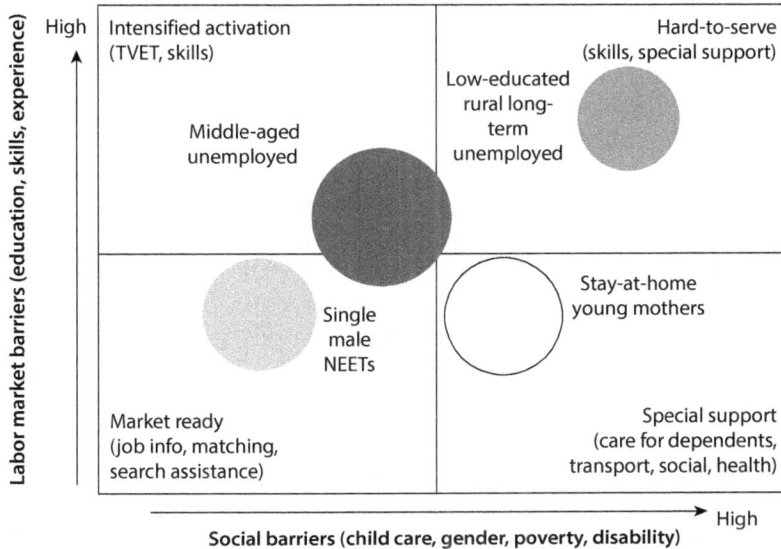

Source: World Bank staff analysis and assessment 2014.
Note: TVET = technical and vocational education and training.

Household Income Composition

When analyzing the 2011 household income of the groups, we realize that benefits are the major income source for only two of them (*retired women* and *low-educated early-retired and disabled*). For the large prioritized groups, no immediate benefit or incentive-trap picture emerges from the overview. Households of *middle-aged unemployed* rely on pensions for 14 percent of their income, but in terms of actual numbers, only 7 percent receive old-age benefits. For *retired women*, old-age benefits make up 46 percent of household income, consistent with the fact that 97 percent of the group is retired and 86 percent is 60-plus years old.

Stay-at-home young mothers have the lowest benefit incidence among all groups (23 percent of household income) while *single male NEETs* are close behind, with 24 percent of household income. Old-age benefits make up 8 and 11 percent of the household income in these groups, an understandable fact since someone older than 64 is present in 19 and 23 percent of these households, respectively. These are interesting household composition effects, but they present no immediate labor market participation disincentives for the young women and men in the *stay-at-home young mothers* and *single male NEETs* groups.

Retired and early-retired men receive 29 percent of old-age benefits, 40 percent if old-age and disability benefits are combined. The same figure for the *low-educated early-retired and disabled* is 44 percent (with disability benefits making up 26 percent of the total). Among the *low-educated rural long-term unemployed*, incidence of family/child benefits is rather high (13 percent of household income) and old-age benefit income comparatively low. This could reconfirm the hypothesis that many Roma and Turkish minority citizens are part of this group, as their benefit receipt patterns show greater use of family/child than of old-age benefits.

Given the overall picture of benefit receipt revealed by EU-SILC data, no immediate need for action emerges when looking just at these groups of inactive and out-of-work residents.

Suggestions for Activation Measures and Further Analysis

This section sets out a set of potential activation measures for each of the priority groups. Areas for further policy dialogue with respect to improving the implementation of activation policies are also outlined.

The suggestions below should be considered as a *starting point for further policy dialogue* between EC DG EMPL, the World Bank, and the Bulgarian authorities, bearing in mind that the groups identified still have some heterogeneity that may affect the level of support required. Accordingly, these suggestions are not meant to be an exhaustive set of possible activation measures.

It should be kept in mind that the class descriptions are derived from 2011 EU-SILC data. Since then, general economic development, policy actions by the government of Bulgaria, and European Commission country-specific recommendations might already have reflected some of the policy suggestions or rendered them obsolete.

Middle-aged unemployed (23 percent, Priority: High). This group is characterized by a middle-aged (66 percent between 35 and 54 years) and mainly rural (64 percent) profile comprising both men and women who are unemployed (83 percent). Their mid-level skill profile and average of 18 years of work experience makes them a ready-to-work group. They have an elevated need for activation, as only a small majority (52 percent) have working spouses, and with 37 percent in the poorest income quintile, their poverty risk is high. Potential activation measures for this group include the following:

- *Build activation on previous work experience and skills.* Owing to the fact that labor market integration is as much about hard skills as it is about self-esteem and self-motivation, activation measures for the *middle-aged unemployed* could start by reconnecting with the jobseekers' previous industry or skill profile. It will be important for employment counselors or training providers to avoid narrowly looking at the occupation held, but rather attempt to reconnect, update, and extend the skills that the worker exercised during the last job. In light of the potential for informal economy employment for this group, efforts to formalize employment ought to be promoted, for example through the introduction of in-work benefits and greater use of part-time employment. Generally, however, formalized employment must be supported from a multitude of angles (taxes, labor inspection, benefit systems, and so on).

- *Facilitate part-time work and temporary placement in companies.* In order to enable jobseekers to reconnect with the labor market and with specific (new) industries or employers, part-time work experiences or temporary placements could be encouraged. This would require working arrangements through the local regional employment commissions or district development councils.

- *Mobility and training schemes.* For individuals in households with limited family commitments (at least 48 percent do not have caregiving responsibility for children[20]), training combined with (regional) mobility support could enhance the labor market prospects of some jobseekers in this class, overcoming the shortage of employment in rural areas.

Single male NEETs (15 percent, Priority: High). Two-thirds of this group's members are unemployed (68 percent), 43 percent for more than one year; an additional 31 percent are inactive. The class is 73 percent male, between 16 and 34 years old, and has generally never married or is without a partner. The majority (61 percent) have no work experience. Their qualification level is more heterogeneous than that of the *middle-aged unemployed*, with close to one-third having no more than a lower secondary education and one-sixth having a tertiary degree. While the activation need for this group is high (long periods of unemployment during youth can have detrimental effects on lifetime employment and earnings prospects), their activation potential is lower, owing to their lack of labor market experience and relatively high (32 percent[21]) receipt of social assistance benefits, which might not encourage job seeking. Following are some proposed activation policies for this group.

- *Second-chance programs.* In light of the recent educational experience of some of the group's members, programs to reconnect with technical schools or professional education colleges could be attempted with this target group. For "older" candidates and those with low educational attainment, these second-chance programs would need to take the form of traditional training and work placement schemes, and be strongly complemented by basic life and occupational behavior and motivation elements.

- *Mobility and young-adult housing in cities.* In order to provide an orderly and supported channel for rural to urban migration and professional experience, a "foyer" model could be introduced which provides low-cost housing, professional orientation, and general guidance for young people moving from rural areas to live and work in major cities. This mobility support would need to be integrated with general public employment service programs and "foyers" would need to draw on a network of partner employers to place and train young people.

- *Language skills and training for (temporary) migration.* Given the low level of caregiving responsibility for this group, labor market integration could also evolve around (temporary) migration to other European Union countries and placement into jobs that have the potential to provide mid- to high-level employment in Bulgaria. Activation and training measures for jobseekers could focus on language skills and job-search skills. The government should seek agreements with receiving countries to ensure investment in qualification and adequate treatment of jobseekers during the work placement abroad. In 2014, Bulgarian nationals will enjoy freedom of movement and occupation within the European Union. LMP could complement this opening of opportunities.

- *Youth volunteer mobilization programs.* In light of the high proportion of inactive members and the low level of work experience in this group, another axis of activation and labor market attachment is volunteering and community organizing projects. Such programs, which provide a combination of community work, minimal remuneration, and elements of training on basic skills, self-esteem, and physical exercise could be supported by public employment services, municipalities, or cultural and educational NGOs.

Low-educated rural long-term unemployed (12 percent, Priority: High). This group has the highest poverty risk in the sample (69 percent fall in the poorest income quintile), a very low education level, high unemployment, and inactivity. The class is more rural (70 percent) and tends to belong to households with caregiving responsibility for children (70 percent live in a household with at least one child). The high poverty risk coincides with a substantial self-declared share of social assistance receipts (64 percent[22]). While no "Roma" indicator is contained in the EU-SILC data, this profile suggests that Roma might make up a significant part of this group. Any activation policy targeted toward this group would need to be closely coordinated with national and international efforts to improve Roma integration and access to services. Among our proposed policies for this group are:

- *Integrate basic education into training and employment programs.* Given the low level of secondary educational attainment in this group, activation measures would need to include adult-learning modules and "second chance" opportunities for basic numeracy, literacy, and general knowledge. If an important share of ethnic minority members (Roma) are to be found in this class, appropriate linkage with resident and embedded coordinators inside employment offices or social assistance agencies should be ensured.

- *Provide local employment and training.* Given the high share of family-bound members in this group, wider mobility support will likely be ineffective. Instead, local employment creation and "enhanced" public works programs (for example, combined morning training modules and afternoon work modules) could maintain labor market linkage and provide support locally or regionally.

- *Build on existing work experience.* As prime-aged (25–54 years) unemployed, many in this group can count on a relatively long tenure of work experience (15 years on average). While some of the skills gained in that work experience might have become obsolete or atrophied during extended unemployment, re connecting with prior firms, industries, and occupational communities can be an important step for this group. Active labor market programs should support this through self-help support or direct training/individual coaching.

- *Address discrimination.* It is possible that some members of this group are subject to labor market discrimination because of their regional or ethnic origin. Discrimination in the workplace would need to be addressed as part of a wider anti-discrimination policy in the country.

Stay-at-home young mothers (15 percent, priority: medium). This group of women is relatively young, with 75 percent between the ages of 16 and 34 years. Eighty-three percent are likely to have caregiving responsibility for children (54 percent live in households with children below six years of age). Their activation potential is gauged as slightly lower, owing to such family commitments. Although their risk of poverty is similar to that of the *middle-aged unemployed* or *single male NEETs*, a great majority (79 percent) of the members of this group have at least one working adult in the household. Some possible activation policies for this group include:

- *Linkage of child-care offerings with (re)-qualifications for mothers.* Given the fact that the majority of women in this group may remain inactive as a result of caregiving responsibilities and the fact that at least one adult in the household is already working, one of the key steps to enable activation and labor market participation is to make available sufficient good-quality child-care offerings. Provision of child care could be coupled with training and refresher education classes for women.

- *Volunteering, self-organization, and training in social services or entrepreneurship.* In light of the very high level of inactive (67 percent) women in this group, novel forms of "activity" attachment could be supported through local public employment services or municipalities. Given available free time (that is, if child care is provided), women could be encouraged to volunteer in community causes or be supported in self-organization of cooperatives or small businesses. This volunteering could be combined with on-the-job training units in the respective services (for example child care, elderly care, community work, and so on).

- *(Temporary) part-time employment as a first step into the labor market.* Taking a part-time contract (and expanding it to full time after some years) can be an appropriate means to maintain labor market engagement for mothers. As a subject of labor law policy, this flexibility should be explored, while at the same time creating incentives for employers and employees to switch to full-time employment as soon as possible[23] (given the upcoming labor shortage in the overall economy and expected shortfall in retirement income for women with a part-time work history).

• *General work placement and training courses.* When courses are available, women from this group should be given the opportunity to receive training and qualification courses by the PES.

The latent classes of *retired women* (19 percent), *retired and early-retired men* (13 percent), and *low-educated early-retired and disabled* (3 percent) are not further considered for activation policies in this study. Together, these classes represent 36 percent of the out-of-work working-age population in Bulgaria. Given the extreme demographic challenges in the country, the recently approved increase in the retirement age to around 65 for men by 2018 and 63 for women by 2021 is a necessary step. This increase will need to be matched by policies to maintain the skills and employment of workers 54 years of age and older, along with better integration of people with disabilities into the workforce, in order to counter the projected decline in the overall working-age population.

In general, further policy dialogue with the Bulgarian authorities ought to focus on areas that enable the government and its agencies, municipalities, and other labor market actors to better deploy their resources, increase coordination, and improve the staffing and resource situation of services. Some of the areas for future dialogue include:

• *Ensuring the basis for activation policies.* When delivering activation policies, local and regional actors (Public Employment Service, social assistance offices, municipalities, and so on) need to be equipped and organized in a way that jobseekers and inactive citizens find the right support networks and are not facing "silos" of different public administration. Potential areas of improvement include but are not limited to (1) focusing social workers in the GMI program more on activation than on rule enforcement, (2) enhancing collaboration with nonprofits and social economy organizations for delivery of community and training programs and the development of an ALMP provider ecosystem, (3) reviewing the staffing level in the public employment service.

• *Changing the balance between passive and active spending.* Even within its current budget, Bulgaria could strengthen spending on active labor market measures and reduce spending on passive measures (benefits), setting a path for further (potential) overall increases in resources for activation policies. Given the extremely low level of benefits, there are natural limits to this strategy.

- *Maintaining and extending institutional anchors for disadvantaged groups.* Building on the experience with Roma mediators in public employment offices, Bulgaria ought to explore other ways to improve outreach to inactive and hard-to-place groups in the labor market, either through facilitators or through collaboration with specific community organizations or social economy providers.

In summary, Bulgaria could benefit from improving the activation approach toward its out-of-work population, especially in light of the projected demographic shift. To maintain its growth potential and ensure adequate development for all its citizens, Bulgaria must muster "all hands on deck" to increase the number and qualifications of workers. Allowing high numbers of citizens to remain inactive or unemployed and not included in the labor market will exacerbate the grave development challenges ahead.

Notes

1. Individuals ages 16–24 years who are out of work and enrolled in education are excluded from the sample; they are considered to be investing in their final stages of human capital formation and therefore are not a particular target group for activation policies. Individuals enrolled in school who are between 25 and 64 years old are, however, included in the latent class analysis and will be grouped under "other inactive." It is important to note that these students (those who are older than 24 years of age) account for less than 1 percent of total working-age population.

2. For the latest developments on active inclusion in Bulgaria, see EC (2013b).

3. This variable is constructed using the self-reported current work status in the EU-SILC survey that has four categories: at work, unemployed, retired, and inactive. The unemployed are further classified into short- and long-term based on how long they have been actively looking for a job. The inactive is combined with another question to separate this group into students, disabled, military, and other inactive.

4. In order to construct this variable, individuals aged 25 or older are considered adults.

5. This is a binary variable that takes the value one if an individual answered "yes, strong limitations" to whether they had been hampered in their usual activities because of health problems for at least the last six months. The value is zero if the answer is "yes, limited" or "no, not limited."

6. The equivalized household income takes into account an equivalence factor to weight the number of household members used in the denominator when calculating household income per capita. The first adult age 18 years or older has a weight of 1.0, children younger than 14 years old have a weight of 0.3, and other individuals 14 and older have a weight of 0.5. The sum of the weights of all household members is equal to the equivalent household size.

7. Note that income reported in EU-SILC surveys is for the year preceding the survey year.

8. Total household gross income is defined as the sum of: (at the individual level) gross employee cash or near-cash income; company car, gross cash benefits or losses from self-employment (including royalties); unemployment benefits; old-age benefits;

survivor benefits; sickness benefits; disability benefits; education allowances; and (at the household level) income from rental of property or land; family/children related allowances; social exclusion not elsewhere classified; housing allowances; regular inter-household cash transfers received; interests, dividends, profit from capital investments in unincorporated business; pensions from individual private plans; and income received by people under 16. Total household net income, in turn, was calculated by subtracting from total household gross income regular taxes on wealth, taxes on income and social insurance contributions, and regular inter-household case transfers paid.

9. Social benefits are aggregated in eight branches using the European System of integrated Social PROtection Statistics (ESSPROS) definitions. For more information, see Eurostat (2011).

10. According to EU-SILC guidelines, dense areas have more than 500 inhabitants per square kilometer, where the total population for the set is at least 50,000 inhabitants. Intermediate areas have more than 100 inhabitants per square kilometer, and either a total population for the set of at least 50,000 inhabitants or a location adjacent to a dense area. The remaining areas are categorized as sparsely populated.

11. The EU-SILC longitudinal survey consists of a four-year rotating panel. In each year, approximately three-quarters of individuals present in the previous year are retained. The samples used in the latent class analysis include about 3,000 observations for each year in the cross-sectional analysis and 500 observations in the longitudinal analysis. The population is weighted with individual weights.

12. Sixty-one percent are 16–24 years old, and another 35 percent are 25–34 years old.

13. From 2008 to 2011, the number of (early) retired men and women in our sample rose by 2 percent; in contrast, the number of short-term and long-term unemployed increased by 6 percent.

14. In 2011, 42 percent of this group was younger than 35, and 36 percent was between the ages of 35 and 54 years.

15. The current retirement age in Bulgaria is 60 for women and 63 for men.

16. The labor force participation rate for men ages 55–64 years is about 4 percentage points lower than the EU27 average; for women ages 60–64 years, labor force participation is about 5 percentage points below the EU27 average.

17. The data do not include individuals 62 years of age and older in 2008, who would be dropped from the sample in 2010 because they are older than 64 years of age. Also, students younger than 25 years old in 2010 are excluded from this analysis because they are not considered a target group for activation policies.

18. http://www.ssa.gov/policy/docs/progdesc/ssptw/2012–2013/europe/bulgaria.html

19. The current retirement age for men in Bulgaria is 63 years.

20. Almost half of this group have no children, and the proportion without child-care responsibilities could be even higher: only 19 percent live in households with children younger than six years of age.

21. Twenty-eight percent receive family benefits and 11 percent receive social exclusion benefits; together, 32 percent receive at least one of these two benefits.

22. Fifty-three percent receive a family child benefit and 23 percent receive a social exclusion benefit; together, 64 percent receive at least one of these two benefits.

23. That is, as care-giving responsibilities start to diminish.

References

Collins, L. M., and S. T. Lanza. 2010. *Latent Class and Latent Transition Analysis: With Applications in the Social, Behavioral, and Health Sciences.* Hoboken, NJ: Wiley.

Dimitrov, Y., and N. Duell. 2013. *Activating Vulnerable Groups in Bulgaria.* Washington, DC: World Bank.

EC (European Commission). 2013a. "EU Measures to Tackle Youth Unemployment." MEMO, Brussels.

———. 2013b. "Assessment of the Implementation of the European Commission Recommendation on Active Inclusion: A Study of National Policies: Country Report—Bulgaria." DG Employment, Social Affairs & Inclusion, European Commission, Brussels.

Eurofound. 2012. *NEETs—Young People Not in Employment, Education or Training: Characteristics, Costs and Policy Responses in Europe.* Luxembourg: Publications Office of the European Union.

Eurostat. 2011. *ESSPROS Manual: The European System of Integrated Social PROtection Statistics.* Luxembourg: European Union.

Kaufman, L., and P. J. Rousseeuw. 1990. *Finding Groups in Data.* New York: Wiley.

Magidson, J., and J. Vermunt. 2002. "Latent Class Modeling as a Probabilistic Extension of K-Means Clustering." Quirk's Marketing Research Review, March 20, 77–80. http://statisticalinnovations.com/technicalsupport/kmeans2a.htm.

Packard, T. G., J. Koettl, and C. Montenegro. 2012. *In from the Shadow: Integrating Europe's Informal Labor.* Washington, DC: World Bank.

Vermunt, J. K., and J. Magidson. 2005. *Latent GOLD 4.0 User's Guide.* Belmont, MA: Statistical Innovations Inc.

World Bank. 2010. *Roma Inclusion: An Economic Opportunity for Bulgaria, Czech Republic, Romania and Serbia.* Policy Note Europe and Central Asia Region, Human Development Sector Unit, Washington, DC.

———. 2012. *Bulgaria: Household Welfare during the 2010 Recession and Recovery.* Report 63457-BG. Washington, DC: World Bank.

———. 2013a. *Gender at a Glance: Bulgaria.* Europe and Central Asia Region Poverty Reduction and Economic Management Sector Unit, Washington, DC.

———. 2013b. *Mitigating the Economic Impact of an Aging Population: Options for Bulgaria.* Washington, DC: World Bank.

CHAPTER 4

Latent Class Analysis of the Out-of-Work Population in Estonia, 2007–11

Background

Estonia entered the global financial crisis following a long period of high growth. According to the World Bank's World Development Indicators, between 2000 and 2007, the country was one of the fastest growing economies in the world, growing at an average rate of about 8 percent per year, with a peak of more than 10 percent in 2006. These figures are all the more impressive if compared to the growth rates observed by the EU-28 as a whole, or the euro area (which expanded 0–3 percent per year over the same period).

Estonia saw a significant downturn associated with the global economic crisis, but it rebounded quite quickly, at least in terms of GDP growth. The cyclical downturn of the economy started earlier in Estonia than in neighboring countries. By 2008, the country had already felt the effects of the global downturn, with GDP growth for the year settling at negative 4 percent, in stark contrast to neighboring Lithuania, which displayed 3 percent GDP growth for the same year. The Estonian economy suffered its worst year in 2009, when output contracted by a staggering 14.1 percent, only slightly better than Lithuania's 14.8 percent. As with other countries in the region, this decline was mostly due to Estonia's strong dependence on exports, which collapsed in the 2008–09 period. While neighboring Latvia fared somewhat worse, the Estonian economy's dip was much more severe than those suffered by the average EU-28 country or euro-area member, which witnessed negative growth rates in the 5 percent region in 2009. However, like nearby countries with similar income levels (for example, Lithuania and Latvia), Estonia recovered from the shock faster than its European partners. GDP growth was back into positive territory by mid-2009, settled at almost 3 percent in 2010, and reached a staggering 9.6 percent by 2011—almost twice the rates of Latvia and Lithuania—making the country the fastest growing economy in the EU. Growth rates returned to more modest levels by 2012 and 2013, at 3.9 and 0.8, respectively.

Unemployment levels, which saw a dramatic increase, are taking much longer to recover. Paralleling the developments observed in Lithuania and Latvia, unemployment in Estonia had been decreasing since the early 2000s, settling at a little more than 4 percent in 2007. However, as the effects of the global financial crisis unraveled, the country suffered a large and extremely rapid increase in unemployment; by the end of 2008, joblessness had risen to about 6 percent, climbing to 14 percent in 2009 and eventually peaking at 17 percent in 2010. Such increases were considerably larger than those in the EU-28 or the euro area as a whole, but comparable to what other countries in the region of similar income levels witnessed. However, unemployment started decreasing in late 2010. By 2013, the average rate reached 8.9 percent, which is still above pre-crisis levels, but considerably lower than the joblessness rate observed in the region.

As in Lithuania and Latvia, young Estonians were particularly affected by the downturn. Like the overall unemployment rate, joblessness among those between the ages of 15 and 24 declined steadily in the pre-crisis period, reaching 10 percent in 2007. As the recession hit, youth unemployment skyrocketed to 29 percent in 2009 and 33 percent in 2010. However, by 2013 unemployment in the 15–24 cohort had significantly recovered, reaching 19 percent or so, still almost 10 percentage points above the 2007 level but considerably lower that the rates observed in Lithuania and Latvia (22–24 percent).

Men were generally more affected than women by the crisis, at least in terms of unemployment. As figure 4.1 below shows, at all age levels, Estonian men suffered larger increases than women in their rate of unemployment. Both men and women in the 25–64 age category entered the crisis with unemployment rates close or slightly below 5 percent; however, by late 2010, women in this age group displayed unemployment rates hovering around 13 percent, as opposed to the 18 percent or so registered among men of the same age. Among young Estonians, men were also affected much more than women, with the rate of joblessness among 15- to 24-year-old men peaking at 35 percent, as opposed to 30 percent

Figure 4.1 Unemployment Rates by Age and Gender in Estonia, 2003–13
percent

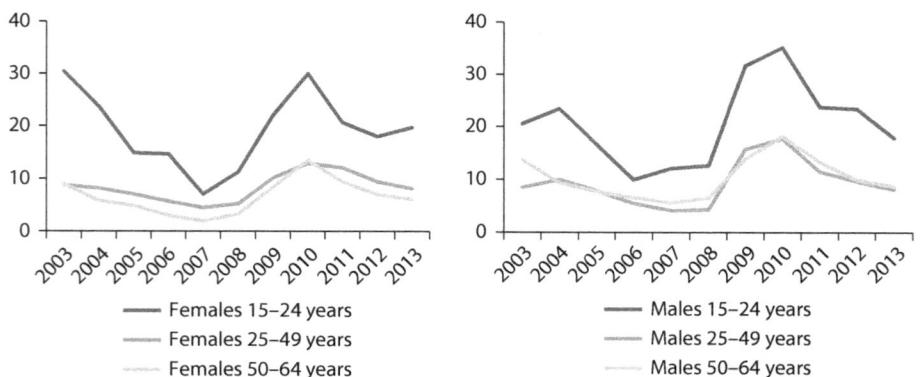

Females 15–24 years
Females 25–49 years
Females 50–64 years

Males 15–24 years
Males 25–49 years
Males 50–64 years

Source: Eurostat, EU-LFS.

among women of the same cohort. Based on data from *Statistics Estonia*, the OECD (2012) also points to labor market discrepancies between Estonians and ethnic non-Estonians. Whereas about 10 percent of Estonians were unemployed in 2011, ethnic non-Estonians were unemployed in about 18 percent of the cases.

One of the most worrying developments of the crisis was the significant increase in the share of long-term unemployed. In 2013, according to Eurostat and as shown in figure 4.2, in the average EU-28 country almost 48 percent of the unemployed had been looking for work for more than 12 months, up from 35 percent in 2009. In Estonia however, the long-term unemployment share, which had declined all the way to about 27 percent in 2009, reached a staggering 57 percent in 2011 and settled at 54 percent in 2012, a development comparable to those observed in Latvia and Lithuania, before declining to 45 percent in 2013.

Another troubling change in the Estonian labor market since 2007 is the rapid increase in both the absolute number of out-of work individuals and in the share of out-of-work population relative to total population and working-age population. European Union Statistics of Income and Living Conditions (EU-SILC) data reveal that the number of the out-of-work population between the ages of 16 and 64 (excluding students) increased steadily between 2007 and 2011, going from slightly more than 167,000 to slightly more than 224,000.[1] This is all the more alarming as it occurred in a period during which both the total size of the population and the total number of working-age individuals in Estonia remained essentially unchanged (at about 1.34 million and about 0.8 million, respectively). This resulted in the share of out-of-work population relative to all working-age population increasing from 21 percent to 28 percent.

The 2007–11 period witnessed a sizeable increase in the number and relative importance of unemployment (particularly long-term unemployment). Figure 4.4 and figure 4.5 below show the composition of working-age and of out-of-work Estonians in 2007 and 2011, respectively. Not only, as figure 4.3 above shows, did the size of the out-of-work population increase between 2007 and 2011 relative

Figure 4.2 Long-Term Unemployment as a Share of Total Unemployment, 2003–13
percent

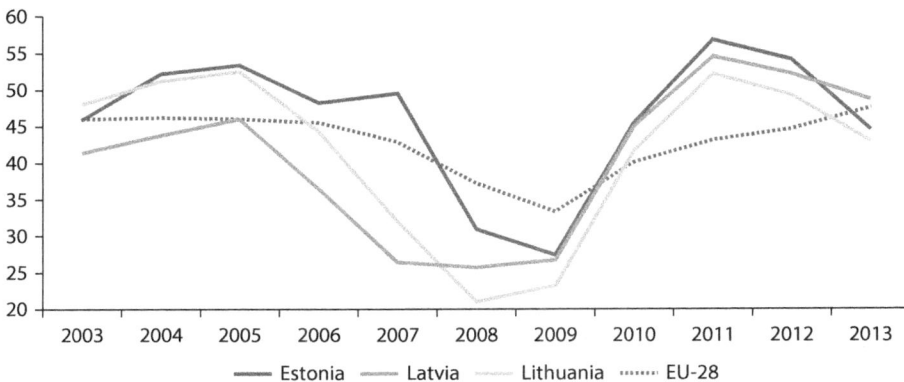

Source: Eurostat, EU-LFS.

Figure 4.3 Evolution of Out-of-Work Population in Estonia, 2007–11
percent

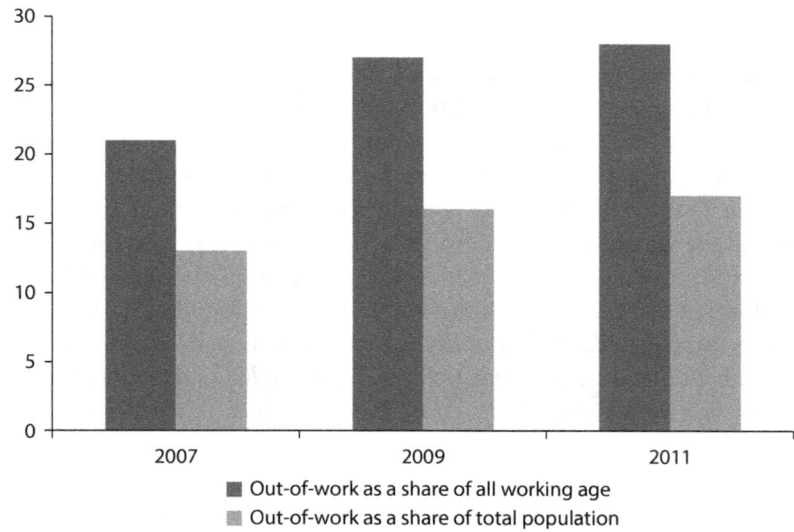

- ■ Out-of-work as a share of all working age
- ▨ Out-of-work as a share of total population

Source: World Bank staff analysis based on EU-SILC.

Figure 4.4 Composition of Working-Age Population (Ages 16–64 Years) by Labor Market Attachment in Estonia, 2007 and 2011
percent

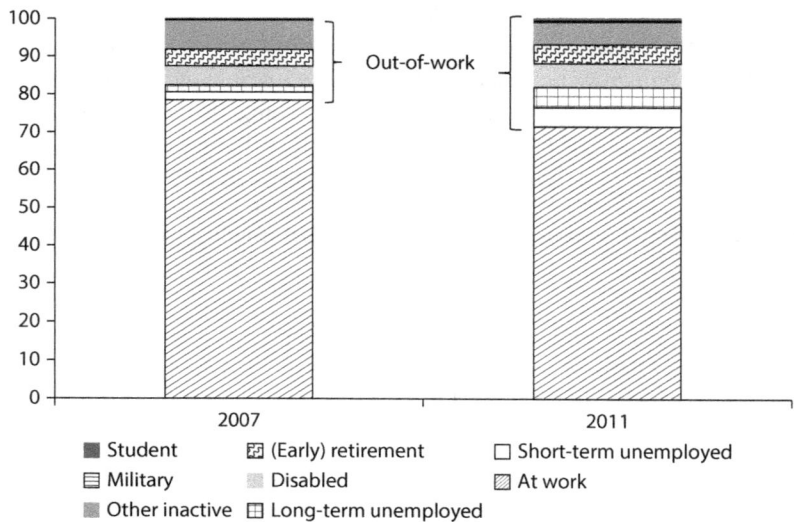

- ■ Student
- 目 Military
- ▨ Other inactive
- ▦ (Early) retirement
- ▨ Disabled
- ▦ Long-term unemployed
- □ Short-term unemployed
- ▨ At work

Source: World Bank staff analysis based on EU-SILC.

to working-age population, but long-term unemployment represented a greater share of Estonians, with the share of those at-work losing ground. While the share of long-term unemployed relative to total working-age people was about 2 percent in 2007, the figure had increased to more than 5 percent in 2007;

Figure 4.5 Distribution of Out-of-Work Population in Estonia, 2007 and 2011
percent

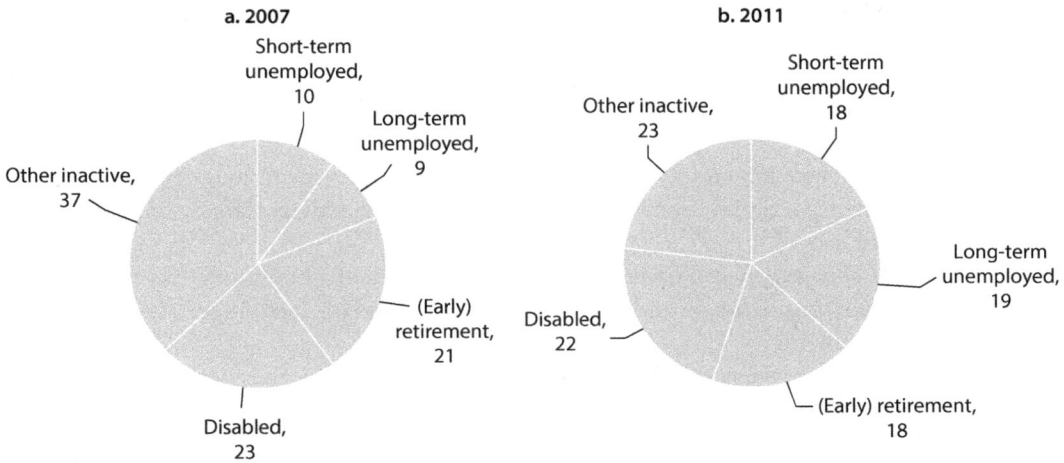

Source: World Bank staff analysis based on EU-SILC.

similarly, long-term unemployed accounted for 9 percent of the out-of-work population in 2007, but for 19 percent in 2011. The share of total unemployment (long-term and otherwise) among working-age individuals (excluding students between 15 and 24[2]) also more than doubled over the period, increasing from 4 percent to 10 percent; jobless individuals accounted for 18 percent of the out-of-work population in 2007, but for 37 percent in 2011.

The developments highlighted above, in particular the increase in the size and relative weight of the out-of-work population and the unemployed, point to a deterioration in the Estonian labor market from 2007 to 2011. A deeper analysis of the out-of-work population, and understanding of its composition, is in fact key to ensuring that the right policy measures are taken and that priorities are set in an appropriate manner.

Methodology: Latent Class Analysis

In chapter 1 a general overview of the latent class analysis methodology was presented. This section explains in detail the variables and covariates used to identify classes or groups of out-of-work individuals that are as homogeneous as possible within each class according to a set of observable characteristics, and as distant as possible between classes. The emerging profiles can then be contrasted with the design and targeting of current activation policies, in order to identify the potential gaps and to enhance their design features.

Variable Selection

The definition of latent classes relies on a number of indicator variables to capture different "symptoms" of an overall latent condition (in this case, the typology of joblessness). The challenge in such models is to identify a discrete number of variables that can best explain the heterogeneity of individual outcomes. In this case, two sets of categorical variables were selected: the first set to show the extent of labor market distance and the other to capture some of the main factors that can affect employment on the supply side, such as labor supply conditions (household-level incentives to work and physical ability to work).

- *Distance from labor market*: short-term unemployment, long-term unemployment, (early) retirement, disability, and other inactivity (largely unpaid domestic work).[3]
- *Labor supply conditions:* whether the individual's household has at least one working adult,[4] and perceived limitations on activities due to health problems.[5]
- *Work experience:* if the individual has worked before and, in this case, whether he or she worked for two or more months in the last year.

In addition to indicators, the model includes active covariates, which are used to improve the classification of individuals in each class. In this case the active covariates are the demographic variables that are normally used to disaggregate labor market outcomes:

- Age-group category (four groups)
- Gender
- Human capital: the highest educational level achieved (three groups)
- Degree of urbanization[6]: densely populated, intermediate area, sparsely populated

Once the latent classes have been defined, inactive covariates that were not included in the model can be used to characterize the individuals in each class and the households in which they live. The inactive covariates chosen describe those characteristics that may provide valuable information for the design of tailored policies that address barriers to employment, including income level. They include:

- Household welfare conditions:
  - Income quintile (defined by equivalized disposable household income[7,8])
  - Labor, benefit, and other income as share of total gross household income[9]
  - Labor market status of partner
  - Tenure status
  - Household ability to keep dwelling warm
  - Partner's labor income
  - Quintile of partner's labor income
  - Binary variables for beneficiaries of social protection benefits[10]
  - Share of each benefit over the household's total gross income

- Household demographics:
  - Household size
  - Household family types
  - Binary variable showing whether there are children younger than 6 years of age in the household
  - Binary variable denoting whether there are three or more under-16 children in the household
  - Children younger than 13 years of age in the household receiving child care: all, some, or none of the children
  - Older person (65 years of age and older) in the household
- Other individual-level demographics:
  - More refined age groups (eight groups)
  - Marital status
- Individual human capital:
  - More refined highest educational level achieved (six groups)
  - Whether the individual is enrolled in school
  - Dummy for previous work experience
- Household location:
  - Urban/rural status

Group Labeling

The resulting groups are then labeled according to the greatest proportional characteristics within groups that also aid in distinguishing among groups. Granted, a large number of characteristics describe these groups, and only a few are taken into account for the purpose of labeling. In part, some of these characteristics may exhibit a large degree of heterogeneity and may thus not be relevant for defining a group. In addition, some characteristics may be more relevant for the purposes of policy design than others. In short, though the labeling of groups can be considered more an art than a science, when taken together with detailed descriptions of a group's most prominent characteristics, labeling can serve as an important starting point in the design and prioritization of activation policies.

The analysis relies on cross-sectional as well as panel data from the EU-SILC surveys for 2008–11, which combine individual-level information with household characteristics. The first part of the note presents a cross-sectional analysis for the years 2008, 2009, 2010, and 2011. In particular, the latent class analysis on 2008 data shows the main characteristics of the out-of-work before the global economic crisis hit Estonia, and thus highlight what could be considered more structural issues of the country's labor market. The 2011 latent class analysis will contrast this initial assessment with more recent developments. The second part of the note exploits longitudinal data between 2008 and 2010[11] to trace the prior labor market status of individuals observed last in 2010 in various classes, and will shed light on the relative persistence in the out-of-work status among different classes of individuals. The set of variables chosen for the cross-section and the longitudinal analysis are slightly different, due to minor differences in the set of variables recorded in each of the two types of data sets.

Main Findings

Out-of-Work Population: Group Profiles

The latent class analysis supports the classification of the out-of-work into seven main groups, some of which have remained stable over time. The groups were named according to their most salient characteristics. Figure 4.6 shows the shares of each of the seven classes identified for the year 2011 and table 4.1 presents their most salient characteristics.

The eight main clusters emerging from the LCA can be characterized as follows for the year 2011 (for more detail, see Appendix A for a link to the online-only annexes):

- Cluster 1: *Middle-aged educated disabled with previous work experience.* This group represents 21 percent of the out-of-work population in 2011. Most individuals in this group report their labor market status as disabled (92 percent)

Figure 4.6 Classes of Out-of-Work Individuals in Estonia, 2011

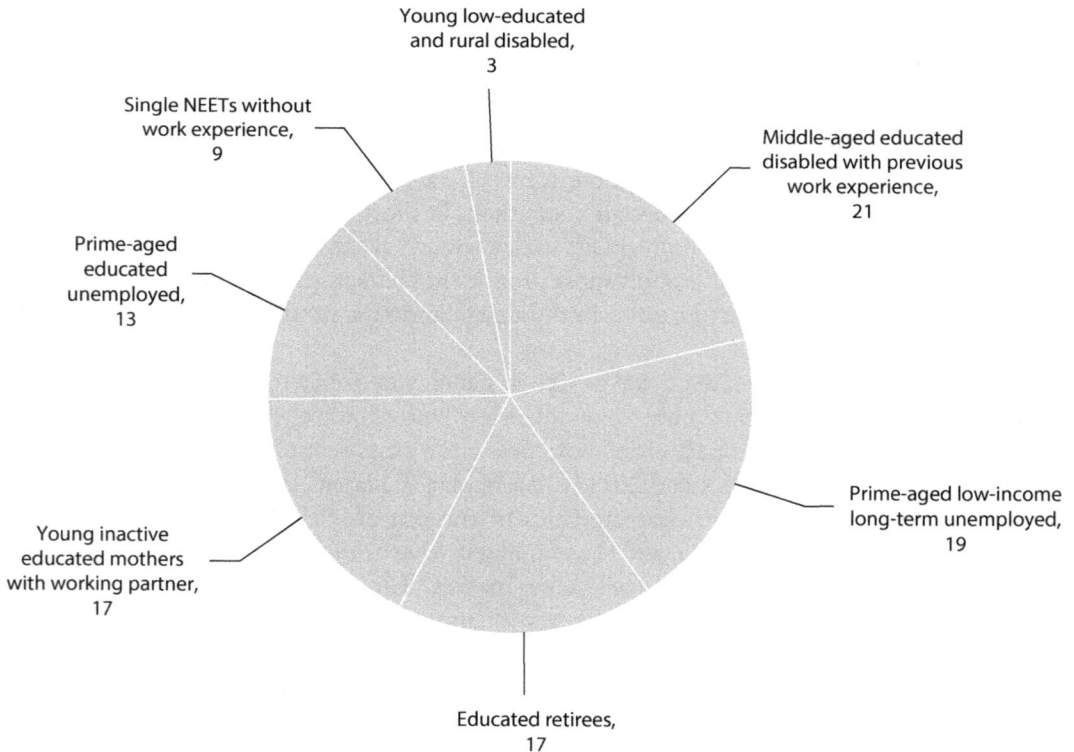

Source: World Bank staff analysis based on EU-SILC.

Portraits of Labor Market Exclusion • http://dx.doi.org/10.1596/978-1-4648-0539-4

Table 4.1 Summary Characteristics of Latent Classes of Out-of-Work Population in Estonia, 2011

1: Middle-aged educated disabled with previous work experience (21%)

- 92% are disabled
- 86% are 35–59 years old
- Another 10% 60–64 years old
- 64% have secondary education and another 14% have tertiary education
- 62% live in rural areas
- 77% belong to the first two income quintiles
- 90% have prior work experience
- 93% receive disability benefits
- 98% receive some benefit
- Benefits represent almost 70% of household income

2: Prime-aged low-income long-term unemployed (19%)

- 85% are long-term unemployed
- Two-thirds are male
- About 75% are 35–59 years old
- Another 25% are 25–34 years old
- 81% are in the first two income quintiles
- Only 20% receive unemployment benefits

3: Educated retirees (18%)

- 100% are retired
- 92% are 60–64 years old
- Almost 65% are female
- 84% have completed secondary or tertiary education
- 59% are married and another 18% are widowed
- 98% of them receive old-age benefits
- 87% live in a household without dependent children
- They mostly live in small sized households
- Benefits make up almost 74% of total household income
- 60% are in the first two income quintiles

4: Young inactive educated mothers with working partner (17%)

- 92% are engaged in domestic or other activities
- 94% are female
- 85% live in a household with a working adult
- 52% have tertiary education
- 97% have work experience and 26% have worked in the previous year
- 93% are 25–55 years old
- 69% are 25–34 years old
- 33% are in the top two income quintiles
- 78% have a child below 6 in their household
- 92% receive at least one benefit; 84% receive family/child benefits

5: Prime-aged educated unemployed (13%)

- 90% are unemployed
- 63% are male
- 84% are 25–59 years old
- 27% have tertiary education and another 56% have completed secondary education
- 70% receive at least one benefit
- 33% receive unemployment benefits
- 85% live in a household with 1 or 2 dependent children
- 36% are in the first income quintile

6: Single NEETs without work experience (9%)

- 35% are unemployed; 25% are long-term unemployed
- The remaining 40% are engaged in domestic or other activities
- All are 16–35 years old
- 82% are 16–24 years old
- 80% have never worked
- Almost 90% are single
- 60% belong to the first two income quintiles
- 51% have secondary education and 31% only primary education
- 76% live in a household with a working adult

7: Young low-educated and rural disabled (3%)

- 76% are disabled
- 96% have never worked
- 70% are under the age of 34
- 75% are in the first two income quintiles
- 71% have only primary education
- About 75% live in urban areas
- 95% receive benefits; 80% receive disability benefits
- 82% are single

Source: World Bank staff analysis based on EU-SILC.

Note: Percentages in parentheses following the group names refer to the share of the total out-of-work population. "Years of work experience" refer only to those individuals who have worked before. "Dependent children" include children younger than 18 years of age and household members ages 18–24 years who are economically inactive and living with at least one parent. "Working adult" refers to adults ages 25 years and older. For this report's purposes, we define the at-risk-of-poverty rate as the relative risk of being in the first quintile of the income distribution. The reference period for income reported in EU-SILC surveys is the year preceding the survey year.

and the majority are between 35 and 59 years of age (86 percent). However, only 43 percent report having strong limitations in their ability to work. As table 4.1 shows, this cluster is *relatively* well educated as 64 percent have secondary education and another 14 percent tertiary education. About 62 percent of individuals in this group live in rural areas. The group also appears to be quite poor, with 51 percent belonging to the first income quintile. The large majority of these individuals (93 percent) receive disability benefits,[12] and almost all (98 percent) of them receive at least one benefit. Finally, benefits account for a large share of these individuals' household incomes: almost 70 percent.

- Cluster 2: *Prime-aged low-income long-term unemployed*. This group, accounting for 19 percent of the out-of-work population, is made up overwhelmingly (85 percent) of long-term unemployed. Two-thirds of the individuals in this cluster are men, and about 70 percent live in rural areas. Three out of four are between 35 and 59 years old and the remaining 25 percent are between 25 and 34. This cluster also appears to be at very high risk of poverty, given that 66 percent of individuals belong to the lowest income quintile. Importantly, only 20 percent receive unemployment benefits; however, about 60 percent receive some form of benefit, even though benefits make up on average less than 50 percent of household income.

- Cluster 3: *Educated retirees*. This third cluster, which makes up 18 percent of the out-of-work population, is composed exclusively of retired individuals, of which almost 65 percent are women. More than 90 percent of those in this group are between 60 and 64 years old. Most of them hold relatively high levels of education (84 percent of them have completed secondary or tertiary education). They are mostly married (59 percent) and another 18 percent are widowed. Ninety-eight percent receive old-age benefits, which tend to be particularly generous, as benefits make up 74 percent of their total household incomes.

- Cluster 4: *Young inactive educated mothers with a working partner*. This group includes 17 percent of the out-of-work population and is for the large part made up of women (94 percent), in their prime age and young (93 percent are between 25 and 55, and almost 70 percent are between 25 and 34), and mostly engaged in domestic or other activities (92 percent). About 85 percent live in a household with a working adult, and are relatively well off, as about one-third belong to the top two income quintiles. This group is well educated, as more than 50 percent have tertiary education. Almost 80 percent of the individuals in this group have a child below 6 in their household and 92 percent receive some benefit, while another 84 percent receive family/child benefits.

- Cluster 5: *Prime-aged educated unemployed*. This group, of which 90 percent is unemployed, makes up 13 percent of the out-of-work population and includes a majority of men (63 percent). Almost two-thirds of them are between 35 and 59 years old and another 22 percent are between 25 and 34 years old; like Group 4, they are well educated, as 56 percent have completed upper or postsecondary education and 27 percent tertiary. Also, most of them (85 percent) live in households with one or more children. Interestingly, 70 percent receive social benefits, but only one-third receive unemployment benefits, and, overall, benefits make up only slightly more than 20 percent of household income.

- Cluster 6: *Single NEETs without work experience*. This group accounts for 9 percent of out-of-work individuals and is mostly composed of unemployed individuals (60 percent of the cluster, with 40 percent of the unemployed being long-term unemployed). The remaining 40 percent are engaged in domestic or other activities. All individuals are between 16 and 35 years old, and 82 percent of them are between 16 and 24, making this cluster the youngest one by far on average. About 80 percent have never worked and almost 90 percent are single, with three out of four living in a household with a working adult. This cluster is also quite low-income, with 60 percent of it falling in the first two income quintiles. This cluster is also not particularly well educated, as 51 percent have an upper secondary education, but a sizeable portion (36 percent) have only primary education.

- Cluster 7: *Young low-educated and rural disabled*. Members of this cluster, 76 percent of which report their labor market status as disabled, account for the last 3 percent of the Estonian out-of-work population in 2011. Nearly all in this cluster, 96 percent, have never worked despite the fact that only half report a strong limitation on daily activities; 82 percent are single and 70 percent are below 35 years of age. The individuals in this group, which is for the most part rural (75 percent live in rural areas), tend to be both low-income (as 75 percent fall in the first two income quintile) and low-educated (with 71 percent having completed only primary education). Importantly, 80 percent of them receive disability benefits, and 95 percent receive at least one benefit. These benefits make up almost 70 percent of the average household income.

The following tables present the main characteristics of each group in 2011. For a complete table including the inactive covariates, see Appendix A for a link to the online-only annexes.

The composition of the classes has also experienced considerable change over the last few years. Table 4.4 shows the evolutions of the classes from 2007 to 2011 as a share of total out-of-work population, while figure 4.7 graphs the absolute numbers. As mentioned before, one important development between 2007 and 2011 was the noticeable increase in the size of the out-of-work population, from about 167,000 to roughly 224,000 individuals. Furthermore, it is interesting how some of the clusters identified by analyzing the 2011 data could also be identified (broadly speaking) in the 2007 and 2009 data,

Table 4.2 **Latent Classes of Out-of-Work Population in Estonia: Indicators, 2011**

	All out-of-work	1. Middle-aged educated disabled with previous work experience	2. Prime-aged low-income long-term unemployed	3. Educated retirees	4. Young inactive educated mothers with working partner	5. Prime-aged educated unemployed	6. Single NEETs without work experience	7. Young low-educated and rural disabled
Cluster size (%)	100	21	19	18	17	13	9	3
Population	224,738	47,694	43,446	39,221	37,108	29,421	20,656	7,192
Indicators (%)								
Labor market attachment								
Unemployed	18	3	4	0	7	90	35	4
Long-term unemployed	19	1	85	0	0	0	25	6
Retired	18	3	0	100	0	0	0	0
Disabled	22	92	0	0	0	0	1	76
Other inactive	13	1	11	0	92	10	39	14
Work experience								
Never worked	11	0	0	0	3	0	79	96
Less than 2 months in last year	68	94	100	87	72	1	20	3
Two or more months in last year	21	6	0	13	26	99	0	1
Self-assessed physical capacity								
Strongly limited	13	43	2	11	0	2	0	51
None/limited	85	57	98	89	100	98	100	49
At least one working adult in household								
No	48	3	4	0	7	90	35	4
Yes	52	1	85	0	0	0	25	6

Source: World Bank staff analysis based on EU-SILC.

Table 4.3 Latent Classes of Out-of-Work Population in Estonia: Active Covariates, 2011

	All out-of-work	1. Middle-aged educated disabled with previous work experience	2. Prime-aged low-income long-term unemployed	3. Educated retirees	4. Young inactive educated mothers with working partner	5. Prime-aged educated unemployed	6. Single NEETs without work experience	7. Young low-educated and rural disabled
Cluster size (%)	**100**	**21**	**19**	**17**	**17**	**13**	**9**	**3**
Population	**224,738**	**47,694**	**43,446**	**39,221**	**37,108**	**29,421**	**20,656**	**7,192**
Active covariates (%)								
Age groups (years)								
16–24	11	0	3	0	5	13	82	23
25–34	23	4	25	0	69	22	18	46
35–59	47	86	73	8	26	62	0	31
60–64	19	10	0	92	0	3	0	0
Gender								
Male	46	58	63	37	6	63	47	54
Female	54	42	37	63	94	37	53	46
Education								
Primary	20	21	22	16	7	15	36	71
Secondary	56	64	68	55	40	56	51	28
Tertiary	23	14	10	29	52	27	9	1
Never studied before/ illiterate/not available	1	0	0	0	1	2	4	0
Location								
Urban	47	38	53	44	55	58	37	27
Rural	53	62	47	56	45	42	63	73

Source: World Bank staff analysis based on EU-SILC.

Table 4.4 Classes of Out-of-Work Individuals in Estonia as a Percentage of Total Out-of-Work Population, 2007, 2009, and 2011

percent

Name of cluster	2007	2009	2011
Middle-aged educated disabled with previous work experience	23	19	21
Prime-aged low income long-term unemployed (2011)	n.a.	n.a.	19
Middle-aged long-term unemployed men (2007 and 2009)	11	9	n.a.
Educated retirees (2009 and 2011)	n.a.	18	18
Educated retired women (2007)	22	n.a.	n.a.
Young inactive educated mothers with working partner	21	18	17
Prime-aged educated unemployed	13	29	13
Single NEETs without work experience (2007 and 2011)	7	n.a.	9
Single uneducated and rural NEETs without work experience (2009)	n.a.	7	n.a.
Young low-educated and rural disabled (2011)	n.a.	n.a.	3
Low-educated and rural disabled youth (2007)	3	n.a.	n.a.
Total	100	100	100

Source: World Bank staff analysis based on EU-SILC.
Note: n.a. = not applicable; NEET = not in employment, education, or training.

although the relative sizes of such clusters might have changed. In particular:

- *The most worrying development, arguably as a result of the crisis, is the emergence in 2011 of a large cluster of young long-term unemployed individuals.* As shown in the first section, the relative weights of long-term unemployment and of overall unemployment as a share of the out-of-work population have doubled between 2007 and 2011, from 19 percent to 37 percent and from 9 to 19 percent, respectively. Within these groups, by 2011 a cluster of mostly young (between 16 and 34 years of age) and long-term unemployed individuals, accounting for about 19 percent of the out-of-work population in Estonia, had emerged.

- *Similarly, and just as worryingly, the last few years have witnessed the steady increase in the size and weight of the clusters of young Estonians who are not employed, in education, or in training.* In 2007, the young people not in employment, education or training (NEET) cluster accounted for about 11,000 individuals (or 7 percent of the out-of-work population). By 2011, this cluster had grown to include more than 20,000 people, almost doubling in size. And while it should be noted that in 2009 the cluster of NEETs was somewhat different than the clusters of NEETs observed in 2007 and 2011 (that is, it was "more rural" and "less educated"), the fact that the ranks of young NEETs with no prior work experience have grown so substantially in such a short time span is troubling from a policy and social perspective.

- *Furthermore, at least in part as a result of the crisis, the cluster of prime-aged unemployed individuals has witnessed a considerable amount of movement.*

Figure 4.7 Classes of Out-of-Work Individuals in Estonia, 2007, 2009, and 2011
Number of individuals

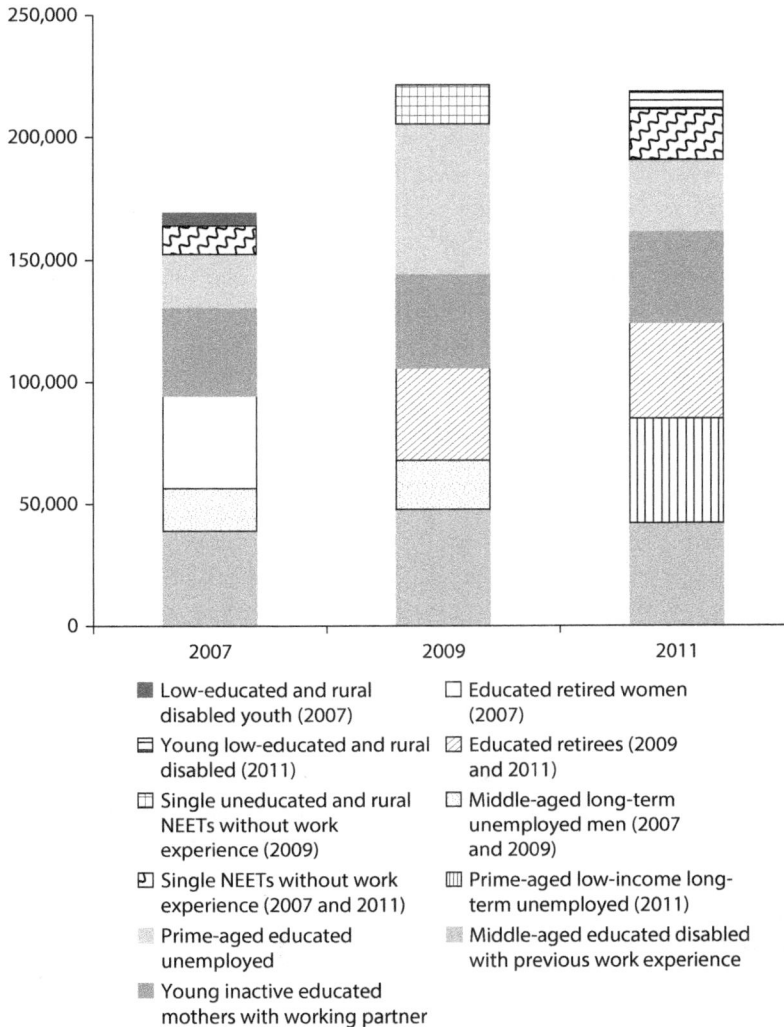

Legend:
- ■ Low-educated and rural disabled youth (2007)
- ▤ Young low-educated and rural disabled (2011)
- ▦ Single uneducated and rural NEETs without work experience (2009)
- ▣ Single NEETs without work experience (2007 and 2011)
- Prime-aged educated unemployed
- Young inactive educated mothers with working partner
- □ Educated retired women (2007)
- ▨ Educated retirees (2009 and 2011)
- □ Middle-aged long-term unemployed men (2007 and 2009)
- ▥ Prime-aged low-income long-term unemployed (2011)
- Middle-aged educated disabled with previous work experience

Source: World Bank staff analysis based on EU-SILC.

Such cluster, which included roughly 22,000 people in 2007, almost tripled in size in a two-year period, increasing to more than 61,000 people in 2009, before declining all the way back to 29,000 by 2011, still marking a 30 percent increase in absolute size from the 2007 figures.

- *The number of disabled individuals has also increased significantly over the last few years.* Over the 2007–11 period there were two clusters of disabled individuals, the combined size of which steadily increased from about 43,000 to more than 54,000 individuals. The first cluster, which increased by about 25 percent, from 38,000 individuals to 47,000 and can be observed throughout the period, was composed of middle-aged educated disabled. The second cluster changed somewhat during the period and could not be observed in 2009, but essentially included young, low-educated disabled individuals. This cluster also increased in size, from 5,000 to 7,000.

• *The number of adult retirees receiving benefits has been generally stable over the years, although with some changes in the features of the cluster.* In 2007, the cluster including retirees numbered about 38,000 people; by 2011 this cluster had only slightly increased to about 39,000. As a result, the share of retirees in the out-of-work population decreased from about 22 percent to 17 percent. Furthermore, while the cluster of retirees was mostly made of women in 2007, by 2011 this group had become more gender-balanced.

Structural Aspects and Emerging Trends in the Profiles of the Out-of-Work

The analysis of the EU-SILC data using latent class methodology reveals the existence of a number of clusters or groups of out-of-work individuals that can be more or less clearly defined and that differ from one another in important characteristics. Some of the features that we have highlighted are more permanent in nature, while others can most likely be ascribed to the global downturn and might therefore be more cyclical.

On the structural side, first and foremost, our analysis shows that young Estonians fare quite poorly in the labor market in absolute terms, although better than youth in neighboring countries. Their performance is also in line with EU-wide averages. The unemployment rate in the 15- to 24-year-old cohort was about 19 percent in 2013, after peaking at more than 35 percent among males and 30 percent among females in 2010. Noticeably, the 2013 data, while quite alarming per se, is better than that registered for the EU as a whole, and for Lithuania and Latvia (22–23 percent). Employment rates in Estonia among those between 15 and 24 years of age peaked, in fact, at 36 percent in 2008, before dropping to 26 percent in 2010 and recovering somewhat to 32 percent in 2013. Again, such figures are aligned with the EU-28 average (32 percent), and stand in stark contrast to those recorded in Lithuania (25 percent). Similarly, as figure 4.8 shows, labor force participation among youth between 15 and 24 years of age is in line with the rest of the European Union; in 2013, youth labor force participation rates settled at about 40 percent in Estonia, considerably lower than the rate registered in some Nordic and continental European countries, but almost 10 percentage points higher than countries such as Lithuania and Bulgaria. The female participation rate for this age cohort was 38 percent in 2013, 1 percentage point lower than the EU-28, and more than 10 points higher than countries such as Lithuania and Bulgaria.

Second, disabled individuals have been and will continue to be a sizeable portion of the out-of-work population, and population aging will only increase Estonia's expenditure on disability benefits. EU-SILC data shows that the number

Figure 4.8 Labor Force Participation among Youth Ages 15–24 Years, European Countries, 2013
percent

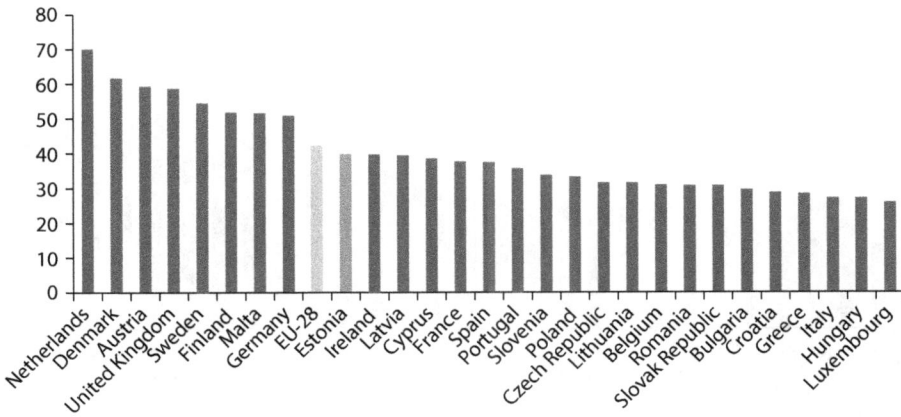

Source: Eurostat, EU-LFS.

of individuals who report their labor market status as disabled (the majority of whom also receive benefits) settled at just under 50,000 in 2011, a year in which there were two distinct clusters of mostly disabled individuals. In 2007, however, the number of disabled individuals totaled less than 40,000. Thus, even though the share of disabled in the out-of-work population marginally decreased over the last few years (from 23 to 22 percent between 2007 and 2011, and mostly because of the large increase in the total out-of-work population), the absolute number of those classified as disabled increased considerably, with the increase occurring entirely between 2009 and 2011. Furthermore, as seen, disabled Estonians tend for the most part to have little or no work experience and to be above 35 years of age. The majority of such individuals benefit from disability or other benefits, which tend to be quite generous (making up on average 70 percent of household income). These factors combined (no work experience, age, and benefit availability) point to high (and growing) impediments for entering or re-entering the labor market, even when disabilities are not too severe. These patterns are somewhat troubling, given the rapid aging the Estonian society will undergo in the coming decades; projections based on current census data show that in the 2001–11 decade alone, the share of Estonian permanent residents older than 65 years of age rose from 15 to 18 percent. According to the Center for International Futures at the University of Denver, this number will almost double by 2060 to about 33 percent. At the same time, the number of working-age people will decline from 66 percent to 52 percent. The most recent census (2011) also shows that over the last decade the country has lost 5.5 percent of its population (from 1.37 million to 1.295 million) and, using the Center for International Futures' data once again, by 2060 only 0.86 million people will likely live in the country, down from 1.3 million in 2011. The combination of increasing numbers of disabled individuals with an aging and shrinking population will likely increase the

Figure 4.9 Expenditures on Disability Benefits as a Share of GDP in Europe, 2008 and 2010
percent

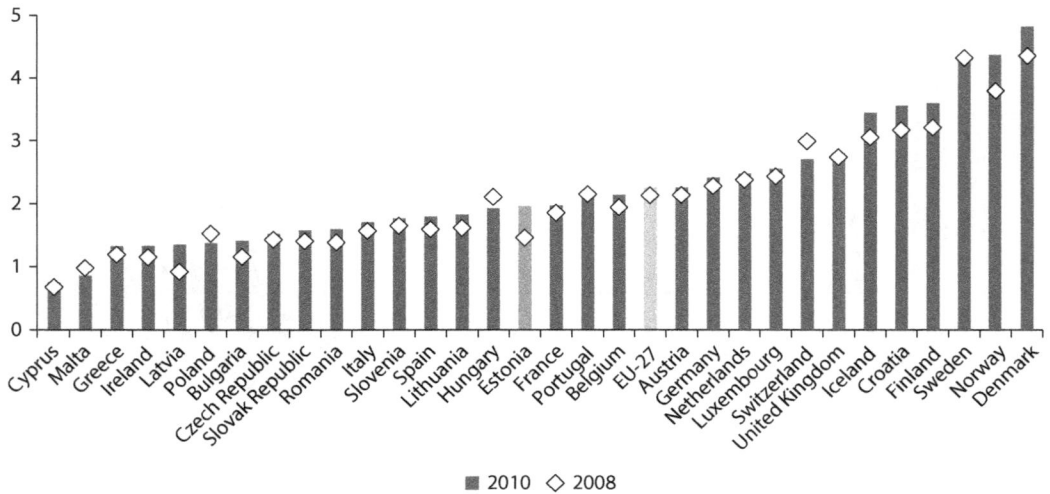

■ 2010   ◇ 2008

Source: Eurostat, EU-LFS.

expenditure on disability benefits that the government will have to undertake in the coming decades. Figure 4.9 below shows that expenditure on disability benefits as a share of GDP, while lower than the EU average, had already increased between 2008 and 2010, going from 1.4 percent to 1.9 percent.

Third, a number of negative developments can be observed within the unemployed category, all of which pose significant and urgent challenges for policymakers. In particular:

- *As already noted above, one of the most striking developments between 2007 and 2011 is the dramatic increase in the size and share of the unemployed, especially long-term unemployed, in Estonia.* Not only, as shown above, have the number of unemployed and their share of the out-of-work population increased dramatically in Estonia from 2007 to 2011 but, across all clusters of unemployed individuals, an extremely worrying phenomenon is the growing share of individuals in long-term unemployment, the absolute numbers of which have almost tripled over the period, according to EU-SILC data.[13] Long-term unemployment not only imposes a significant financial burden on households, but also affects the long-term health status of jobseekers, negatively affects government finances, and results in a lower overall long-term level of skills among a country's workforce, with permanent negative effects on productivity (Katz 2010). Once more, addressing the plight of the long-term unemployed should be among the policy priorities for Estonian policy makers.

- *A further concerning development is the significant increase in the size of the NEETs group, the size of which almost doubled over the last few years.* About 80 percent of the individuals in this cluster have no prior work experience, and 60 percent of them belong to the first two income quintiles; activating these clusters should therefore be another policy priority for Estonian policy makers, to avoid the further depreciation of the stock of human capital among these young individuals and to promote their long-term well-being.

- *In line with the first point above, the global downturn is likely at least partly responsible for the rise of a group of young long-term unemployed*, a cluster that did not exist in 2007 or in 2009 but represented a staggering 19 percent of the out-of-work population in 2011. With about two-thirds of them being men in their prime (hence many of them likely to be heads of households), and given the high risk of poverty within this group (as shown, 80 percent of these individuals fall in the first two income quintiles), facilitating the transition of this group into the labor market is key to the long-term well-being of these individuals and their families.

- *The downturn is also probably responsible for at least part of the increase in the size of the group of well-educated, unemployed individuals in their prime.* Despite the fact that this cluster tripled in size between 2007 and 2009, and reverted back to "only" 30 percent above its pre-crisis level by 2011, the existence of a large and increasing number of well-educated, mostly prime-aged, jobless men is now a structural feature of the Estonian labor market.

Out-of-Work Population: Group Profiles from Longitudinal Analysis

Finally, by looking at longitudinal EU-SILC data for the period 2008–10, one can better understand the in-cluster dynamics, as well as notice other movements in the labor market. EU-SILC allows for the tracking of a number of out-of-work individuals between 2008 and 2010. Of course, because of the difficulties in tracking people across time, the sample size of the panel data set is considerably smaller than the cross-section surveys; the 2008–10 longitudinal data set includes in fact about 560 observations, as opposed to 2,400 observations for 2011. However, the panel data confirm the existence of some latent classes that emerged in the cross-sectional analysis. And even though the smaller sample size forced us to lower the number of clusters identified, some clear patterns emerged. Through longitudinal data five classes can be defined, some of which can also be found in the cross-section data sets:

- *Prime-aged educated unemployed* (38 percent)
- *Educated retirees* (21 percent)
- *Young inactive educated mothers with working partner* (17 percent)
- *Middle-aged low-educated and rural disabled* (15 percent)
- *Single NEETs without work experience* (9)

Annex 3 (see Appendix A for a link to the online-only annexes) shows the statistical description of the latent classes in full while table 4.5 summarizes the key features of each group.

Table 4.5 Longitudinal Analysis: Summary Characteristics of Latent Classes of Out-of-Work Population in Estonia, 2010

1: Prime-aged educated unemployed (38%)	*2: Educated retirees (21%)*
• 90% are unemployed	• 85% are retired and the rest disabled
• 93% are 25–59 years old, and 63% are 35–59 years old	• 96% are age 60 and older
• 31% have tertiary education	• 60% are female
• 70% are male	• 70% have upper and postsecondary education
• 50% are in the first two income quintiles	• 60% are in the first two income quintiles
• Three out of four receive at least one benefit	• 97% receive at least one benefit
3: Young inactive educated mothers with working partner (17%)	*4: Middle-aged low-educated and rural disabled (15%)*
• 75% are inactive and another 20% unemployed	• 60% are disabled, 23% unemployed, and another 15% inactive
• Almost 80% are younger than 34 years old	• About 75% live in a household without at least one working adult
• 97% are female	• More than 85% reside in rural areas
• Almost 40% have tertiary education	• 92% are 35–59 years old
• Almost 95% receive some benefit, and about 85% receive family benefits	• 85% receive at least one benefit
• 39% are in the first two income quintiles	• Almost 80% belong to the two poorest income quintiles
5: Single NEETs without work experience (9%)	
• 85% are unemployed	
• 80% are male	
• About 60% live in a household with at least one working adult	
• 53% have never worked	
• 80% are 16–24 years old, and the remaining 20% are 25–34 years old	
• 65% live in rural areas	
• Almost 90% are single	
• 52% are in the first two income quintiles	

Source: World Bank staff analysis based on EU-SILC.
Note: "Years of work experience" refers only to those individuals who have worked before. "Dependent children" include children younger than 18 years of age and household members ages 18–24 years who are economically inactive and living with at least one parent. "Working adult" refers to adults ages 24 years and older.

A further advantage of the panel analysis is to provide information on the movement of individuals in and out of certain clusters and in and out of jobs between 2008 and 2010. Table 4.6 shows the flow of individuals into the different clusters as of 2010, according to their labor market status in 2008. The most interesting column is the one relative to those that were employed in 2010. According to the panel data, among those categorized as employed in 2010, 81 percent were also employed in 2008; however, and somewhat encouragingly, almost 30 percent of those unemployed in 2008 moved into employment by 2010, while 55 percent of those classified as "other inactive" in 2008 had become employed by 2010. However, 19 percent of those employed in 2008 had fallen into one of the out-of-work categories by 2010.

Table 4.7, on the other hand, shows a considerable amount of movement out of employment between 2008 and 2010. For instance, 80 percent of those in the *prime-aged educated unemployed* cluster were actually employed in 2008.

Table 4.6 Estonia: Composition of 2010 Clusters Based on 2008 Labor Market Status (Column Percentages)

Cluster	Working-age population in 2010	Unemployed	Retired	Disabled	Other inactive	Employed	Total
1	Prime-aged educated unemployed	27	3	2	5	12	11
2	Educated retirees	8	92	26	1	2	5
3	Young inactive educated mothers with working partner	3	0	7	19	2	5
4	Middle-aged low-educated and rural disabled	19	0	60	6	2	6
5	Single NEETs without work experience	14	0	0	15	1	4
NC	Employed	29	5	6	55	81	69
	Total	100	100	100	100	100	100

Source: World Bank staff analysis based on EU-SILC.
Note: For 2010, students 16–24 years old who are inactive are excluded from the sample. Numbers referred to in the text appear shaded in gray; NEET = not in employment, education, or training.

Table 4.7 Estonia: Composition of 2010 Clusters Based on 2008 Labor Market Status (Row Percentages)

Cluster	Working-age population in 2010	Unemployed	Retired	Disabled	Other inactive	Employed	Total
1	Prime-aged educated unemployed	11	1	1	7	80	100
2	Educated retirees	6	36	24	4	29	100
3	Young inactive educated mothers with working partner	2	0	7	60	31	100
4	Middle-aged low-educated and rural disabled	14	0	51	14	21	100
5	Single NEETs without work experience	17	0	0	61	22	100
NC	Employed	2	0	0	12	85	100
	Total	5	2	5	16	73	100

Source: World Bank staff analysis 2014.
Note: For 2010, students 16–24 years old who are inactive are excluded from the sample. Numbers referred to in the text appear shaded in gray; NEET = not in employment, education, or training.

Similarly, 22 percent of the 2010 NEETs cluster were employed in 2008, and more than 30 percent of the young, inactive mothers had also left the ranks of the gainfully employed between 2008 and 2010.

From Profiling to Activation

Activation and Inclusion Policies in Estonia

Expenditures on active labor market policies (ALMPs) are relatively low but have been scaled up since 2008. Up until the crisis, employment services and activation policies for the unemployed had not been a particular concern in Estonia;

in 2008, for instance, ALMP expenditures accounted for 0.1 percent of GDP, half of which was covered through EU funds (OECD 2010). More than half of that amount was spent on employment services, counseling, and job-search activities, and no more than 0.5 percent of the total workforce benefited from labor market policies (LMPs). Few of the unemployed received benefits, either contributory or noncontributory. The effects of the financial crisis underlined the need for labor market reforms, for greater resources to support the unemployed; accordingly, in 2009, the country underwent an extensive reform process that affected labor market regulations, contractual agreements, labor compensation and wage policies, unemployment insurance, social protection and insurance schemes, and so on.

In the post-2009 scenario, the main agency in charge of employment services and unemployment benefits is the Unemployment Insurance Fund (UIF). Until 2009 the country had a self-standing public employment service (PES) under the Ministry of Social Affairs; however, with the advent of the crisis and the increasing need to tighten the link between unemployment assistance, unemployment insurance, and employment services, the PES was merged with the UIF. After the merge, the UIF, a public agency fully financed by employers' and employees' contributions, became a "tripartite" organization in charge of all active and passive LMPs. The merged UIF, which remained under the supervision of the Ministry of Social Affairs, maintained its 15 regional and 26 local labor offices, 80 percent of which provide information and job counseling and manage job-seekers and employers' cases through their front-line staff (OECD 2010).

As a result of the crisis, the range of active and passive LMPs and employment services offered by the UIF is now wide. In particular, examples of services and programs offered by UIF include (OECD 2010):

- *Supported Employment Programs/Measures.* These include career counseling, job-search assistance, job-broking services, measures for disabled jobseekers, and public works in selected municipalities;
- *Training Schemes* in the form of benefits for both employers and employees, workplace trainings, and so on;
- *Support Schemes for Job Creation*, such as start-up incentives, support to employers in finding suitable workers;
- *Passive measures* such as unemployment benefits.

Estonia traditionally spends much less on LMPs than other OECD countries; this pattern still holds despite the fact that the crisis resulted in a notable increase in such expenditures. As figure 4.10 shows, in 2011 Estonia spent little more than 0.6 percent of GDP on LMPs, two-thirds of which was devoted to unemployment benefits and early retirement. The average OECD country, on the other hand, spent more than 1.4 percent of GDP in LMPs, almost two and a half times the Estonian figure. Looking at the evolution of such expenditures between 2003 and 2011, it is immediately noticeable that the downturn was associated with a massive increase in unemployment and early retirement

Figure 4.10 Labor Market Policy (LMP) Spending in Estonia as a Share of GDP
percent

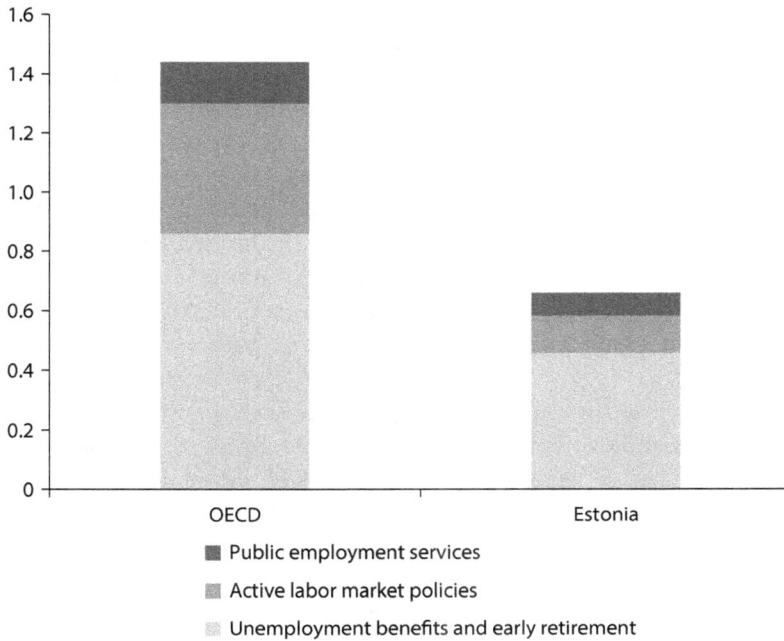

- Public employment services
- Active labor market policies
- Unemployment benefits and early retirement

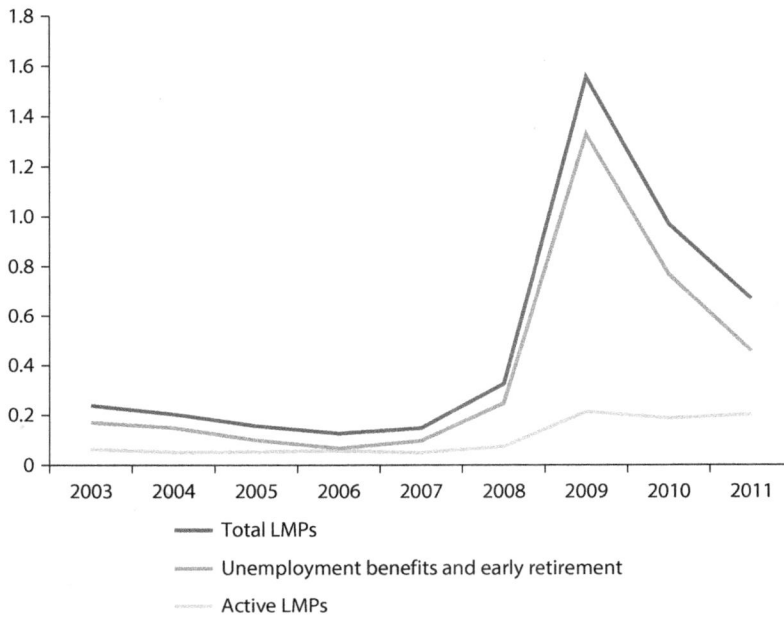

- Total LMPs
- Unemployment benefits and early retirement
- Active LMPs

Source: Eurostat and OECD.

benefits. In the pre-crisis period, total LMP expenditure was extremely low; it ranged between 0.1 and 0.2 percent of national GDP, with unemployment and early benefits absorbing about three-quarters of the expenditures (0.07–0.15 percent of GDP). By 2009, at the peak of the crisis, the share of these benefits had increased more than tenfold, reaching 1.6 and 1.3 percent of GDP, respectively. By 2012, unemployment and early retirement benefits as a share of GDP were still three times as much as the pre-crisis level (Eurostat and OECD data). It should be noted as a positive that Estonia did not respond to the crisis with a decrease in relative activation spending, but rather increased such expenditures; the share of ALMP spending in GDP quadrupled between 2007 and 2012 (from about 0.05 to 0.2 percent of GDP). *Overall, then, even though the range of LMPs offered by the UIF is now quite wide and comparable to the packages offered by the LMP systems of other OECD countries, the scale of such programs is much more limited.*

The large increase (and then decrease) in the share of total LMP costs that went toward unemployment benefits was matched by a dramatic rise (and then fall) in the number of beneficiaries. As figure 4.11 shows, while the 2003–11 period did witness an increase (although from a very low basis) in the number of ALMP beneficiaries from about 1,000 in 2003 to 6,000 in 2011, the downturn was clearly linked to a spike in the number of those receiving unemployment or early retirement benefits, with almost 30,000 individuals joining the ranks of the beneficiaries between 2008 and 2009 alone.

As previously mentioned, the level of ALMP spending has increased considerably as a result of the global financial crisis, albeit from a very low base; furthermore, the composition and source of such expenditures have changed.

Figure 4.11 Labor Market Policy Beneficiaries in Estonia (Annual)

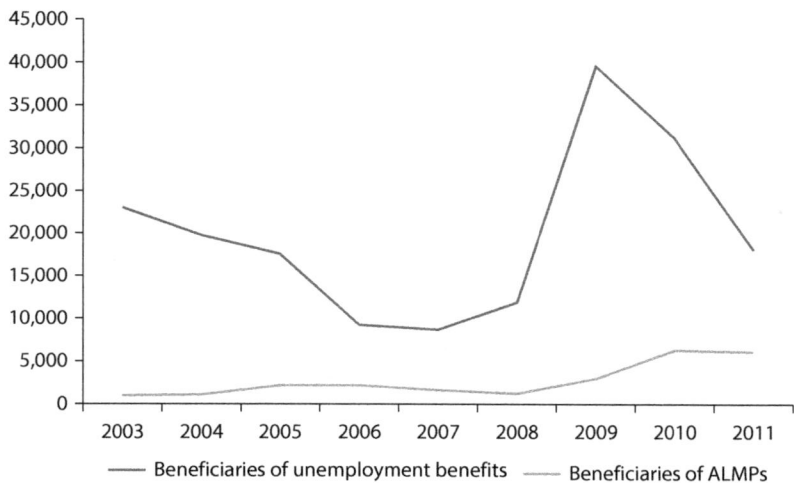

Source: Eurostat, OECD.

Figure 4.12 Composition of Spending on ALMPs in Estonia, 2008 and 2011
Euros (millions)

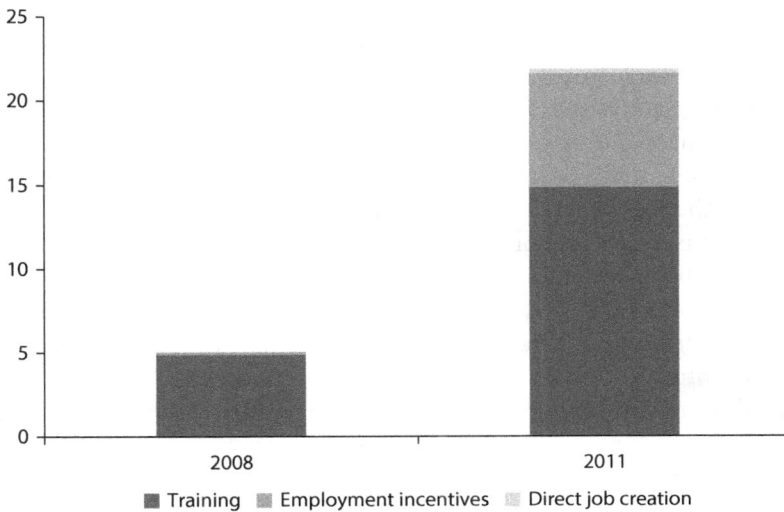

Training ■ Employment incentives ▨ Direct job creation

Source: Eurostat, OECD.

As depicted in figure 4.12, spending on training, which made up virtually all of ALMP expenditures in 2008, increased threefold. On the other hand, spending on employment incentives became a sizeable budget item in 2001, but was almost negligible in 2008 (Eurostat 2011). In addition to the new composition of LMP spending, the crisis also led to a change in the financing of the inclusion measure: after 2009, a major funding source has in fact now become the EU structural funds, which currently support projects that provide vocational training, improve the quality of working life, facilitate job creation, and so on.

Activation Priority, Activation Type, and Benefit Receipt by Group

When further considering the approach to labor market integration, an assessment of the priorities and potential of the identified groups needs to be undertaken. Given the cautious increase in nominal resources for activation programs, further prioritization of intervention is all the more important. After a *first step* ("activation priority") of prioritizing the intervention along activation need and activation potential, a *second step* ("activation type") will attempt to classify the groups according to the kind of activation intervention needed, depending on social or labor market barriers to be overcome. Lastly, as a *third step*, information on the *household income composition* of the different groups will be used to assess potential cross-dependencies of the benefit system with the labor market status and activation approaches.

Activation Priorities

Table 4.8 gives an overview of the identified out-of-work classes and their respective activation need and activation potential. The total number of persons estimated in these clusters was about 224,000 in 2011, representing 28 percent of the working-age (16–64-year-old) population of Estonia in 2011.

In the table, "activation need" refers to a group's level of need for inclusion in the labor market in order to achieve earnings and reduce or end poverty. "Activation potential" describes that group's ability or motivation to be included in the labor market. A high activation need could be driven by high poverty risk (as in the case of the *prime-aged low-income long-term unemployed*) whereas a high activation potential could be driven by previous work experience or a relatively good educational base (for example, the *prime-aged educated unemployed*). Overall priority for action can also be supported by the size of the group.

From this prioritization exercise, a set of five groups emerges with "high" or "medium" priority for action. *Middle-aged disabled with previous work experience* are a large group with a relatively high share of benefit receipts and prima-facie work limitations. At the same time, they have previous work experience and a relatively high educational status (14 percent even have tertiary degrees). *Prime-age low-income long-term unemployed* have a high activation need among other factors, owing to their high exposure to poverty. At the same time, they report almost no work limitation because of disabilities and have a good education status. *Young inactive educated mothers with working partner* show a medium activation need, less so because of their poverty risk but more because of their labor market contribution potential (52 percent have tertiary education!). Their activation potential is high but their overall priority should be set to "medium" in light of their households' relatively secure position. *Prime-aged educated unemployed* and *single NEETs without work experience* are both rated as "high priority" because of either good work experience and maintenance of human capital or young age and avoidance of "scarring" effects.

Table 4.8 Activation Need and Potential of Different Clusters in Estonia

| Share %
(2011) | Cluster | Activation
need | Activation
potential | Priority
for action |
|---|---|---|---|---|
| 21 | Middle-aged educated disabled with previous work experience | Medium | Medium | Medium |
| 19 | Prime-aged low-income long-term unemployed | High | High | High |
| 18 | Educated retirees | Low | Low | Low |
| 17 | Young inactive educated mothers with working partner | Medium | High | Medium |
| 13 | Prime-aged educated unemployed | High | High | High |
| 9 | Single NEETs without work experience | High | Medium | High |
| 3 | Young low-educated rural disabled | Medium | Low | Low |

Source: World Bank staff analysis and assessment 2014.
Note: NEET = not in employment, education, or training.

Educated retirees and *young low-educated rural disabled* are not prioritized for further action owing, respectively, to their officially achieved retirement status and extreme distance (via very low educational attainment and self-declared disability) from the labor market.

Activation Type

As a second step, the relative severity of labor market or social obstacles to be overcome for labor market integration will serve as an orientation for activation approaches. Figure 4.13 depicts the prioritized clusters along the labor market and social barrier dimensions; the size of the bubbles correspond to their relative group size.

When mapping the respective barriers for labor market integration faced by the five prioritized groups, we can see that while many of them have severe labor market distance and attachment challenges, only the *middle-aged educated disabled with previous work experience* emerge as a group that will face severe social barriers owing to the high share of disability within the group. The *young inactive educated mothers with working partner* could be described as facing a "social" barrier because of the relative importance of paid maternity leave compared with the availability of public child-care offerings in Estonia. On the other hand, their satisfactory household welfare situation (only 19 percent in bottom income quintile) could lead to the conclusion that their social situation might be in part self-chosen or driven by "cultural norms," if not that potential combined household income will not be perceived as sufficient to cover

Figure 4.13 Activation Types of Prioritized Clusters in Estonia

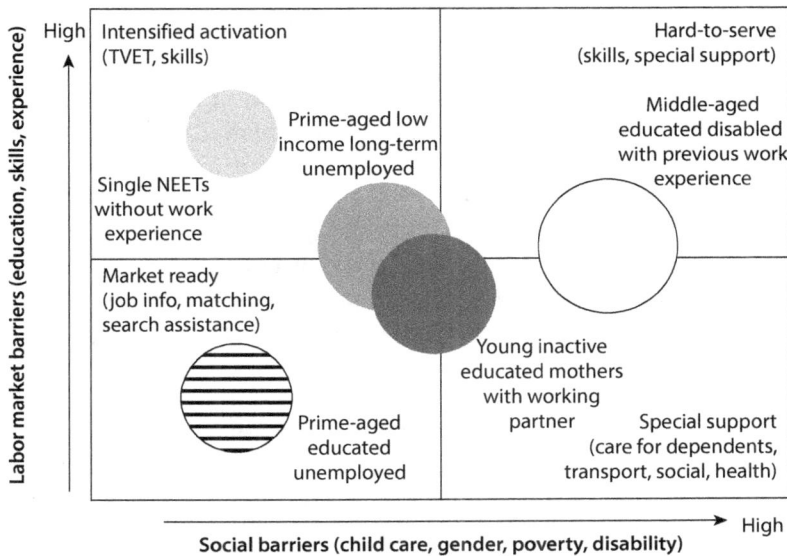

Source: World Bank staff analysis and assessment 2014.
Note: NEET = not in employment, education, or training; TVET = technical and vocational education and training.

eventual private child-care costs. Nevertheless it should be kept in mind that Estonia has higher female labor market participation than Europe as a whole (71.5 percent versus 65.5 percent for EU-28 for 2012). The female participation is even greater in the 25- to 64-year-old cohort at almost 80 percent, 10 points higher than the region's average.

Finally, the three groups of *single NEETs without work experience*, *prime-aged low-income long-term unemployed*, and *prime-aged educated unemployed* can be distinguished by their relative distance from the labor market (in terms of qualification and work experience). However, the *prime-aged low-income long-term unemployed* face significantly higher poverty.

Household Income Composition

When analyzing the 2011 household income of the prioritized groups, it is a striking feature that most households have a relatively high share of labor income. This is related to the low level and degree of coverage of unemployment and social assistance benefits in Estonia (EC 2013b). Among the prioritized groups, only the *middle-aged educated disabled with previous work experience* (29 percent) have a low share of labor income, a fact certainly corresponding to the 62 percent of household income stemming from disability and old-age benefits. With 92 percent of this group's individuals reporting their labor market status as "disabled," but only 43 percent strongly limited in their capacity to work because of their physical or mental condition, there appears to be some potential for labor market mobilization and benefit rationalization in this group.

Apart from this observation, the general level of benefit receipt in the prioritized groups is small to nonexistent. The *single NEETs without work experience* are the only group with a noticeable amount (1 percent (!)) of household income stemming from social exclusion benefits. In light of the fact that, with the exception of the *young, educated mothers with working partner*, all of the groups are severely overrepresented in the two bottom-income quintiles, this pattern of benefit receipts certainly falls short on any social inclusion target.

Given the overall picture of benefit receipt revealed by EU-SILC data, a key need for action emerges around a potential review of disability benefit allocation among *middle-aged educated disabled with previous work experience* and on the coverage and generosity of the unemployment and social exclusion benefits in general.

Suggestions for Activation Measures and Further Analysis

This section sets out a set of potential activation measures for each of the priority groups. Areas for further policy dialogue are also outlined. Any suggestion or policy discussion around concrete measures will need to take into account that the Estonian authorities have introduced a recent set of reforms and changes to existing programs in the field of employment and labor market inclusion (EU 2013b).

The suggestions below should be considered as a starting point for further policy dialogue between the EC, the World Bank, and Estonia, bearing in mind that the groups identified still carry heterogeneity that may affect the type of support required. Accordingly, these suggestions are also not meant to be an exhaustive set of possible activation measures.

It is important to keep in mind that the groups have been derived from EU-SILC data from the year 2011. Since then, general economic development, policy actions by the government of Estonia, and European Commission country-specific recommendations might reflect some of these policy suggestions or render them obsolete. Among the policy changes that the government of Estonia has initiated since 2011 that ought to improve the labor market integration or activation of some of the groups is a major reform of the incapacity-for-work scheme and the implementation of measures to prevent youth unemployment, support youth who are NEET, and include a wage subsidy for the employer and reimbursement of training costs for people between 17 and 29 years old.

Middle-aged educated disabled with previous work experience (21 percent, Priority: Medium). This is the largest group among the identified and prioritized groups. Its almost 48,000 members make up about 5 percent of the total working-age population in Estonia. Forty-three percent of this group report severe limitations in their capacity to work. While this is significantly lower than the share of individuals reporting their activity status as disabled (93 percent), any improved labor market integration of this group is likely going to require a complex set of social, medical, and therapeutic support actions.

At any rate, this significant group of out-of-work citizens needs to be followed more closely, and any new applicants for disability benefits closely monitored and controlled. Limiting the inflows into this group (via more stringent disability benefit criteria) will be easier than forcing the activated exit from members of this group. Potential activation measures for the inactive who remain in this group will largely depend on the ability of local governments to provide and finance services for disabled (transport, social and medical care, and so on), but also on the integration of national policies with local service standards and adequate financing. In light of the potentially high integration cost for and potential discrimination against disabled workers, local social services cannot be expected to finance these approaches without support from central government. Potential activation measures include:

- *Review disability status but continue benefits (for now).* While continuing to provide current benefits, the government could make the members of this group eligible for a review of their disability and work-ability status. When considered "fit to work" in this review, a set of support measures and continuing benefits (potentially with a phase-out period) ought to be provided to cushion the transition to labor market integration. According to Estonian officials, measures along these lines are currently under consideration and changes in the way the country supports and integrates disabled individuals will be introduced.

- *Mobility support.* Given the fact that the majority of this population lives in rural contexts, support for labor market access and mobility could be an important service. When providing transport or mobility solutions, local authorities could draw on social enterprises or cooperatives, providing additional opportunities for local employment.

- *Standard PES job search assistance and placement support.* Building on the strong previous work experience of this group and starting with the "nondisabled" members, integration into the standard (or emerging) activation regime of the Estonian UIF, the PES in Estonia.

- *Social economy support and sheltered employment as time-limited transition offerings.* For members of this group who are subjected to transition from "disabled" to "unemployed" labor market status, temporary placement in social economy enterprises or "sheltered" employment could provide a first step back into a fully competitive labor market. Special care needs to be taken that these offerings are time-limited and linked to clear activation regimes.

Prime-aged low-income long-term unemployed (19 percent, Priority: High). This middle-aged group shows strong work availability, is majority male, and has a nearly 50/50 urban-rural split. It has the highest poverty risk among all the groups identified.

- *Improve social inclusion benefit and link to activation.* In light of the extremely high poverty faced by this group, a targeted expansion of coverage and generosity of an activating social inclusion benefit (conditional on job search) could improve the household welfare condition. This would require improved collaboration of the Estonian Unemployment Insurance Fund and municipal social welfare offices.
- *Reconnect with previous employment experience.* Building on previous employment experience, this group could be equipped with missing functional or technical skills, second-chance apprenticeship programs, and higher secondary school certificates. Ideally, these programs would relate to industry experience already gained in previous employment spells.
- *Combined professional training and public works.* In order to combat any behavioral and attitudinal detachment from the labor market that may result after long periods of unemployment, it may be warranted to subject some of the members of this group to a (time-limited) public works requirement, combining this offering with training, job search, and skills support.
- *Mobility and training.* Questions of geographic mobility are of great importance for this group of unemployed. Linking mobility to training offerings, enabling some of these jobseekers to participate in higher-quality training in central places can be an important addition to the menu of LMPs locally. Encouragingly, training needs are already assessed individually by local PESs, and transportation costs related to training will be reimbursed up to EUR 26 per day.

Young inactive educated mothers with working partner (17 percent, Priority: Medium). Given their excellent educational status, relatively low poverty, and the high income of their working partners, some of these women could be more or less voluntarily inactive. In terms of their labor market status, they could be regarded as "market" type customers for the Estonian Unemployment Insurance Fund, needing limited and self-driven forms of job search support and reconnection with previous employment and education experience, as long as any service needs (child care, elderly care in family, and so on) are taken care of.

- *Child care and early childhood development.* Extension of accessible child-care offerings will play an important role in enabling earlier labor market integration for these women. Given their above-average household income, an income-graded cost for participation could pay for the necessary child-care services. It is likely that such policies will be supported by European Social Funds during the 2014–20 period.

- *Reconnection with previous employment.* With 93 percent of the women having worked before, linking women to their previous industry or profession after maternity leave or family time can build on existing ties and professional knowledge. These interventions should ideally be employer-driven and only marginally supported by public intervention (for example, voucher systems), and focus on women who have been detached from their industry or employer for many years and have difficulties reconnecting.[14]

- *Group-specific job-search support.* Support from PES counselors in job search techniques, soft skills, self-presentation, and update of certain functional skills may help members of this group reconnect with the labor market and attack the necessary challenges in a group-specific support network (for example, "young mothers job club," and so on)

Prime-aged educated unemployed (13 percent, Priority: High). This group should be among the highest priority customers of the PES since they boast a very good education level and relatively recent work experience. Building on these assets, this group's integration in the benefit and activation system of the UIF should be strengthened. Currently, this group receives very limited social assistance benefits.

- *Job-search support through PES.* Standard measures of job-search support, regular updates on personal progress, and personal action plans need to be the central pillar of activation support. Nevertheless, these should be seen as a "second level" option, to be used after a self-driven job search fails. As evidenced in EC (2013b), Estonia has already taken important steps in this direction with recent changes to unemployment and labor market programs.

- *Placement in private enterprises.* Job placement and training that occur within labor market activation programs need to be linked to employers' needs for skills and workers. Given the good educational endowment of these unemployed, supporting employers with skills upgrades for their existing workforces, together with these unemployed, could facilitate their access to companies.

- *Mobility and training.* Questions of geographic mobility are of great importance for this group of unemployed. Linking mobility to training offerings, enabling some of these jobseekers to participate in higher-quality trainings in central places can be an important addition to the menu of LMPs locally.

Single NEETs without work experience (9 percent, Priority: High). This group is mainly challenged with getting its first foothold in the labor market and building on recent educational experience.

- *Internet and social network-based activation and information offerings.* Promotion of online job portals, potentially linked with "game-ification" of job search offerings, mobile CV submission, application, and so on.
- *Group job search.* Mobilizing young people to continue job searching and not retreat to their homes can be an important measure to keep NEETs "engaged."
- *Reconnect programs with educational history.* Building on educational history, training and job-search offerings could help to build the functional skills necessary for related industries.
- *School-to-work transition, first work experience.* Estonia has already taken initial steps to strengthen this critical area.
- *Youth guarantee programs.* Importantly, these programs are set to be introduced in 2015. The services, which will combine training and wage subsidies, aim to increase the number of active young people in the labor market.

In general, further policy dialogue with the Estonian authorities ought to focus as much on the general level and setup of resources devoted to labor market integration and activation of the inactive and out-of-work as on the ongoing improvement of services on the national and local levels. Within this discussion, a dialogue around specific measures for specific groups could be deepened. The following items appear especially important:

- *Consistent local service delivery.* According to EC (2013b), Estonia is intending to take steps to ensure consistent service delivery levels across the country. Given the fact that the majority of the country's out-of-work population is situated in rural areas and many members of these groups require social and other public services for improved labor market integration, the adequate financing and equipment of local services (for example, support to disabled, child care, and so on) can be an important prerequisite and complement to any activation policy.

- *Labor market (re-)entry policies.* Several groups face barriers to labor market entry postschool or postwork interruption. Giving special attention to school-to-work transitions and supporting fast reentry into the labor market after unemployment or maternity spells will address the activation needs of many prioritized groups (*young mothers* as well as *NEETs*).

In summary, Estonia could benefit from accompanying the ongoing improvement of its labor market services and social inclusion policies with an enhanced knowledge about the composition and socioeconomic situations of the different groups of out-of-work citizens. This notably relates to a unified view across traditional labor market categories (employed/unemployed) and social inclusion dimensions (poverty, living conditions, and access to services) because the two are intrinsically linked, especially for the labor market's most marginalized participants.

Notes

1. According to Estonian officials, in 2013 the out-of-work population accounted for less than 200,000 people. The analysis that follows is based on EU-SILC 2011 data, the most recent and the only harmonized survey across the EU at the time of publication. All the numbers are likely to have changed since.

2. Individuals ages 16–24 years who are out of work and enrolled in education are excluded from the sample; they are considered to be investing in their final stages of human capital formation and therefore are not a particular target group for activation policies. In 2011, there were close to 88,170 youth ages 16–24 years who were out of work and enrolled in education, representing 53 percent of the total population in this age category and 28 percent of the total out-of-work population of working age. Military personnel are included in the sample but considered "at-work," and therefore do not feature in the latent class analysis below. Individuals enrolled in school who are older than 24 years and younger than 65 years are, however, included in the latent class analysis and will be grouped under "other inactive." It is important to note that the two groups combined (military and students older than 24 years) account for less than 1 percent of total population of working age.

3. This variable is constructed using the self-reported current work status in the EU-SILC survey that has four categories: at work, unemployed, retired, and inactive. The unemployed are further classified into short- and long-term based on how long they have been actively looking for a job. The inactive is combined with another question to separate this group into students, disabled, military, and other inactive.

4. In order to construct this variable, individuals age 25 years or older are considered adults.

5. This is a binary variable that takes the value one if an individual answered "yes, strong limitations" to whether they had been hampered in their usual activities because of health problems for at least the last six months. The value is zero if the answer is "yes, limited" or "no, not limited."

6. According to EU-SILC guidelines, dense areas have more than 500 inhabitants per square kilometer, where the total population for the set is at least 50,000 inhabitants. Intermediate areas have more than 100 inhabitants per square kilometer, and either

a total population for the set of at least 50,000 inhabitants or a location adjacent to a dense area. The remaining areas are categorized as sparsely populated.

7. The equivalized household income takes into account an equivalence factor to weight the number of household members used in the denominator when calculating household income per capita. The first adult 18 years of age or older has a weight of 1.0, children younger than 14 years old have a weight of 0.3, and other individuals 14 years of age and older have a weight of 0.5. The sum of the weights of all household members is equal to the equivalent household size.

8. Note that income reported in EU-SILC surveys is for the year preceding the survey year.

9. Total household gross income is defined as the sum of: (at the individual level) gross employee cash or near-cash income; company car, gross cash benefits or losses from self-employment (including royalties); unemployment benefits; old-age benefits; survivor benefits; sickness benefits; disability benefits; education allowances; and (at the household level) income from rental of property or land; family/children related allowances; social exclusion not elsewhere classified; housing allowances; regular inter-household cash transfers received; interests, dividends, profit from capital investments in unincorporated business; pensions from individual private plans; and income received by people under 16. Total household net income, in turn, was calculated by subtracting from total household gross income regular taxes on wealth, taxes on income and social insurance contributions, and regular inter-household case transfers paid.

10. Social benefits are aggregated in eight branches using the European System of integrated Social PROtection Statistics (ESSPROS) definitions. For more information, see Eurostat (2011).

11. The EU-SILC longitudinal survey consists of a four-year rotating panel. In each year, approximately three-quarters of individuals present in the previous year are retained. The samples used in the latent class analysis include about 3,000 observations for each year in the cross-sectional analysis and 600 observations in the longitudinal analysis. The population is weighted with individual weights.

12. It should be kept in mind that the EU-SILC activity status is self-reported. Therefore, the disabled population figure may not be accurate when compared to administrative data. Furthermore, in Estonia there are different benefits that are probably being captured as disability benefits: the incapacity-for-work pension and the disability benefit for people who incur additional costs due to their disability.

13. By 2013 the number of long-term unemployed had decreased significantly. According to Estonian Labor Force Survey data, there were 48,600 long-term unemployed in 2011, but just over 26,100 in 2013.

14. Currently, parents retain the right to rejoin their employer for up to three years after the birth of a child, with access to the same job.

References

Brixiova, Z., and B. Egert. 2012. "Labour Market Reforms and Outcomes in Estonia." IZA Discussion Paper 6336.

Collins, L. M., and S. T. Lanza, 2010. *Latent Class and Latent Transition Analysis: With Applications in the Social, Behavioral, and Health Sciences.* Hoboken, NJ: Wiley.

EC (European Commission). 2013a. "EU Measures to Tackle Youth Unemployment." MEMO, Brussels, 28 May.

———. 2013b. "Assessment of the Implementation of the European Commission Recommendation on Active Inclusion: A Study of National Policies: Country Report—Estonia." DG Employment, Social Affairs & Inclusion, European Commission, Brussels.

Eurofound. 2012. *NEETs—Young People Not in Employment, Education or Training: Characteristics, Costs and Policy Responses in Europe*. Luxembourg: Publications Office of the European Union.

Eurostat. 2011. *ESSPROS Manual: The European System of integrated Social Protection Statistics*. Luxembourg: European Union.

Katz, L. 2010. "Long-Term Unemployment in the Great Recession." Testimony for the Joint Economic Committee, U.S. Congress Hearing on Long-Term Unemployment: Causes, Consequences and Solutions." April 29.

Kaufman, L., and P. J. Rousseeuw. 1990. *Finding Groups in Data*. New York: Wiley.

Magidson, J., and V. Jeroen. 2002. *Latent Class Modeling as a Probabilistic Extension of K-Means Clustering*. Quirk's Marketing Research Review, March 20, 77–80. http://statisticalinnovations.com/technicalsupport/kmeans2a.htm.

Masso, J., R. Eamets, and P. Motsmees. 2013. "The Effect of Migration Experience on Occupational Mobility in Estonia." IZA Discussion Paper 7482.

OECD (Organisation for Economic Co-operation and Development). 2010. "OECD Reviews of Labor Market and Social Policies: Estonia." http://www.oecd-ilibrary.org/docserver/download/8110061e.pdf?expires=1387213871&id=id&accname=ocid195787&checksum=9F87DC8BFF74755DC339F9D137FEF4A3.

———. 2012. OECD Economic Surveys: *Estonia*. OECD.

Vermunt, J. K., and J. Magidson. 2005. *Latent GOLD 4.0 User's Guide*. Belmont, MA: Statistical Innovations Inc.

Latent Class Analysis of the Out-of-Work Population in Greece, 2007–11

Background

While most countries in the region have been able to recover after the global financial crisis, Greece is still in recession. Greece had a moderate growth rate of over 4.3 percent from 2003 to 2007, above the 2.2 percent average among the EU-28 Member States during the same period. Like most of Europe, in 2009 the country was hit by the crisis and the economy contracted 3.1 percent. Nonetheless, unlike other European countries, whose growth started recovering soon afterward, Greece's economy continued its downturn, contracting during 2010, 2011, 2012, and 2013.

As it entered its sixth year of recession in 2013, Greece also witnessed a steady deterioration of employment outcomes, particularly since 2010. From 2004 to 2008, unemployment of 15- to 64-year-olds slowly decreased, reaching 7.8 percent. Following the onset of the crisis, unemployment rose rapidly, increasing more than 16 percentage points to 27.5 percent in 2013. This is more than twice the average rate that EU-28 countries had in 2013. Labor force participation is also low by European standards. In 2013, 32 percent of Greece's working-age population was inactive, compared to a 28.1 percent average for the EU-28 countries.

Conversely, unemployment rates rose steadily and disproportionately affected those segments of the working-age population traditionally at higher labor market risk in Greece (OECD 2013b). In 2013, a staggering 68.3 percent of young people ages 15–24 years were unemployed, and among them, more than 60 percent were long-term unemployed (12 months or more), compared to about a third in 2008. Perhaps more tellingly, the share of youth not in education, employment, or training (NEET rate) nearly doubled, from 11.7 percent in 2008 to 20.6 percent in 2013. Greece has among the highest NEET rates in the EU. Another telling example of the social consequences of the crisis is that the share of children 0–17 who live in households with no employed member increased from 3.6 percent in 2008 to 12.9 percent in 2012.

A look at unemployment rates disaggregated by gender shows that women were particularly affected by the crisis. As figure 5.1 shows, unemployment rates are generally higher for women, independent of age. While men in the 25–64 age category entered the crisis with unemployment rates close to 4.3 percent, the share of unemployed women in this same age group was close to 10.1 percent. By 2013 these rates had jumped to 19.9 and 25.7 percent, respectively. Among young Greeks, women were also affected more than men, with the rate of joblessness among 15- to 24-year-old men reaching 53.6 percent in 2013, as opposed to 64.2 percent for women of the same cohort.

In Greece, long-term unemployment as a share of total unemployment has usually been higher than the average for the EU-28 countries. In 2013, according to Eurostat and as shown in figure 5.2, in the average EU-28 country 47.5 percent of the unemployed had been looking for work for more than 12 months, up from 33 percent in 2009. The long-term unemployment in Greece has been considerably higher than that during the last 10 years. In 2009, it declined to 41 percent—still 6 percentage points higher than the average EU-28 country— but by 2013 67.5 percent of the unemployed were long-term.

Following the crisis, low-educated individuals were especially affected by the rise in unemployment. Unemployment rates were already increasing for the group of less-educated individuals. After the crisis hit in 2009 this trend was somewhat accentuated. However, all educational groups saw an increase in unemployment rates during the period from 2008 to 2013. For those with a tertiary education, unemployment more than tripled, from 6.3 to 20.3 percent of the working-age population. Those with lower educational levels witnessed a greater increase in their unemployment rate, making the gap between low- and high-educated groups bigger during the period. The gap also reflects structural

Figure 5.1 Unemployment Rates by Age and Gender in Greece, 2007–13
percent

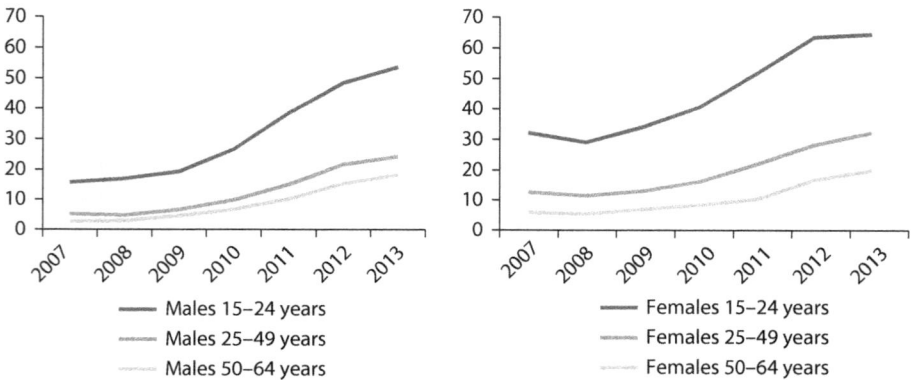

Source: Eurostat, EU-LFS.

Figure 5.2 Long-Term Unemployment as a Share of Total Unemployment, 2003–13

percent

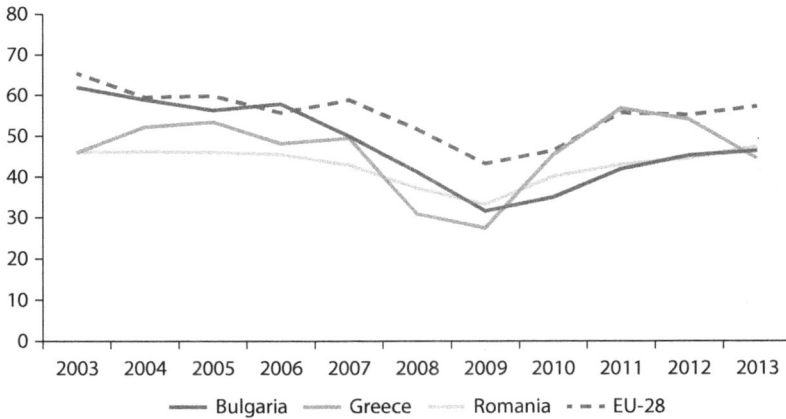

Bulgaria —— Greece —— Romania - - - EU-28 - - -

Source: Eurostat, EU-LFS.

changes that increased the demand for more skilled workers. The difference in unemployment rates for low- and high-educated workers grew from 1.3 percentage points in 2008 to 9.8 percentage points in 2013.

As a result of the crisis, employment rates also deteriorated. The employment rate of individuals ages 15–64 years, which peaked in 2008 at 61.9 percent, reached their lowest level in 2013 at 49.3 percent, notably with no major distinction across educational categories.

Although Greeks with lower educational levels suffered the most as a result of the crisis, their share of the active population has been decreasing over time. The percentage of people who have only lower secondary education or less has fallen almost 10 points since 2003, reaching 28.2 percent in 2013. Similarly, those with tertiary education have increased from 21 percent in 2003 to 30.5 percent 2013.

During the period from 2007 to 2011, the size of the out-of-work population considered in this note increased, from 2.139 to 2.695 million individuals. The analysis of the out-of-work population in this note focuses on the working-age population (16–64 years old). Specifically, only individuals ages 25–64 years who are not employed and individuals ages 16–24 years who were neither employed nor in education or training were considered.[1] Only the working-age population (16–64-year-olds) is analyzed, as labor activation options—the main policy focus of this note—are only viable for that segment of the population. The group in need of opportunities has substantially increased since 2007, as the profiles of working-age population by labor market status show (see figure 5.3). Table 5.1 shows that the groups of unemployed (short and long term), and even of early retirees, have increased, while the share of disabled individuals and other inactive has decreased. Nonemployment,[2] defined here as neither at work nor in military service, rose from 33 percent in 2007 to 41 percent in 2011.

Figure 5.3 Distribution of Working-Age Population (Ages 16–64 Years) by Labor Market Attachment in Greece, 2007 and 2011

percent

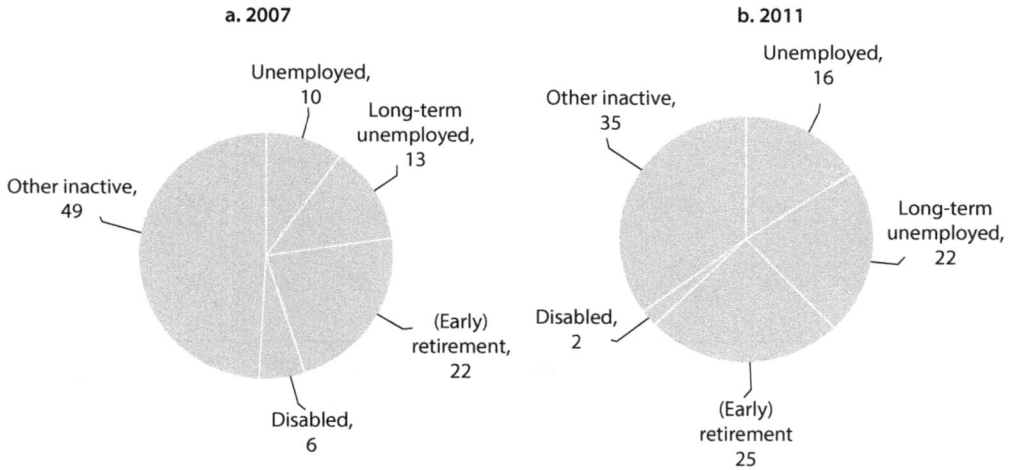

a. 2007

Unemployed, 10
Long-term unemployed, 13
Other inactive, 49
(Early) retirement, 22
Disabled, 6

b. 2011

Unemployed, 16
Other inactive, 35
Long-term unemployed, 22
Disabled, 2
(Early) retirement 25

Source: World Bank staff analysis based on EU-SILC.
Note: Data do not include inactive individuals ages 16–24 years who are enrolled in education.

Table 5.1 Number and Percentage of Working-Age Individuals (Ages 16–64 Years) by Labor Market Attachment in Greece, 2007 and 2011

	2007	2011	Percent change 2007–11
At work	4,379	3,871	−11.6
	67.2%	59.0%	
Unemployed	204	435	113.1
	3.1%	6.6%	
Long-term unemployed	275	588	113.8
	4.2%	9.0%	
(Early) retirement	477	670	40.3
	7.3%	10.2%	
Disabled	134	61	−54.7
	2.1%	0.9%	
Other inactive	1,048	941	−10.3
	16.1%	14.3%	
Total	6,518	6,565	0.7
	100%	100%	

Source: World Bank staff analysis based on EU-SILC.

Methodology: Latent Class Analysis

In chapter 1 a general overview of the latent class analysis methodology was presented. This section explains in detail the variables and covariates used to identify classes or groups of out-of-work individuals that are as homogeneous as possible within each class according to a set of observable characteristics, and as distant as possible between classes. The emerging profiles can then be contrasted with the design and targeting of current activation policies, in order to identify the potential gaps and to enhance their design features.[3]

Variable Selection

The definition of latent classes relies on a number of indicator variables to capture different "symptoms" of an overall latent condition (in this case, the typology of joblessness). The challenge in such models is to identify a discrete number of variables that can best explain the heterogeneity of individual outcomes. In this case, two sets of categorical variables were selected: the first set to show the extent of labor market distance and the other to capture some of the main factors that can affect employment on the supply side, such as labor supply conditions (household-level incentives to work and physical ability to work).

- *Distance from labor market*: short-term unemployment, long-term unemployment, (early) retirement, disability, and other inactivity (largely unpaid domestic work).[4]
- *Labor supply conditions*: whether the individual's household has at least one working adult,[5] and perceived limitations on activities due to health problems.[6]

In addition to indicators, the model includes active covariates, which are used to improve the classification of individuals in each class. In this case the active covariates are the demographic variables that are normally used to disaggregate labor market outcomes:

- Age-group category (four groups)
- Gender
- Human capital: the highest educational level achieved (three groups)
- Urban/rural location

Once the latent classes have been defined, inactive covariates that were not included in the model can be used to characterize the individuals in each class and the households in which they live. The inactive covariates chosen describe those characteristics that may provide valuable information for the design of tailored policies that address barriers to employment, including income level. They include:

- Household welfare conditions:
    - Income quintile (defined by equivalized disposable household income[7,8])
    - Labor, benefit, and other income as share of total gross household income[9]
    - Binary variable denoting whether at least one working adult (age 25 years and older) is present in the household

     – Tenure status
     – Household able to keep dwelling warm
     – Partner's labor income
     – Quintile of partner's labor income
     – Binary variables denoting whether individuals or their households are beneficiaries of any of eight social protection benefits[10]
- Household demographics:
     – Household size
     – Household composition
     – Binary variable showing whether there are children younger than six years of age in the household
     – Binary variable denoting whether there are three or more children younger than 16 years old in the household
     – Children younger than 13 years old in the household receiving child care: all, some, or none of the children
     – Older person (65 years of age and older) in the household
- Other individual-level demographics:
     – More refined age groups (seven groups)
     – Marital status
- Individual human capital:
     – More refined highest educational level achieved (six groups)
     – Work experience in years
     – Binary variable for previous work experience
- Household location:
     – Degree of urbanization[11]: densely populated, intermediate area, sparsely populated
     – Regional breakdown: northern and eastern, southwestern and south-central

Group Labeling

The resulting groups are then labeled according to the greatest proportional characteristics within groups that also aid in distinguishing among groups. Granted, a large number of characteristics describe these groups, and only a few are taken into account for the purpose of labeling. In part, some of these characteristics may exhibit a large degree of heterogeneity and may thus not be relevant for defining a group. In addition, some characteristics may be more relevant for the purposes of policy design than others. In short, though the labeling of groups can be considered more an art than a science, when taken together with detailed descriptions of a group's most prominent characteristics, labeling can serve as an important starting point in the design and prioritization of activation policies.

    The analysis relies on cross-sectional as well as panel data from the European Union Statistics of Income and Living Conditions (EU-SILC) surveys for 2008–11, which combine individual-level information with household characteristics. The first part of the note presents a cross-sectional analysis for the years 2008, 2009, 2010, and 2011. In particular, the latent class analysis on 2008 data shows the main characteristics of the out-of-work before the global economic crisis hit Greece, and thus highlight what could be considered more structural issues of the country's labor market. The 2011 latent class analysis will contrast this initial assessment with more recent developments. The second part of the note exploits longitudinal data between 2008 and 2010[12] to trace the prior labor market status of individuals observed last in 2010 in various classes, and will shed light on the relative persistence in the out-of-work status among different classes of individuals. The set of variables chosen for the cross-section and the longitudinal analysis are slightly different, due to minor differences in the set of variables recorded in each of the two types of data sets.

Main Findings

Out-of-Work Population: Group Profiles from Cross-Sectional Analysis

The latent class analysis supports the categorization of the out-of-work into seven major groups, some of which have remained stable over time. Figure 5.4 shows the shares of each of these seven classes in the year 2011 while table 5.2 presents their most salient characteristics.

Figure 5.4 Classes of Out-of-Work Individuals in Greece, 2011
percent

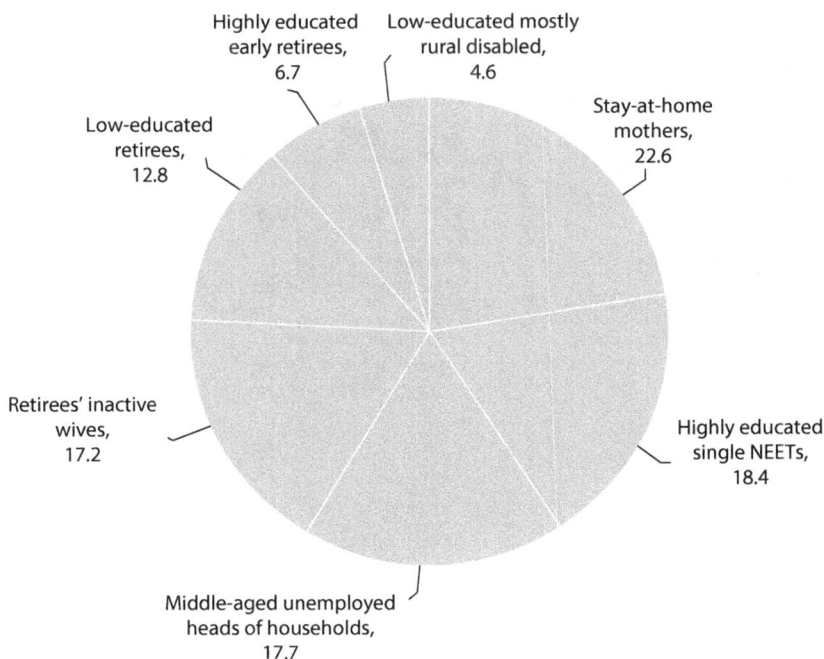

Highly educated early retirees, 6.7

Low-educated mostly rural disabled, 4.6

Stay-at-home mothers, 22.6

Low-educated retirees, 12.8

Retirees' inactive wives, 17.2

Highly educated single NEETs, 18.4

Middle-aged unemployed heads of households, 17.7

Source: World Bank staff analysis based on EU-SILC.

Table 5.2 Summary Characteristics of Latent Classes of Out-of-Work Population in Greece, 2011

1: Stay-at-home mothers (23%)

- 76% are inactive
- 86% have a working partner
- 99% are married
- Mid-skilled: 48% have completed upper secondary education while only 21% have completed tertiary or postsecondary education
- 11% have no working adult in household
- 63% are 35–54 years old
- They are all female
- 56% have worked before; 11 years of experience on average
- 67% live with children; 29% with children younger than 6 years old
- Moderate poverty risk: 28% in poorest income quintile

2: Highly educated single NEETs (18%)

- 43% are long-term unemployed, unemployed (29%)
- 94% have never married (94%)
- High-skilled: 55% have completed tertiary or post-secondary education
- 40% have no working adult in household
- 60% are 25–34 years old
- 59% are male
- 53% have worked before; 5 years of experience on average
- 63% live in urban areas
- Moderate poverty risk: 29% in poorest income quintile

3: Middle-aged unemployed heads of households (18%)

- 29% are unemployed; 54% are long-term unemployed
- 67% don't have a partner or partner not working
- 56% have no working adult in household
- 69% are married
- Mid-skilled: 38% have upper secondary education; 25% tertiary or postsecondary
- 71% are 35–54 years old
- 61% are male
- 93% have worked before; 17 years of experience on average
- 71% live in urban areas
- Very high poverty risk: 44% in poorest income quintile
- 19% receive unemployment benefits

4: Retirees' inactive wives (17%)

- 69% are inactive
- 76% are married; 62% have a retired partner
- Low-skilled: 64% have below upper secondary education
- 68% have no working adult in household
- 71% are 55–64 years old
- 100% are female
- 55% have worked before; 21 years of experience on average
- 58% live in urban areas
- Moderate poverty risk: 27% in poorest income quintile

5: Low-educated retirees (13%)

- 90% are retired
- 72% live in households without a working partner
- 90% are married
- Low-skilled: 52% have below upper secondary education
- 58% have no working adult in household
- 59% are 60–64 years old
- 86% are male
- 97% have worked before; 34 years of experience on average
- 62% live in urban areas
- Low poverty risk: 19% in poorest income quintile
- 71% receive old-age benefits

6: Highly educated early retirees (7%)

- 99% are retired
- 61% live in a household without a working partner
- 85% are married
- High-skilled: 76% have tertiary or postsecondary education
- 44% have no working adult in household
- 83% are 45–59 years old
- 61% are female
- 98% have worked before; 29 years of experience on average
- 71% live in urban areas
- Very low poverty risk: 4% in poorest income quintile
- 79% receive old-age benefits

7: Low-educated mostly rural disabled (5%)

- 44% report their labor market status as disabled; 25% are retired
- 67% report a strongly limited capacity to work
- 86% live in a household without a working partner
- 61% have never married
- Low-skilled: 68% have below upper secondary education
- 64% have no working adult in household

table continues next page

Table 5.2 Summary Characteristics of Latent Classes of Out-of-Work Population in Greece, 2011 *(continued)*

7: Low-educated mostly rural disabled (5%)

- 72% are 35–59 years old
- 63% are male
- 59% have worked before; 20 years of experience on average
- 58% live in rural areas
- High poverty risk: 34% in poorest income quintile
- 51% receive disability benefits; 26% receive family/child benefits

Source: World Bank staff analysis based on EU-SILC.
Note: Percentages in parentheses following the group names refer to the share of the total out-of-work population. "Years of work experience" refer only to individuals who have worked before. "Dependent children" include children younger than 18 years of age and household members ages 18–24 years who are economically inactive and living with at least one parent. "Working adult" refers to adults ages 25 years and older. For this report's purposes, we define the at-risk-of-poverty rate as the relative risk of being in the first quintile of the income distribution. The reference period for income reported in EU-SILC surveys is the year preceding the survey year.

The seven main groups emerging from the LCA analysis in 2011 can be characterized as follows (for more detail, see Appendix A for a link to the online-only annexes):

- Cluster 1: *Stay-at-home mothers.* This group, representing 23 percent of the out-of-work sample in 2011, consists largely of out-of-the-labor-force women (77 percent) in their prime age (35–54 years). Two-thirds of this group have children (almost one-third have children younger than 6 years of age), more than half have an upper secondary education, and only 56 percent claim to have worked before. Another robust characteristic of this group is a working partner who earns, on average, a medium level of annual income (EUR 17,000). This group has the lowest share of the "no working adult in the household" indicator (11 percent). However, as these women's households tend to be relatively large (3.5 members on average), it is not surprising that in terms of welfare, more than 50 percent of the class members live in the bottom 40 percent of the income distribution. Overall, although some individuals in this group receive family/child benefits, this group can least rely on public transfers, owing to the fact that their partners are employed.

- Cluster 2: *Highly educated single NEETs.* This group represented 18 percent of the out-of-work population in 2011. Members of this class are largely younger than 35 years of age and resemble other unemployed youth who have been particularly hit by the economic crisis across the EU, as 40 percent of them are long-term unemployed and another 30 percent short-term unemployed. The protracted employment crisis is also evident through a relatively high (and rising) average age. In 2010, less than one-third of this group was younger than 25 years old, while more than 60 percent was between 25 and 34 years of age. In 40 percent of these group's households, there is no working adult. Moreover, this group is relatively highly educated; more than half have either tertiary education or a postsecondary degree. Another defining characteristic of the *highly educated single NEETs* is that they have never been married and live in large households without children (probably their household of origin). Overall this group has a moderate poverty risk; 27 percent of them are in the poorest income quintile.

- Cluster 3: *Middle-aged unemployed heads of households.* This group made up 18 percent of the out-of-work in 2011. This group comprises individuals who are almost entirely middle-aged (35–59 years), majority male (61 percent), unemployed (more than half long-term, that is, unemployed for more than 12 months). Together with the *highly educated single NEETs* they constitute more than 80 percent of the unemployed in the country.[13] Unlike their younger counterparts, however, this group comprises individuals who have left their birth households, made the transition to marriage, and largely have children. They are also fairly heterogeneous in terms of educational attainment: 36 percent have not completed upper secondary and 25 percent have completed postsecondary or tertiary education. And while half of the NEETs never worked before, this group is composed almost entirely of job losers, with 17 years of experience on average. Their joblessness and family status explain why they are by far the worst-off in the whole sample of the out-of-work in terms of welfare (44 percent belonged to the bottom income quintile in 2011). In this context, it is noteworthy that only one-fifth of them receive unemployment benefits and only a small fraction receive family/child benefits. In 56 percent of these group's households, there is no working adult, the second-highest share among the nonretiree groups.

- Cluster 4: *Retirees' inactive wives.* Representing 17 percent of the out-of-work population of 2011, this group consists of low-educated, inactive women, mostly close to or at retirement age, who live in small households and are married to retired men. Just over half of this group reports having worked in the past, but only 30 percent describe themselves as retired. Over all, this group has a moderate poverty risk; 27 percent of them live in the poorest income quintile.

- Cluster 5: *Low-educated retirees.* The fifth-largest group can be considered the male counterpart of the previous one, sharing similar household characteristics. They have low educational attainment: more than half did not finish upper secondary school. Interestingly, a third of the members in this group are less than 60 years old, but almost all of them (84 percent) receive either a permanent (pension, disability pension) or unemployment-related income replacement benefit. In fact, this group figures among those least likely to be in poverty or near poverty, with only 19 percent in the bottom income quintile. Their retirement status and previous work experience make them likely to be the main owners of pension rights for their households. Thirteen percent of them claim to have limited capacity to work due to illness or disability, a rather high share compared to most groups.

- Cluster 6: *Highly educated early retirees.* This group represented 7 percent of the out-of-work population in 2011. Its members are characterized by a relatively low age for people in retirement (29 percent between 45 and 54, and another 53 percent between 55 and 59), all of them self-defining as retired, and about 85 percent of them receiving either old-age or disability benefits. They are by far the most highly educated (69 percent have tertiary education), urbanized (60 percent live in the capital of Athens), and highest-income group, with 54 percent in the top income quintile and only 4 percent in the bottom.

- Cluster 7: *Low-educated mostly rural disabled.* This group, representing from 4 to 5 percent of the out-of-work population, reports its labor market status as disabled (44 percent) or retired (25 percent), with very low education levels. A majority (67 percent) also report strongly limited work ability due to a health condition. In 65 percent of this group's households, there is no working adult, the highest share among the nonretiree groups. Most of these individuals receive at least one social benefit: the most common are disability benefits (51 percent) and family/child benefits (26 percent). The members of this group are also characterized by the absence of a partner and live in households without a working adult. They are the group next at risk of falling into poverty after the *middle-aged unemployed heads of households,* with 34 percent belonging to the poorest income quintile. A majority live in rural areas.

Table 5.3 and table 5.4 present the main characteristics of each group in 2011. Annex 2 (see Appendix A for a link to the online-only annexes) provides tables with the full characteristics of the identified groups for the years 2007, 2009, and 2011.

Table 5.3 Latent Classes of Out-of-Work Population in Greece: Indicators, 2011

	All out-of-work	1. Stay-at-home mothers	2. Highly educated single NEETs	3. Middle-aged unemployed heads of households	4. Retirees' inactive wives	5. Low-educated retirees	6. Highly educated early retirees	7. Low-educated mostly rural disabled
Cluster size (%)	100	22.6	18.4	17.7	17.2	12.8	6.7	4.6
Population	2,694,563	608,102	496,828	476,621	464,496	345,139	179,709	123,668
Indicators (%)								
Labor market attachment								
Unemployed	16	11	29	45	0	3	0	2
Long-term unemployed	22	13	43	54	0	4	0	21
Retired	25	0	2	0	30	90	99	25
Disabled	2	0	0	0	0	2	0	44
Domestic tasks/other	35	76	27	1	69	2	0	8
Education								
Primary	36	32	5	37	68	52	1	74
Secondary	44	56	54	48	32	37	30	26
Tertiary	19	13	41	16	1	11	69	0

table continues next page

Table 5.3 Latent Classes of Out-of-Work Population in Greece: Indicators, 2011 *(continued)*

	All out-of-work	1. Stay-at-home mothers	2. Highly educated single NEETs	3. Middle-aged unemployed heads of households	4. Retirees' inactive wives	5. Low-educated retirees	6. Highly educated early retirees	7. Low-educated mostly rural disabled
Working partner								
Yes	32	86	0	33	5	19	39	15
No	34	14	0	35	71	71	46	7
Not applicable	34	0	100	32	25	10	15	78
Self-assessed physical capacity								
None/limited	92	99	99	97	90	87	99	33
Strongly limited	8	1	1	3	10	13	1	67

Source: World Bank staff analysis based on EU-SILC.

Table 5.4 Latent Classes of Out-of-Work Population in Greece: Active Covariates, 2011

	All out-of-work	1. Stay-at-home mothers	2. Highly educated single NEETs	3. Middle-aged unemployed heads of households	4. Retirees' inactive wives	5. Low-educated retirees	6. Highly educated early retirees	7. Low-educated mostly rural disabled
Cluster size (%)	**100**	**22.6**	**18.4**	**17.7**	**17.2**	**12.8**	**6.7**	**4.6**
Population	**2,694,563**	**608,102**	**496,828**	**476,621**	**464,496**	**345,139**	**179,709**	**123,668**
Acitve Covariates (%)								
Age group								
16–24 years	7	3	32	4	0	0	0	1
25–34 years	20	25	60	15	0	0	0	19
35–59 years	55	72	8	81	57	31	86	72
60–64 years	18	1	0	0	43	69	14	7
Gender								
Female	62	100	41	39	100	14	61	37
Male	38	0	59	61	0	86	39	63
Urbanization degree								
Densely populated	46	35	49	55	48	51	37	35
Intermediate areas	15	18	14	16	10	11	34	7
Sparsely populated	39	47	37	29	42	38	29	58
At least one working adult in household								
No	45	12	40	56	68	58	45	65
Yes	55	88	60	44	32	42	55	35

Source: World Bank staff analysis based on EU-SILC.

Table 5.5 Classes of Out-of-Work Population in Greece, as a Percentage of Total Out-of-Work Population, 2007, 2009, and 2011

percent

Name of cluster	2007	2009	2011
Stay-at-home mothers	31	28	23
Highly educated single NEETs	18	19	18
Retirees' inactive wives	17	22	17
Low-educated retirees	16	12	13
Low-educated mostly rural disabled	6	6	5
Early retirees/poor unemployed (2007 and 2009)	13	13	n.a.
Highly educated early retirees (2011)	n.a.	n.a.	7
Middle-aged unemployed heads of households (2011)	n.a.	n.a.	18

Source: World Bank staff analysis based on EU-SILC.
Note: n.a. = not applicable.

Although a small number of the identified classes of out-of-work have been quite stable over the last few years, most of the identified classes experienced changes in composition and also in the share they represent of the total out-of-work. Table 5.5 shows the evolution of the groups' classifications from 2007 to 2011 as a share of the total out-of-work population, while figure 5.5 shows the absolute numbers. From the graph, the first important observation is that the size of the out-of-work population has increased from 2.142 million to 2.695 million individuals, almost a 27 percent increase. Some clusters have changed across time; for example, clusters identified in 2011 that were present in previous years underwent changes in relative size and also in composition. The fact that the composition of the groups changes over time is particularly important to keep in mind when interpreting changes in group size. For instance, significant increases (decreases) in group size are sometimes due to reassignments of individuals across groups, resulting in changes in group composition. Thus, although some groups may retain similar names across years due to their most salient characteristics, they may nonetheless vary in composition across years. The evolution in terms of group size and group composition over the 2007–11 period can be summarized as follows:

- The major difference across time is the division of *early retirees/poor unemployed* cluster into two parts in 2011. Up until 2009 this group represented almost 13 percent of the out-of-work population. In 2011, this group splits into a smaller group of *highly educated early retirees* and a new, relatively large group comprising *middle-aged unemployed heads of households.* This new group captures the increase in unemployment among prime-aged individuals following the crisis.

- The *highly educated single NEETs* cluster share of the total out-of-work population remained stable at around 18 percent during the 2007–10 period. Nevertheless, the group had absolute growth of 25 percent in the same period (the population in this group was around 394,000 in 2007 and grew to 497,000

Figure 5.5 Classes of Out-of-Work Population in Greece, 2007, 2009, and 2011
Thousands of individuals

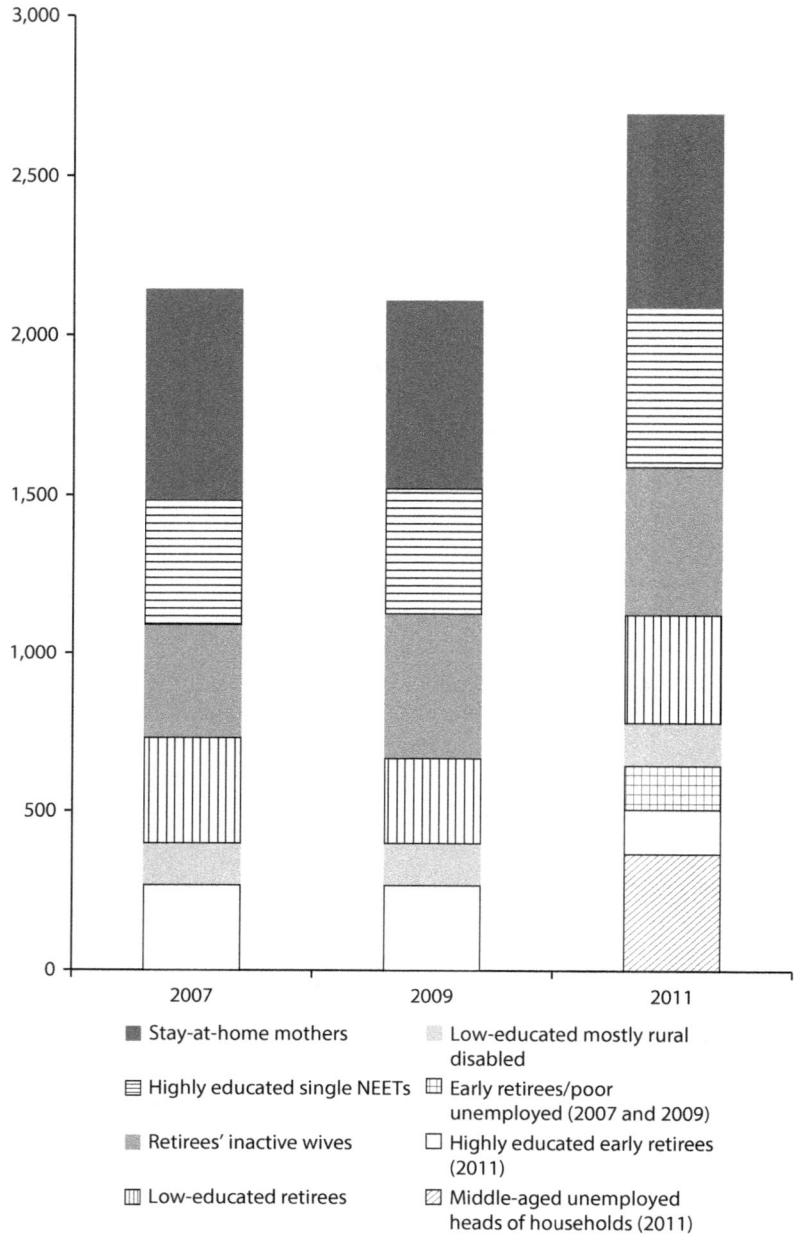

Stay-at-home mothers

Highly educated single NEETs

Retirees' inactive wives

Low-educated retirees

Low-educated mostly rural disabled

Early retirees/poor unemployed (2007 and 2009)

Highly educated early retirees (2011)

Middle-aged unemployed heads of households (2011)

Source: World Bank staff analysis based on EU-SILC.

in 2011). The composition of the group also experienced some changes from 2007 to 2010. In 2011 this cluster had more males than in previous years, increasing from 46 to 59 percent. Also, the share of people with tertiary or post-secondary education increased to 57 percent in 2011, up from 33 percent in 2007.

- There has been a slight decrease in the absolute size of the group of *stay-at-home mothers*. It is notable that this group represented 30 percent of the out-of-work in 2007, but due to the growth in other groups as a direct result of the crisis, its relative size shrank to 23 percent after the crisis. Interestingly, the group also decreased in absolute size, possibly because of changes in incentives for labor supply due to the loss of income of the partner, along with a general trend toward higher female labor force participation. Indeed, while in 2007 88 percent declared themselves to be inactive, in 2010 only 76 percent did so. Conversely, the group of stay-at-home mothers that claimed to be unemployed grew 11 percent. This group also became slightly more educated. In 2010, 17 percent had only a primary education (compared to 29 percent in 2008), and 48 percent had upper secondary (compared to 39 percent).

- The *retirees' inactive wives* share of the out-of-work population oscillated between 17 and 22 percent from 2007 to 2009. Although the share of this cluster in 2011 with respect to that of 2007 did not vary significantly (17 percent), in absolute numbers this group grew almost 29 percent, an additional 103,000 people. In terms of composition there were also considerable changes. First, the percentage of individuals that were classified as retired increased from 3 percent to 30 percent between 2007 and 2011. The share of inactive decreased from 96 to 69 percent during the same period. In addition, the members of this group became more likely to have worked before and the share of them that received old-age benefits increased from 4 to 21 percent.

- The *low-educated retirees* and *low-educated mostly rural disabled* groups remained stable in terms of absolute size. Although the relative size of both groups fell over time, the absolute numbers varied very little. The share of the out-of-work population for *low-educated retirees* decreased from 16 to 13 percent while growing 14 percent in absolute numbers. In terms of composition, the share of individuals with secondary education increased by 13 percentage points, and were more likely to be male—86 percent in 2011 compared to 72 percent in 2007. On the other hand, the *low-educated mostly rural disabled* group reduced its share from 6 to 4 percent, which in absolute numbers represented a 6 percent decrease. The share of individuals in the *low-educated mostly rural disabled* who were between 35–54 years old increased from 63 to 72 percent, and 65 percent said there was no working adult in the household in 2011, compared with 46 percent in 2007. A larger share of this group have never married—the percentage increased from 44 to 61—and the group is also more likely to be living in urban areas than before.

Structural Aspects and Emerging Trends in the Profiles of the Out of-Work

The clusters identified in the out-of-work population for the period from 2007 to 2011 reflect both structural and cyclical aspects of the labor market. This section identifies some of the key structural aspects of the Greek labor market and uses cross-sectional and longitudinal analysis of clusters of the out-of-work population to further examine the effects of the crisis.

Even in time of protracted economic crisis, only just over one-third of the out-of-work population reports being actively searching for work. Out of the seven classes identified in 2011, the first (largest) class, together with the last four (smallest) classes, comprise individuals with either low or no labor force partici-pation, and with limited incentives to join the labor force. Limited incentives to work are found especially among the four smallest classes, all of which are made up of retired individuals and their wives or individuals on disability. The first (largest) group is composed of *stay-at-home mothers* who could potentially be pushed into the labor market in the case of loss of income from their partners, as well as if barriers, such as lack of child care, were removed. The two middle-sized groups of largely unemployed individuals *(highly educated single NEETs and middle-aged unemployed heads of households)* are only just above a third of the total unemployed (36 percent).

The low activity rates of some latent classes are associated with structural aspects of the labor market that preceded the crisis. The first issue relates to very limited female labor force participation, highlighted by the fact that the top group of the out-of-work population is made up of largely inactive women. In fact, the labor force participation rate for women of working age in Greece is 7 percentage points below that of the European Union average (see figure 5.6).

Figure 5.6 Female Labor Force Participation Rate, Ages 55–64 Years, 2012

percent

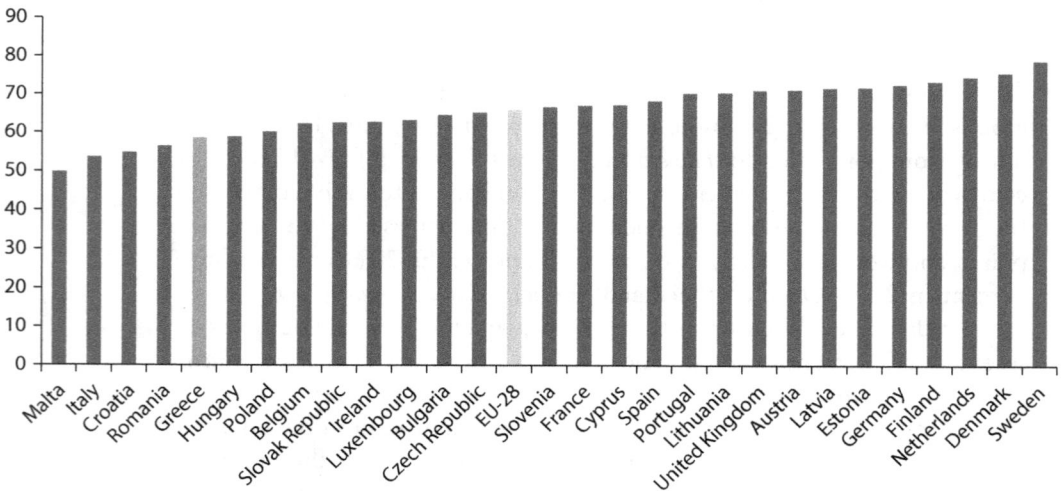

Source: Eurostat, EU-LFS.

The *stay-at-home mothers* depend on their partner's income, and nearly half of them have never worked before despite being of prime working age. As noted below, however, their absolute number fell after the crisis, consistent with the fact that the female labor force participation rate has been rising in recent years.

The structure of social protection benefits, particularly pensions, is directly linked with the very high levels of inactivity in the working-age population, especially among those between 55 and 64 years old. *Low-educated retirees, highly educated early retirees, retirees' inactive wives*, and the *low-educated mostly rural disabled* make up 42 percent of the out-of-work population. It is interesting that their absolute number has been increasing since the crisis, probably as the low labor demand drove down incentives for remaining in the labor force and increased pressure to enter the pension system at an early age. As a relative number, these groups of retired individuals shrank compared to earlier years because of the large inflows of job losers in the out-of-work population. It is noteworthy that retirees and their wives are the groups that are best protected from the risk of poverty in the out-of-work population. In fact, the labor force participation rate for the population ages 55–64 years, at 42.5 percent in 2013, is almost 12 percentage points lower than the average for the European Union (figure 5.7). In contrast, the *low-educated mostly rural disabled* are at the highest risk of poverty, but make up only 5 percent of the out-of-work, versus 37 percent in the case of (early) retirees and their inactive wives.

Unemployment has changed in nature and size as a result of the crisis, with middle-aged job losers acquiring new importance. Almost all of the groups of

Figure 5.7 Labor Force Participation Rate, Ages 55–64 Years, 2013

percent

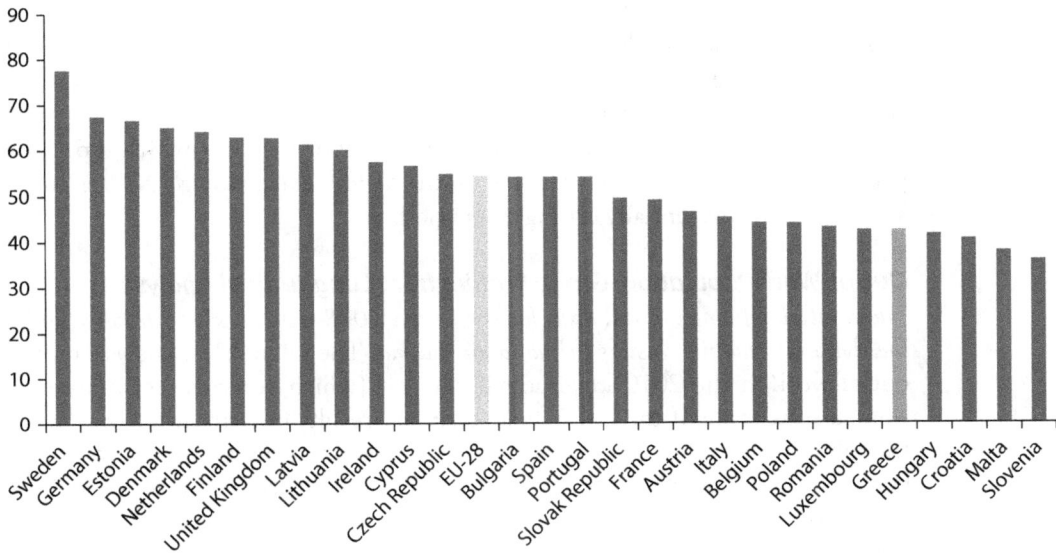

Source: Eurostat, EU-LFS.

out-of-work individuals remained largely stable over time, though the crisis saw a rise in unemployed, middle-aged poor. The population comprised six similar groups in 2007 and 2009, expanding to seven well-defined groups in 2011, due to the increase in the size and the nature of joblessness. The crisis also reduced the affordability of inactivity among middle-class inactive mothers, and saw a significant reduction in the share of *stay-at-home mothers.*

Middle-aged unemployed heads of households appear to be at highest risk of falling into poverty. The significant share of inactive in this group that receive retirement benefits at a relatively young age appear to be at less risk of poverty than those who are out of work but staying in the labor market. In the middle lie *stay-at-home mothers* and *highly educated single NEETs,* who, although not as protected from poverty as retirees and their wives, are at less relative risk of poverty.

Household composition patterns appear to be endogenous products of the protracted employment crisis. Across groups, with the exception of *stay-at-home mothers* and *middle-aged unemployed heads of households,* households mainly comprise at least two adults and no children, even in the case of *highly educated single NEETs.* Of these, about 32 percent still live with their parents. This suggests that out-of-work individuals live with their families, which play the role of a safety net. In the case of *stay-at-home mothers,* although the great majority (67 percent) live in households with children, an even larger proportion (86 percent) have a working partner. This is in contrast with *middle-aged unemployed heads of households,* for whom living with their families largely implies having dependents (only one third have a working spouse and a majority live in households with children) and thus a higher risk of falling into poverty.

The most discernible change between 2007 and 2011 is the emergence of the *middle-aged unemployed heads of households* and the large growth of *highly educated single NEETs* (figure 5.5). Models for 2007 and 2009 indicated the existence of six latent classes, while in 2011 the most fitting model supported seven classes. The main difference resulted from the clear growth in size of a new class of *middle-aged unemployed heads of households,* who represent the main departure from existing structural issues in the labor market—which especially penalized youth and women. The size of the *highly educated single NEETs* group also increased substantially during the period.

Out-of-Work Population: Group Profiles from Longitudinal Analysis

The analysis of longitudinal data for the period 2008–10 can shed further light on the dynamics within clusters in the labor market. The latent class analysis on the out-of-work in the 2010 longitudinal data set (which comprises 600 observations, a subsample of the total) yielded similar results in terms of latent classes, though in light of the reduced sample size, some categories of out-of-work were combined into one class: early retirees were put together with retirees, and the unemployed (nonsingle NEET) together with the disabled. Given the qualitative similarity between the size and characteristics of these five clusters compared to those found in the cross-sectional analysis, the findings from the panel data are here used to understand further the dynamics of the previously described sample. Overall the five classes include, in order of magnitude:

- *Stay-at-home mothers* (28 percent)
- *Highly educated single NEETs* (24 percent)
- *Retired and early retired men* (18 percent)
- *Retirees' inactive wives* (17 percent)
- *Low-educated unemployed or disabled* (13 percent)

Annex 3 (see Appendix A for a link to the online-only annexes) shows the statistical description of the latent classes in full while table 5.6 summarizes the main key characteristics of the five classes.

A further advantage of the panel analysis is to provide information on the flow of individuals among clusters and in and out of employment. Table 5.7 shows the flow of individuals into each cluster of the out-of-work population or into employment in 2010 according to their labor market status in 2008. Between 2008 and 2010, 88 percent of the employed remained at work. About 6 percent moved into unemployment, either to the group of the *highly educated single NEETs* or to the *low-educated unemployed or disabled*, while another 7 percent moved into inactivity: 3 percent into retirement, 1 percent into the *retirees' inactive wives* group, and an additional 3 percent into the *stay-at-home mothers* group. There is also an interesting flow into employment among those who were unemployed or inactive in 2008. In 2010, 34 percent of those who were classified as unemployed and 21 percent who were classified as inactive in 2008 were found to be employed. The sample size of individuals who were inactive in 2010 and for whom we had information in 2008 is about 600.

Job losses hit all identified groups to some extent, but they were more pronounced among the *low-educated unemployed or disabled* and *highly educated single NEETs*. Table 5.7 shows the labor market status in 2008 for each cluster and at-work population in 2010.

Table 5.8 identifies the 2010 population groups that were most affected by job loss. The fifth (and smallest) class of low-educated unemployed or disabled were those who were hardest hit, as close to half of them changed status from employment to nonemployment during this period. Young people were the second hardest-hit group, as one-third of *highly educated single NEETs* lost their jobs.

On the other hand, the lack of flow into employment was pronounced.

Table 5.8 also shows that of those employed in 2010, only 8 percent had been out of work in 2008. In addition, from the previous table it is clear that only one-third of the unemployed and one-fifth of the inactive moved into a job between 2008 and 2010. This suggests that the lack of job creation and the structural rigidities of the labor market reinforced the divide between the employed and the nonemployed during this period.

Self-employment and the "informal economy." Any discussion of the Greek economy and its labor market will need to take into account the presence of high self-employment and a variety of informal activities. For the purpose of the segmentation of the out-of-work population, EU-SILC data should be indifferent

Table 5.6 Longitudinal Analysis: Summary Characteristics of Latent Classes of the Out-of-Work Population in Greece, 2010

1: Stay-at-home mothers (28%)

- 86% are inactive
- 94% have a working partner
- Low-to-mid-skilled: 44% have primary education; 44% have upper secondary
- 88% are 25–54 years old
- All are female
- 10 years of work experience on average
- 63% live in households with children; 29% live with children younger than 6 years old
- 64% live in rural areas
- High poverty risk: 36% in poorest income quintile

2: Highly educated single NEETs (24%)

- 64% are unemployed; 36% are inactive
- 99% do not have a partner
- High-skilled: 25% have completed tertiary education; 44% have upper secondary or postsecondary
- 89% are 20–34 years old
- 56% are female
- 4 years of work experience on average
- 54% live in urban areas
- Low poverty risk: 24% in poorest income quintile

3: Retired and early retired men (18%)

- 76% are retired; 20% are unemployed
- 54% have a partner that is not working
- 90% are married
- Low-to-mid-skilled: 52% have below upper secondary education; 23% have tertiary
- 47% are 45–59 years old; 17% are 60–64 years old
- 73% are male
- 29 years of work experience on average
- 53% live in urban areas
- Low poverty risk: 22% in poorest income quintile
- 59% receive old-age benefits; 42% social assistance benefits

4: Retirees' inactive wives (17%)

- 82% are inactive
- 97% do not have a working partner; 63% have a retired partner
- 76% are married
- Low-skilled: 79% have below upper secondary education
- 75% are 55–64 years old
- All are female
- 18 years of work experience on average
- 59% live in rural areas
- Moderate poverty risk: 28% in poorest income quintile

5: Low-educated unemployed or disabled (13%)

- 57% are unemployed; 35% report their labor market status as disabled
- 29% have strongly limited capacity to work
- 74% do not have a working partner
- 57% have never married
- Low-skilled: 59% have below upper secondary education
- 75% are 35–54 years old
- 73% are male
- 18 years of experience on average
- 61% live in rural areas
- High poverty risk: 40% in poorest income quintile
- 49% receive social assistance; 26% sickness benefits

Source: World Bank staff analysis based on EU-SILC.

Note: "Years of work experience" refer only to those individuals who have worked before. "Dependent children" include children younger than 18 years of age and household members ages 18–24 years who are economically inactive and living with at least one parent. "Working adult" refers to adults ages 24 years and older.

to the formality or informality of work performed or income received. In an OECD working paper on the subject, Andrews, Caldera Sánchez, and Johansson (2011) give an overview of different measures for informality in EU and OECD countries and report the share of employees not covered by social security contributions in Greece to be 37.3 percent in 2008 (with an OECD average of 32 percent). At the same time, the authors question the reliability of the data in terms of the question design in the EU-SILC questionnaire. In a 2007 Eurobarometer study on "undeclared work," Greece reported the highest number (16 hours) of undeclared hours per week in the European OECD sample.

Table 5.7 Greece: Composition of 2010 Clusters Based on 2008 Labor Market Status (Column Percentages)

Cluster	Working-age population in 2010	Labor market status in 2008				
		Unemployed	Retired	Disabled	Other inactive	Employed
1	Stay-at-home mothers	18	0	0	33	3
2	Highly educated single NEETs	29	1	0	17	3
3	Retired and early retired men	3	71	17	1	3
4	Retirees' inactive wives	0	21	4	27	1
5	Low-educated unemployed or disabled	16	5	79	1	3
NC	Employed	34	2	0	21	88
	Total	100	100	100	100	100

Source: World Bank staff analysis based on EU-SILC.
Note: For the year 2010, inactive individuals ages 16–24 years enrolled in education are excluded from the analysis. Numbers referred to in the text appear shaded in gray.

Table 5.8 Greece: Composition of 2010 Clusters Based on 2008 Labor Market Status (Row Percentages)

Cluster	Working-age population in 2010	Labor market status in 2008					
		Unemployed	Retired	Disabled	Other inactive	Employed	Total
1	Stay-at-home mothers	8	0	0	72	20	100
2	Highly educated single NEETs	16	0	0	49	34	100
3	Retired and early retired men	2	58	3	2	35	100
4	Retirees' inactive wives	0	15	1	77	8	100
5	Low-educated unemployed or disabled	16	7	22	8	47	100
NC	Employed	2	0	0	6	92	100

Source: World Bank staff analysis based on EU-SILC.
Note: Students ages 16–24 years who were inactive or unemployed are excluded from the sample. Numbers referred to in the text appear shaded in gray.

The high prevalence of nonagricultural self-employment in Greece (higher than 35 percent) and the almost 40 percent of workers without an employment contract (ibid., pp. 17 and 18, respectively) indicate the main driver of informality in Greece, self-employment.

From Profiling to Activation

Overall, the profiles of the out-of-work resulting from this analysis indicate that an important share of this population has very low activation potential, especially in the current dire labor market situation. Many of the groups that are not working now are inactive either from choice or from a combination of choice and labor market conditions. This section will start with (a) a short overview of the current state of activation and inclusion policies and programs in Greece, then (b) gauge the activation need and potential of the different groups, and conclude with

(c) a focused set of suggestions for further analysis, policy approaches, and activation opportunities for the different groups. The suggested interventions are meant only as a starting point in a discussion with country authorities on general activation policies and their respective priorities. While the latent classes identified in this exercise can point to a general direction in terms of effective tailored policies, it would be beneficial to conduct a more detailed profiling exercise at the individual level. Latent class analysis allows for the classification of a vast population into broad meaningful categories, but there is still variation within groups, with resulting implications for the appropriate level of support required for activation.

Activation and Inclusion Policies in Greece

The current state of social inclusion and activation policies in Greece can best be described as fragmentary (EC 2013b). Without a general minimum income scheme for social assistance and a very limited and uncoordinated set of active labor market policies (ALMPs), the country is ill equipped to withstand the current social crisis by means of formal state intervention (Matsaganis 2012, 4). According to the OECD database on ALMPs, Greece spent 0.22 percent of GDP on ALMPs in 2010, vs. an OECD average of 0.49 percent (excluding public employment services (PES) operation, respectively). The ALMPs offered by the Greek public employment service (Organismou Apascholisis Ergatikou Dynamikou, or OAED) are in many cases funded from the European Social Fund (EC 2013b, 18) but can provide help for some unemployed (table 5.9).

According to the EC DG EMPL, since 2010, about 1.2 million persons have benefited from OAED training and placement schemes at a total budget of

Table 5.9 Number of Beneficiaries and Budget of Selected ALMP Interventions of OAED, 2013

Program	Number of beneficiaries	Total budget (m EUR)
Subsidy program for social security contributions (2 years)	25,000	170.9
Subsidy program for social security contributions (4 years)	40,000	501.4
Work experience program for 16–24 -year-old labor market entrants; traineeships of 6–12 months at 80 percent of national minimum wage; 100% subsidy of social security contributions.	5,000	1.4
Hiring subsidy for university and technical higher education graduates up to 35 years of age; twenty-four months part of wage subsidized.	7,200	40.1
Labor market entry voucher for training and work experience (up to 5 months) up to 29 years of age.	35,000	130.0
Public Works Program. Jobs in local institutions and NGOs; EUR 625 / month allowance for maximum 5 months; payroll and insurance contributions covered.	57,400	188.3
Training program for the unemployed in the tourism sector	n.a.	n.a.
Wage subsidy for older people, between 1 and 60 months for approximately 40 percent of wage bill.	n.a.	n.a.
Placement program for older workers in local authority enterprises.	5,000	75.0

Source: EC DG EMPL Country Unit Greece.
Note: n.a. = not available.

EUR 3.87 billion. Evaluation of the programs by OAED finds that they have resulted in the retention of approximately 340,000 jobs, vocational training for 625,000 persons, and initial vocational training for 42,000 young people. It should be noted that the majority of vocational training institutions in the country are in fact run by the OAED organization. At the same time, the provider landscape for training, placement, and accompanying activation work is clearly underdeveloped.

Moreover, the Greek social protection model has at its core always relied on maintenance of primary breadwinner employment, family-based solidarity patterns (Amitsis 2012, 6), and a strong role for social insurance benefits, while granting generous payments and treatments to privileged insider groups (bankers, senior civil servants, certain professions, and so on).

Much like the entire country and its budgets, the current social protection system is under severe financial stress, contributing to the fiscal contraction agreed upon with EU authorities (Amitsis 2012, 5). At the same time, the crisis has forced changes in many social programs in Greece, especially in the field of social insurance (pensions, health) and the related general budget subsidies for these programs. *Given these fiscal constraints, many of the proposed activation and support measures must be designed in a very cost-conscious way*, giving initial preference to group interventions, self-help approaches, and self-service online services rather than customized and individual case manager approaches.

Over the next two years, the government of Greece has committed to the introduction of a *pilot program for a means-tested minimum income benefit* (European Commission 2013c, 40). If successfully rolled out on a national scale to low-income individuals and households, this benefit could provide effective poverty relief and be a backstop against the deprivation currently experienced by some of the out-of-work groups identified in this note.[14] With a benefit of this type, Greece would close its gap with the European standard for inclusion policies, providing generalized income support instead of insurance-based and categorical payments.

Concurrently, the government of Greece has announced an emergency public works program, the details of which are still being negotiated with EU authorities. Owing to the fact that this program will be limited in run time and volume, it will be considered only as a part of the policy approaches to address specific activation needs of the inactive groups in this survey, and not as a main line of policy response.

Activation Priority, Activation Type, and Benefit Receipt by Group

When further considering the approach toward labor market integration, an assessment of the priorities and potential of the identified groups needs to be undertaken. In the current context in Greece, a prioritization of intervention is very important. After a first step ("activation priority") of prioritizing the intervention along activation need and activation potential, a second step ("activation type") will attempt to classify the groups according to the kind of activation intervention needed, depending on social or labor market barriers to be overcome. Lastly, as a third step, information on *household income composition* of the different groups will be used to assess potential cross-dependencies of the benefit system with groups' labor market status and activation approaches

Activation Priority

Table 5.10 provides an overview of the seven primary groups of out-of-work persons among the population of working age according to their activation need and potential. The total number of individuals included is 2.695 million, representing 25 percent of the total population in Greece in 2011, and 46 percent of the population of working age.

"Activation need" describes a group's need for inclusion in the labor market to achieve income and dampen or end poverty. "Activation potential" describes that group's ability or motivation to be included in the labor market again. A high activation potential could indicate good qualifications and labor market experience (as in the case of the *highly educated early retirees*) or previous work experience and high household-level incentives to work (due to low employment) (as is the case of *middle-aged unemployed heads of households*).

From this simple overview of need and potential, a clear set of prioritizations arises. The groups *highly educated single NEETs* and *middle-aged unemployed heads of households* emerge as the *top priority target groups* for potential activation measures. The latter group is considered a particular priority due to its income situation and potential for activation. While *highly educated single NEETs* largely rely on other household members as a safety net, they are also considered a priority because their current unemployment status and difficulty in acquiring work experience could have long-lasting societal consequences, including negative effects on future employment outcomes and earnings for the economy as a whole. *Stay-at-home mothers* represent the largest group among the out-of-work population and are largely inactive, with the presence of a working member/partner reducing their incentive to join the labor force. The presence of children also implies caregiving responsibilities that may serve as a barrier to labor force participation. Because activation is more difficult in an environment of labor-demand shortage, they are considered second in line in terms of activation priorities.

Table 5.10 Activation Need and Potential of Different Clusters in Greece

Share % (2011)	Cluster	Activation need	Activation potential	Priority for action
23	Stay-at-home mothers	Medium	Medium	Medium
18	Highly educated single NEETs	High	Medium	High
18	Middle-aged unemployed heads of households	High	High	High
17	Retirees' inactive wives	Low	Low	Low
13	Low-educated retirees	Low	Medium	Low
7	Highly educated early retirees	Low	High	Low
5	Low-educated, mostly rural disabled	Medium	Low	Low

Source: World Bank staff analysis and assessment 2014.

Last, nonactivation target groups in the current state (thus considered as priority C) include *retirees' inactive wives, low-educated retirees, highly educated early retirees,* and *low-educated mostly rural disabled.* As a whole, these groups will likely lack incentives to return to work. Nonetheless, they have also grown in size over the last four years and the majority of their members receive old age or disability benefits, resulting in fiscal pressures on the pension system. Reducing the inflow of individuals into these groups is thus also a policy priority for Greece.

When looking at these groups in greater detail, special consideration needs to be given to the significant shares of early retirees in the groups of *low-educated retirees* and *highly educated early retirees.* The *highly educated early retirees* pose an especially striking example, with 83 percent of them 45–59 years old. This effect is less pronounced for the *low-educated retirees,* of whom 29 percent are in this age group. As discussed below, this pattern is a clear cause for concern because significant numbers of potential workers have been allowed to enter old-age benefit systems during their productive work years. While activating these groups out of the retirement status will be difficult, special care needs to be taken to limit further inflow into these groups.

Activation Type

As a second step, the relative severity of labor market or social obstacles to labor market integration will serve as an orientation for activation approaches of the prioritized groups of *stay-at-home mothers, highly educated single NEETs* and *middle-aged unemployed heads of households.* Figure 5.8 depicts the prioritized clusters along the labor market and social barrier dimensions; the size of the bubbles correspond to their relative group size.

Figure 5.8 Activation Types of Prioritized Clusters, Greece

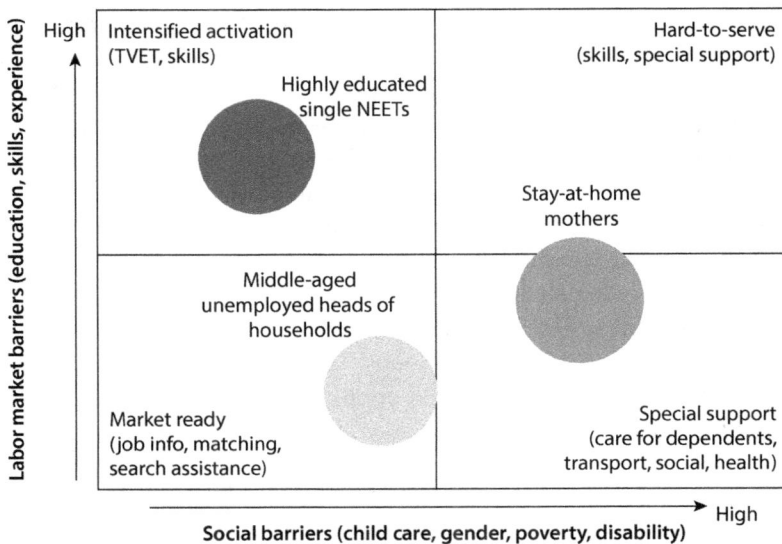

Source: World Bank staff analysis and assessment 2014.
Note: NEET = not in employment, education, or training; TVET = technical and vocational education and training.

By mapping the respective barriers for labor market integration faced by the three prioritized groups, we can quickly discern the respective types of activation that could be undertaken for them. The areas of activation are very broad and will need to be refined more narrowly when considering individual or group-based intervention patterns for the different groups. Whereas the *middle-aged unemployed heads of households* probably require more "market-based" types of interventions because of their work experience, the *highly educated single NEETs* will need more intensified labor market entry support, adding practical and usable skills to their (often academic) education. *Stay-at-home mothers* require more social support (for child care, care of other dependents, and so on) but can build on previous work experience to gain labor market entry.

Household Income Composition

In the third step, planning and consideration of activation approaches, an over-view of the 2011 household income of the groups can be conducted. In the first three groups (*stay-at-home mothers, highly educated single NEETs*, and *middle-aged unemployed heads of households*), labor income represents the majority of household income. The situation reverses for the remaining four groups, with old-age and disability benefit payments consistently contributing between 50 and 65 percent of household income.

The striking feature of the receipt of benefits for groups four through seven is the high prevalence of old-age benefits. In the group of the *low-educated mostly rural disabled*, disability benefits come into play (representing 25 percent of total household income), but for the *retirees' inactive wives*, the *low-educated retirees*, and the *highly educated early retirees*, old-age benefits contribute to 51, 55, and 51 percent of household income, respectively. As briefly discussed before, this type of income will also fall to many of the below-64 years of age members in these groups, and will in fact act as a disincentive to labor market participation.

In the prioritized groups, old-age benefits play a significant role only for the households of the *highly educated single NEETs* (representing close to one-fourth of total household income), implicitly suggesting the use of them as retirement income for older household members (20 percent of this group live in households with at least one member older than 64 years of age). While this benefit income helps to stabilize household welfare, it can take away from job search or work incentives for younger household members (the identified *highly educated single NEETs*).

Lastly, it is striking that all other forms of benefits, that is, those not associated with old age or disability, contribute an almost negligible proportion to the total household incomes of the identified groups. This highlights the fact that social protection in Greece is largely centered upon pensions, providing little protection in terms of unemployment insurance or social assistance.

Suggestions for Activation Measures and Further Analysis

The following sections set out a short set of potential activation measures for each of the priority groups. All of the suggestions below should be considered as a *starting point for further policy dialogue* between EC DG EMPL, the World Bank, and the Greek authorities, bearing in mind that the groups identified still carry some heterogeneity that may affect the level of support required. Accordingly, these suggestions are also not meant to be an exhaustive set of possible activation measures.

It should also be kept in mind that the recommendations are based on clusters derived from 2011 EU-SILC data. Since then, policy actions by the government of Greece and the European Commission's country-specific recommendations might have reflected some of these policy suggestions or rendered them obsolete.

Highly educated single NEETs (18 percent, priority: high). This group is characterized by a relatively high education standard and lack of independence (most are still living at home). The majority are unemployed, although a non-negligible 29 percent are inactive. Potential activation measures for this group include the following:

- Assist in developing a qualification in a field related to the one studied, but promote technical or professional skills rather than further acquisition of academic qualifications.
- Support skill development through work experience for postsecondary or tertiary degree holders. Examples include internship and "second-chance" programs that enable youth to enhance and make use of analytical skills, while facilitating the transition between school and work.
- Support mobility within Greece and the EU (including foreign language training) that is aimed at placing highly qualified individuals.
- Enable participation in the intended public works program for the 45 percent of NEETs who only have an upper secondary education or below, or for the 40 percent who do not have at least one working adult in their household.

Middle-aged unemployed heads of households (18 percent, priority: high). This group represents probably the most traditional group of activation-policy clients, having formed families and gained work experience, and having now lost their jobs in the crisis. Given the lack of other income support, it is here that the threat to welfare is especially severe. As an emergency backstop, this group will need to be made aware of its right to family benefits (by entering a tax return and applying for the reformed family benefit). Their high poverty risk also implies that members of this group might also participate in the planned public works program, or apply for a yet-to-be-introduced minimum income benefit in 2015 or later. When considering integration of this group with a new version of the public works program, the public works engagements could be combined with short training seminars, job-search clubs, or seminar offerings for participants. Focusing these complimentary offerings on participants with recent work experience will help to self-select "market-type" clients into the offers. Potential activation measures for this group include the following:

- OAED training measures (opening OAED-run vocational schools to adults and "second chance" candidates)
- "Job-search club" group interventions for men from different professions
- Update of formal professional skills (certificates, new qualifications), including foreign language skills training aimed toward employment in the tourism industry
- Limited offer of self-employment training/start-up support (making this highly selective of clients with a good chance for success)
- Mobility support within Greece and within the EU (including foreign language training)

Stay-at-home mothers (23 percent, Priority: Medium). This group presents a heterogeneous picture and would most likely need further analysis through a more qualitative approach. Activation should focus on the 50 percent of women in this group who have previous work experience. The respective pathways of women who successfully transitioned from inactivity to contingent breadwinner in response to partner job loss during the crisis might yield clues as to activation strategies for other women in this cohort. In general, potential activation measures could include:

- "Reconnection" programs to seek contact with previous employer, industry, or colleagues and assess skill needs, availability, and so on for reentry.
- "Family enterprise and self-employment" programs to explore self-employment or joint employment with other family members.
- "Job club for experienced women": multisession group activity for teaching job-search skills, resume and job interview training, and so on.
- Provision of free or subsidized child care for mothers of young children, using a means-tested approach targeted toward low-income households and low-skilled women who engage in work or a job search.

Retirees' inactive wives (17 percent, Priority: Low). This group is characterized by very low activation needs and potential, due to their low education levels and close-to-retirement age.

- Offer self-help portal on OAED website to assist in restarting their careers (but only opportunistically and without new resources).

Low-educated retirees (13 percent, Priority: Low). This group is also a low priority for current activation-policy planning. Their retirement income is mostly sufficient to make any public transfers beyond the pension payment nonessential.

Highly educated early retirees (7 percent, Priority: Low). Although their high educational attainment and work experience drive up its activation potential, this group is also very unlikely to have an interest in activation policies. Over 50 percent are in the richest income quintile and only 4 percent are in the bottom quintile.

Low-educated mostly rural disabled (5 percent, Priority: Low). While the welfare of this group could certainly be enhanced by strengthening mobile and decentralized assistance services to disabled citizens (67 percent report "severe limitations" on taking up employment), the current focus on out-of-work groups does not mesh with the lack of employment prospects for this group.

Retirees' inactive wives (17 percent), *low-educated retirees* (13 percent), *highly educated early retirees* (7 percent), and the *low-educated mostly rural disabled* (5 percent) are not further considered for activation policies for the purposes of this study. Together, these clusters together represent more than a third of the out-of-work and their absolute size has been growing over time, with implications for fiscal expenditures. As mentioned above, however, given their overall low need and potential for activation, these groups are not considered a priority for activation during times of low labor demand and high unemployment. Moreover, international experience shows that stemming the outflow of new retirees and disability benefit recipients from work into inactivity may be more effective than attempting to increase inflows into activity.[15] Stanching outflows is especially important in times of high unemployment if long-term disability or early retirement have become more attractive than work for the long-term unemployed. Policies can and should be implemented to delay early retirement, including the promotion of skill maintenance and lifelong learning, along with flexible work schedules and the ability to work from home. Prevention of long-term disability benefit dependency should also be addressed through a review of work capacity assessment, together with the early identification of people with disabilities who can work and their integration into the workforce through financial incentives for disabled workers and their employers. Greek authorities note that there is a limited culture of workplace integration of disabled or (partly) incapacitated workers. Setting out to change this would require a long-term and very difficult effort in the current economic situation.

In summary, while each cluster of the out-of-work has particular characteristics that need to be considered in the activation policy design, there are some overarching policy options that could cater to several groups at once. All poor households or individuals among the currently identified groups of out-of-work citizens are likely to benefit from the guaranteed minimum income program to be introduced in 2015 or later. The program is being piloted in 2014, and will potentially be taken to a national scale in the following years. LCA analysis has shown that the groups of out-of-work individuals most at risk of falling into poverty are *middle-aged unemployed heads of households* (of which 56 percent do not have another working adult in the household) and the *low-educated mostly rural disabled*, whereas the groups of (early) retirees are in least need of social assistance.

In general, current and future policy discussions between the government of Greece and international partners could focus on a set of policy areas where potential activation linkages can emerge. These include, but are not limited to:

- *Emergency public works program.* Responsible authorities ought to provide more details on the planned size, scope, and target groups of the program. If possible, the targeting mechanism for enrollment in the program ought to focus on the group of *middle-aged unemployed heads of households* but should also be open to *highly educated single NEETs* and *stay-at-home mothers.* The inherent self-targeting mechanism (effort, stigma, crowding-out of informal employment) of a well-managed public works program will most likely help to focus program participation on the truly needy (bottom quintiles) among the identified inactive groups

- *Reform of the public employment service (PES) and the unemployment insurance agency OAED.* In 2011, Greece initiated a reform of its PES, supported by technical assistance from EU partner countries. Currently, OAED offers only limited activation support in the form of active labor market programs and is focusing many of its resources on administering the unemployment insurance benefit, which is limited to a year (OECD 2013a, 50). Work-streams 4 through 6 of the current OAED reform ("Active labor market measures design, adjusted to market needs"; "Service provision related to the needs of jobseekers"; and "Support of young apprentices") can form a central piece of the activation response for the group of excluded and out-of-work identified in this note.

- *Integration with employment demand generation and competitiveness policies.* While ALMPs, activation, and job-matching support can help smooth frictions in the labor market, they will not lead to stable and sustainable employment. Demand for jobs comes from the economic activity of firms and the social sector. This integration with regional economic development policy is especially important and has been recognized by the authorities.

In summary, Greece could benefit from focusing activation policies on the target groups identified, enhancing the opportunity for labor market inclusion and stabilizing welfare for poor and inactive households.

Notes

1. Individuals ages 16–24 years who are out of work and enrolled in education are excluded from the sample; they are considered to be investing in their final stages of human capital formation and therefore are not a particular target group for activation policies. Individuals enrolled in school between 25 and 64 years of age are, however, included in the latent class analysis and will be grouped under "other inactive." It is important to note that the group of students older than 24 years of age account for only 1 percent of total population of working age.

2. Throughout this report, this population is also referred to as the out-of-work population.

3. For the latest developments on active inclusion in Greece, see EC (2013b).

4. This variable is constructed using the self-reported current work status in the EU-SILC survey that has four categories: at work, unemployed, retired, and inactive. The unemployed are further classified into short- and long-term based on how long they have been actively looking for a job. The inactive is combined with another question to separate this group into students, disabled, military, and other inactive.

5. In order to construct this variable, individuals 25 years of age or older are considered adults.

6. This is a binary variable that takes the value one if an individual answered "yes, strong limitations" to whether they had been hampered in their usual activities because of health problems for at least the last six months. The value is zero if the answer is "yes, limited" or "no, not limited."

7. The equivalized household income takes into account an equivalence factor to weight the number of household members used in the denominator when calculating household income per capita. The first adult 18 years of age or older has a weight of 1.0, children younger than 14 years old have a weight of 0.3, and other individuals 14 years of age and older have a weight of 0.5. The sum of the weights of all household members is equal to the equivalent household size.

8. Note that income reported in EU-SILC surveys is for the year preceding the survey year.

9. Total household gross income is defined as the sum of: (at the individual level) gross employee cash or near-cash income; company car, gross cash benefits or losses from self-employment (including royalties); unemployment benefits; old-age benefits; survivor benefits; sickness benefits; disability benefits; education allowances; and (at the household level) income from rental of property or land; family/children related allowances; social exclusion not elsewhere classified; housing allowances; regular inter-household cash transfers received; interests, dividends, profit from capital investments in unincorporated business; pensions from individual private plans; and income received by youth younger than 16 years of age. Total household net income, in turn, was calculated by subtracting from total household gross income regular taxes on wealth, taxes on income and social insurance contributions, and regular inter-household case transfers paid.

10. Social benefits are aggregated in eight branches using the European System of integrated Social PROtection Statistics (ESSPROS) definitions. For more information, see Eurostat (2011).

11. According to EU-SILC guidelines, dense areas have more than 500 inhabitants per square kilometer, where the total population for the set is at least 50,000 inhabitants. Intermediate areas have more than 100 inhabitants per square kilometer, and either a total population for the set of at least 50,000 inhabitants or a location adjacent to a dense area. The remaining areas are categorized as sparsely populated.

12. The EU-SILC longitudinal survey consists of a four-year rotating panel. In each year, approximately three-quarters of individuals present in the previous year are retained. The samples used in the latent class analysis include about 3,000 observations for each year in the cross-sectional analysis and 600 observations in the longitudinal analysis. The population is weighted with individual weights.

13. As shown in table 5.1, there were 1.023 million unemployed individuals in our sample of the working-age population in 2011. As many as 98 percent of the *middle-aged*

unemployed heads of households and 71 percent of the *highly educated single NEETs* are reported to be unemployed; together, these two clusters are a concentration of 80 percent of the unemployed.

14. The means-tested minimum income benefit will not necessarily be exclusively targeted toward the out-of-work population; it will be targeted toward individuals and households living in extreme poverty in general.

15. For the case of disability benefit recipients, see, for example, OECD (2010).

References

Amitsis, G. 2012. "Developing Activation Discourses in an Era of Fiscal Constraints—Policy Challenges for the Rudimentary Greek Welfare State." Paper for the 10th Annual Conference of the European Social Policy Network, Edinburgh. http://www.espanet 2012.info/__data/assets/word.../Amitsis_-_Stream_7.doc.

Andrews, D., A. Caldera Sánchez, and Å. Johansson. 2011. "Towards a Better Understanding of the Informal Economy." OECD Economics Department Working Papers 873, OECD Publishing. http://dx.doi.org/10.1787/5kgb1mf88x28-en.

Collins, L. M., and S. T. Lanza. 2010. *Latent Class and Latent Transition Analysis: With Applications in the Social, Behavioral, and Health Sciences.* Hoboken, NJ: Wiley.

EC (European Commission). 2013a. "EU Measures to Tackle Youth Unemployment." MEMO, Brussels, 28 May.

———. 2013b. "Assessment of the Implementation of the European Commission Recommendation on Active Inclusion: A Study of National Policies: Country Report—Greece." DG Employment, Social Affairs & Inclusion, European Commission, Brussels.

———. 2013c. "The Second Economic Adjustment Program for Greece." Second Review Directorate General for Economic and Financial Affairs Occasional Paper 148. European Commission, Brussels.

Eurofound. 2012. *NEETs—Young People Not in Employment, Education or Training: Characteristics, Costs and Policy Responses in Europe.* Luxembourg: Publications Office of the European Union.

Eurostat. 2011. *ESSPROS Manual: The European System of Integrated Social PROtection Statistics.* Luxembourg: European Union.

Kaufman, L., and P. J. Rousseeuw. 1990. *Finding Groups in Data.* New York: Wiley.

Magidson, J., and J. Vermunt. 2002. *Latent Class Modeling as a Probabilistic Extension of K-Means Clustering.* Quirk's Marketing Research Review, March 20, 77–80. http://statisticalinnovations.com/technicalsupport/kmeans2a.htm.

Matsaganis, M. 2012. "Social Policy in Hard Times: The Case of Greece." *Critical Social Policy* 32 (3): 406–21.

Moschou, A. 2012. *Country Sheet on Youth Policy in Greece.* Youth Partnership, EU.

OECD. 2010. *Sickness, Disability and Work: Breaking the Barriers.* Paris: OECD.

———. 2013a. *Greece: Reform of Social Welfare Programmes.* OECD Public Governance Reviews, OECD Publishing.

———. 2013b. *OECD Employment Outlook 2013.* OECD Publishing. http://dx.doi.org/10.1787/empl_outlook-2013-en

Vermunt, J. K., and J. Magidson. 2005. *Latent GOLD 4.0 User's Guide.* Belmont, MA: Statistical Innovations Inc.

Latent Class Analysis of the Out-of-Work Population in Hungary, 2007–11

Background

Following the world financial crisis, Hungary's economy underwent severe economic contraction in 2009, and it has not fully recovered since then. Over the 2003–08 period, the Hungarian economy grew by an annual average of 2.9 percent, not too far from the 2.2 percent average among EU-28 Member States during this same period. And as in other countries in the region, in 2009 the crisis hit hard and output contracted by 6.8 percent. By the end of 2011 Hungary was one of the most financially vulnerable countries in Europe outside the euro area (EEAG 2012) and growth has not recovered yet, as GDP declined 1.7 percent in 2012 and grew 1.1 percent in 2013.

Unemployment started rising during the mid-2000s with a sharper increase in 2009, following the fall in output. In 2003 and 2004, unemployment (for those between 15 and 64 years old) was slightly below 6 percent. From 2005 to 2008, it rose to an average of 7.5 percent. After the crisis hit the Hungarian economy in 2009, unemployment increased by 2.2 percentage points, reaching a high of 11.2 percent in 2010. It remained steady at 11 percent till 2012, and fell to 10.3 percent in 2013. Unemployment in Hungary can be considered moderate when compared to the average of 11 percent for the EU-28 countries in 2013. And despite the fact that labor force participation is low by European standards— in 2013, the working-age population in the EU-28 countries was on average 71.9 percent—it remained fairly constant during the crisis, at 61.6 percent in 2009.[1] By 2013, it had slightly increased to 65.1 percent.

Young workers experienced a sharp rise in unemployment when compared to the overall working-age population. In 2003 unemployment rates were 7.1 percentage points higher for individuals ages 15–24 years than for individuals ages 15–64 years. Youth were clearly disproportionately affected by the increase in unemployment. In 2012, the gap in the unemployment rates observed for these two groups reached 17.1 percentage points, when youth unemployment reached 28.1 percent. In 2013 the gap fell to 16.9 as youth unemployment fell slightly to 27.2 percent. The percentage of young individuals ages 15–24 years that were not in employment, education, or training (the NEET rate) reached its lowest level for the decade in 2007—11.3 percent. After a downward trend between 2003 and 2008, the NEET rate also increased, reaching 15.4 percent in 2013.

A look at unemployment rates disaggregated by age and gender shows that young men were generally more affected by the crisis. As shown in figure 6.1, the economic downturn of 2009 also affected men the most, especially those in the 15- to 24-year-old group, whose unemployment rate grew from 19 to 28 percent between 2008 and 2009, representing an increase of 48 percent. In contrast, unemployment for women in this age group only increased by 16 percent. Men ages 25–49 years and 50–64 years also experienced higher proportional increases in unemployment than women in the same age group.

In Hungary, long-term unemployment as a share of total unemployment has usually been higher than the average for the EU-28 countries. In 2010, it peaked at 49.3 percent but has decreased again to the same level as in 2005, around 45 percent. Unfortunately, in 2013 the percentage of long-term unemployed increased once more, reaching 48.6 percent (see figure 6.2). Even if there was no sharp increase in the share of long-term unemployment in the economy during the decade (on average), there is still a concern due to the high share of individuals who have been without a job for at least 12 months.

Following the crisis, low-educated individuals were especially affected by the rise in unemployment. Unemployment rates were already increasing for the group of

Figure 6.1 Unemployment Rate by Age and Gender in Hungary, 2007–13
percent

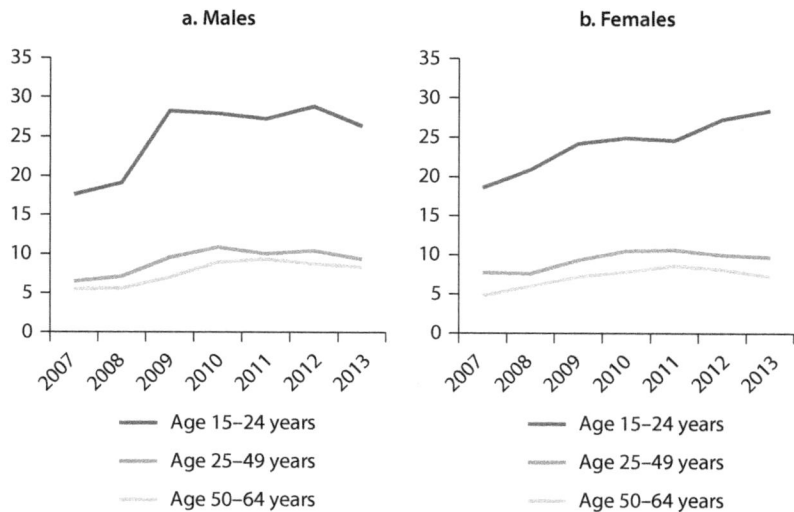

Source: Eurostat, EU-LFS.

Figure 6.2 Long-Term Unemployment as a Share of Total Unemployment, 2003–13
percent

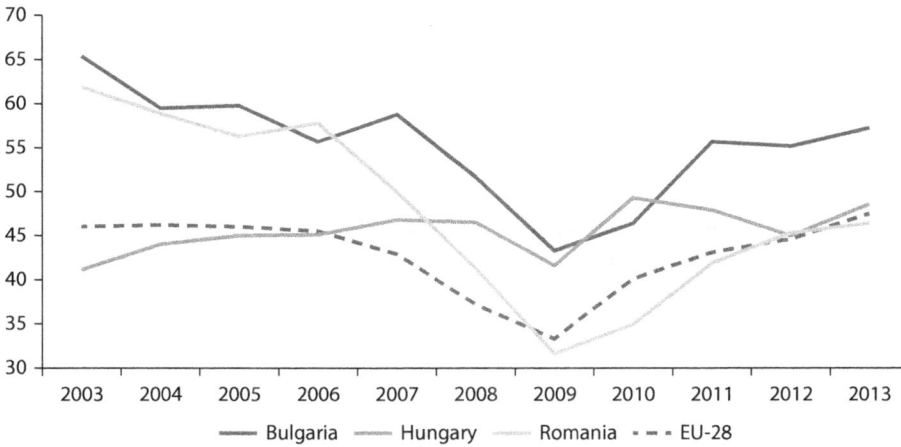

less-educated individuals; after the crisis hit in 2009 this trend was rather accentuated. However, all educational groups saw an increase in unemployment rates during the period from 2008 to 2013. For those with tertiary education, the unemployment rate increased 50 percent, from 2.8 to 4.1. But the gap between the groups became bigger during the period, which reflects structural changes that increased the demand for more skilled workers. The difference in unemployment rates for low- and higher-educated workers grew from 16.1 percentage points in 2008 to 20.1 percentage points in 2013.

Overall employment levels remained relatively stable before and following the crisis, slightly decreasing during the period for individuals in all educational levels. Employment levels have decreased slightly for all educational levels, not only after the crisis in 2009, but this trend had been in place since the mid-2000s. The educational composition of the working-age population in Hungary, on the other hand, has changed during the last decade. The share of the working-age population with less than an upper secondary education fell from 30.3 in 2003 to 22.6 percent in 2013, while the share with tertiary education increased from 12.9 percent to 19.5 during the same period.

During the period from 2008 to 2011, the sample of the out-of-work population considered in this note increased, from 2.25 to 2.28 million individuals. The analysis of the out-of-work population in this note focuses on the working-age population (16–64 years old). Specifically, only individuals ages 25–64 years who are not employed, and individuals ages 16–24 years who were neither employed nor in education nor training were considered.[2] Only the working-age population (16–64 year-olds) is analyzed, as labor activation options—the main policy focus of this note—are only viable for that segment of the population. As a percentage of the population of working age under analysis, the out-of-work population rose from 37 percent to 38.1 percent. The two groups of the out-of-work population that became smaller during this period were the groups of disabled and other inactive, which decreased in size by 32 and 23 percent, respectively. On the other hand, the groups of (short-term) unemployed, long-term unemployed, and (early) retired grew by 99, 58, and 14 percent, respectively (see table 6.1). Figure 6.3 shows the composition of the out-of-work population in Hungary in 2008 and 2011.

Table 6.1 Number and Percentage of Working-Age Individuals (Ages 16–64 Years) by Labor Market Attachment in Hungary, 2008 and 2011
Number in thousands

	2008	2011	Percent change 2008–11
	3,834	3,702	3.4
At work	63%	62%	
	184	367	99.2
Unemployed	3%	6%	
	194	307	57.9
Long-term unemployed	3%	5%	
	599	681	13.7
(Early) retirement	10%	11%	
	664	454	−31.6
Disabled	11%	8%	
	610	469	−23.2
Other inactive	10%	8%	
	6,086	5,979	−1.7
Total	100%	100%	

Source: World Bank staff analysis based on EU-SILC.
Note: Individuals ages 16–24 years who are out of work and enrolled in education (0.75 million individuals) are excluded from the sample.

Figure 6.3 Distribution of Out-of-Work Population in Hungary, 2008 and 2011
percent

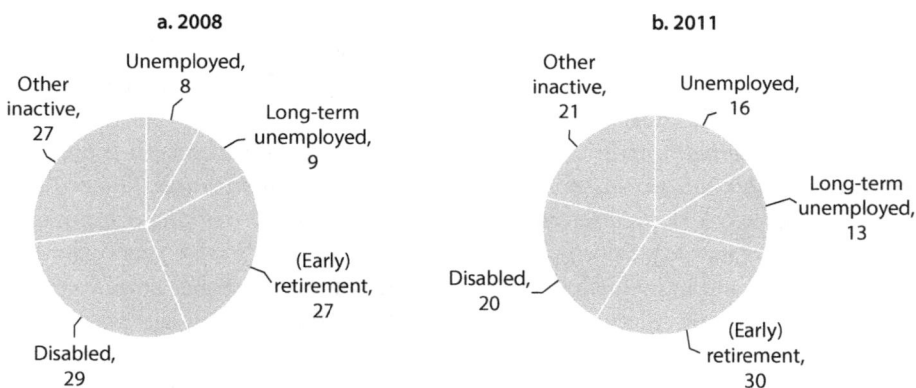

a. 2008

Other inactive, 27
Unemployed, 8
Long-term unemployed, 9
(Early) retirement, 27
Disabled, 29

b. 2011

Other inactive, 21
Unemployed, 16
Long-term unemployed, 13
(Early) retirement, 30
Disabled, 20

Source: World Bank staff analysis based on EU-SILC.

Methodology: Latent Class Analysis

In chapter 1 a general overview of the latent class analysis methodology was laid out. This section explains in detail the variables and covariates used to identify classes or groups of out-of-work individuals that are as homogeneous as possible within each class according to a set of observable characteristics, and as distant as possible between classes. The emerging profiles can then be contrasted with the design and targeting of current activation policies, in order to identify the potential gaps and to enhance their design features.[3]

Variable Selection

The definition of latent classes relies on a number of indicator variables to capture different "symptoms" of an overall latent condition (in this case, the typology of joblessness). The challenge in such models is to identify a discrete number of variables that can best explain the heterogeneity of individual outcomes. In this case, two sets of categorical variables were selected: the first set to show the extent of labor market distance and the other to capture some of the main factors that can affect employment on the supply side, such as labor supply conditions (household-level incentives to work and physical ability to work).

- *Distance from labor market:* short-term unemployment, long-term unemployment, (early) retirement, disability, and other inactivity (largely unpaid domestic work).[4]
- *Work experience:* if individual has worked before and, in this case, whether he or she worked for two or more months in the last year.
- *Labor supply conditions:* whether the individual's household has at least one working adult,[5] and perceived limitations on activities due to health problems.[6]

In addition to indicators, the model includes active covariates, which are used to improve the classification of individuals in each class. In this case the active covariates are the demographic variables that are normally used to disaggregate labor market outcomes:

- Age-group category (four groups)
- Gender
- Human capital: the highest educational level achieved (three groups)
- Urban/rural location

Once the latent classes have been defined, inactive covariates that were not included in the model can be used to characterize the individuals in each class and the households in which they live. The inactive covariates chosen describe those characteristics that may provide valuable information for the design of tailored policies that address barriers to employment, including income level. They include:

- Household welfare conditions:
  - Income quintile (defined by equivalized disposable household income[7,8])
  - Labor, benefit, and other income as share of total gross household income[9]
  - Working status of the partner
  - Household ability to keep dwelling warm
  - Partner's labor income
  - Quintile of partner's labor income
  - Tenure status
  - Binary variables denoting whether individuals or their households are beneficiaries of any of eight social protection benefits[10]
  - Share of benefits over the total household gross income
- Household demographics:
  - Household size
  - Household composition
  - Binary variable showing whether there are children younger than six years old in the household
  - Binary variable denoting whether there are three or more children younger than 16 years old in the household
  - Children younger than 13 years old in the household receiving child care: all, some, or none of the children
  - Older person (65 years of age and older) in the household
  - Presence of individual's parents in the household
- Other individual-level demographics:
  - More refined age groups (eight groups)
  - Marital status
- Individual human capital:
  - More refined highest educational level achieved (six groups)
  - Work experience in years
- Household location:
  - Degree of urbanization[11]: densely populated, intermediate area, sparsely populated
  - Regional breakdown

Group Labeling

The resulting groups are then labeled according to the greatest proportional characteristics within groups that also aid in distinguishing among groups. Granted, a large number of characteristics describe these groups, and only a few are taken into account for the purpose of labeling. In part, some of these characteristics may exhibit a large degree of heterogeneity and may thus not be relevant for defining a group. In addition, some characteristics may be more relevant for the purposes of policy design than others. In short, though the labeling of groups can be considered more an art than a science, when taken together with detailed descriptions of a group's most prominent characteristics, labeling can serve as an important starting point in the design and prioritization of activation policies.

The analysis relies on cross-sectional as well as panel data from the European Union Statistics of Income and Living Conditions (EU-SILC) surveys for 2008–11, which combine individual-level information with household character-istics. The first part of the note presents a cross-sectional analysis for the years 2008, 2009, 2010, and 2011. In particular, the latent class analysis on 2008 data shows the main characteristics of the out-of-work before the global economic crisis hit Hungary, and thus highlight what could be considered more structural issues of the country's labor market. The 2011 latent class analysis will contrast this initial assessment with more recent developments. The second part of the note exploits longitudinal data between 2008 and 2010[12] to trace the prior labor market status of individuals observed last in 2010 in various classes, and will shed light on the relative persistence in the out-of-work status among different classes of individuals. The set of variables chosen for the cross-section and the longitu-dinal analysis are slightly different, due to minor differences in the set of variables recorded in each of the two types of data sets.

Main Findings

Out-of-Work Population: Group Profiles from Cross-Section Analysis

The latent class analysis supports the classification of the out-of-work into ten major groups, some of which have remained stable over time. The groups were named according to their most salient characteristics. Figure 6.4 shows the shares of each of the ten classes identified for the year 2011 while table 6.2 presents their most salient characteristics.

The ten main groups emerging from the LCA analysis in 2011 can be charac-terized as follows (for more detail, see Appendix A for a link to the online-only annexes):

- Cluster 1: *Disabled with previous work experience.* This group, representing almost one fifth of our sample of the out-of-work in 2011, reports its economic status as disabled and most of them (89 percent) receive disability benefits,[13] despite the fact that only 35 percent report strong physical limitations on their ability to carry out daily activities. A majority (63 percent) live in rural areas. It is likely that many in this group could be work-ready: most have worked before, with 25 years of work experience on average, and educational attainment is in the low to mid-range: 37 percent have not completed upper secondary, while 58 percent have complete upper secondary or postsecond-ary. The group is equal parts men and women and most (78 percent) are between 45 and 59 years of age. Just over half do not report at least one adult working in the household, and overall benefits amount to 64 percent of total gross household income.[14] Their risk of poverty[15] is high, with 36 percent living in the first income quintile.

Figure 6.4 Classes of Out-of-Work Population in Hungary, 2011
percent

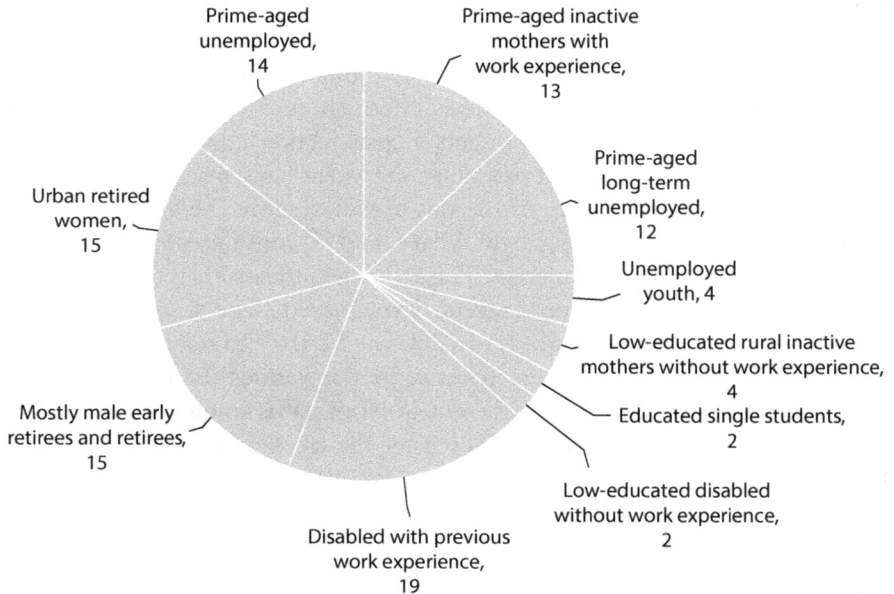

Prime-aged unemployed, 14

Prime-aged inactive mothers with work experience, 13

Prime-aged long-term unemployed, 12

Urban retired women, 15

Unemployed youth, 4

Low-educated rural inactive mothers without work experience, 4

Educated single students, 2

Mostly male early retirees and retirees, 15

Low-educated disabled without work experience, 2

Disabled with previous work experience, 19

Source: World Bank staff analysis based on EU-SILC.

Table 6.2 Summary Characteristics of Latent Classes of the Out-of-Work Population in Hungary, 2011

1: Disabled with previous work experience (19%)	*2: Mostly male early retirees and retirees (15%)*
• 94% report their labor market status as disabled • 50% are male; 50% are female • 78% are 45–59 years old • 60% are married; 32% are without a partner • 35% report strongly limited capacity to work • 55% have no working adults in household • Low-to-mid-skilled: 37% have not completed upper secondary education; 58% have completed upper or postsecondary • 100% worked before; 98% worked less than 2 months in the previous year; 25 years of experience on average • 72% live in households without dependent children; 11% live alone • 63% live in rural areas • High poverty risk: 36% are in poorest income quintile • 89% receive disability benefits • Total household benefits represent 64% of gross household income	• 100% are retired • 62% are male • 57% are 60–64 years old; 31% are 55–59 years old • 70% are married • 12% report strongly limited capacity to work • Low-to-mid-skilled: 29% have not completed upper secondary education; 59% have completed upper or postsecondary • 99% have worked before, 90% worked less than 2 months in the previous year; 36 years of experience on average • 79% live in households without dependent children • 54% live in rural areas • Very low poverty risk: 13% are in poorest income quintile • 90% receive old-age benefits • Total household benefits represent 67% of gross household income

table continues next page

Table 6.2 Summary Characteristics of Latent Classes of the Out-of-Work Population in Hungary, 2011 *(continued)*

3: Urban retired women (15%)

- 95% are retired; 5% report their labor market status as disabled
- 80% are female
- 96% are 60–64 years old
- 60% are married; 21% are widowed
- 79% have no working adults in household
- Low-to-mid-skilled: 21% have not completed upper secondary education; 62% have completed upper or postsecondary
- 98% have worked before, but less than 2 months in the previous year; 36 years of experience on average
- 91% live in households without dependent children; 23% live alone
- 64% live in urban areas
- Very low poverty risk: 12% in poorest income quintile
- 94% receive old-age benefits
- Total household benefits represent 83% of gross household income

4: Prime-aged unemployed (14%)

- 97% are unemployed
- 60% are male
- 76% are 25–54 years old
- 55% have no working adults in household
- Low-to-mid-skilled: 36% have not completed upper secondary education; 59% have completed upper or postsecondary
- 100% have worked before, 93% 2 or more months in the previous year; 16 years of experience on average
- 51% live in households with dependent children; 18% live in households with children younger than 6 years old
- 59% live in rural areas
- Very high poverty risk: 49% in poorest income quintile
- 55% receive unemployment benefits; 50% receive family/child benefits
- Total household benefits represent 35% of gross household income

5: Prime-aged inactive mothers with work experience (13%)

- 94% are inactive
- 100% are female
- 91% are 25–54 years old
- 82% have at least one working adult in household
- 73% have a working partner
- Mid-to-high-skilled: 57% with complete upper or postsecondary education; 24% with complete tertiary
- 100% have worked before, 89% have worked less than 2 months in the previous year; 11 years of experience on average
- 91% live in households with dependent children; 72% live in households with children younger than 6 years old
- High poverty risk: 32% in poorest income quintile
- 92% receive family/child benefits
- Total household benefits represent 40% of gross household income

6: Prime-aged long-term unemployed (12%)

- 86% are long-term unemployed; 14% are inactive
- 57% are male
- 75% are 25–54 years old; 18% are 54–59 years old
- 59% have no working adults in household
- Low-to-mid-skilled: 38% have not completed upper secondary education; 56% have completed upper or postsecondary
- 99% worked before, but less than 2 months in the previous year; 18 years of experience on average
- 50% live in households with dependent children; 19% live in households with children younger than 6 years old
- 50% live in rural areas
- Extreme poverty risk: 65% in poorest income quintile
- 49% receive unemployment benefits; 49% receive family/child benefits
- Total household benefits represent 56% of gross household income

7: Unemployed youth (4%)

- 47% are long-term unemployed; 43% are unemployed
- 56% are male
- 91% are 16–24 years old
- 78% have at least one working adult in household
- 57% are married
- Mid-skilled: 66% have completed upper or post-secondary education
- 18% have worked before, but less than 2 months in the previous year; 2 years of experience on average
- 89% live with at least one parent
- High poverty risk: 44% in poorest income quintile
- Total household benefits represent 33% of gross household income

8: Low-educated rural inactive mothers without work experience (4%)

- 88% are inactive; 12% are long-term unemployed
- 90% are female
- 84% are 16–34 years old
- 62% are never married; 63% have a partner
- 53% have at least one working adult in household
- Low-skilled: 78% have not completed upper secondary education
- 78% have never worked before
- 88% live in households with dependent children; 62% live in households with children younger than 6 years old
- 70% live in rural areas
- Extreme poverty risk: 77% in poorest income quintile
- 86% receive family/child benefits; 38% receive housing allowance; 29% receive social exclusion benefits
- Total household benefits represent 57% of gross household income

table continues next page

Table 6.2 Summary Characteristics of Latent Classes of the Out-of-Work Population in Hungary, 2011 *(continued)*

9: Educated single students (2%)	*10: Low-educated disabled without work experience (2%)*
• 90% are inactive	• 85% report their labor market status as disabled
• 63% are male	• 52% are female
• 91% are 25–29 years old	• 88% are 20–54 years old
• 79% have at least one working adult in household	• 67% report strongly limited capacity to work
• Mid-to-high-skilled: 68% with complete upper or postsecondary education; 32% with complete tertiary	• 58% have no working adults in the household
	• 100% have never worked before
• 99% have never worked before	• Low skilled: 60% have not completed upper secondary education; an additional 15% have never studied before
• 81% are enrolled in education	
• 82% live with at least one parent	• 76% live with at least one parent
• 94% are single	• High poverty risk: 46% in poorest income quintile
• 77% live in urban areas	• 74% receive disability benefits; 59% receive family/child benefits; 45% receive old-age benefits at household level
• Moderate poverty risk: 23% in poorest income quintile	
• 23% receive education allowance	• Total household benefits represent 71% of gross household income
• Total household benefits represent 22% of gross household income	

Source: World Bank staff analysis based on EU-SILC.

Note: Percentages in parentheses following the group names refer to the share of the total out-of-work population. "Years of work experience" refers only to those individuals who have worked before. "Dependent children" include children younger than 18 years of age and household members ages 18–24 years who are economically inactive and living with at least one parent. "Working adult" refers to adults ages 25 years and older. For this report's purposes, we define the at-risk-of-poverty rate as the relative risk of being in the first quintile of the income distribution. The reference period for income reported in EU-SILC surveys is the year preceding the survey year.

- Cluster 2: *Mostly male early retirees and retirees.* This group represented 15 percent of the out-of-work population in 2011. It comprises mostly men (62 percent), and all of its members are retired, with 90 percent receiving old-age benefits. A slim majority (57 percent) are 60–64 years old, meaning that they are likely to have reached the retirement age of 62. The remaining 43 percent can be considered early retired, of which the majority are in the 55- to 59-age range. Because they are retired, this group's members all have work experience, but only 9 percent report having worked for two or more months during the last year. They are low to mid-skilled: almost one-third have not completed upper secondary school; the majority (59 percent) have completed upper or postsecondary education. Just over one-half do not report any working adults in the household. The benefit levels received by this group and their households appear to be generous: benefits represent 67 percent of total gross household income, and only 13 percent of individuals in this group are in the poorest income quintile.

- Cluster 3: *Urban retired women.* Like cluster 2 (*mostly male early retirees and retirees*), this group of retirees represented 15 percent of the out-of-work sample in 2011. In contrast to that group, however, nearly all the retirees in this group have reached retirement age, as 96 percent are 60–64 years old. They are also predominantly female (80 percent) and mostly live in urban areas (64 percent). Another characteristic that distinguishes them from cluster 2 is that 79 percent do not have any working adults in their households. As such, total benefits represent 83 percent of gross household income, the highest

share among all identified groups. Benefits also appear to be sufficiently generous, as only 12 percent of this group live among the poorest income quintile.

- Cluster 4: *Prime-aged unemployed.* This group made up 14 percent of the out-
of-work in 2011. Its members are newly unemployed individuals who worked
for two or more months during the last year, and who, on average, have 16 years
of work experience. They are mostly men (60 percent) in their prime age and
are concentrated in rural areas (59 percent). Over one-third have not completed upper secondary school, and 59 percent have completed upper or postsecondary studies, making this a low-to-mid-skilled group. Half of this group
lives in households with dependent children. One-half also receive family/
child benefits, and a small majority receive unemployment benefits. One-half
of the group's members (55 percent) do not have any working adults in the
household, and over all, benefits make up just over a third of their total household income. The group has a very high risk of poverty, as 49 percent live in
the poorest income quintile.

- Cluster 5: *Prime-aged inactive mothers with work experience.* This group of prime-
aged (ages 25–54 years) women represented 13 percent of the out-of-work in
2011. Given that 91 percent live in households with dependent children
(72 percent live in households with children younger than six years old), and
that, for the most part, these inactive women have working partners, they are
likely to be stay-at-home mothers. However, their work experience and relatively high educational attainment—24 percent of them have completed a tertiary degree—make the members of this group labor market ready. Ninety-two
percent receive family/child benefits, and, on average, total household benefits
represent 40 percent of gross household income. Perhaps due to a relatively
large average household size of 4.2 members, this group has a high risk of poverty, with 32 percent in the poorest income quintile.

- Cluster 6: *Prime-aged long-term unemployed.* This group represented 12 percent of the out-of-work in 2011 and resembles the larger group of *prime-aged
unemployed.* Like its newly unemployed counterparts, the long-term unemployed members of this group comprise mostly men (57 percent) who for the
most part are in their prime (ages 25–54 years). This group, however, is somewhat skewed toward older individuals, and a non-negligible 18 percent are
54–59 years old. Furthermore, the group is less rural, with a 50/50 urban/rural
split, and a slightly larger majority (59 percent) of households are without any
working adults. However, the educational attainment of this group is very
similar, with 36 percent having not completed an upper secondary education
and 59 percent having completed upper or postsecondary school. The members of this group are just as likely as the larger group to have dependent
children in their households (50 percent), as well as to receive family/child
benefits. Interestingly, they are only marginally less likely to receive unemployment benefits (49 percent), despite the fact that they have been

unemployed for at least 12 months. Again, total household benefits make up a very similar percentage of total household income (57 percent). Nonetheless, despite having slightly smaller households (3.4 members, versus 3.5 for their newly unemployed counterparts) this group is more likely to be living in poverty. With 65 percent in the poorest income quintile, this group has the second highest risk of poverty among the ten identified groups.

- Cluster 7: *Unemployed youth.* Making up just 4 percent of the out-of-work in 2011, this group comprises both long-term and newly unemployed youth ages 16–24 years and resembles the unemployed youth who have been largely affected by the crisis in Europe. Owing to their young age, this group has very little work experience, with only 18 percent having worked before. They are for the most part mid-skilled, as 66 percent have completed upper or postsecondary education. More than half are also in households that receive family/child benefits and one-fifth receive unemployment benefits. Despite the fact that these never-married individuals are still living in their birth households—78 percent of which have at least one working adult—they remain at a high risk for poverty: 44 percent live in the poorest income quintile. With benefits making up 33 percent of total household income, their benefit dependence is low in comparison to most other groups.

- Cluster 8: *Low-educated rural inactive mothers without work experience.* This group, amounting to about 4 percent of the out-of-work population in 2011, is composed of relatively young (16–35 years old), inactive women living in rural areas. They are likely to be mothers, as 88 percent live in households with dependent children (62 percent with children younger than six years old). In contrast to the larger group of *prime-aged inactive mothers with work experience*, this group has lower prospects for labor market insertion, as they do not have previous work experience and have low educational attainment, with the great majority (78 percent) having not finished upper secondary school. Another distinguishing feature of this group is that the majority (62 percent) has never been married and just over half do not have a working adult in their households. Like their counterparts with work experience, the great majority receive family/child benefits. However, 29 percent also receive social exclusion benefits and 38 percent receive housing allowances, perhaps reflecting their lower socioeconomic status. Benefits make up more than half (57 percent) of household income. Nonetheless, this group has the highest risk of poverty among the ten identified groups: 77 percent live in the poorest income quintile.

- Cluster 9: *Educated single students.* This group only amounted to 2 percent of the out-of-work in 2011 and comprises students (81 percent) who are between 25 and 29 years old (91 percent). This group is the most educated of the ten, with close to one-third having completed tertiary education; an additional 68 percent have completed upper or secondary education. Despite being over 24 years of age, the members of this group have never worked before. Like the *unemployed youth,* they have also never married and for the most part are still living with their parents, in households that predominantly have at least one working adult. However, unlike their unemployed youth counterparts, they tend to live in urban areas, where educational opportunities are likely to be more abundant. Twenty-three percent of them receive an educational allowance, and benefits make up 22 percent of total gross income, the lowest share among all groups. With 23 percent in the poorest income quintile, this group has a moderate risk of poverty.

- Cluster 10: *Low-educated disabled without work experience.* Like the group of young students, this group represented only 2 percent of the out-of-work in 2011. Its members report their labor market status as disabled, but unlike the larger group of disabled (*disabled with previous work experience*), none have ever worked before and most (67 percent) report that their capacity to work is strongly limited. Nonetheless, the percentage that reports receiving disability benefits (74 percent) is lower than that of the *disabled with previous work experience* (89 percent). Just over half are women, and their ages span a larger range, with 80 percent between 20 and 54 years of age. Likely due to their disability status, their educational attainment is low: 15 percent have never attended school, 22 percent have never finished primary school, and another 38 percent have never finished lower secondary. Another characteristic that distinguishes this group from their disabled counterparts with work experience is that they have never married and are still living with their parents. Just over half report having at least one working adult in their households, and benefit dependency is high: 71 percent of total gross household income is composed of benefits, second only to the group of *urban retired women.* This group is also at a high risk for poverty, as 46 percent of them live among the poorest income quintile.

Tables 6.3 and 6.4 present the main characteristics of each group in 2011. For the complete table, including inactive covariates, see Appendix A for a link to the online-only annexes.

Although a small number of the identified classes of the out-of-work population have been quite stable over the last few years, most of the identified classes experienced changes in their composition and also in the share they represent among the out-of-work. In table 6.5, clusters are compared over time between 2008 and 2011 as a share of the total out-of-work population, while figure 6.5 shows the absolute numbers. From the graph, the first important observation is that the size of the out-of-work population has just slightly increased—by 1 percent between 2008 and 2011. However, some clusters have changed across time; for example, clusters identified in 2011 that were present in previous years underwent changes in relative size and also in composition. The fact that the composition of the groups changes over time is particularly important to keep in mind when interpreting changes in group size. For instance, significant increases (decreases) in group size are sometimes due to reassignments of individuals across groups,

Table 6.3 Latent Classes of Out-of-Work Population in Hungary: Indicators, 2011

	All out-of-work	1. Disabled with previous work experience	2. Mostly male early retirees and retirees	3. Urban retired women	4. Prime-aged unemployed	5. Prime-aged inactive mothers with work experience	6. Prime-aged long-term unemployed	7. Unemployed youth	8. Low-educated rural inactive mothers without work experience	9. Educated single students	10. Low-educated disabled without work experience
Cluster size (%)	**100**	**19**	**15**	**15**	**14**	**13**	**12**	**4**	**4**	**2**	**2**
Population	**2,277,342**	**432,012**	**351,394**	**346,839**	**318,600**	**301,065**	**265,310**	**95,648**	**91,094**	**39,170**	**36,210**
Indicators (%)											
Labor market attachment											
Unemployed	16	1	0	0	97	3	0	43	0	6	1
Long-term unemployed	13	3	0	0	0	3	86	47	12	3	6
Retired	30	0	100	95	0	0	0	0	0	0	2
Disabled	20	94	0	5	0	0	0	0	0	1	85
Other inactive	21	2	0	0	3	94	14	11	88	90	6
At least one working adult in household											
No	51	55	52	79	55	18	59	22	47	21	58
Yes	49	45	48	21	45	82	41	78	53	79	42
Work experience											
Never worked	10	0	0	1	0	0	1	82	78	99	100
Less than 2 months in last year	73	98	90	98	7	89	99	18	21	1	0
2 or more months in last year	16	2	9	1	93	11	0	0	2	0	0
Self-assessed physical capacity											
Strongly limited	12	35	12	8	3	2	3	0	0	0	67
None/limited	88	65	88	92	97	98	97	100	100	100	33

Source: World Bank staff analysis based on EU-SILC.

Table 6.4 Latent Classes of Out-of-Work Population in Hungary: Active Covariates, 2011

	All out-of-work	1. Disabled with previous work experience	2. Mostly male early retirees and retirees	3. Urban retired women	4. Prime-aged unemployed	5. Prime-aged inactive mothers with work experience	6. Prime-aged long-term unemployed	7. Unemployed youth	8. Low-educated rural inactive mothers without work experience	9. Educated single students	10. Low-educated disabled without work experience
Cluster size (%)	100	19	15	15	14	13	12	4	4	2	2
Population	2,277,342	432,012	351,394	346,839	318,600	301,065	265,310	95,648	91,094	39,170	36,210
Active covariates (%)											
Age groups (years)											
16–24	9	0	0	0	14	3	5	91	52	0	31
25–34	17	2	0	0	25	50	20	9	32	100	33
35–59	48	88	43	4	60	45	73	0	15	0	34
60–64	26	10	57	96	1	1	2	0	1	0	2
Gender											
Male	42	50	62	20	60	0	57	56	10	63	48
Female	58	50	38	80	40	100	43	44	90	37	52
Education											
Primary	32	37	29	21	36	19	38	20	78	0	60
Secondary	57	58	59	62	59	57	56	60	21	68	23
Tertiary	11	5	12	17	5	24	6	20	2	32	1
Never studied before/ illiterate/not available	0	0	0	1	0	0	0	1	0	0	15
Location											
Urban	48	37	46	64	41	52	50	45	30	77	47
Rural	52	63	54	36	59	48	50	55	70	23	53

Source: World Bank staff analysis based on EU-SILC.

Table 6.5 Classes of Out-of-Work Population in Hungary, as a Percentage of Total Out-of-Work Population, 2008–11

percent

Name of cluster	2008	2009	2010	2011
Disabled with previous work experience	29	25	17	19
Mostly male early retirees and retirees (2011)	n.a.	n.a.	n.a.	15
Early retirees and retirees (except 2011)	28	13	19	n.a.
Urban retired women (except 2008)		18	15	15
Prime-aged unemployed	10	10	13	14
Prime-aged inactive mothers with work experience	14	14	13	13
Prime-aged long-term unemployed	9	10	11	12
Unemployed youth (2010 and 2011)	n.a.	n.a.	3	4
Low-educated rural inactive mothers without work experience (2011)	n.a.	n.a.	n.a.	4
Low-educated inactive young women without work experience (except 2011)	8	8	7	n.a.
Educated single students (2011)	n.a.	n.a.	n.a.	2
Low-educated disabled without work experience	2	2	2	2

Source: World Bank staff analysis based on EU-SILC.
Note: n.a. = not applicable.

resulting in changes in group composition. Thus, although some groups may retain similar names across years due to their most salient characteristics, they may nonetheless vary in their composition across years. The evolution in terms of group size and group composition over the 2008–11 period can be summarized as follows:

- The composition of the group of *disabled with previous work experience* has been quite stable over time, but its relative and absolute size has decreased. The share of this cluster in the out-of-work population was 29 percent in 2008. In 2011, it reached 19 percent (although it was still the largest cluster). This represented an approximate 33 percent decline in absolute numbers. More than 90 percent of the individuals in this cluster reported being disabled and around 35 percent of them claimed to have a strong limitation on work capacity due to their health. Indeed, 84 and 89 percent of them were receiving disability benefits in 2008 and 2011, respectively. Among the characteristics that have been quite stable, more than 80 percent are between 35 and 59 years old, around 40 percent live in urban areas, and a minimum of 60 percent have at least an upper secondary education.

- The *early retirees and retirees* were a single group from 2008 to 2009. In 2011, retirees were classified as either *mostly male early retirees and retirees* or *urban retired women*. Taken together, they represent an absolute size increase of 11 percent when compared to the original group in 2008. The cluster of *early retirees and retirees* changed in size and composition over time. In 2011, it was

Figure 6.5 Classes of Out-of-Work Population in Hungary, 2008–11
number of individuals

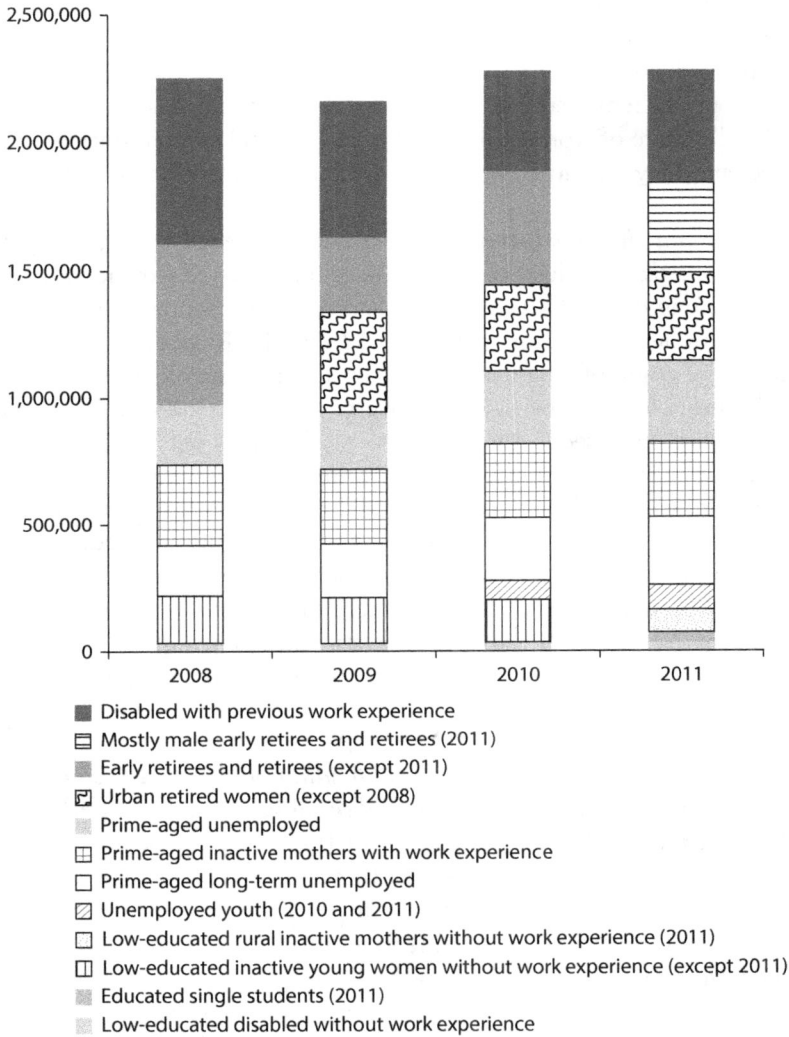

- ■ Disabled with previous work experience
- ⊟ Mostly male early retirees and retirees (2011)
- ▨ Early retirees and retirees (except 2011)
- ⊡ Urban retired women (except 2008)
- ▨ Prime-aged unemployed
- ⊞ Prime-aged inactive mothers with work experience
- ☐ Prime-aged long-term unemployed
- ▨ Unemployed youth (2010 and 2011)
- ☐ Low-educated rural inactive mothers without work experience (2011)
- ⊞ Low-educated inactive young women without work experience (except 2011)
- ▨ Educated single students (2011)
- ▨ Low-educated disabled without work experience

Source: World Bank staff analysis based on EU-SILC.

called *mostly male early retirees and retirees* because the female share fell from 62 percent in 2008 to only 38 percent in 2011. This group also became less urban—the share of individuals living in urban areas fell from 59 to 46 percent over the period. It also became relatively younger—in 2008, 28 and 70 percent were 45–59 and 60–64 years old, respectively; in 2011 these shares changed to 39 and 57 percent. Despite those differences in composition over time, around 90 percent of the individuals in this cluster are receiving old-age benefits and have on average more than 35 years of work experience.

- In its turn, the cluster of *urban retired women*—which appeared as a separate group beginning in 2009—became more urban, female, and older. From being 18 percent of the out-of-work population in 2009, this cluster lost almost 50,000 individuals, reducing its share to 15 percent in 2011. Not only has its size changed, but individuals classified in this cluster became older—in 2011, 96 percent of them were between 60 and 64 years old, against 76 percent in 2009—the share of women increased from 68 to 80 percent during the same period, and they are more likely to be living in urban areas than before.

- *One important change observed is the increase in unemployment among prime-aged individuals.* Two clusters of prime-aged unemployed were identified in all the years: one of newly unemployed and the other representing those who have been unemployed for more than 12 months. Regardless of the year of analysis, the group of long-term unemployed comprises older individuals who are also more likely to be living in poverty. And from 2008 to 2011, both of these clusters increased in size. The *prime-aged unemployed* faced an increase of 37 percent during this period, while the *prime-aged long-term unemployed* grew around 35 percent. However, not only did these clusters increase in size, but the composition of their members' labor market status changed. Among the *prime-aged unemployed*, the share of individuals who reported being inactive fell from 31 to 3 percent, while the share of unemployed grew from 64 to 97 percent. Among the *prime-aged long-term unemployed* the share of inactive fell from 27 to 14 percent, while the share of long-term unemployed increased from 70 to 86 percent.

- *Across time, different clusters of young individuals were found. It can be noticed that they have become relatively more likely to be unemployed and less likely to be inactive.* Until 2009, 8 percent of the out-of-work population was represented by the *low-educated inactive young women without work experience*, but in the next years the composition of the clusters of younger individuals would become more defined and new clusters could be identified. Indeed, in 2010, this cluster of inactive young women itself represented a higher percentage of females, increasing from 69 to 81 percent of the total. In 2011, this cluster was replaced by the *low-educated rural inactive mothers without work experience*. Women represented 90 percent of this group, whose members were more likely to be living in rural areas. Sixty-three percent lived with a partner (regardless of marital status). This group was also less likely to report living with parents in the same household, and was less educated (78 percent had completed up to lower secondary education). In 2010, the cluster of *unemployed youth* appeared, representing 3 percent of the out-of-work population. In 2011, more than 20,000 young individuals were added to this cluster, an increase of more than 30 percent. So, in the last year analyzed, three clusters of young individuals were identified: *unemployed youth* (4 percent), *low-educated rural inactive mothers without work experience* (4 percent), and *educated single youth* (2 percent).

Even accounting for the presence of inactive youth in the cluster of unemployed and for the unemployed youth in the cluster of inactive, the percentage of young individuals that were classified as unemployed increased from 25 percent to 44 percent from 2008 to 2011. In addition, the absolute size of these youth clusters has become 22 percent larger during this same period.

- Finally, the *prime-aged inactive mothers with work experience* and the *low-educated disabled without work experience* clusters remained most stable during the period in analysis, both in size and in composition. The cluster of *inactive mothers with work experience* represented around 13 percent of the out-of-work individuals between 2008 and 2011, which in absolute numbers accounted for a slight decrease of 7 percent in its size—a reduction of around 23,000 people. Not only has its share been maintained, its composition also has not experienced considerable changes. For the group of *disabled without work experience*, which represented only 2 percent of the out-of-work population during these four years, characteristics have only changed slightly. This group reported an increase in the share of people with a strong limitation on ability to work, from 61 to 67 percent; its members became more likely to be living in urban areas—from 37 percent in 2008 to 47 percent in 2011—and the share of women also rose, from 41 to 52 percent.

Structural Aspects and Emerging Trends in the Profiles of the Out-of-Work

The clusters identified in the out-of-work population for the period from 2008 to 2011 reflect both structural and cyclical aspects of the labor market. This section identifies some of the key structural aspects of the Hungarian labor market and uses cross-sectional and longitudinal analysis of clusters of the out-of-work population to further examine the effects of the crisis.

The youth labor force participation rate in Hungary was the second lowest in Europe in 2013. Since 2007, Hungary's NEET rate has increased, reaching 15.4 percent in 2013. The youth labor force participation rate, at only 27.2 percent in 2013, is the second lowest among the countries in the region (figure 6.6), and pales in comparison to the EU average of 42.2 percent. Two aspects might account for the low activity rate among the youth. In many EU countries, youth have higher labor force participation rates partly because they are able to combine their studies with part-time work. For example, as many as 75 percent and 40 percent of youth in the Netherlands and Slovenia, respectively, reported working part-time (Dimitrov and Duell 2013). However, in 2013, only about 10 percent of the youth in Hungary (15–24 years old) reported working part-time (Eurostat 2013). Also, the labor tax wedge[16] is one of the highest in the European Union (figure 6.7). Lower take-home wages reduce labor supply at the extensive margin, primarily for younger and older workers (EEAG 2012).

Low participation rates among the older working-age population in Hungary can be explained by changes in both the demand for and the supply of labor in the economy.

Figure 6.6 Labor Force Participation Rate, Ages 15–24 Years, European Countries, 2013

percent

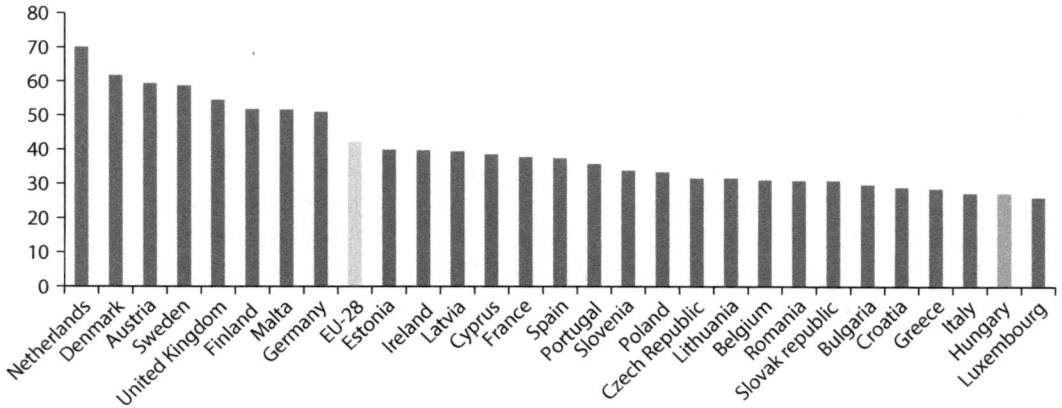

Source: Eurostat, EU-LFS.

Figure 6.7 Labor Tax Wedges in Europe, 2008 and 2010

percent

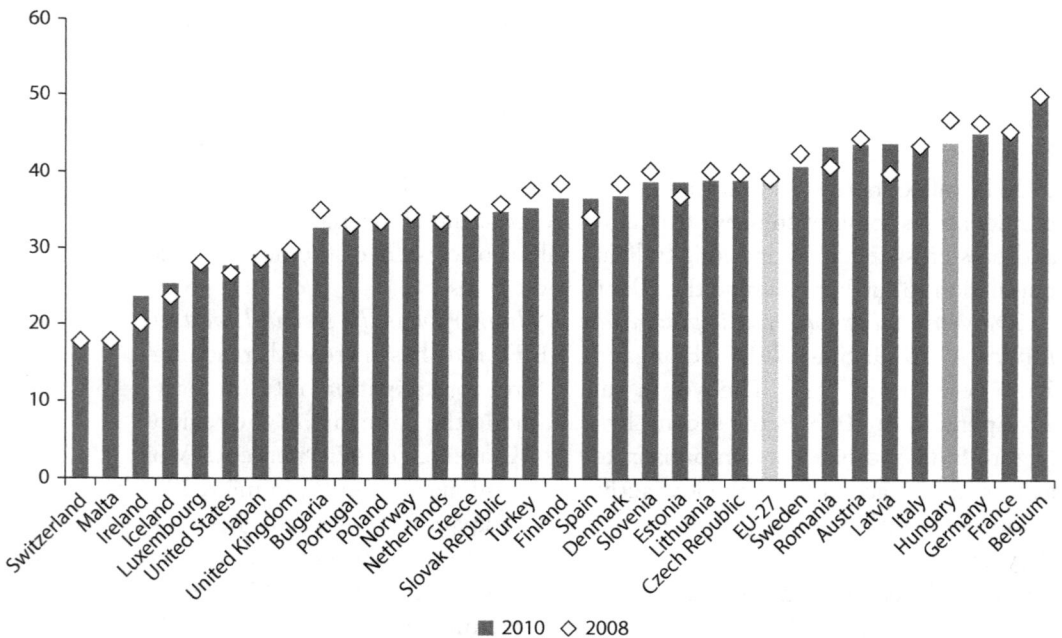

■ 2010   ◇ 2008

Source: Eurostat, EU-LFS.

The transition to a market economy and privatization schemes that led to increased competition among firms generated the restructuring and reallocation of resources in the economy. There was a decline in employment, particularly in the agricultural and industrial sectors, and a shift in the labor demand toward more skilled workers. From the supply side, a relatively low retirement age,[17] and the possibility of retiring earlier than the legal age with little or no penalty in terms of a lower pension, also contributes to explaining the low participation rates observed among older workers (EEAG 2012).

Retired and disabled individuals make up more than half of the out-of-work population analyzed in this note. In the working-age sample used in this analysis, three clusters of retirees or disabled individuals with previous work experience emerge, representing almost half of the out-of-work population—or more than 50 percent if we consider a small group of disabled without work experience. However, about half of them are younger than 60 years of age; in other words, they are under the legal retirement age. If we consider the two main clusters found—and exclude the cluster of *urban retired women*—this share reaches almost 70 percent. In the cluster of *disabled with previous work experience*, which represents almost one-fifth of the out-of-work sample analyzed, 88 percent are between 35 and 59 years old, and 35 percent of them reported being strongly limited in work capacity due to a health condition. The second cluster— *mostly male early retirees and retirees*—represents 15 percent of the out-of-work population sample; 43 percent of the individuals in this group are between ages 35 and 59.

Labor force participation rates for older people are among the lowest in Europe. In 2013, Hungary showed a labor force participation rate of only 63.5 percent among the group of people ages 55–59 years old (figure 6.8). In the case of individuals 55–64 years old, rates are only 41.7 percent, much lower than the EU-28 average of 54.3 percent. Nevertheless, this difference has been decreasing over time, since in 2008 activity rates were only 33 and 48 percent in Hungary and the EU-28, respectively. Figure 6.9 shows that for other European countries, expenditures on old-age pensions as a share of the GDP have been increasing.

Figure 6.8 Labor Force Participation Rate, Ages 55–59 Years, European Countries, 2013
percent

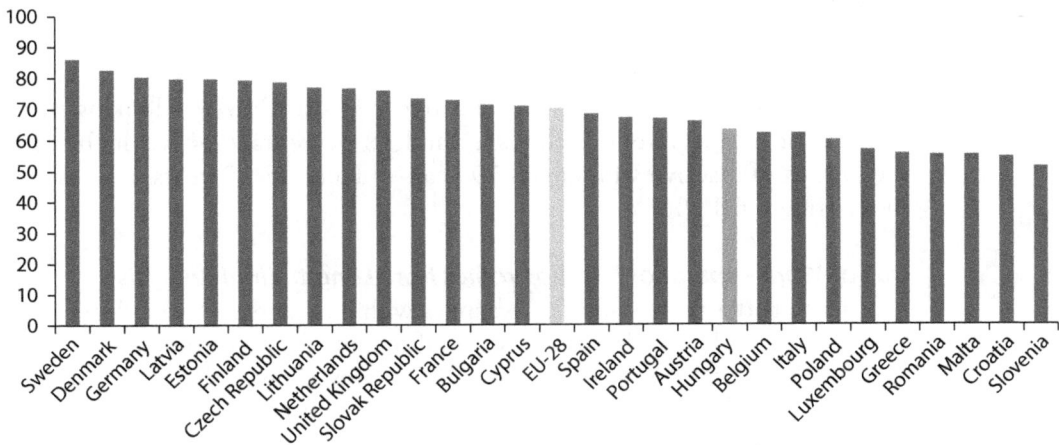

Source: Eurostat, EU-LFS.

Figure 6.9 Expenditures on Old-Age Benefits as a Share of GDP in Europe, 2008 and 2010

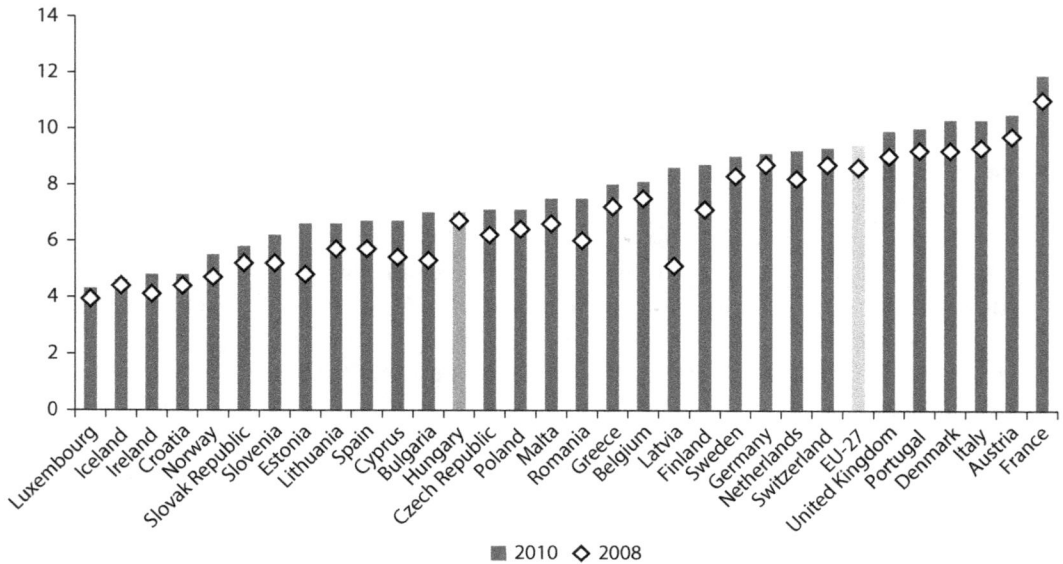

■ 2010 ◇ 2008

Source: Eurostat.

As the working-age population shrinks and life expectancy rises, raising the retirement age and increasing labor force participation among older individuals may counteract a shrinking workforce and rising old-age benefit outlays.

Inactive women account for 17 percent of the out-of-work population, and 84 percent of them are in their prime age. High inactivity rates are an issue in Hungary, and this is no different for women of working age. Labor force participation rates for women between 15 and 64 years old have increased 3 points, from around 56 percent since before the crisis. Data from Eurostat show that in Hungary the percentage of children with access to formal child care is one of the lowest among European countries (figure 6.10). Indeed, in comparison to the average in the EU-28, in Hungary the percentage of women who report being inactive because they are looking after children or incapacitated adults is 11 and 18 percentage points higher, for the groups of inactive women 15–39 years old and 25–49 years old, respectively (figure 6.11).

Out-of-Work Population: Group Profiles from Longitudinal Analysis

In order to better understand the dynamics within clusters and other labor market movements, latent class analysis was also applied to longitudinal EU-SILC data for the period 2008–10. The EU-SILC survey allows the tracking of individuals in both 2008 and 2010, albeit with a smaller sample size than that available in the cross-section surveys. The latent class analysis of the out-of-work population in 2010 yielded similar results in terms of clusters, although due to

Figure 6.10 Formal Child Care as a Percentage of All Children Younger than 3 Years Old, European Countries, 2011

percent

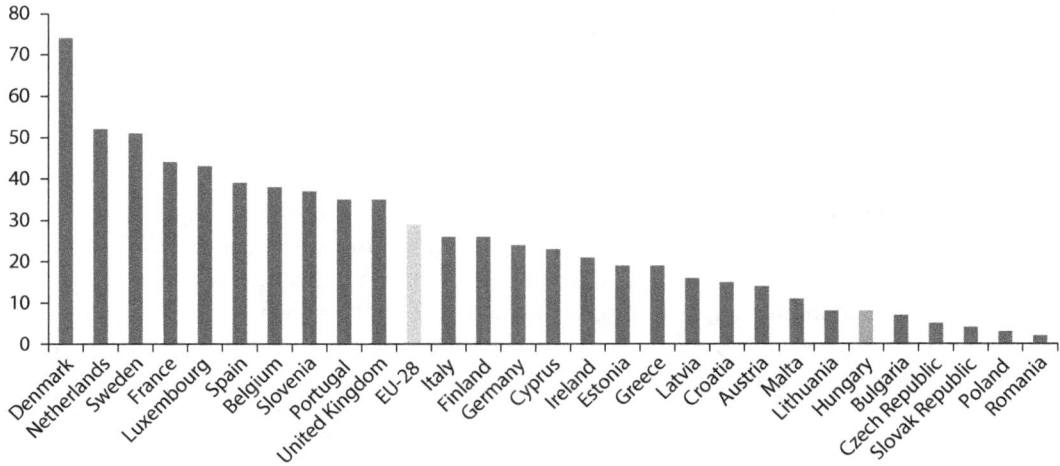

Source: Eurostat, EU-LFS.

Figure 6.11 Percentage of Inactive Women Who Report Looking after Children or Incapacitated Adults as the Main Reason for Not Seeking Employment, European Countries, 2013

percent

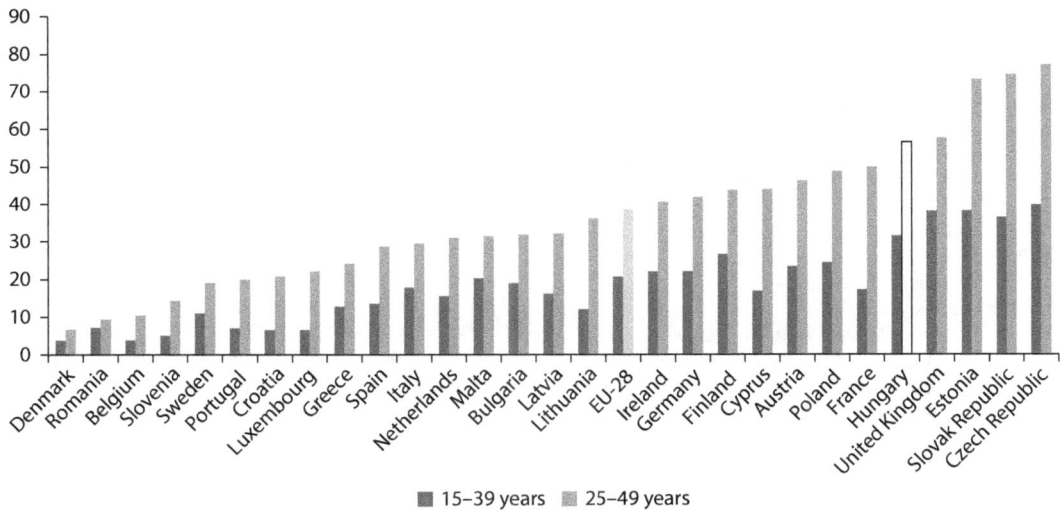

■ 15–39 years   ■ 25–49 years

Source: Eurostat.

the reduced sample size, the number of clusters was also smaller. For a sample of around 1,150 observations, six classes were defined:

- *Mostly rural retired and disabled with previous work experience* (28 percent)
- *Retirees* (25 percent)
- *Middle-aged unemployed* (17 percent)

- *Prime-aged inactive mothers with work experience* (16 percent)
- *Inactive young single women without work experience* (8 percent)
- *Unemployed rural single young men* (6 percent)

Annex 3 (see Appendix A for a link to the online-only annexes shows the full statistical description of the latent classes, while table 6.6 summarizes the key features of each cluster.

A further advantage of the panel analysis is to provide information on the flow of individuals among clusters and in and out of employment. Table 6.7 shows the flow of individuals into each cluster of the out-of-work population or into employment in 2010 according to their labor market status in 2008. Between 2008 and 2010, 85 percent of the employed remained at work. Indeed, there is also an interesting flow into employment among those who were unemployed or inactive in 2008. In 2010, 41 percent of those who were classified as unemployed and 53 percent who were classified as inactive in 2008 were found to be employed. In other words, more than half of the inactive individuals in 2008 were reported as employed in 2010. An additional 15 percent of those inactive in 2008 moved to a cluster of unemployed individuals in 2010, meaning that around 68 percent left inactivity.

On the other hand, table 6.8 shows the labor market status in 2008 for each cluster and at-work population in 2010. Three main results emerge from the dynamics presented. First, for the cluster of *middle-aged unemployed*, 50 percent were employed in 2008, which makes them the most affected by employment

Table 6.6 Longitudinal Analysis: Summary Characteristics of Latent Classes of Out-of-Work Population in Hungary

1: Mostly rural retired and disabled with previous work experience (28%)	*2: Retirees (25%)*
• 70% report their labor market status as disabled; 27% are retired	• 98% are retired
• 55% are female	• 63% are female
• 85% are 45–64 years old	• 88% are 60–64 years old
• 64% are married; 34% are without a partner	• 67% are married; 31% without a partner
• 33% report strongly limited capacity to work	• 11% report strongly limited capacity to work
• 54% have no working adults in household	• Low-to-high-skilled: 23% have not completed upper secondary education; 61% have completed upper or postsecondary; 16% have completed tertiary
• Low-to-mid-skilled: 35% have not completed upper secondary education; 59% have completed upper or postsecondary	• 100% have worked before, 97% worked less than 2 months in the previous year; 36 years of experience on average
• 99% worked before; 91% worked less than 2 months in the previous year; 26 years of experience on average	• 96% live in households without dependent children, 18% live alone
• 82% live in households without dependent children; 11% live alone	• 62% live in urban areas
• 66% live in rural areas	• Very low poverty risk: 12% are in poorest income quintile
• High poverty risk: 28% are in poorest income quintile	• 92% receive old-age benefits
• 71% receive disability benefits	• Total household benefits represent 77% of gross household income
• Total household benefits represent 67% of gross household income	

table continues next page

Table 6.6 Longitudinal Analysis: Summary Characteristics of Latent Classes of Out-of-Work Population in Hungary *(continued)*

3: Middle-aged unemployed (17%)
- 84% are unemployed
- 60% are male
- 76% are 35–59 years old
- 53% are married; 38% are without a partner
- 59% have no working adults in household
- Low-to-mid-skilled: 32% have not completed upper secondary education; 63% have completed upper or postsecondary
- 100% have worked before; 63% have worked 2 or more months in the previous year; 20 years of experience on average
- 57% live in households without dependent children
- 66% live in rural areas
- Very high poverty risk: 50% in poorest income quintile
- 48% receive unemployment benefits
- Total household benefits represent 45% of gross household income

4: Prime-aged inactive mothers with work experience (16%)
- 88% are inactive
- 99% are female
- 82% are 25–54 years old
- 76% are married; 14% are without a partner
- 82% have at least one working adult in household
- Mid-to-high-skilled: 59% have completed upper or postsecondary education; 28% have completed tertiary
- 100% have worked before; 83% less than 2 months in the previous year; 11 years of experience on average
- 87% live in households with dependent children; 60% live in households with children younger than 6 years old
- 57% live in rural areas
- High poverty risk: 31% in poorest income quintile
- 95% receive family/child benefits
- Total household benefits represent 36% of gross household income

5: Inactive young single women without work experience (8%)
- 81% are inactive
- 76% are female
- 79% are 16–29 years old
- 73% are never married; 60% are without a partner
- 54% have at least one working adult in household
- Low-to-mid-skilled: 42% have not completed upper secondary education; 46% have completed upper or postsecondary
- 91% have never worked before; 6 years of experience on average
- 53% live in households with dependent children; 43% live in households with children younger than 6 years old
- 60% live with at least one parent
- Very high poverty risk: 43% in poorest income quintile
- 66% receive family/child benefits; 39% receive housing allowance
- Total household benefits represent 51% of gross household income

6: Unemployed rural single young men (6%)
- 100% are unemployed
- 77% are male
- 94% are 20–24 years old
- 98% are never married
- 76% have no working adults in household
- Low-to-mid-skilled: 24% have not completed upper secondary education; 71% have completed upper or postsecondary
- 51% have never worked before; 45% worked 2 or more months in the previous year; 2 years of experience on average
- 71% live in households without dependent children
- 98% live with at least one parent
- 73% live in rural areas
- Very high poverty risk: 49% in poorest income quintile
- 65% receive family/child benefits; 22% receive unemployment benefits
- Total household benefits represent 35% of gross household income

Source: World Bank staff analysis based on EU-SILC.
Note: Percentages in parentheses following the group names refer to the share of the total out-of-work population. "Years of work experience" refers only to those individuals who have worked before. "Dependent children" includes children younger than 18 years of age and household members ages 18–24 years who are economically inactive and living with at least one parent. "Working adult" refers to adults ages 24 years and older.

losses. Second, the group of *prime-aged inactive mothers with work experience* was the second most likely to have been employed in 2008. This may be reflecting incentives for women of child-bearing age to drop out of the labor force. Finally, 71 percent of the individuals in the group of *unemployed rural single young men* were inactive in 2008, a reflection of the fact that youth tend to be new to the labor market and lack work experience (in contrast, only 21 percent of the *middle-aged unemployed* were inactive in 2008).

Table 6.7 Hungary: Composition of 2010 Clusters Based on 2008 Labor Market Status (Column Percentages)

Cluster	Working-age population in 2010	Labor market status in 2008					
		Unemployed	Retired	Disabled	Other inactive	Employed	Total
1	Mostly rural retired and disabled with previous work experience	5	15	66	3	3	11
2	Retirees	3	76	24	1	4	10
3	Middle-aged unemployed	32	1	2	8	6	7
4	Prime-aged inactive mothers with work experience	11	0	0	17	2	5
5	Inactive young single women without work experience	3	0	3	10	0	2
6	Unemployed rural single young men	5	0	0	7	0	2
NC	Employed	41	8	5	53	85	63
Total	100	100	100	100	100	100	

Source: World Bank staff analysis based on EU-SILC.
Notes: Students aged 16–24 who were inactive or unemployed are excluded from the sample. Numbers referred to in the text appear shaded in gray.

Table 6.8 Hungary: Composition of 2010 Clusters Based on 2008 Labor Market Status (Row percentages)

Cluster	Working-age population in 2010	Labor market status in 2008					
		Unemployed	Retired	Disabled	Other inactive	Employed	Total
1	Mostly rural retired and disabled with previous work experience	3	9	65	5	18	100
2	Retirees	2	50	25	2	22	100
3	Middle-aged unemployed	25	1	3	21	50	100
4	Prime-aged inactive mothers with work experience	12	0	1	61	26	100
5	Inactive young single women without work experience	6	0	12	79	3	100
6	Unemployed rural single young men	13	0	0	71	15	100
NC	Employed	3	1	1	15	80	100
	Total	5	7	11	18	60	100

Source: World Bank staff analysis based on EU-SILC.
Notes: Students ages 16–24 years who were inactive or unemployed are excluded from the sample. Numbers referred to in the text appear shaded in gray.

From Profiling to Activation

Activation and Inclusion Policies in Hungary

Active labor market policies (ALMPs) are not a strategy per se in Hungary, but their elements are integrated into national policy making and should be further enhanced. The Hungarian employment level is low when compared to other

European countries. The main challenge has been to increase the labor market participation of specific disadvantaged groups, such as low-skilled, older workers, young career starters, women with small children, and the disabled (EC 2013b). Therefore, several reforms have been introduced in order to make work attractive to the inactive and promote employment.

In 2011, expenditures on labor market policies (LMPs) in Hungary corresponded to 70 percent of the total for the OECD countries, and unemployment and early retirement benefits accounted for more than half of these expenditures. Figure 6.12 shows the spending on different LMPs as a share of GDP in Hungary and compared to OECD countries (in 2011). From 2008 and 2010, there was an increase of 112 percent in the amount spent on ALMPs as a share of GDP. Unemployment and early retirement benefit values rose by 95 percent in the same period. And, while ALMPs represented around one-third of the total LMPs in 2011, unemployment and early retirement benefits accounted for 65 percent, an increase in comparison with a share of 51 percent in 2008.

Structural reforms have been introduced to raise the effective retirement age, increase employment, and promote sustainability. As a response to a high inflow into disability schemes and a widespread use of early retirement options, reforms affecting the pension, disability, and social benefit systems were introduced. The value of benefits is decreasing while the criteria for accessing them has become stricter and more work-oriented (EC 2013b). Furthermore,

Figure 6.12 Labor Market Policy (LMP) Spending in Hungary as a Share of GDP
percent

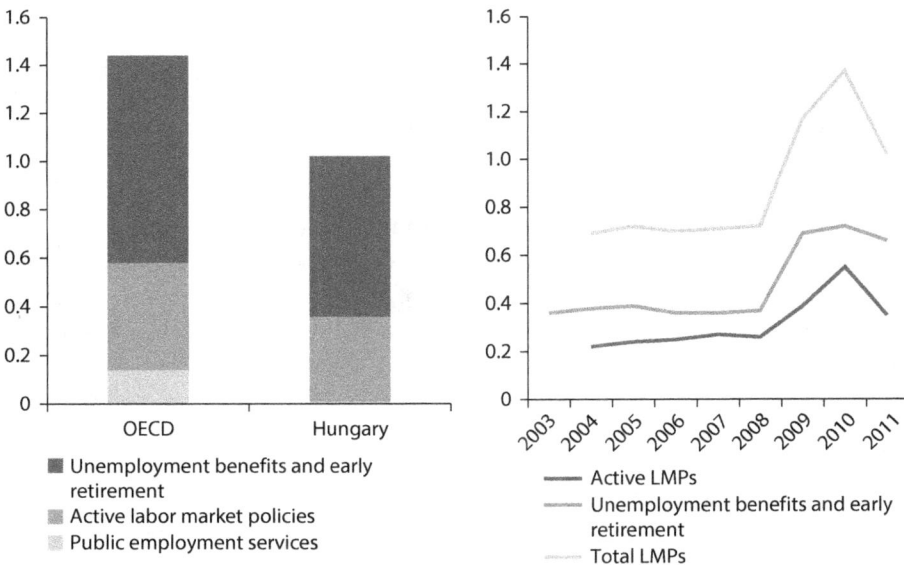

Legend:
- Unemployment benefits and early retirement
- Active labor market policies
- Public employment services

- Active LMPs
- Unemployment benefits and early retirement
- Total LMPs

Source: Eurostat, OECD.

in order to activate those capable of work, some measures listed in the Hungarian Work Plan include:

- Strengthen ALMPs, reinforcing services and supports available to jobseekers;
- Increase labor market flexibility through the promotion of flexible forms of employment and flexible workplaces, ease return of young parents, and support companies in adjusting working hours for flexibility;
- Continue targeted tax allowance for employers who employ young career starters, and support their acquisition of work experience;
- Modernize the education and training system to improve the skills of the labor force;
- Strengthen the social economy and social cooperatives;
- Promote public works.

Public work became an important activation measure in 2009 with the launch of the "Pathway to work" *program.* The idea was to assist those capable of work to find some form of public employment, reducing the duration of unemployment and breaking long-term benefit dependency, while making it easier for them to find a job on the open labor market through the improvement in their skills. Figure 6.13 shows the composition of spending on ALMPs in Hungary and how direct job creation was almost two times more expensive than employment incentives and training together. Indeed, among different LMP measures available, the share of participants in training activities, for example, is one of the lowest in Europe (figure 6.14). Therefore, while the majority of financial resources is spent on public work, there is less left for training, rehabilitation programs, or significant contribution allowances, although these latter are proved to be efficient in promoting labor market participation (EC 2013b). In the case of Hungary, low effectiveness, high selectivity of inclusion, and sometimes discriminating practices by local authorities have been outlined by OECD (2014) and Kierzenkowski (2012). The government of Hungary has signaled its response to these observations by better combining the public works program with training offerings.

Activation Priority, Activation Type, and Benefit Receipt by Group

When further considering the approach toward labor market integration, an assessment of the priorities and potentials of the identified groups needs to be undertaken. Given the limited increase in nominal resources for activation programs, further prioritization of intervention is all the more important. After a *first step* ("activation priority") of prioritizing the intervention along activation need and activation potential, a *second step* ("activation type") will attempt to classify the groups according to the kind of activation intervention needed, depending on social or labor market barriers to be overcome. Lastly, as a *third step*, information on *household income composition* of the different groups will be used to assess potential cross-dependencies of the benefit system with the labor market status and activation approaches.

Figure 6.13 Composition of Spending on ALMPs in Hungary, 2008 and 2011

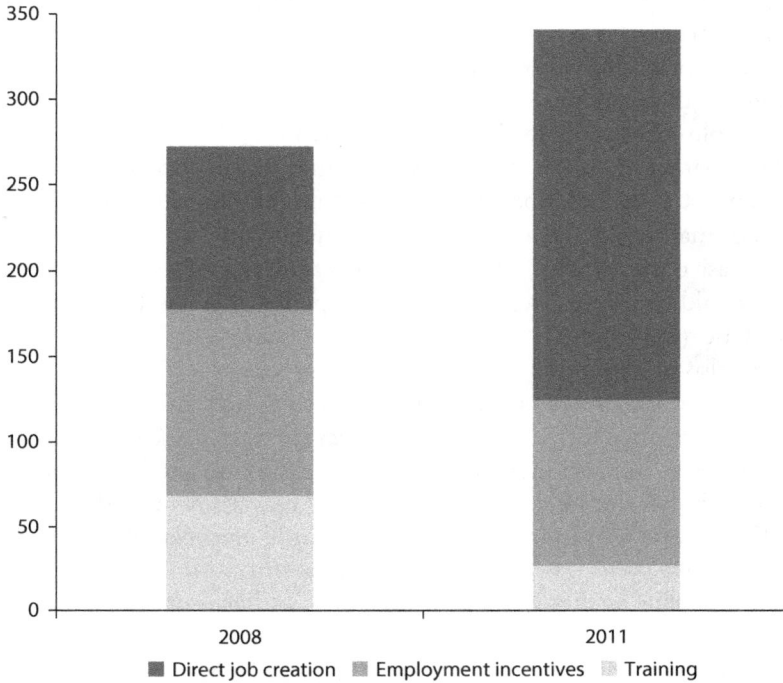

Direct job creation   Employment incentives   Training

Source: Eurostat, OECD.

Figure 6.14 Share of Participants in Training as an Active Labor Market Tool, European Countries, 2011

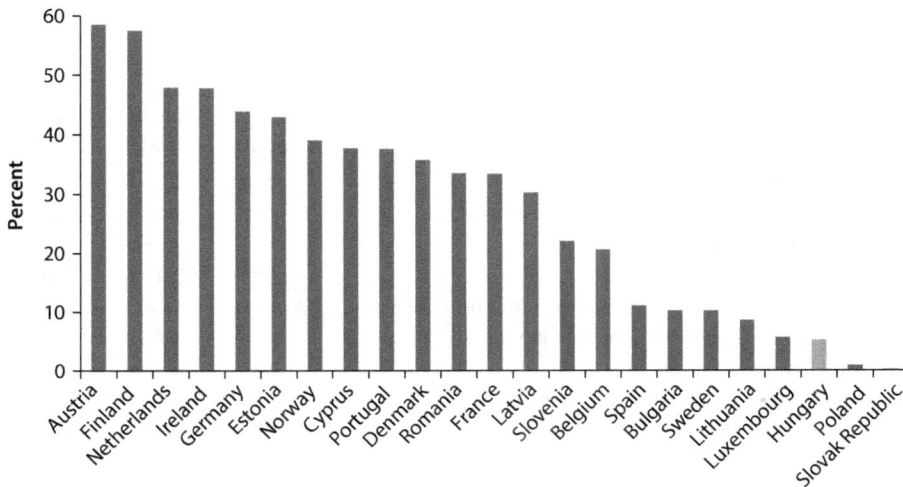

Source: Eurostat.

Activation Priorities

Table 6.9 gives an overview of the identified out-of-work classes and their respective activation need and activation potential. The total number of persons estimated in these clusters was about 2.28 million in 2011, representing about 38 percent of the working-age (16–64) population of Hungary in 2011.

In the table, "activation need" refers to a group's level of need for inclusion in the labor market in order to achieve income and reduce or end poverty. "Activation potential" describes that group's ability or motivation to be included in the labor market. A high activation need could be driven by high poverty risk (as in the case of the *prime-aged long-term unemployed*), whereas a high activation potential could be driven by previous work experience or a relatively good educational base (for example, the *educated single students*). Overall priority for action can also be supported by the size of the group.

From this prioritization exercise, a set of seven groups emerges with a "high" or "medium" priority for action. *Disabled with previous work experience* have a medium priority because their potential reinsertion into the labor market will most probably have to be achieved via a forced reassessment of their disability status. This can be a protracted process. *Prime-aged unemployed* and *prime-aged long-term unemployed* are considered high priority for further activation. *Prime-aged inactive mothers with work experience* and *low-educated rural inactive mothers without work experience* are both ranked "medium" priority but should still be included in the roster of prioritized groups. They present very different socio-economic challenges. *Unemployed youth* and *educated single students* form prioritized groups because of the potential scarring effects of labor market detachment for young people at an early age. From the view of the Hungarian authorities, *educated single students* do not constitute a prioritized group for further action in 2014 or later, because one of their main labor market barriers (language completion requirement) was addressed through dedicated programs after 2011.

Table 6.9 Activation Need and Potential of Different Clusters in Hungary

Share % (2011)	Cluster	Activation need	Activation potential	Priority for action
19	Disabled with previous work experience	Medium	Medium	Medium
15	Mostly male early retirees and retirees	Low	Medium	Low
15	Urban retired women	Low	Low	Low
14	Prime-aged unemployed	High	Medium	High
13	Prime-aged inactive mothers with work experience	Medium	High	Medium
12	Prime-aged long-term unemployed	High	Medium	High
4	Unemployed youth	High	Medium	High
4	Low-educated rural inactive mothers without work experience	High	Low	Medium
2	Educated single students	Low	High	Medium
2	Low-educated disabled without work experience	Medium	Low	Low

Source: World Bank analysis and assessment 2014.

Mostly male early retirees and retirees, urban retired women, and *low-educated disabled without work experience* are not prioritized for further action owing, respectively, to their officially achieved retirement status and extreme distance (via very low educational attainment and self-declared disability) from the labor market.

Activation Type

As a second step, the relative severity of labor market or social obstacles to be overcome for labor market integration will serve as an orientation for activation approaches. Figure 6.15 depicts the prioritized clusters along the labor market and social barrier dimensions; the size of the bubbles corresponds to their relative group size.

When mapping the respective barriers for labor market integration faced by the seven prioritized groups, we can see that their challenges are quite evenly distributed across the matrix. *Unemployed youth* and *educated single students* have similar social barriers but differ in their potential labor market proximity, the *students* being much closer to a job start. The two groups of the *prime-aged long-term unemployed* and the *prime-aged unemployed* face similar social barriers. The same can be said for the two groups of *inactive mothers*, with the *prime-aged inactive mothers with work experience* being much closer to the labor market. The large group of the *disabled with previous work experience* probably faces the strongest social hurdles for labor market integration: overcoming their disability status and reintegrating in mid-life.

Figure 6.15 Activation Types of Prioritized Clusters in Hungary

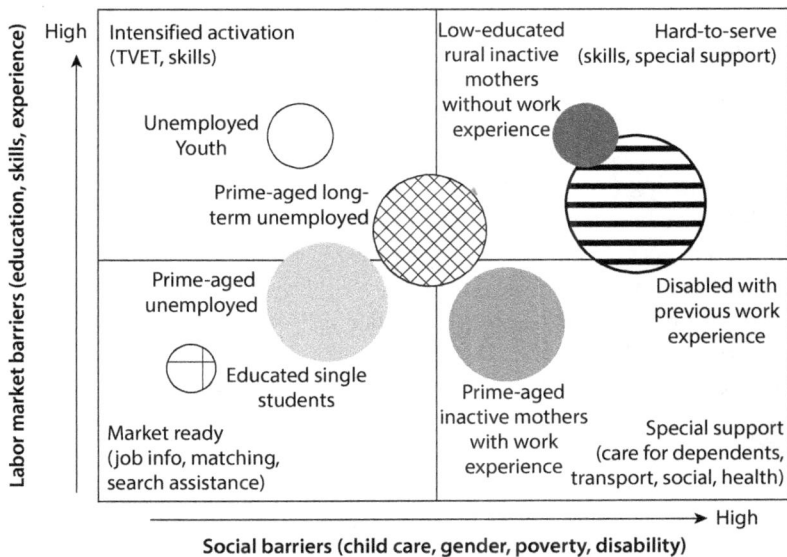

Source: World Bank analysis and assessment 2014.
Note: TVET = technical and vocational education and training.

Household Income Composition

When analyzing the 2011 household income of the prioritized groups, one notices a relatively high share of benefit income among many groups. For the three nonprioritized groups (*mostly male early retirees and retirees, urban retired women,* and *low-educated disabled without work experience*) this does not present a major problem because their pattern of benefit receipt corresponds to their sociodemographic situation. The *prime-aged unemployed* and *prime-aged long-term unemployed* each have about 50 percent of income from unemployment benefits. Following recent policy changes to reduce the unemployment benefit payment to only three months, this figure may be lower.

As already mentioned, the *disabled with previous work experience* ought to be examined again as to their disability status. With only 35 percent reporting any limitation on daily activities, yet 89 percent receiving disability benefits, there appears to be some potential for labor market mobilization and benefit rationalization in this group.

Given the overall picture of benefit receipt revealed by EU-SILC data, the key need for action emerges around a potential review of disability benefit allocation.

Suggestions for Activation Measures and Further Analysis

This section sets out a set of potential activation measures for each of the priority groups. Areas for further policy dialogue are also outlined. Any suggestion or policy discussion around concrete measures will need to take into account that the Hungarian authorities have introduced a set of reforms since 2012, and changes to existing programs in the field of employment and labor market inclusion (EC 2013; OECD 2014).

The suggestions below should be considered as a starting point for further policy dialogue between the EC, the World Bank, and Hungary, bearing in mind that the groups identified still may have heterogeneities that affect the type of support required. Accordingly, these suggestions are not meant to be an exhaustive set of possible activation measures.

When discussing potential activation approaches for the identified groups, it is important to keep in mind that the groups have been derived from EU-SILC data from the year 2011. Since then, general economic development, policy actions by the government of Hungary, and European Commission country specific recommendations might have reflected some of the policy suggestions or rendered them obsolete.

More concretely, since 2011 the government of Hungary has taken a number of steps and has initiated policy changes that ought to improve the labor market integration or activation of some of the groups. Notably, these reforms were taken in the fields of (1) access to disability insurance—with a change from disability pensions to rehabilitation benefits and the revision of the health status of the recipients, emphasizing working capacity rather than loss of skills; (2) early retirement—where rules of early retirement were tightened and the retirement age will be raised from 62 to 65 years (box 6.1); (3) linkage of social assistance

Box 6.1 Retirement-Income Systems in Hungary

The following provides details about some recent changes in the retirement system in Hungary.

Old-age pensions

In Hungary, the retirement age was equalized at 62 for both men and women (from 60 and 55, respectively). The age for men reached 62 in 2000; for women, it occurred in the beginning of 2009. After 2010, the statutory unisex retirement age is being increased gradually, reaching 65 by 2022.

In addition, 20 years of service are required for both the earnings-related pension and the minimum pension. Fifteen years of service are required to receive a partial pension.

The pension payment has been indexed, half to wages and half to prices, since 2001, but further ad hoc increases were applied. As of 2010 indexation will be linked to GDP growth.

From 2006 to 2009, all pensioners received an additional month's (13th-month) pension. On January 1, 2009, the rules on eligibility to 13th month pension changed. As of 2010, the 13th month pension was totally abolished.

Early retirement:

In 2008, early retirement was possible for men at age 60 and for women at age 57 without actuarial reduction. When pension ages were equalized at 62 in 2009, early retirement became available at 59 for women and 60 for men. According to newly adopted legislation, the retirement age will gradually increase to 65 years. And, as of 2010, advanced pension rules were also tightened along with the increase in standard retirement age.

Unemployment:

Older unemployed people can receive special pre-retirement benefits if they have received unemployment insurance benefits for 140 days, will reach pensionable age within five years, have exhausted their unemployment benefit entitlement within eight years of pensionable age, and have contributed to the pension scheme for at least 20 years.

Source: World Bank staff analysis 2014.

beneficiaries with activation services—eligibility rules for unemployment assistance became stricter and recipients were obliged to participate in public works or other activation programs for at least 30 days a year; and (4) reconciliation of work and family life, allowing parents who receive child-care benefits to pursue gainful activity without time limitation (box 6.2), and by the development of day-care services. When discussing the results of the LCA analysis, the potential impact of these reforms on current (2013/2014) inactivity figures will need to be discussed.

Disabled with previous work experience (19 percent, Priority: Medium). This is the largest group among the identified and prioritized groups, with 432,000 members in 2011. On the face of things, the group does have strong work experience in light of middle to low educational achievement. The large majority of

Box 6.2 Child Benefit Systems in Hungary

The following provides details about some recent changes occurring in other benefits such as maternity leave.

Child care:

People can take the following benefits: pregnancy confinement, child-care fee, child-care allowance, and child-raising support.

The pregnancy confinement benefit is for women who are pregnant or giving birth, for 24 weeks (168 days). The benefit is 70 percent of the daily average gross earnings of the previous year.

The child-care fee may be claimed by one parent the day after the pregnancy confinement benefit expires. The entitlement runs to the second birthday of the child (maximum 24 months). The benefit amount is 70 percent of the daily average gross earnings of the previous year, up to a maximum of twice the minimum wage.

The child-care allowance is for a parent who cares for the child until the child's third birthday (maximum 36 months); or in the case of twin children, until the end of the year they reach school age; or in the case of a permanently ill or seriously disabled child, until the child is ten years of age (maximum 120 months). The monthly amount is equal to the minimum old-age pension, irrespective of the number of children in the family; and in the case of twins, the amount is twice the minimum old-age pension. After a child's first birthday, a grandparent may claim the benefit.

Child-raising support is for a parent who raises three or more underage children in the period between the third and eighth birthday of the youngest child (maximum 60 months). The monthly amount is equal to the minimum old-age pension, irrespective of the number of children.

Source: OECD 2011.

---

them live in rural areas and about 35 percent of them report strong physical limitations on their ability to work, a much lower rate than the 89 percent claiming a disability benefit.

At any rate, this significant group of out-of-work citizens needs to be followed more closely and any new applicants for disability benefits closely monitored and controlled (as recent policy changes by the Hungarian authorities suggest). Limiting the inflows into this group (via more stringent disability benefit criteria) will be easier than forcing the activated exit of members from this group. Nevertheless, this effort ought to be undertaken in light of the demographic profile of the group (many members are still in their forties). Potential activation measures for the inactive who remain in this group will largely depend on the ability of local governments to provide and finance services for the (formerly) disabled (rehabilitation, transport, social and medical care, and so on), but also on the integration of national policies with local service standards and adequate financing. In light of the potentially high integration cost for and potential discrimination against disabled workers, local social services cannot be expected to finance these approaches without support from central government. Potential activation measures include:

- *Review disability status but continue benefits (for now)*. Continuing to provide the current benefits, the members of this group could be made eligible for a review of their disability and work-ability status. When considered "fit to work" in this review, a set of support measures and continuing benefits (potentially with a phase-out period) ought to be provided to cushion the transition toward labor market integration. Since 2012, the incapacity benefit administration has been reformed; it is more focused on "work ability" checks and is supposed to tighten the access to the program.
- *Integration into standard public employment services (PES) offerings*. After reassessment of their labor market status, the members of the group ought to be made part of the normal client base of the public employment service (at medium priority), offering training and job placement experience.
- *Participation in (reformed!) public works program*. In light of the strong rural living pattern of the group, a participation in the (reformed! more training!) public works program could be an option to supplement potential social assistance income levels after withdrawal of the disability pension.
- *PES does provide a mobility subsidy to jobseekers who have found a job outside of their home city*. However, this does not address the general lack of public transportation in the country nor its high cost.
- *Enhanced and cheaper mobility in rural and peri-urban areas*. Given the relative high cost of mobility using public transport in Hungary (OECD 2014), this group might find itself at a disadvantage owing to its rural living pattern. Any progress in the field of public transport could certainly help to improve regional mobility and labor matching.
- The "Rehabilitation card" issued for persons with health problems by the national tax authority, which provides support to employers for the employment of disabled/incapacitated workers. In February 2014 more than 23,000 employees in almost 6,000 companies benefited from this program.

Prime-aged unemployed (14 percent, Priority: High). These newly unemployed have solid work experience (16 years on average) and mainly live in rural areas. Many of them have dependent children, reducing their geographic mobility. Their risk of poverty is high, with 49 percent living in the poorest income quintile.

Prime-aged long-term unemployed (12 percent, Priority: High). This group resembles the previous group but is slightly older and less rural. Potential activation measures for the two groups include:

- *Availability of public transportation and rental offers*. Increasing the availability of public transportation can improve the quality of life and people's chances of finding a job and staying employed—for example, taking advantage of opportunities in particular geographic areas. The Hungarian authorities noted that many rental offers and incomes are in fact part of the "gray" economy, so the real availability of rental offers in the market might be higher than perceived but might be unsuitable for any type of mobility support due to lack of documentation. Nevertheless the government of Hungary introduced in 2012 a housing allocation for jobseekers who cannot find jobs locally, to be used to rent accommodations for up to 18 months in the case of employment.

- *Enhanced and cheaper mobility in rural and peri-urban areas.* Given the relative high cost of mobility using public transport in Hungary (OECD 2014), this group might find itself at a disadvantage owing to its rural living pattern. Any progress in that field of public transport could certainly help to improve regional mobility and labor matching.

- *Job-to-job matching by PES.* The rather recent fall into unemployment by this group (*prime-aged unemployed*) underlines the necessity for the PES to take customers in charge early on, ideally when they are still employed in their previous job, and help with "job-to-job" transitions to avoid long spells of unemployment in the first place. This requires immediate notification on the part of the (future) jobseeker and immediate action by the PES when it learns about the upcoming joblessness of a potential client.

- *Reconnection with previous field of employment.* Given the strong work experience of this group, building any future development on their acquired skills can strengthen their case with new employers.

- *Linkage with regional economic development activities.* For both groups, a linkage with regional economic development activities (investment, self-employment promotion, enhanced public works schemes, and so on) will be important, regardless of urban or rural living pattern.

Prime-aged inactive mothers with work experience (13 percent, Priority: Medium). This group of women could certainly benefit from improved child-care offerings and reconnection programs with their fields of previous employment or study. Potential and current activation measures include:

- *Standard PES job-search assistance.* Given their good work experience and (on average) high educational attainment, job searches by this group could be expected to be conducted independently, with little supervision and support from the PES authorities.

- *Linkage of PES job-search assistance with child-care offerings.* Linking any activation attempt to provision of child care will be critical.

- *Continue to expand child-care facilities.* Seventy-five percent of children ages three to six years were enrolled in formal child care in 2011, which was below the EU average of 83 percent. During the joint country mission, the Hungarian authorities noted that child-care offerings had been expanded since 2011. More challenging is child care for younger children, which according to Eurostat is provided to around 8 percent of children younger than three years old, compared to 30 percent of children in the EU in 2011. In 2009–10 an action plan was launched to increase the capacity of day care by 3,200–3,500 new places before 2013 (European Union 2014).[18]

- *Greater flexibility in parental leave and benefit policies.* In January 2014, parents were allowed to return to work more quickly while still receiving their benefit for the full two years. At the same time, low-income mothers were able to receive a "child-care allowance" for three years. There are fears that the latter might act as a work disincentive, a view not shared by the Hungarian authorities due to the very low level of the benefit, at about one-fourth of the minimum wage.
- *The* "Job Protection Act" *introduced an employment subsidy for disadvantaged jobseekers,* including those returning from child care and those without qualifications, among others.

Unemployed youth (4 percent, Priority: High). This group urgently needs to be connected to the labor market to avoid any "scarring" effect on their life chances. Very few of them have initial work experience, but the group has medium-level educational attainment. Potential activation measures include:

- *Job placement and job-start programs.* Placement through subsidized internships with accompanying professional and life skills training could be a promising line of action, breaking the common barrier of required work experience for many entry-level positions.
- *Job-search offerings by PES and via virtual platforms.* Any PES offering for this group will have to take into account that the use of mobile technology (for localized job search, initiation of employer contact, and so on) will be taken for granted by many members of this group.
- *The* "Job Protection Act" *introduced an employment subsidy for young people.* The subsidy is time-limited and targeted to younger-than-25-year-olds to incentivize sustainable employment.

Low-educated rural inactive mothers without work experience (4 percent, Priority: Medium). This group presents much greater integration challenges than the larger group of inactive mothers. They are a group of much younger women who mainly live in rural areas. They have almost no work experience and much lower educational attainment. Potential activation measures include:

- *(Reformed) Public-works* "window" *for mothers.* Opening a "mothers" window in a reformed public works program that includes child-care offerings and training opportunities might help some of these women get initial work experience and address their dire poverty situation. Most likely, this will call for reform of the local selection practices of the public works program by municipalities.

- *Remedial education.* In light of the extremely low educational attainment among this group, offerings of remedial secondary education could be quite well placed for this group. Again, these offerings would probably have to be accompanied by child-care offerings.

Educated single students (2 percent, Priority: Medium). This group has a high educational standard but no work experience and will, in the coming years, leave school and enter either unemployment or inactivity. Similar to the *unemployed youth*, they will need a quick start and work attachment to avoid any "scarring." Potentially, programs for the *unemployed youth* and the *educated single students* could be offered along the same program lines (in the same ESF OP or the like), with participants self-selecting into specific courses or programs based on educational background or living area (rural/urban). Potential activation measures include:

- *Promotion of part-time work during studies.* Allowing students to gain firsthand work experience during their studies might help with initial labor market insertion upon graduation.
- *Standard job-search support.* Helping the members of this group with basic job-search skills could already be helpful.
- *Offer support to students in order to comply with language requirements needed to receive their university diplomas (already addressed).* In order to get their university degree, students in Hungary must pass an intermediate-level language exam in the foreign language of their choice. Offering more support for these language requirements could help provide many students with the necessary formal credentials for labor market entry. In March 2014, the government of Hungary launched the *Diploma Rescue Program*, which supports those who have completed their tertiary education and only require a certificate of foreign language to get their degree, by covering their language course cost and, for registered jobseekers, the cost of the (first) language exam.

In summary, Hungary could benefit from accompanying the ongoing improvement of its labor market services and social inclusion policies with enhanced knowledge about the composition and socioeconomic situation of the different groups of out-of-work citizens.

Notes

1. Prior to the crisis, the labor force participation rate in 2008 was 61.5 percent.
2. Individuals ages 16–24 years who are out of work and enrolled in education are excluded from the sample; they are considered to be investing in their final stages of human capital formation and therefore are not a particular target group for activation policies. In 2011, there were 741,817 youth ages 16–24 years who were out of

work and enrolled in education, representing 62 percent of the total population in this age category and 25 percent of the total out-of-work population of working age. Individuals between 25 and 64 years of age who are enrolled in school are included in the latent class analysis, and will be grouped under "other inactive." It is important to note that this group of students (older than 24) accounts for only 1 percent of total population of working age.

3. For the latest developments on active inclusion in Hungary, see EC (2013b).

4. This variable is constructed using the self-reported current work status in the EU-SILC survey that has four categories: at work, unemployed, retired, and inactive. The unemployed are further classified into short- and long-term based on how long they have been actively looking for a job. The inactive is combined with another question to separate this group into students, disabled, military, and other inactive. In the case of Hungary, the retired category also includes disabled.

5. In order to construct this variable, individuals ages 25 years or older are considered adults.

6. This is a binary variable that takes the value one if an individual answered "yes, strong limitations" to whether they had been hampered in their usual activities because of health problems for at least the last six months. The value is zero if the answer is "yes, limited" or "no, not limited."

7. The equivalized household income takes into account an equivalence factor to weight the number of household members used in the denominator when calculating household income per capita. The first adult 18 years of age or older has a weight of 1.0, children younger than 14 years old have a weight of 0.3, and other individuals 14 years of age and older have a weight of 0.5. The sum of the weights of all household members is equal to the equivalent household size.

8. Note that income reported in EU-SILC surveys is for the year preceding the survey year.

9. Total household gross income is defined as the sum of: (at the individual level) gross employee cash or near-cash income; company car, gross cash benefits or losses from self-employment (including royalties); unemployment benefits; old-age benefits; survivor benefits; sickness benefits; disability benefits; education allowances; and (at the household level) income from rental of property or land; family/children related allowances; social exclusion not elsewhere classified; housing allowances; regular inter-household cash transfers received; interests, dividends, profit from capital investments in unincorporated business; pensions from individual private plans; and income received by youth younger than 16 years of age. Total household net income, in turn, was calculated by subtracting from total household gross income regular taxes on wealth, taxes on income and social insurance contributions, and regular inter-household case transfers paid.

10. Social benefits are aggregated in eight branches using the European System of integrated Social PROtection Statistics (ESSPROS) definitions. For more information, see Eurostat (2011).

11. According to EU-SILC guidelines, dense areas have more than 500 inhabitants per square kilometer, where the total population for the set is at least 50,000 inhabitants. Intermediate areas have more than 100 inhabitants per square kilometer, and either a total population for the set of at least 50,000 inhabitants or a location adjacent to a dense area. The remaining areas are categorized as sparsely populated.

12. The EU-SILC longitudinal survey consists of a four-year rotating panel. In each year, approximately three-quarters of individuals present in the previous year are retained. The samples used in the latent class analysis include about 6,000 observations for each year in the cross-sectional analysis and 1,150 observations in the longitudinal analysis. The population is weighted with individual weights.

13. It should be kept in mind that the EU-SILC activity status is self-reported; therefore, the disabled population count may not be accurate when compared with administrative data.

14. Disability benefits amount to 38 percent of total gross household income.

15. Risk of poverty is here understood as the relative probability of living in the poorest income quintile. By definition, 20 percent of the population lives in this quintile; risk is thus gauged relative to a benchmark of 20 percent.

16. The tax wedge is defined as the difference between labor's cost to the employer and the corresponding net take-home pay of the employee.

17. The legal retirement age is 62 for both men and women.

18. Furthermore, the government has installed "sure start" centers for vulnerable communities (modeled after a UK example) that provide additional social support for poor children and their families.

References

Collins, L. M., and S. T. Lanza. 2010. *Latent Class and Latent Transition Analysis: With Applications in the Social, Behavioral, and Health Sciences*. Hoboken, NJ: Wiley.

Dimitrov, Y., and N. Duell. 2013. *Activating Vulnerable Groups in Bulgaria*. Washington, DC: World Bank.

EC (European Commission). 2013a. "EU Measures to Tackle Youth Unemployment." MEMO, Brussels, 28 May 2013.

———. 2013b. "Assessment of the Implementation of the European Commission Recommendation on Active Inclusion: A Study of National Policies: Country Report—Hungary." DG Employment, Social Affairs & Inclusion, European Commission, Brussels.

EEAG. 2012. *The EEAG Report on the European Economy, "The Hungarian Crisis."* Munich, Germany: CESifo, 115–30.

Eurofound. 2012. *NEETs—Young People Not in Employment, Education or Training: Characteristics, Costs and Policy Responses in Europe*. Luxembourg: Publications Office of the European Union.

European Union. 2014. "Hungary: Developing Child Care Services to Help Parents Back to Work." European Platform for Investing in Children. Country Profile (last updated in February 2014). http://europa.eu/epic/countries/hungary/index_en.htm.

Eurostat. 2011. *ESSPROS Manual: The European System of Integrated Social PROtection Statistics*. Luxembourg: European Union.

Katz, L. 2010. "Long-Term Unemployment in the Great Recession." Testimony for the Joint Economic Committee, U.S. Congress Hearing on "Long-Term Unemployment: Causes, Consequences and Solutions." April 29.

Kaufman, L., and P. J. Rousseeuw. 1990. *Finding Groups in Data*. New York: Wiley.

Kierzenkowski, R. 2012. "Towards a More Inclusive Labour Market in Hungary." OECD Economics Department Working Papers 960, OECD, Paris.

Magidson, J., and J. Vermunt. 2002. "Latent Class Modeling as a Probabilistic Extension of K-Means Clustering." Quirk's Marketing Research Review, March 20, 77–80. http://statisticalinnovations.com/technicalsupport/kmeans2a.htm.

OECD. 2011. "Hungary." In *Pensions at a Glance 2011: Retirement-Income Systems in OECD and G20 Countries*. OECD Publishing. http://dx.doi.org/10.1787/pension_glance-2011–58-en.

———. 2014. *Economist Surveys: Hungary*. Paris: OECD.

Vermunt, J. K., and J. Magidson. 2005. *Latent GOLD 4.0 User's Guide*. Belmont, MA: Statistical Innovations Inc.

Latent Class Analysis of the Out-of-Work Population in Lithuania, 2007–11

Background

Lithuania approached the global financial crisis following a decade of high growth. According to the World Bank's World Development Indicators, between 1998 and 2008, the country was one of the fastest growing economies in the world, displaying an average GDP growth rate of about 7 percent per year. In the 2003–08 period, the country grew between 6 and 10 percent per year, in sharp contrast to the anemic growth rates observed by the EU-28, or the euro area (which expanded between 0 and 3 percent per year).

Lithuania was hit hard by the downturn but appears to have recovered fairly rapidly, at least as far as output growth is concerned. Even though the country entered the storm later compared to many other countries (GDP growth in 2008 still settled at an acceptable 3 percent), the Lithuanian economy suffered a severe recession in 2009, when output contracted by a staggering 14.8 percent. This was mostly due to the country's strong dependence on exports, which collapsed in the 2008–09 period. While neighboring Latvia fared somewhat worse, the dip witnessed by the Lithuanian economy was much more severe than the one suffered by the average EU-28 country or euro-area member, which witnessed negative growth rates in the 5 percent region in 2009. However, like neighboring countries with similar income levels (for example, Estonia and Latvia), Lithuania recovered from the shock faster than its European partners; GDP growth was back into positive territory by mid-2009 and remained comfortably positive throughout 2010, before settling at about 6 percent in 2011. Growth rates returned to more modest levels by 2012 and 2013, at about 3–4 percent.

While GDP growth resumed quite rapidly, unemployment deteriorated sharply as a result of the downturn and is struggling to revert to pre-crisis levels. The rate of joblessness in Lithuania had declined steadily since the early 2000s, settling at a little over 4 percent in 2007. However, as the effects of the global financial crisis unraveled, the country suffered a large and extremely rapid increase in unemployment; by the end of 2008, joblessness had risen to about 6 percent, climbing to 14 percent in 2009 and eventually peaking at 18 percent in 2010. Such increases are considerably larger than those observed in the EU-28 or the euro area as a whole, but comparable to what other countries in the region of similar income levels witnessed. Unemployment began to slowly decrease in late 2010, but the average rate in 2013 was still 12 percent, about 8 percentage points above the pre-crisis levels.

Young Lithuanians were particularly affected by the global downturn. Like the overall unemployment rate, the joblessness rate among Lithuanians between the ages of 15 and 24 had declined steadily in the pre-crisis period, reaching 8 percent in 2007. As the global recession hit, youth unemployment skyrocketed to 29 percent in 2009 and then 35 percent in 2010. Encouragingly, however, as unemployment started to fall in 2010, the rate of joblessness among young Lithuanians followed suit; by 2012, unemployment in the 15–24 cohort had recovered somewhat to 26 percent—still more than 15 percentage points above the 2007 pre-crisis level. However, youth unemployment declined somewhat to 22 percent, and was slightly lower than the rate registered for the EU-28 as a whole (23 percent).

As far as joblessness goes, men were generally more affected than women. As figure 7.1 shows, at all age levels, Lithuanian men suffered larger increases in their rate of unemployment relative to women. Both men and women in the 25–64 age category entered the crisis with unemployment rates close to 5 percent; however, by late 2010, women in this age group displayed unemployment rates in the 12–15 percent range, as opposed to 15–20 percent among men of the same age. Among young Lithuanians, men were also affected much more

Figure 7.1 Unemployment Rates by Age and Gender in Lithuania, 2007–13
percent

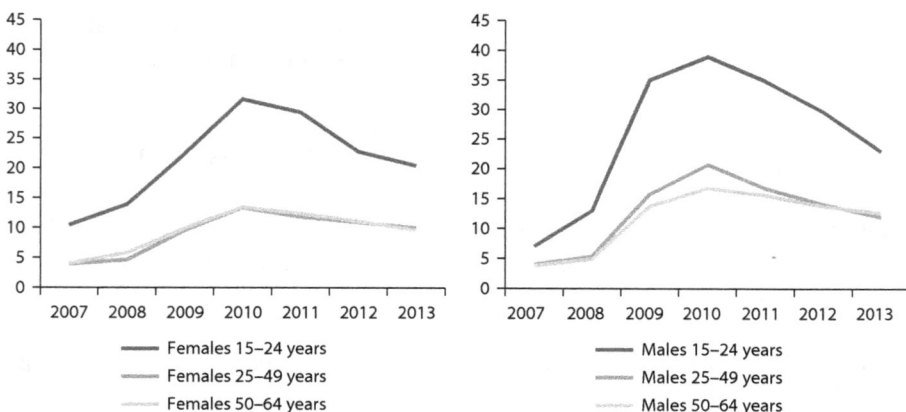

Source: Eurostat, EU-LFS.

than women, with the rate of joblessness among 15- to 24-year-old men peaking at 45 percent, as opposed to 35 percent among women of the same cohort.

One of the most worrying developments as a result of the crisis was the significant increase in the share of long-term unemployed. In 2013, according to Eurostat and as shown in figure 7.2, in the average EU-28 country almost 48 percent of the unemployed have been looking for work for more than 12 months, up from 35 percent in 2009. In Lithuania, where the long-term unemployment rate had declined all the way to just over 20 percent in 2009, the figure reached 52 percent in 2011 and settled at 50 percent in 2012, a development comparable to those observed in Latvia and Estonia, before declining to 43 percent in 2013.

A further troubling change in the Lithuanian labor market since 2007 is the rapid increase in both the absolute number of out-of work individuals and in the share of the out-of-work population relative to total population and working-age population. European Union Statistics of Income and Living Conditions (EU-SILC) data reveal that the number of the out-of-work population between the ages of 16 and 64 years (excluding students) had been increasing steadily between 2007 and 2011, going from slightly more than 450,000 to slightly less than 610,000. This is all the more alarming as it occurred during a period in which both the total size of the population and the total number of working-age individuals in Lithuania actually shrank (from about 3.375 to about 3.285 million and from 1.985 to 1.9 million, respectively). This resulted in the share of out-of-work population relative to the total working-age population increasing from 23 percent to 32 percent.

The 2007–11 period witnessed a sizeable increase in the number and relative importance of unemployment (particularly long-term unemployment), at the expense of employment. Figures 7.4 and 7.5 show the composition of working-age and of out-of-work Lithuanians in 2007 and 2011, respectively. Not only, as figure 7.3 above shows, did the size of the out-of-work population increase between 2007

Figure 7.2 Long-Term Unemployment as a Share of Total Unemployment, 2003–13
percent

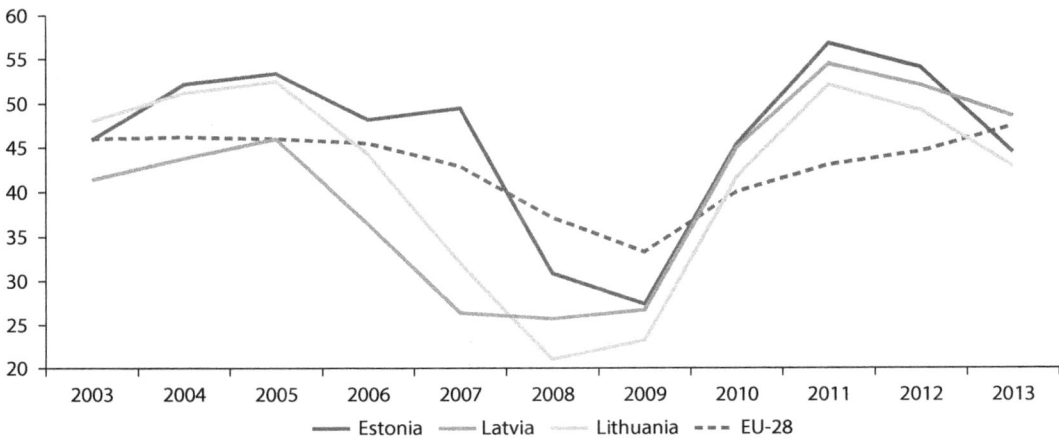

Source: Eurostat.

Figure 7.3 Evolution of Out-of-Work Population (Ages 16–64 Years) in Lithuania, 2007, 2009, and 2011

percent

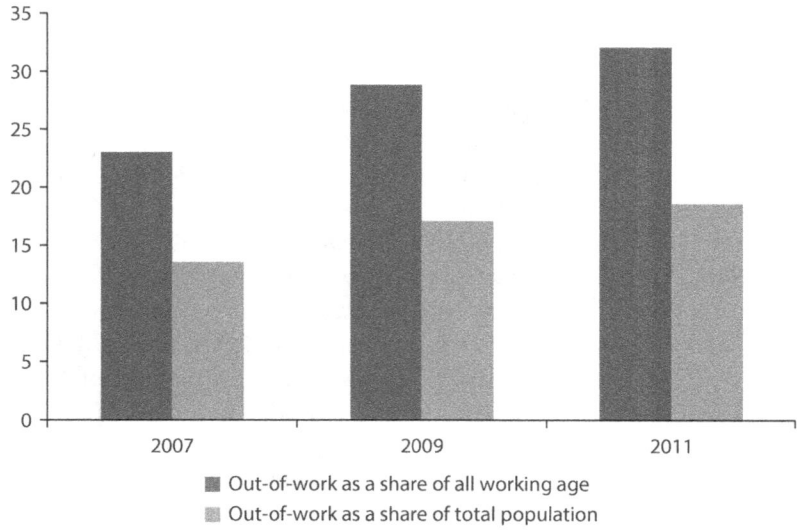

Source: World Bank staff analysis based on EU-SILC.

Figure 7.4 Composition of Working-Age Population (Ages 16–64 Years) by Labor Market Attachment in Lithuania, 2007 and 2011

percent

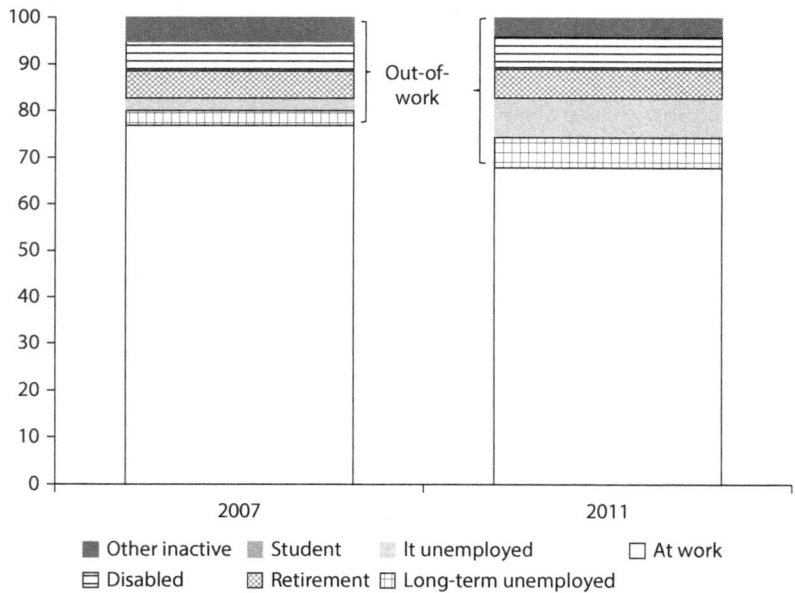

Source: World Bank staff analysis based on EU-SILC.

Figure 7.5 Distribution of Out-of-Work Population in Lithuania, 2007 and 2011
Percent

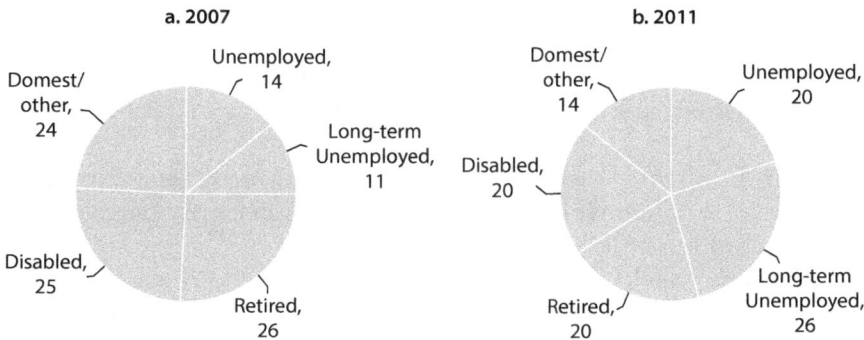

a. 2007

Domest/other, 24

Unemployed, 14

Long-term Unemployed, 11

Disabled, 25

Retired, 26

b. 2011

Domest/other, 14

Unemployed, 20

Disabled, 20

Long-term Unemployed, 26

Retired, 20

Source: World Bank staff analysis based on EU-SILC.

and 2011 relative to the working-age population, but long-term unemployment became relatively more common among Lithuanians, while the share of those at work has been losing ground. While the share of long-term unemployed relative to total working-age people was about 2.5 percent in 2007, the figure had increased to over 8 percent in 2011; similarly, long-term unemployed accounted for 11 percent of the out-of-work population in 2007, but for 26 percent in 2011. The share of total unemployment (long-term and non) among working-age individuals (excluding students[1]) also more than doubled over the period, increasing from 6 percent to 15 percent; jobless individuals accounted for 25 percent of the out-of-work population in 2007, but for 46 percent in 2011.

The developments highlighted above, in particular the increase in the size and relative weight of the out-of-work population and the unemployed, point to a deterioration in the Lithuanian labor market over the last few years. A deeper analysis of the out-of-work population is therefore urgently needed; understanding the composition of these groups is in fact key to ensuring that the right policy measures are taken and that priorities are set in an appropriate manner.

Methodology: Latent Class Analysis

In chapter 1 a general overview of the latent class analysis methodology was presented. This section explains in detail the variables and covariates used to identify classes or groups of out-of-work individuals that are as homogeneous as possible within each class according to a set of observable characteristics, and as distant as possible between classes. The emerging profiles can then be contrasted with the design and targeting of current activation policies, in order to identify the potential gaps and to enhance their design features.

Variable Selection

The definition of latent classes relies on a number of indicator variables to capture different "symptoms" of an overall latent condition (in this case, the typology of joblessness). The challenge in such models is to identify a discrete number of variables that can best explain the heterogeneity of individual outcomes. In this case, two sets of categorical variables were selected: the first set to show the extent of labor market distance and the other to capture some of the main factors that can affect employment on the supply side, such as labor supply conditions (household-level incentives to work and physical ability to work).

- *Distance from labor market:* short-term unemployment, long-term unemployment, (early) retirement, disability, and other inactivity (largely unpaid domestic work).[2]
- *Labor supply conditions:* whether the individual's household has at least one working adult,[3] and perceived limitations on activities due to health problems.[4]

In addition to indicators, the model includes active covariates, which are used to improve the classification of individuals in each class. In this case the active covariates are the demographic variables that are normally used to disaggregate labor market outcomes:

- Age-group category (four groups)
- Gender
- Human capital: the highest educational level achieved
- Degree of urbanization[5]: densely populated, intermediate area, sparsely populated

Once the latent classes have been defined, inactive covariates that were not included in the model can be used to characterize the individuals in each class and the households in which they live. The inactive covariates chosen describe those characteristics that may provide valuable information for the design of tailored policies that address barriers to employment, including income level. They include:

- Household welfare conditions:
  - Income quintile (defined by equivalized disposable household income[6,7])
  - Labor, benefit, and other income as share of total gross household income[8]
  - Working status of the partner
  - Tenure status
  - Household ability to keep dwelling warm
  - Partner's labor income
  - Quintile of partner's labor income
  - Binary variables denoting whether individuals or their households are beneficiaries of any of eight social protection benefits[9]
  - Share of each benefit over the household's gross income
- Household demographics:
  - Household size
  - Household composition

- Binary variable showing whether there are children younger than 6 years old in the household
- Binary variable denoting whether there are three or more children younger than 16 years old in the household
- Children younger than 13 years old in the household receiving child care: all, some, or none of the children
- Older person (65 years of age and older) in the household
- Other individual-level demographics:
  - More refined age groups (eight groups)
  - Marital status
- Individual human capital:
  - More refined highest educational level achieved (six groups)
  - Work experience in years
  - Binary variable for previous work experience
- Household location:
  - Urban/rural status

The analysis relies on cross-sectional as well as panel data from the EU-SILC surveys for 2008–11, which combine individual-level information with household characteristics. The first part of the note presents a cross-sectional analysis for the years 2008, 2009, 2010, and 2011. In particular, the latent class analysis on 2008 data shows the main characteristics of the out-of-work before the global economic crisis hit Lithuania, and thus highlight what could be considered more structural issues of the country's labor market. The 2011 latent class analysis will contrast this initial assessment with more recent developments. The second part of the note exploits longitudinal data between 2008 and 2010[10] to trace the prior labor market status of individuals observed last in 2010 in various classes, and will shed light on the relative persistence in the out-of-work status among different classes of individuals. The set of variables chosen for the cross-section and the longitudinal analysis are slightly different, due to minor differences in the set of variables recorded in each of the two types of data sets.

Main Findings

Out-of-Work Population: Group Profiles
The latent class analysis supports the classification of the out-of-work into eight major groups, some of which have remained stable over time. The groups were named according to their most salient characteristics. Figure 7.6 shows the shares of each of the eight classes identified for the year 2011 while table 7.1 presents their most salient characteristics.

The eight main clusters emerging from the latent class analysis can be characterized as follows (for more detail, see Appendix A for a link to the online-only annexes):

- Cluster 1: *Middle-aged poor rural long-term unemployed.* This group represents 28 percent of the out-of-work population in 2011. The increase of the

Figure 7.6 Classes of Out-of-Work Individuals in Lithuania, 2011

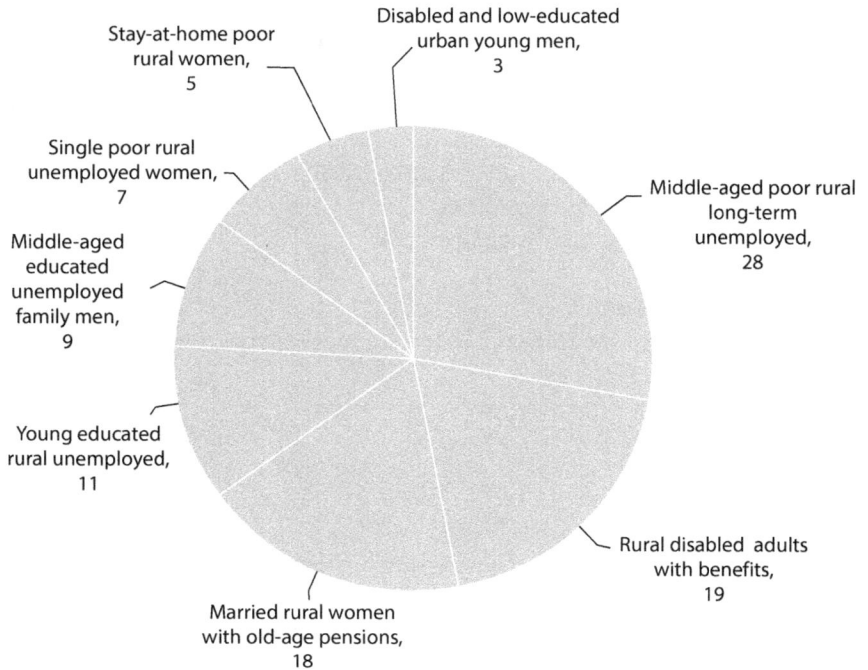

Stay-at-home poor rural women, 5

Disabled and low-educated urban young men, 3

Single poor rural unemployed women, 7

Middle-aged educated unemployed family men, 9

Middle-aged poor rural long-term unemployed, 28

Young educated rural unemployed, 11

Rural disabled adults with benefits, 19

Married rural women with old-age pensions, 18

Source: World Bank staff analysis based on EU-SILC.

out-of-work population from 2007 to 2011 can be mainly ascribed to the increase in the size of this particular cluster of people. Individuals in this group are mostly between 25 and 59 years of age, and more than 60 percent are between 35 and 59. About 29 percent of them are unemployed while, most worryingly, the majority of them (71 percent) are long-term unemployed. Sixty-six percent of the members of this group live in rural areas and they tend to be low-income, as almost 80 percent of them belong to the first two income quintiles. About 45 percent have upper secondary education, and almost 25 percent lower secondary. This group is composed of both men and women (58 and 42 percent, respectively).

- Cluster 2: *Rural disabled adults with benefits.* This group, accounting for 19 percent of the out-of-work population, is almost completely (90 percent) made up of disabled people who receive benefits: 84 percent of them receive a disability benefit; 96 percent receive some sort of benefit. The benefits also appear quite generous, as they comprise over 70 percent of total household income. However, surprisingly, only 42 percent of the individuals in this group claimed to have strong limitations on their daily activities due to health conditions. This cluster comprises few young individuals, as 99 percent are between 25 and 64 years old. Similarly to the first and third groups, the level of education attained is mainly

Table 7.1 Summary Characteristics of Latent Classes of the Out-of-Work Population in Lithuania, 2011

1: Middle-aged poor rural long-term unemployed (28%)

- Almost all are unemployed
- High proportion of long-term unemployed (more than 70% of all the cluster or three-fourths of the unemployed in the cluster)
- 45% have upper secondary education, and almost 25% lower secondary
- Almost 70% live in rural areas
- About 65% are 35–59 years old
- Another 24% are 25–34 years old
- Almost 80% are in the first two income quintiles
- Almost 60% are male

2: Rural disabled adults with benefits (19%)

- 90% report their labor market status as disabled
- 85% are 35–59 years old
- Another 11% are 60–64 years old
- 75% reside in rural areas
- 84% receive disability benefits
- 96% receive some benefit
- Benefits make up almost 75% of total household income

3: Married rural women with old-age pensions (18%)

- 99% are retired
- 91% are between 60 and 64 years old
- Almost 70% are female
- 65% live in rural areas
- 60% are married and another 20% are widowed
- 77% of them receive old-age benefits
- 85% live in a household without children
- They mostly live in small-sized households
- Benefits make up almost 75% of total household income

4: Young educated rural unemployed (11%)

- 77% are unemployed
- All are 16–35 years old
- 53% are 16–24 years old
- Almost 60% are single
- 44% have tertiary education and 10% postsecondary
- Almost 90% of them live in a household with a working adult

5: Middle-aged educated unemployed family men (9%)

- 66% are unemployed
- 61% are male
- Two-thirds live in rural areas
- 99% are 35–59 years old
- 30% have tertiary education
- 87% are married
- 81% have a working spouse
- 70% receive some benefit
- Almost 60% live in a household with 1 or 2 kids

6: Single poor rural unemployed women (7%)

- 40% are unemployed and 60% are engaged in domestic activities
- None live in a household with a working adult
- 62% are female
- 86% live in rural areas
- 80% are in the first two income quintiles
- 60% are single, divorced, or widowed
- Almost a third have no previous work experience

7: Stay-at-home poor rural women (5%)

- 99% are engaged in domestic activities
- All are female
- All live in a household with a working adult
- 83% live in rural areas
- 80% are 25–55 years old
- 45% are 25–34 years old
- 60% have upper secondary education, 20% postsecondary
- 90% are in the bottom three income quintiles
- 80% receive some benefit, 70% child benefits

8: Disabled and low-educated urban young men (3%)

- 95% report their labor market status as disabled
- 95% suffer from severe disabilities
- 99% are younger than 34 years old
- More than 80% are male
- About 77% live in urban areas
- Almost all receive benefits; 81% receive disability benefits
- 96% are single

Source: World Bank staff analysis based on EU-SILC.
Note: Percentages in parentheses following the group names refer to the share of the total out-of-work population. "Years of work experience" refer only to those individuals who have worked before. "Dependent children" include children younger than 18 years of age and household members ages 18–24 years who are economically inactive and living with at least one parent. "Working adult" refers to adults ages 25 years and older. For this report's purposes, we define the at-risk-of-poverty rate as the relative risk of being in the first quintile of the income distribution. The reference period for income reported in EU-SILC surveys is the year preceding the survey year.

secondary (71 percent), and most live in rural areas (76 percent). The individuals in this cluster are in the middle of the income distribution, as 70 percent of them have an income belonging to the second to fourth quintiles.

- Cluster 3: *Married rural women with old-age pensions.* This third cluster, which makes up 18 percent of the out-of-work population, is composed almost exclusively of retired individuals, of whom almost 70 percent are women. More than 90 percent of those in this group are between 60 and 64 years old, and almost 55 percent belong to the first two quintiles of the income distribution. Most of them live in rural areas (65 percent) and hold relatively high levels of education (71 percent of them have completed secondary or tertiary education). They are mostly married (61 percent) and about 40 percent of them live with a retired spouse. Most of them receive generous (75 percent of total household income) benefits; 91 percent receive at least one assistance benefit, 77 percent receive some form of old-age payment, and 13 percent receive survivor benefits.

- Cluster 4: *Young educated rural unemployed.* This group, which emerged in 2011 probably as a result of the crisis, includes 11 percent of the out-of-work population and comprises young individuals, as all are between 16 and 35, and 53 percent are between 16 and 24. Most of the individuals in this cluster are unemployed (45 percent), while 22 percent are long-term unemployed. However, this group tends to be quite evenly distributed among income quintiles. Almost two out of three live in rural areas and almost 90 percent of them live in a household with a working adult. Compared to the first three groups, individuals in this class have a relatively high level of education: 44 percent have completed tertiary education and 44 percent have completed upper or postsecondary. When it comes to their marital status, almost 60 percent of them are single. While family and social exclusion benefits make up 13 percent of their household income, unemployment benefits only contribute 2 percent.

- Cluster 5: *Middle-aged educated unemployed family men.* This group, of which 66 percent are unemployed, makes up 9 percent of the out-of-work population and includes a majority of men (61 percent). Twenty-two percent of those in this cluster are long-term unemployed and two-thirds live in rural areas. Almost all of them are between 35 and 59 and, like cluster 4, they are well educated: 64 percent have completed upper or postsecondary education and 30 percent tertiary. Their income status does not appear to be very informative, as this groups is relatively evenly distributed among quintiles. Also, most of them live in households composed of two adults and one or more children (60 percent). Interestingly, 70 percent receive social assistance benefits and 45 percent receive child or family benefits.

- Cluster 6: *Single poor rural unemployed women.* This group accounts for 7 percent of out-of-work individuals and the majority are women (62 percent). Forty percent are unemployed while 60 percent are engaged in domestic activities. They are of prime working age, as 90 percent are between 25 and 59 years old. Similarly to most of the other clusters, they mainly live in rural areas (86 percent); however, more than a third hold only a primary education, and 70 percent are in the first income quintile. About 60 percent are either single, divorced, or widowed, and around one-fifth have no prior work experience. Importantly, more than 70 percent receive at least one benefit, and 64 percent of the total household income of the individuals in this group is derived from benefits.

- Cluster 7: *Stay-at-home poor rural women.* Members of this cluster, covering about 5 percent of the out-of-work population, are all women, engaged in domestic activities and predominantly living in rural areas (83 percent). Eighty percent are between 25 and 54 years old, but 40 percent are between 25 and 34. Almost all women in this group have at least a secondary education (15 percent at the lower level, 59 percent at the upper-secondary level, and 19 percent at the postsecondary level). About 65 percent of them fall in the first two income quintiles. All of them live in households with a working adult, and more than 80 percent in households with at least one child. Like Cluster 1, though, the other important characteristic of this group is its low income level: 66 percent of them have incomes in the two lowest quintiles of the income distribution. Eighty percent receive at least one benefit, and 70 percent receive family/child benefits. The main difference between this cluster and the previous one lies in two variables: first, this cluster is made up exclusively of women, as opposed to Group 6, which does include some men (38 percent). Second, this cluster includes stay-at-home women, while the previous one includes unemployed individuals as well.

- Cluster 8: *Disabled and low-educated urban young men.* The last group emerged in 2011. It represents 3 percent of the out-of-work population. It is composed of single men between 16 and 34 years old, almost all of whom are extremely disabled. Almost all are single and live with other family members. Unlike the other seven groups, the individuals in this cluster live mostly in urban areas (77 percent) and have very low levels of education (only one-third have completed at least lower secondary school), but seem to live in better-off households (as almost 60 percent of these households belong to the top two income quintiles). In addition, 96 percent of this group have never worked. As said previously, their main characteristic is that most are disabled and, as opposed to cluster 3, 94 percent of them claim to suffer from strong limitations on daily activity due to health conditions. Even though almost all individuals in this group receive at least one benefit, just 81 percent of individuals in this group receive a disability benefit, as opposed to 84 percent of individuals in cluster 2.

Tables 7.2 and 7.3 present the main characteristics of each group in 2011. For the complete table, including inactive covariates, see Appendix A for a link to the online-only annexes.

Table 7.2 Latent Classes of the Out-of-Work Population in Lithuania: Indicators, 2011

	All out of work	1. Middle-aged poor rural long-term unemployed	2. Rural disabled adults with benefits	3. Married rural women with old-age pensions	4. Young educated rural unemployed	5. Middle-aged educated unemployed family men	6. Single poor rural unemployed women	7. Stay-at-home poor rural women	8. Disabled and low-educated urban young men
Cluster size (%)	100	28	19	18	11	9	7	5	3
Population	609,134	173,299	113,969	111,715	67,187	52,446	44,345	30,639	15,472
Indicators (%)									
Labor market attachment									
Unemployed	20	29	1	0	45	44	39	0	0
Long-term unemployed	26	71	8	0	22	22	1	1	0
Retired	19	0	0	99	0	15	0	0	0
Disabled	20	0	89	1	2	9	0	0	95
Other inactive	14	0	1	0	32	10	60	99	5
Self-assessed physical capacity									
Strongly limited	13	2	42	12	0	1	0	0	94
None/limited	87	98	58	88	100	99	100	100	6
At least one working adult in household									
No	52	61	67	68	13	2	100	1	40
Yes	48	39	33	32	87	98	0	99	60

Source: World Bank staff analysis based on EU-SILC.

Table 7.3 Latent Classes of Out-of-Work Population in Lithuania: Active Covariates, 2011

	All out of work	Middle-aged poor rural long-term unemployed	Rural disabled adults with benefits	Married rural women with old-age pensions	Young educated rural unemployed	Middle-aged educated unemployed family men	Single poor rural unemployed women	Stay-at-home poor rural women	Disabled and low-educated urban young men
Cluster size	**100**	**28**	**19**	**18**	**11**	**9**	**7**	**5**	**3**
Population	**609,134**	**173,299**	**113,969**	**111,715**	**67,187**	**52,446**	**44,345**	**30,639**	**15,472**
Active covariates (%)									
Age group									
16–24 years	12	11	1	0	53	0	7	16	52
25–34 years	18	24	3	0	47	0	32	40	46
35–59 years	51	65	85	9	0	99	58	44	0
60–64 years	19	1	11	91	0	1	3	0	1
Gender									
Male	48	58	52	32	48	61	38	0	81
Female	52	42	48	68	52	39	62	100	19
Education level									
Primary	23	27	22	29	0	2	35	18	67
Secondary	63	67	71	58	44	64	50	78	3
Tertiary	14	5	5	13	44	30	11	3	4
Never studied before/ illiterate/NA*		1	2	1	12	4	5	1	26
Urban or rural									
Urban	31	34	24	35	37	34	14	17	77
Rural	69	66	76	65	63	66	86	83	23

Source: World Bank staff analysis based on EU-SILC.
*NA = not available.

Table 7.4 Classes of Out-of-Work Population in Lithuania as a Percentage of Total Out-of-Work Population, 2007, 2009, and 2011

percent

Name of cluster	2007	2009	2011
Married rural women with old-age pensions	25	17	18
Middle-aged educated unemployed family men	8	28	9
Young educated rural unemployed	n.a.	n.a.	11
Stay-at-home (or unemployed) rural married-with-kids young women	13	6	n.a.
Rural disabled adults with benefits	21	17	19
Single poor rural unemployed women	9	14	7
Middle-aged poor rural long-term unemployed	11	5	28
Middle-aged mostly urban low-educated low-income (mostly long-term) unemployed men	4	n.a.	n.a.
Stay-at-home poor rural women	n.a.	n.a.	5
Unemployed urban young women	n.a.	9	n.a.
Stay-at-home (or unemployed) well-educated rural married-with-kids young women	9	n.a.	n.a.
Stay-at-home low-income young women with children	n.a.	4	n.a.
Disabled and low-educated urban young men	n.a.	n.a.	3
Total	100	100	100

Source: World Bank staff analysis based on EU-SILC.
Note: n.a. = not applicable.

The composition of the classes has experienced considerable changes over the last few years. Table 7.4 and figure 7.7 show the evolutions of the classes from 2007 to 2011, as a share of total out-of-work population and in absolute numbers. As mentioned before, one important development between 2007 and 2011 was the noticeable increase in the size of the out-of-work population, from fewer than 460,000 to just under 610,000 individuals. Furthermore, it is interesting how some of the clusters identified by analyzing the 2011 data could also be (broadly speaking) identified in the 2007 and 2009 data, although the relative sizes of such clusters might have changed. In particular:

- The most striking and worrying change is the increase in the size of the *middle-aged poor rural long-term unemployed* group, the size of which more than tripled in absolute numbers over the period (going from just over 50,000 individuals to almost 175,000); this cluster represented 11 percent of the out-of-work population in 2007, but 28 percent in 2011. Interestingly, in 2011 this group was composed of men and women in almost equal shares, while by 2009, 86 percent were men.
- A further significant and negative development was the increase in the number of *middle-aged educated unemployed family men.* This group represented only 8 percent of the working population in 2008, but reached 28 percent in 2009, before returning to 9 percent in 2011. In absolute terms, this group increased from over 36,000 in 2007 to 52,000 in 2011.

Figure 7.7 Classes of Out-of-Work Population in Lithuania, 2007, 2009, and 2010

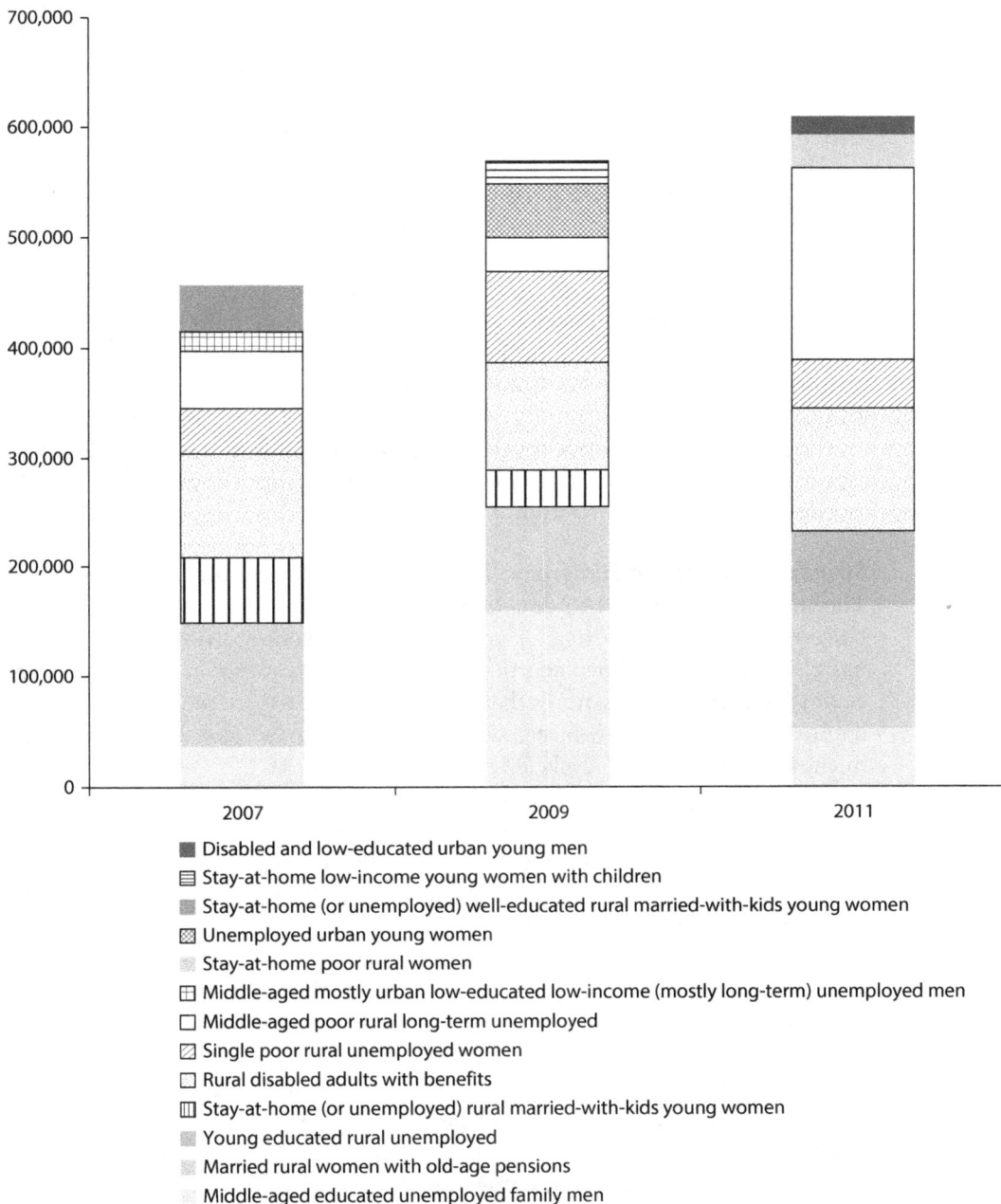

■ Disabled and low-educated urban young men
▤ Stay-at-home low-income young women with children
▨ Stay-at-home (or unemployed) well-educated rural married-with-kids young women
▩ Unemployed urban young women
▨ Stay-at-home poor rural women
⊞ Middle-aged mostly urban low-educated low-income (mostly long-term) unemployed men
☐ Middle-aged poor rural long-term unemployed
▨ Single poor rural unemployed women
☐ Rural disabled adults with benefits
⫼ Stay-at-home (or unemployed) rural married-with-kids young women
▦ Young educated rural unemployed
▨ Married rural women with old-age pensions
  Middle-aged educated unemployed family men

Source: World Bank staff analysis based on EU-SILC.

- The group of *single poor rural unemployed women* also witnessed significant changes over the period, increasing from fewer than 42,000 individuals in 2007 to 82,000 in 2009, but decreasing all the way back to 44,000 by 2011. Somewhat encouragingly, this group's share of the out-of-work population was lower in 2011 than in 2007.
- The cluster of *young educated unemployed* emerged only in 2011, possibly as a result of the crisis. This group was not present in the data from previous years, but represented 11 percent of the out-of-work population in 2011 (67,000 individuals).
- The group of *rural disabled adults with benefits* has been generally stable over the years in relative terms, but has increased in absolute terms. This group represented 21 percent of the out-of-work population in 2007, 17 percent in 2009 and 19 percent in 2011. However, the total size of this group increased from 96,000 in 2007 to 114,000 in 2011.
- The well-established group of *married rural women with old-age pensions* did not change much in absolute terms. The absolute number of individuals in this group has in fact been stable over the period at about 110,000; however, its relative size has declined from 25 percent in 2007 to 18 percent in 2011.

Structural Aspects and Emerging Trends in the Profiles of the Out-of-Work

The analysis of the EU-SILC data using latent class methodology reveal the existence of a number of clusters or groups of out-of-work individuals that can be more or less clearly defined and that differ from one another in important characteristics. Some of the features that we have highlighted are more permanent in nature, while others can most likely be ascribed to the global downturn and might therefore be more cyclical.

On the structural side, first and foremost, our analysis shows that young Lithuanians have fared—and fare—particularly badly in the labor market. As per the graphs above, the unemployment rate in the 15- to 24-year-old cohort was 22 percent in 2013, after peaking at more than 39 percent among males and 32 percent among females in 2010. Although youth unemployment in Lithuania is worrisome, it is in line with the average unemployment rate in the EU-28 among young people in 2013 (23 percent). At the same time, according to Eurostat data, Lithuanian youth display much worse employment rates than their European counterparts. Employment rates in Lithuania among those ages 15–25 years peaked at 27 percent in 2008, before dropping to 18 percent in 2010 and recovering somewhat to 25 percent in 2013; Latvia and Estonia, on the other hand, closed 2013 at 30 and 32 percent, respectively, after peaking at 37 percent in 2008. Similarly, employment rates in the average EU-28 or euro area country are currently 7 percentage points higher than the Lithuanian ones. Finally, as figure 7.8 shows, labor force participation among youth ages 15–24 years is also considerably lower in Lithuania relative to the rest of the European Union; in 2013, youth labor force participation rates reached 30 percent in Lithuania, one of the lowest rates in the European Union, and about 10 percentage points lower than countries such as Latvia and Estonia, and the EU average.

Figure 7.8 Labor Force Participation Rate, Ages 15–24 Years, European Countries, 2013
percent

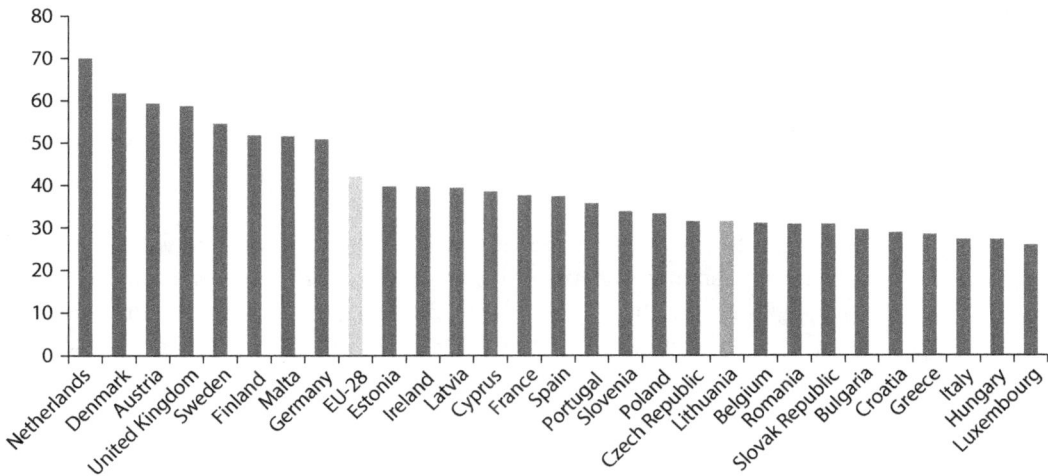

Source: Eurostat, EU-LFS.

Second, disabled individuals have been and will continue to be a sizeable portion of the out-of-work population, and population aging will only increase the expenditures on disability benefits. The cluster of *rural disabled adults with benefits* included almost 114,000 people in 2011, while a second cluster that emerged in the same year of *disabled and low-educated urban young men* accounted for another 15,000 individuals. In 2007, the cluster of *rural disabled adults with benefits* accounted for slightly more than 96,000 people. EU-SILC data also show that those classified as disabled, while decreasing as a share of the out-of-work population from 2007 to 2011 (from 25 to 20 percent), have actually increased in absolute terms, from about 114,000 in 2007 to almost 124,000 in 2011 (a 6 percent increase in four years). Furthermore, disabled Lithuanians tend to be relatively old (85 percent of them were more than 35 years old in 2011 according to EU-SILC data, and 65 percent more than 45). As many as 25 percent of them have no previous work experience, and thereby face high (and growing) impediments to entering or reentering the labor market. Finally, the same data reveal that approximately 24 percent of all the out-of-work population, or about 147,000 individuals, receive disability benefits, up from 123,000 people in 2007 (a 20 percent increase over four years). These patterns are somewhat concerning given the rapid aging that the Lithuanian society will undergo in the coming decades; Eurostat data show that the share of Lithuanian residents over the age of 65 is currently 16 percent of the total population, but this number will double by 2060. At the same time, the number of working-age people will decline from 67 percent to 55 percent. The most recent census also shows that over the last decade the country has lost 13 percent of its population and, using Eurostat data once again, by 2060 only 2.76 million people will likely live in the country, down from 3.29 million in 2011. The combination of increasing numbers of disabled individuals and the aging of the population will likely increase the expenditures on disability benefits that the government will have to undertake in the coming decades. Figure 7.9 shows that expenditure on disability benefits as a share of GDP, while lower than the EU average, has already increased between 2008 and 2010, going from 1.6 percent to 1.8 percent.

Third, a number of negative developments can be observed within the unemployed category, all of which pose significant and urgent challenges for policy makers. In particular:

- As previously noted, one of the most striking developments between 2007 and 2011 is the dramatic increase in the size of the *middle-aged poor rural long-term unemployed* group, the size of which more than tripled in absolute numbers over the period. And while part of this increase can almost certainly be ascribed to the global downturn, the data confirm that the existence of a (depending on the business cycle) more or less sizeable pool of low-income unemployed adults is a structural feature of the Lithuanian labor market, and one that needs to be dealt with urgently as these individuals and their families are probably at high risk of poverty.

- A further concerning development is the significant increase in the size of the *middle-aged educated unemployed family men* group. With about 94 percent of the individuals in this cluster having a secondary education or higher, this group of people probably has a relatively high skills endowment and should therefore be another priority when it comes to activation policies.

Figure 7.9 Expenditures on Disability Benefits as a Share of GDP in Europe, 2008 and 2010
percent

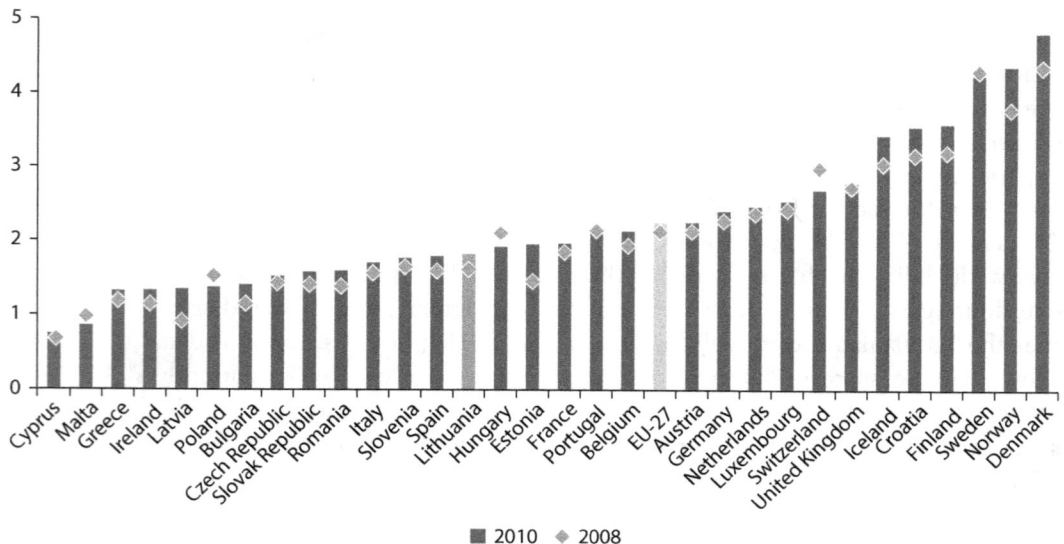

■ 2010 ◆ 2008

Source: Eurostat, EU-LFS.

- The global downturn is likely at least partly responsible for the rise of a group of *young educated rural unemployed*, a cluster that did not exist in previous years but absorbed about 11 percent of the out-of-work population in 2011. With about one-third of them having no prior work experience and with 90 percent having secondary education, facilitating the transition of this group into the labor market is key to the long-term well-being of these individuals.

- The downturn is also probably responsible for at least part of the large increase in the share and number of long-term unemployed in Lithuania. Across all clusters of unemployed individuals, an extremely worrying phenomenon was the growing share of individuals in long-term unemployment over the 2007–11 period. As shown in the first section, the absolute numbers of those who have been looking for a job for over 12 months have also more than doubled. Long-term unemployment not only imposes a significant financial burden on households, but also affects the long-term health status of jobseekers, negatively affects government finances, and results in a lower overall long-term level of skills among a country's workforce, with permanent negative effects on productivity (Katz 2010). Once more, addressing the plight of the long-term unemployed should be among the policy priorities for Lithuanian policy makers.

Out-of-Work Population: Group Profiles from Longitudinal Analysis

Finally, by looking at longitudinal EU-SILC data for the period 2008–10, one can better understand the in-cluster dynamics and notice other movements in the labor market. EU-SILC allows the tracking of a certain number of out-of-work individuals between 2008 and 2010. Of course, because of the difficulties in tracking people across time, the sample size of the panel data set is considerably smaller than the cross-section surveys; the 2008–10 longitudinal data set includes 705 observations, as opposed to the 2,300 observations for 2011. However, the panel data confirm the existence of some latent classes that emerged in the cross-sectional analysis. And even though the smaller sample size forces us to reduce the number of clusters identified, some clear patterns emerge. Through longitudinal data five classes can be defined, all of which can also be found in the cross-section data sets:

- *Middle-aged low income unemployed* (34 percent)
- *Disabled* (21 percent)
- *Married rural women with pensions* (18 percent)
- *Stay-at-home or unemployed rural poor wives* (16 percent)
- *Young rural unemployed men* (11 percent)

Annex 3 (see Appendix A for a link to the online-only annexes) gives the full statistical description of the latent classes, while table 7.5 summarizes the key features of each group.

Table 7.5 Longitudinal Analysis: Summary Characteristics of Latent Classes of Out-of-Work Population in Lithuania, 2010

1: Middle-aged low-income unemployed (34%)

- Almost 90% are unemployed
- Over 90% are 25–59 years old; 70% are 35–59 years old
- 50% are in the first income quintile, and another 20% in the second

2: Disabled (21%)

- Over 95% report their labor market status as disabled
- Half have report limited capacity to work and the other half report strongly limited capacity to work
- Almost 80% are 35–59 years old; 10% are 25–34 years old

3: Married rural women with pensions (18%)

- Almost 90% are retired
- All are 60–64 years old
- Three out of four are female
- Two out of three live in rural areas
- Almost 95% receive some benefit, and more than 80% receive old-age benefits

4: Stay-at-home or unemployed rural poor wives (16%)

- 71% are inactive and another 15% are unemployed
- Three out of four live in a household with at least one working adult
- Almost 85% are female
- Over 85% reside in rural areas
- One-third are 25–34 years old; 90% are 25–59 years old
- Over 60% are married
- Almost 60% belong to the poorest two income quintiles

5: Young rural unemployed men (11%)

- Almost 90% are unemployed
- 93% are male
- Almost 95% live in a household with at least one working adult
- Almost 50% are 16–24 years old; 15% are 25–34 years old
- Three out of four live in rural areas
- Almost 60% are single
- Over 70% belong to the top three income quintiles

Source: World Bank staff analysis based on EU-SILC.
Note: "Years of work experience" refer only to those individuals who have worked before. "Dependent children" include children younger than 18 years of age and household members ages 18–24 years who are economically inactive and living with at least one parent. "Working adult" refers to adults ages 25 years and older.

An further advantage of the panel analysis is to provide information on the movement of individuals in and out of certain clusters and in and out of jobs between 2008 and 2010. Table 7.6 presents the flow of individuals into the different clusters as of 2010 according to their labor market status in 2008. The most interesting column is the one for those employed in 2008 because it generally points to a lot of movement out of employment and into one of the out-of-work statuses. According to the panel data, among those categorized as *middle-aged low-income unemployed* in 2010, 53 percent were employed in 2008; similarly, 45 percent of those falling into the *young rural unemployed men* category were gainfully employed in 2008, and 39 percent of *stay-at-home or unemployed rural poor wives* in 2010 were working in 2008. On the other hand, only 4 percent of those employed in 2010 were unemployed in 2008. Table 7.7 also shows a considerable amount of movement from being out-of-work to employment: 46 percent of those unemployed in 2008 were employed by 2010, while 53 percent of those engaged in domestic activities in 2008 had transitioned to work by 2010. Puzzlingly, these data also show that 63 percent of those retired in 2008 had moved back into employment by 2010.

Table 7.6 Lithuania: Composition of 2010 Clusters Based on 2008 Labor Market Status (Column Percentages)

| Cluster | Working-age population in 2010 | Labor market status in 2008 | | | | | |
		Unemployed	Retired	Disabled	Other inactive	Employed	Total
1	Middle-aged low-income unemployed	21	9	3	14	53	100
2	Disabled	10	12	43	6	29	100
3	Married rural women with pensions	5	35	17	11	32	100
4	Stay-at-home or unemployed rural poor wives	8	9	3	41	39	100
5	Young rural unemployed men	4	9	9	33	45	100
NC	Employed	4	9	2	8	78	100
	Total	6	11	6	10	67	100

Source: World Bank staff analysis based on EU-SILC.
Note: Students ages 16–24 years who were inactive or unemployed are excluded from the sample. Numbers referred to in the text appear shaded in gray.

Table 7.7 Lithuania: Composition of 2010 Clusters Based on 2008 Labor Market Status (Row Percentages)

| Cluster | Working-age population in 2010 | Labor market status in 2008 | | | | | |
		Unemployed	Retired	Disabled	Other inactive	Employed	Total
1	Middle-aged low-income unemployed	30	7	4	11	7	8
2	Disabled	13	9	56	5	3	8
3	Married rural women with pensions	4	15	13	5	2	5
4	Stay-at-home or unemployed rural poor wives	5	3	2	16	2	4
5	Young rural unemployed men	2	3	5	10	2	3
NC	Employed	46	63	20	53	83	72
	Total	100	100	100	100	100	100

Source: World Bank staff analysis based on EU-SILC.
Note: Students ages 16–24 years who were inactive or unemployed are excluded from the sample. Numbers referred to in the text appear shaded in gray.

From Profiling to Activation

Activation and Inclusion Policies in Lithuania

Active labor market policies (ALMPs) are implemented by a variety of actors in Lithuania, but the main institution in charge of ALMPs and public employment services (PES) is the Lithuanian Labor Exchange (LLE). Established in 1991, the LLE operates under the Ministry of Social Welfare and Labor and was restructured in 2010 in response to the economic downturn. The LLE currently comprises one central office and 10 territorial labor exchange offices (TLEs)—down from 46 previously—that serve between three and seven municipalities each (and for a total of 60 municipalities). The LLE maintains the overall responsibility for ALMPs and supervises the activities of the 10 TLEs, which in turn provide employment services and implement labor policies for residents and employers at the district, municipality, and sub-district level (EC 2013b).

The range of ALMPs and employment services is wide. The LLE, in collaboration with local partners and other ministries implements several ALMPs (Eurostat 2010; ILO 2011). In particular:

- *Supported Employment Programs/Measures.* These include subsidized employment programs, support for the acquisition of professional skills, public works programs for the unemployed or employees of firms in financial difficulties, job-rotation or job-sharing schemes, and client services (such as group counseling, vocational counseling, and so forth).
- *Vocational Training Schemes* in the form of benefits for both employers and employees, workplace trainings, institutional trainings, support for apprenticeships, and so on.
- *Support Schemes for Job Creation,* such as subsidies for job creation, support schemes for self-employment, start-up incentives, and local initiatives for employment (such as business development plans for firms and job-placement subsidies).
- *Local Mobility and Commuting Support Schemes,* such as reimbursement of work-related relocation, accommodation, or transportation expenses.
- *New Measures* which have also been implemented in the recent past include employability barometers, employment programs for unemployed individuals 55 years of age and older, first employment programs for youth, and skills upgrade programs for the long-term unemployed.

At the same time, several passive measures, such as unemployment or early retirement benefits, are also available. These include full and partial unemployment benefits, redundancy compensation, bankruptcy compensation, and conditional and unconditional early retirement benefits. Importantly, in 2012, an innovative measure to prevent poverty traps and to give the long-term unemployed an extra incentive to take up employment was introduced in the form of an extra benefit payment for long-term unemployed individuals returning to work. This measure extends six months of benefits to individuals that transition from long-term unemployment to employment and do not earn more than double the monthly minimum wage (Eurostat 2010; ILO 2011).

Lithuania spends little on labor market policies (LMPs) relative to other OECD countries, although the crisis resulted in a notable increase in such expenditures, mostly due to the spike in unemployment and early retirement benefits. As figure 7.10 shows, in 2011 Lithuania spent little more than half a percentage point of GDP on LMPs, almost half of which was devoted to unemployment benefits and early retirement; the average OECD country, on the other hand, spent over 1.4 percent of GDP on LMPs, almost three times the Lithuanian figure. Looking at the evolution of such expenditure items between 2003 and 2011, it is immediately clear that the downturn was associated with a massive

Figure 7.10 Labor Market Policy (LMP) Spending in Lithuania as a Share of GDP
percent

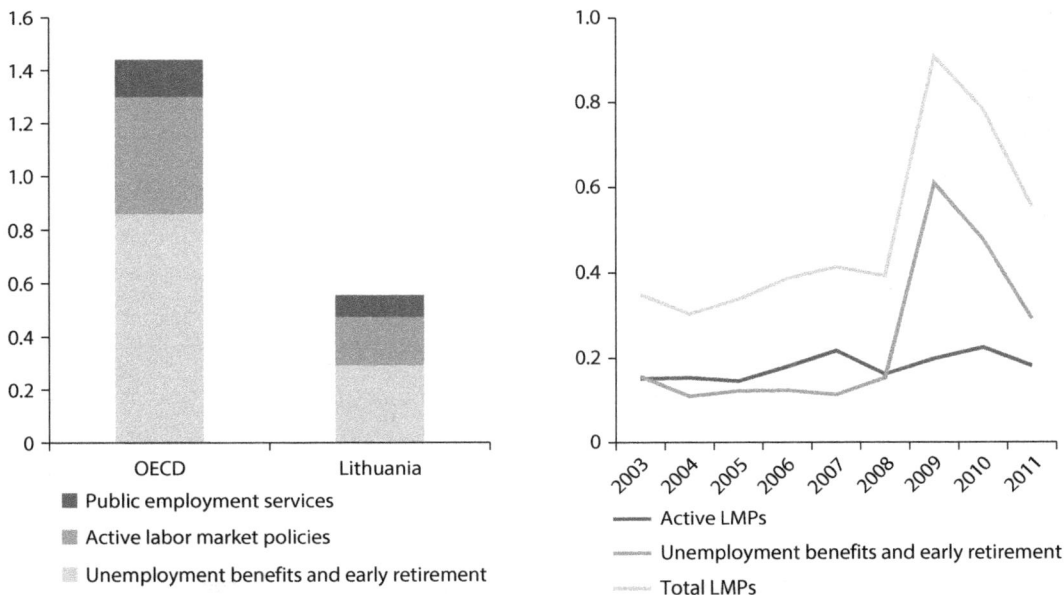

Public employment services
Active labor market policies
Unemployment benefits and early retirement

——— Active LMPs
——— Unemployment benefits and early retirement
·········· Total LMPs

Source: Eurostat, OECD.

increase in unemployment and early retirement benefits. In the pre-crisis period, total LMP expenditure ranged between 0.3 and 0.4 percent of national GDP, while unemployment and early retirement benefits absorbed about 0.1–0.12 percent of GDP; by 2009, at the peak of the crisis, the share of such spending had doubled and then tripled, reaching 0.9 and 0.6 percent of GDP, respectively. In 2012, unemployment and early retirement benefits as a share of GDP were still twice the pre-crisis level (Eurostat and OECD data). It should be noted as positive that Lithuania did not respond to the crisis with a decrease in relative activation spending; the share of ALMPs in GDP remained almost constant at about 0.2 percent GDP.

The large increase in the share of total LMP costs that went toward unemployment benefits was matched by a dramatic rise in the number of beneficiaries. As figure 7.11 shows, while the 2006–11 period did not witness an increase in the number of ALMP beneficiaries, the downturn was clearly linked to a spike in the number of those receiving unemployment or early retirement benefits, with almost 50,000 individuals joining the ranks of the beneficiaries between 2008 and 2009 alone.

More particularly, while the level of ALMP spending has remained relatively low and constant with the crisis, the composition and the source of such expenditures have changed. As depicted in figure 7.12, spending on training fell quite sharply, whereas spending on direct job creation and employment incentives increased (Eurostat 2010). In addition to the new composition, the crisis also

Figure 7.11 Labor Market Policy (LMP) Beneficiaries in Lithuania, 2006–10
thousands

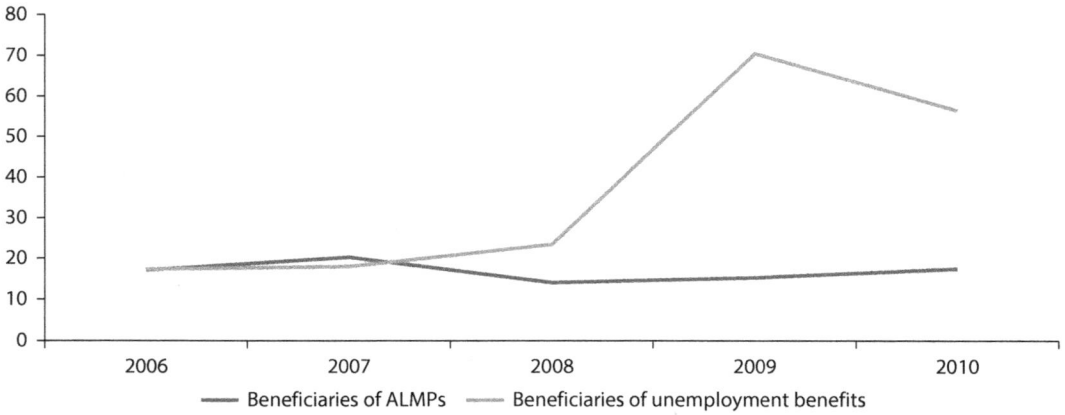

Source: Eurostat, OECD.
Note: ALMP = Active labor market policy.

Figure 7.12 Composition of Spending on ALMPs in Lithuania, 2008 and 2011
percent

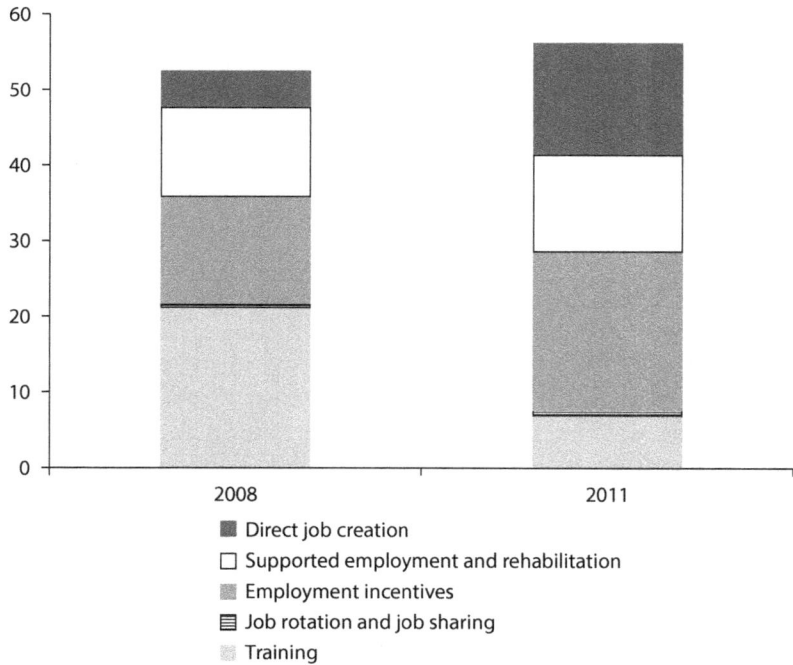

Source: Eurostat, OECD.

led to a change in the financing source of inclusion measures: after 2009, the main funding source became the EU structural funds, which currently support mainly social enterprises and employment programs for people with disabilities and public works programs, as well as projects that provide vocational training, create subsidized employment, and facilitate job rotation and territorial mobility.

Activation Priority, Activation Type, and Benefit Receipt by Group

In further considering labor market integration, an assessment of the priorities and potentials of the identified groups needs to be undertaken. Given the cautious increase in nominal resources for activation programs, further prioritization of intervention is all the more important. After a first step ("activation priority") of prioritizing the intervention along activation need and activation potential, a second step ("activation type") will attempt to classify the groups according to the kind of activation intervention needed, depending on social or labor market barriers to be overcome. Lastly, as a third step, information on *household income composition* of the different groups will be used to assess potential cross-dependencies of the benefit system with the labor market status and activation approaches.

Activation Priorities

Table 7.8 gives an overview of the identified inactive classes and their respective activation need and activation potential. The total number of persons estimated in these clusters was about 610,000 in 2011, representing 32 percent of the working-age (16–64-year-old) population of Lithuania in 2011.

In the table, "activation need" refers to a group's level of need for inclusion in the labor market in order to achieve income and reduce or end poverty. "Activation potential" describes that group's ability or motivation to be included in the labor market. High activation need could be driven by high poverty risk (as in the case of the *middle-aged poor rural long-term unemployed*), whereas high activation potential could be driven by previous work experience or a relatively

Table 7.8 Activation Need and Potential of Different Clusters in Lithuania

Share % (2011)	Cluster	Activation need	Activation potential	Priority for action
27	Middle-aged poor rural long-term unemployed	High	Medium	High
19	Married rural women with old-age pensions	Low	Low	Low
18	Rural disabled adults with benefits	Low	Low	Low
11	Young educated rural unemployed	High	High	High
9	Middle-aged educated unemployed family men	High	High	High
7	Single poor rural unemployed women	High	Medium	High
5	Stay-at-home poor rural women	High	Medium	Medium
3	Disabled and low-educated urban young men	Low	Low	Low

Source: World Bank staff analysis and assessment 2014.

good educational base (for example, the *young educated rural unemployed*). Overall priority for action can also be driven by the size of a group.

From this overview, an initial set of priorities arises, with the *middle-aged poor rural long-term unemployed, young educated rural unemployed, middle-aged educated unemployed family men,* and *single poor rural unemployed women* showing the highest priority for activation. Their high priority stems from their relatively large cohort sizes, high or medium activation needs due to high poverty risk, and activation potential due to labor market proximity, given their work history and/ or education level. *Stay-at-home poor rural women* follow close behind, but are classified as slightly lower priority owing to their nondeclared unemployment and the significant share that have at least one working adult in the household. *Rural disabled adults with benefits, married rural women with old-age pensions,* and *disabled and low-educated urban young men* are not prioritized for activation measures or policies due to lower need and potential (many report strongly limited capacity to work).

In light of the significant portion of disability benefits among the out-of-work population, a potential focus of activation could be the group of *rural disabled adults with benefits,* of which 26 percent are younger than 44 years old but for whom disability benefits make up 49 percent of this group's household income (for year 2011). While it might be difficult to activate some of the members of this group because of their disability despite the fact that they are of prime working age, special attention should be given to not increasing the number of younger disability recipients beyond the minimum necessary, and to tightly controlling the inflow into this group.

Figure 7.13 Activation Types of Prioritized Clusters in Lithuania

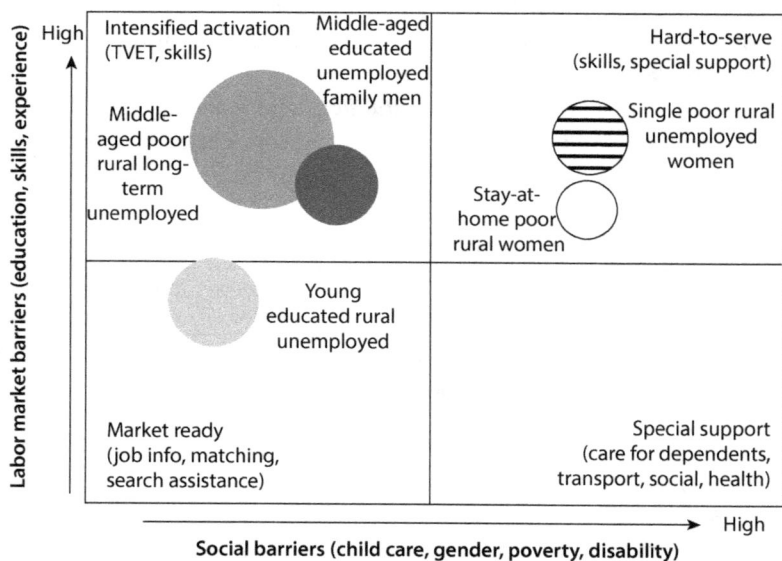

Source: World Bank staff analysis and assessment 2014.
Note: TVET = technical and vocational education and training.

Activation Type

As a second step, the relative severity of labor market or social obstacles to be overcome for labor market integration will serve as an orientation for activation approaches. Figure 7.13 depicts the prioritized clusters along the labor market and social barrier dimensions; the size of the bubbles corresponds to their relative group size.

When mapping the respective barriers for labor market integration faced by the five prioritized groups, we can see that few of the groups face great social barriers. The two groups of rural women have a different connection to the labor market (work experience, education), but both could probably benefit from greater access to social and public services near their homes (for example, child care). Groups of middle-aged unemployed could be supported with standard skill- and mobility-based measures, while the *young educated rural unemployed* could probably benefit from mobility support.

Household Income Composition

When analyzing the 2011 household income of the groups, we can see that three groups have a benefit share of household income that could be an indication of excessive reliance on benefits: 53 percent of the household income of the *middle-aged poor rural long-term unemployed*, 72 percent of the household income of the *rural disabled adults with benefits*, and 64 percent of the household income of the *single poor rural unemployed women* are benefit payments. Other groups (retirees or highly disabled) also have high benefit shares, but this can be seen as a correct function of the social safety net because of legitimate limitations for self-supporting work.

Middle-aged poor rural long-term unemployed adults receive 21 percent of their household income from old-age and disability benefits, although only 1 percent of group members are over the age of 60. This could be an indication that some members of this group are in early retirement. *Single poor rural unemployed women* rely on benefits for 64 percent of their household income, most probably social inclusion benefits for their welfare.

For the interesting phenomenon of the *young educated rural unemployed*, the hypothesis of benefit dependency through intra-family transfers (for example, dependence on old-age pensions or disability pensions of relatives) can most probably be rejected. Only 13 percent of the household income of this group comes from old-age and disability benefits.

Given the overall picture of benefit receipt revealed by EU-SILC data, no actions are needed to counter work disincentives. The pattern of benefits appears to be generally in line with the socioeconomic situation of the specific groups.

Suggestions for Activation Measures and Further Analysis

This section sets out a set of potential activation measures for each of the priority groups. Areas for further policy dialogue are also outlined. The suggestions below should be considered as a starting point for further policy dialogue between the EC, the World Bank, and Lithuania, bearing in mind that the groups identified still possess heterogeneity that may affect the type of support required. Accordingly, these suggestions are not meant to be an exhaustive set of possible activation measures.

It is important to keep in mind that the groups have been derived from EU-SILC data from the year 2011. Since then, general economic development, policy actions by the government of Lithuania, and European Commission country-specific recommendations might have reflected some of these policy suggestions or rendered them obsolete.

Middle-aged poor rural long-term unemployed (28 percent, Priority: High). This is the largest group among the out-of-work in Lithuania, with over 170,000 members. All are unemployed, over 70 percent of them for more than one year. This, together with the fact that 98 percent say they do not have any limitation on capacity to undertake daily activities due to health reasons, confirms their high labor availability and activation potential. Sixty percent of them fall in the lowest income quintile. Age wise, 89 percent of the group is between 25 and 59. The distribution between men and women is somewhat favored towards men, at 58–42 percent, respectively. Primary and secondary education levels dominate in 94 percent of the group. Two-thirds of its members reside in rural areas. Fifty-two percent of the group are single, but the average household size stands at three, which indicates other relatives (17 percent with an adult older than 65 years of age) and children (47 percent with least one child) in the household. Only 14 percent of households have children younger than six years old, indicating reduced caregiving responsibility for children. Potential activation measures for this group include the following:

- *Build activation on previous work experience and skills.* Building on the work experience of 93 percent of this group, training and skill-building offerings should be based on previous experience in the labor market. At the same time, the average age and household composition of this cohort makes many of its members eligible for longer-term intervention such as training in foreign languages or information communication technology, or "second chance" apprenticeship programs. For some of the more intensified training, the educational basis would probably have to be strengthened.
- *Self-employment in and around regional cities.* With the large share of this group living in a rural environment, potential activation measures can focus on self-employment, cooperatives, and services or trades in urban and regional centers. Support for business creation, small loans, or micro-credits could help members of this group engage in self-employed activity.
- *Mobility.* Enabling jobseekers and workers to permanently and temporarily move inside the country could help members of this group. Availability and quality of public transport (not part of specific activation policy, but rather general public infrastructure tasks) and mobility grants for job search or transition into jobs can be possible measures to support this group.

Young educated rural unemployed (11 percent, Priority: High). This group faces the lowest labor market and social barriers, but is also a potential source for further emigration from the country, a fact that has been getting important attention in the years since the start of the financial and economic crisis. In 2011, the group represented about 67,000 members, of which two-thirds were declared as unemployed. None reported any limitations in daily activities due to health reasons, and all of its members are younger than 34 with an almost equal relation between the sexes. An interesting feature of this group is that 44 percent have a tertiary education (making up the relatively low number of unemployed young Lithuanians with a university degree). The majority of the group lives in rural areas (63 percent), is not married (62 percent), and lives in a household of 4.2 average members, hinting at a residence still at the parent(s)' house. The labor share of income in these households is 62 percent and the benefits received appear plausible for the respective socioeconomic situation. Potential activation measures for this group include the following:

- "Top-up" *courses for practical job skills.* Many university graduates lack practical hands-on job skills for a workplace environment. With group intervention training schemes, young jobseekers could be offered supplemental soft and functional skill training on top of their domain knowledge degree.
- *Job fairs.* With formal training apparently not the key labor market barrier for this group, job matching and job information must take center stage. For graduates from rural areas and regional centers, accessibility to job fairs ought to be ensured through "job buses" or other outreach and transportation initiatives.
- *Job placement/internships.* ALMP funds could be used to support the temporary placement of graduates with firms for internships or short-term engagements.
- *Job linkage at university/college.* To prevent joblessness after graduation and to ensure early attachment to companies and industries, universities and colleges need to link students early on to job skills, job search techniques, and work experiences.
- *Mobility support to large cities, near-abroad countries.* With most of the unemployed in this group living in nonurban areas, mobility to potential locations of employment becomes all the more critical. At the same instance, temporary access to subsidized housing for young job starters or "foyer" type housing offerings in larger cities could facilitate the mobility of youths within Lithuania. Promoting labor migration to the near-abroad (while helping temporary migrants to retain their ties to home) can be another measure to prevent critical human capital depreciation at an important time of career formation.

Middle-aged educated unemployed family men (9 percent, Priority: High). Two-thirds of this group are registered as unemployed and despite a disability share of 9 percent, only 1 percent declares to have strong limitations to work. Almost all members of this exclusive 35–59-year-old group live in a household with a working adult, hinting at a supplementary earner model through the household's wife (87 percent are married). A relatively high household income is achieved through mainly labor income (77 percent). Households have relatively few children but 87 percent have a person over 65 years of age. Education level is medium with only 30 percent holding tertiary education. As with all other groups, previous work experience is very high at 94 percent. Potential activation measures for this group include the following:

- *Linkage to previous occupation/industry.* With a working spouse and relatively low risk of poverty (43 percent in bottom two quintiles), this group can be supported in relinking with the qualifications, occupations, and industries that they once gained their work experience in. Reskilling will probably need to update functional skills (languages, communication, writing, information and communications technology).
- *Job clubs and group search.* Building on the life experience of this group, job-search clubs or entrepreneurial start-up groups could be offered to some of this group's members.
- *Self-employment from home.* With spouses of these men employed and providing for the family income, opportunities for self-employment from home or local employment ought to be supported. Medium-sized commuting and mobility support could also be provided to allow for job-uptake in nearby regional centers (or with weekly commute) in towns farther away in case a good-paying job can be secured to cover travel and extra housing costs.

Single poor rural unemployed women (7 percent, Priority: High). Compared to the previous prioritized groups, only a subset (40 percent) of this group is registered as unemployed but no member appears to report strong limitations to taking up work. With none of the households containing a working adult, this group of mainly rural (86 percent) individuals (62/38 percent female/male) has the highest poverty exposure in the sample (81 percent fall in the bottom two quintiles). Owing to the absence or unemployment of spouses, households in this group do not gain income from complementary work uptake. The share of benefit income in total household income is correspondingly very high (64 percent). Members have work experience but 85 percent hold only primary or secondary education. Potential activation measures for this group include the following:

- *Income support coupled with work and training opportunities.* Given the high (and legitimate) benefit share in this group any approach to activation would probably need to be based on the existing income support programs in Lithuania and link them with community work and training offerings. In order to improve the skill and training level of this group, care must be taken to not just operate simple community public works programs.
- *Mobility support and training.* When coupled with training and skill-building, the members of this group could also be helped to find employment in regional or larger cities. This would require additional skill training on job search, basic functional skills, and (temporary) mobility support for transportation or housing.
- *Community employment and self-organization.* Given the recent emphasis on "subsidiarity" and local community decision in social service provision in Lithuania, forms of self-organization for community work and social

entrepreneurship could be promoted with members of this group. Guidance on this would probably need to be provided by PES or municipality staff.

Stay-at-home poor rural women (5 percent, Priority: Medium). This small group among the prioritized shows a similar profile to the previous group of women, with the difference that none of their members is declared as unemployed and all of the households have a working adult in their ranks. The group is 100 percent women and shows a very similar profile to their unemployed "sisters" in terms of rural/urban split, age, and education distribution. The vast majority (79 percent) are married, but poverty exposure is much lower (63 percent in bottom two income quintiles) with 75 percent of spouses working and gaining a decent income (EUR 4,300). The share of labor in household income is correspondingly high (68 percent) and the benefit income can be legitimately attributed to the presence of children (53 percent have children younger than 6 years old) in the household. Potential activation measures for this group include the following:

- *Similar approaches as for the previous group but coupled with child-care offerings and community care provision.* In light of the significant child caregiving responsibility exercised by these households, any approach to further labor market activation must assist these women to combine (part-time) work with child care.

In general, further policy dialogue with the Lithuanian authorities ought to focus on areas that enable the government and its agencies, municipalities, and other labor market actors to better deploy their resources, increase coordination, and improve the staffing and resource situation of services. Some of these areas for future dialogue include:

- *Focus on nonurban areas.* Labor market exclusion in Lithuania is a predominantly rural phenomenon. Almost all of the groups identified in the latent class analysis show a rural share of well over 65 percent, some of the groups prioritized for activation even shares of over 80 percent. Creation of jobs in secondary cities, transport links, and (temporary) mobility support to regional or large centers within Lithuania or toward the neighboring countries must be among the potential answers to this situation
- *Mobility is key.* When considering mobilizing more of its citizens for the labor market, Lithuania ought to make mobility within the country (and to near-abroad countries) a key priority. Being able to connect to regional economic centers or to (temporarily) seek employment in a neighboring country can help to reintegrate the unemployed but also to prevent skill loss and "scarring" among young jobseekers.

In summary, Lithuania could benefit from maintaining a labor market–centric activation approach toward its rural out-of-work population, especially in light of the demographic developments taking place.

Portraits of Labor Market Exclusion • http://dx.doi.org/10.1596/978-1-4648-0539-4

Notes

1. Individuals between 16 and 24 years of age who are out of work and enrolled in education are excluded from the sample; they are considered to be investing in their final stages of human capital formation and therefore also not a particular target group for activation policies. In 2011, this population amounted to about 257,400 individuals, representing 59.5 percent of the total population between 16 and 24 years of age and 30 percent of the total out-of-work population of working age. Individuals enrolled in school who are between 25 and 64 years old are, included in the latent class analysis and grouped under "other inactive." It is important to note that the group of students (older than 24 years) account for less than 1 percent of total population of working age.

2. This variable is constructed using the self-reported current work status in the EU-SILC survey that has four categories: at work, unemployed, retired, and inactive. The unemployed are further classified into short- and long-term based on how long they have been actively looking for a job. The inactive is combined with another question to separate this group into students, disabled, military, and other inactive.

3. In order to construct this variable, individuals ages 25 or older are considered adults.

4. This is a binary variable that takes the value one if an individual answered "yes, strong limitations" to whether they had been hampered in their usual activities because of health problems for at least the last six months. The value is zero if the answer is "yes, limited" or "no, not limited."

5. According to EU-SILC guidelines, dense areas have more than 500 inhabitants per square kilometer, where the total population for the set is at least 50,000 inhabitants. Intermediate areas have more than 100 inhabitants per square kilometer, and either a total population for the set of at least 50,000 inhabitants or a location adjacent to a dense area. The remaining areas are categorized as sparsely populated.

6. The equivalized household income takes into account an equivalence factor to weight the number of household members used in the denominator when calculating household income per capita. The first adult 18 years of age or older has a weight of 1.0, children younger than 14 years old have a weight of 0.3, and other individuals 14 years of age and older have a weight of 0.5. The sum of the weights of all household members is equal to the equivalent household size.

7. Note that income reported in EU-SILC surveys is for the year preceding the survey year.

8. Total household gross income is defined as the sum of: (at the individual level) gross employee cash or near-cash income; company car, gross cash benefits or losses from self-employment (including royalties); unemployment benefits; old-age benefits; survivor benefits; sickness benefits; disability benefits; education allowances; and (at the household level) income from rental of property or land; family/children related allowances; social exclusion not elsewhere classified; housing allowances; regular inter-household cash transfers received; interests, dividends, profit from capital investments in unincorporated business; pensions from individual private plans; and income received by youth younger than 16 years old. Total household net income, in turn, was calculated by subtracting from total household gross income regular taxes on wealth, taxes on income and social insurance contributions, and regular inter-household case transfers paid.

9. Social benefits are aggregated in eight branches using the European System of integrated Social PROtection Statistics (ESSPROS) definitions. For more information, see Eurostat (2011).

10. The EU-SILC longitudinal survey consists of a four-year rotating panel. In each year, approximately three-quarters of individuals present in the previous year are retained. The samples used in the latent class analysis include about 3,000 observations for each year in the cross-sectional analysis and 600 observations in the longitudinal analysis. The population is weighted with individual weights.

References

Collins, L. M., and S. T. Lanza. 2010. *Latent Class and Latent Transition Analysis: With Applications in the Social, Behavioral, and Health Sciences.* Hoboken, NJ: Wiley.

EC (European Commission). 2013a. "EU Measures to Tackle Youth Unemployment." MEMO, Brussels, 28 May.

———. 2013b. "Assessment of the Implementation of the European Commission Recommendation on Active Inclusion: A Study of National Policies: Country Report—Lithuania." DG Employment, Social Affairs & Inclusion, European Commission, Brussels.

Eurofound. 2012. *NEETs—Young People Not in Employment, Education or Training: Characteristics, Costs and Policy Responses in Europe.* Luxembourg: Publications Office of the European Union.

Eurostat. 2010. "Labor Market Policy Statistics—Qualitative Report: Lithuania 2010."

———. 2011. *ESSPROS Manual: The European System of Integrated Social Protection Statistics.* Luxembourg: European Union.

ILO (International Labor Organization). 2011. "Active Labour Market Programmes Implemented by the Lithuanian Labour Exchange." http://www.ilo.org/public/english/region/afpro/cairo/downloads/almp-lithuania-eng.pdf.

Katz, L. 2010. "Long-Term Unemployment in the Great Recession." Testimony for the Joint Economic Committee, U.S. Congress Hearing on "Long-Term Unemployment: Causes, Consequences and Solutions." April 29.

Kaufman, L., and P. J. Rousseeuw. 1990. *Finding Groups in Data.* New York: Wiley.

Magidson, J., and J. Vermunt. 2002. "Latent Class Modeling as a Probabilistic Extension of K-Means Clustering. Quirk's Marketing Research Review. " March 20, 77–80. http://statisticalinnovations.com/technicalsupport/kmeans2a.htm.

Vermunt, J. K., and J. Magidson. 2005. *Latent GOLD 4.0 User's Guide.* Belmont, MA: Statistical Innovations Inc.

Latent Class Analysis of the Out-of-Work Population in Romania, 2008–11

Background

After a period of high growth, Romania experienced a severe economic contraction in 2009 and has not yet recovered to its previous economic growth levels. During the period from 2003 to 2008, the Romanian economy grew at very high rates—an average of 6.6 percent per year, compared to 2.2 percent per year among EU-28 countries. However, as in the other countries in the region, in 2009 the crisis hit hard and output contracted by 6.6 percent. Only in 2011 was GDP growth back to a positive level, of 2.3 percent. In 2013 the economy grew 3.5 percent, only surpassed in the region by Latvia (which grew 4.1 percent).

Unemployment rose following the crisis, but the increase was low in comparison to the sharp fall in output. From 2003 to 2008, unemployment was, on average, 7.3 percent; in 2008 it reached its lowest level at 6.1 percent. After the crisis hit the Romanian economy in 2009, unemployment only marginally increased, reaching 7.6 percent in 2013. This pales in comparison to the dramatic rise in unemployment following the crisis that many European countries witnessed. Moreover, labor force participation, albeit low by European standards, remained fairly constant following the crisis, between 63 and 65 percent.[1]

However, youth experienced a sharp rise in unemployment. Figure 8.1 shows that unemployment rates were falling steadily, particularly among youth, before the crisis. The percentage of young individuals between 15 and 24 years of age who were not in employment, education, or training (the NEET rate) reached its lowest level of the decade in 2008—11.6 percent. However, when the crisis hit Romania, youth felt most of the impact. Overall unemployment reached 7.7 percent in 2011, representing a 1.6 percentage point increase from pre-crisis levels. Youth unemployment, on the other hand, peaked at 23.7 percent in 2011, almost 5 percentage points above its pre-crisis level. After a downward trend between 2003 and 2008, the NEET rate also increased, returning in 2012 to the same level it had been in 2005.

Figure 8.1 Unemployment and NEET Rates in Romania, 2003–13
percent

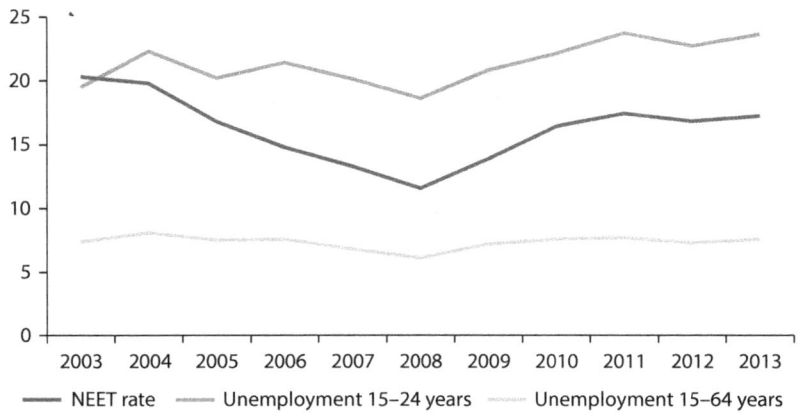

Source: Eurostat, EU-LFS.
Note: While the unemployment rate is calculated as a share of the economically active population in the respective age group, the NEET rate is calculated for the percentage of the population 15–24 years old. NEET = not in employment, education, or training.

Figure 8.2 Unemployment Rates by Age and Gender in Romania, 2007–13
percent

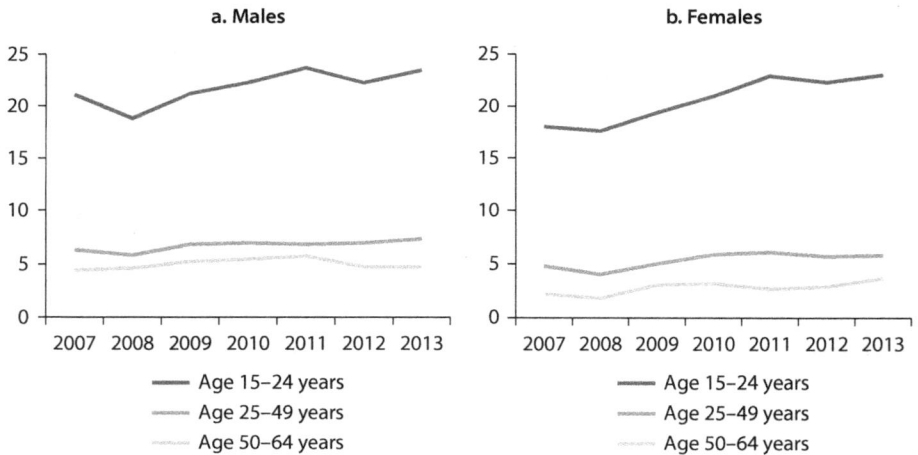

Source: Eurostat, EU-LFS.

A look at unemployment rates disaggregated by gender shows that women were generally more affected by the crisis. As shown in figure 8.2, unemployment rates are usually lower for women. However, the economic downturn affected women most, especially those in the 50- to 64-year-old group, whose unemployment rate grew from 1.9 to 3.3 percent between 2008 and 2010, representing an increase of over 70 percent. Unemployment rates for men in this age group, in contrast, only increased by 18 percent. Women ages 15–24 years and 25–49 years also

Figure 8.3 Long-Term Unemployment as a Share of Total Unemployment, 2003–13

percent

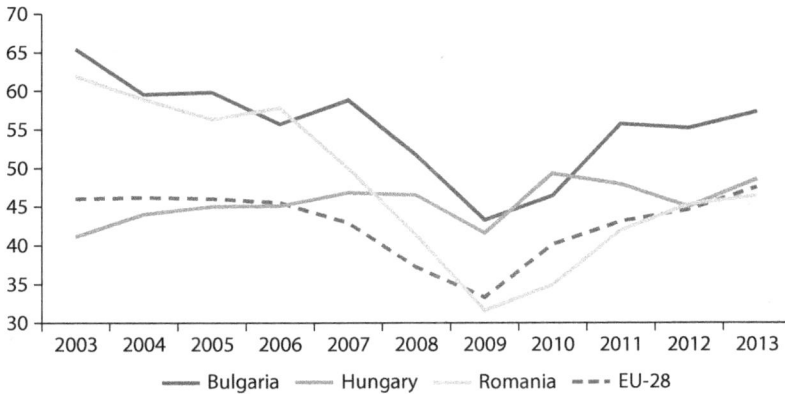

Source: Eurostat, EU-LFS.

experienced higher proportional increases in unemployment than did men in the same age group.

Despite the relatively small change in overall unemployment rates observed during the crisis, one of the most worrisome results was the change in the duration of unemployment, with a significant increase in the share of long-term unemployed. Long-term unemployment as a share of total unemployment hit a low of 31.6 percent in 2009; since then the share has risen to 46.4 percent (as shown in figure 8.3). The relatively small effect of the crisis on unemployment figures thus appears to be hiding more negative conditions in the labor market.

Although overall employment levels remained relatively stable following the crisis, individuals with tertiary education experienced declining employment rates, while their supply increased. After peaking at 59 percent in 2008, employment rates remained relatively unchanged, with their lowest postcrisis rate being 58.5 percent in 2011. In contrast, the employment rate for individuals with tertiary education reached its lowest point for the 2003–13 period in 2013, at 81.4 percent, down from 85.7 percent in 2008.[2]

What is more, between 2008 and 2013, unemployment rates doubled for individuals with tertiary education. Deteriorating labor market outcomes for the most educated might also reflect lower experience, since youth are usually the more educated group. Nonetheless, although those with less education were less affected during the crisis in terms of relative changes, it is worth noting that, at least in terms of levels, labor market outcomes have generally favored those with higher education. In the meantime, the Romanian labor force has become more educated, reflecting the fact that youth entering the labor force (and replacing the workers who retire) are more educated. However, as reported previously, youth have also been the most affected by the crisis, and their higher levels of education have not resulted in improved labor market prospects overall.

Table 8.1 Number and Percentage of Working-Age Individuals (Ages 16–64 Years) by Labor Market Attachment in Romania, 2008 and 2011

thousands

	2008	2011	Percent change 2008–11
At work	8,812	9,023	2.4
	67.7%	68.8%	
Unemployed	192	152	−20.8
	1.5%	1.2%	
Long-term unemployed	275	349	26.9
	2.1%	2.7%	
(Early) retirement	1,950	2,006	2.9
	15.0%	15.3%	
Disabled	160	101	−36.9
	1.2%	0.8%	
Other inactive	1,623	1,486	−8.4
	12.5%	11.3%	
Total	13,012	13,117	0.8
	100%	100%	

Source: World Bank staff analysis based on EU-SILC.
Note: Individuals ages 16–24 years who are out of work and enrolled in education (1.5 million individuals) are excluded from the sample.

During the period from 2008 to 2011, the sample of the out-of-work population considered in this note decreased, from 4.2 to 4.1 million individuals. The analysis of the out-of-work population in this note focuses on the working-age population (16–64 years old). Specifically, only individuals ages 25–64 years who are not employed, and individuals ages 16–24 years who were neither employed nor in education nor training were considered.[3] Only the working-age population (16- to 64-year-olds) is analyzed, as labor activation options—the main policy focus of this note—are only viable for that segment of the population. As a percentage of the population of working age under analysis, the out-of-work population fell from 32.3 percent to 31.2 percent. The three groups of the out-of-work population that became smaller during this period were the groups of disabled, short-term unemployed, and other inactive, which decreased in size by 37, 21, and 8 percent, respectively. On the other hand, the number of long-term unemployed grew by 27 percent (see table 8.1). Figure 8.4 shows the composition of the out-of-work population in Romania in 2008 and 2011.

Methodology: Latent Class Analysis

In chapter 1 a general overview of the latent class analysis methodology was presented. This section explains in detail the variables and covariates used to identify classes or groups of out-of-work individuals that are as homogeneous as possible within each class according to a set of observable characteristics, and as distant as possible between classes. The emerging profiles can then be contrasted with the design and targeting of current activation policies, in order to identify the potential gaps and to enhance their design features.[4]

Figure 8.4 Distribution of Out-of-Work Population in Romania, 2008 and 2011
percent

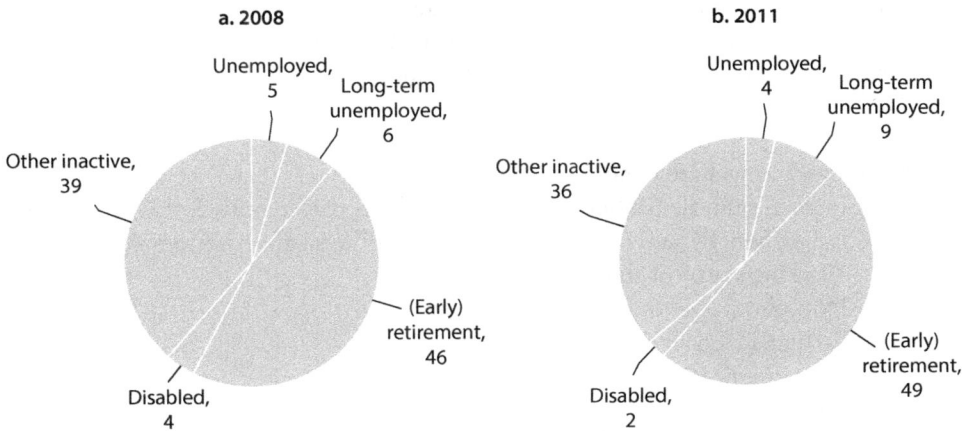

a. 2008

Unemployed, 5
Long-term unemployed, 6
Other inactive, 39
(Early) retirement, 46
Disabled, 4

b. 2011

Unemployed, 4
Long-term unemployed, 9
Other inactive, 36
(Early) retirement, 49
Disabled, 2

Source: World Bank staff analysis based on EU-SILC.

Variable Selection

The definition of latent classes relies on a number of indicator variables to capture different "symptoms" of an overall latent condition (in this case, the typology of joblessness). The challenge in such models is to identify a discrete number of variables that can best explain the heterogeneity of individual outcomes. In this case, two sets of categorical variables were selected: the first set to show the extent of labor market distance and the other to capture some of the main factors that can affect employment on the supply side, such as labor supply conditions (household-level incentives to work and physical ability to work).

- *Distance from labor market*: short-term unemployment, long-term unemployment, (early) retirement, disability, and other inactivity (largely unpaid domestic work).[5]
- *Work experience:* if individual has worked before and, in this case, whether worked for two or more months in the previous year;
- *Labor supply conditions:* whether the individual's household has at least one working adult,[6] and perceived limitations on activities due to health problems.[7]

In addition to indicators, the model includes active covariates, which are used to improve the classification of individuals in each class. In this case the active covariates are the demographic variables that are normally used to disaggregate labor market outcomes:

- Age-group category (four groups)
- Gender
- Human capital: the highest educational level achieved
- Urban/rural location

Once the latent classes have been defined, inactive covariates that were not included in the model can be used to characterize the individuals in each class and the households in which they live. The inactive covariates chosen describe those characteristics that may provide valuable information for the design of tailored policies that address barriers to employment, including income level. They include:

- Household welfare conditions:
  - Income quintile (defined by equivalized disposable household income[8,9])
  - Labor, benefit, and other income as share of total gross household income[10]
  - Working status of the partner
  - Household able to keep dwelling warm
  - Partner's labor income
  - Quintile of partner's labor income
  - Tenure status
  - Binary variables denoting whether individuals or their households are beneficiaries of any of eight social protection benefits[11]
  - Share of benefits in household gross income
- Household demographics:
  - Household size
  - Household composition
  - Binary variable showing whether there are children younger than six years old in the household
  - Binary variable denoting whether there are three or more children younger than 16 years old in the household
  - Children younger than 13 years old in the household receiving child care: all, some, or none of the children
  - Older person (65 years of age and older) in the household
  - Presence of individual's parents in the household
- Other individual-level demographics:
  - More refined age groups (eight groups)
  - Marital status
- Individual human capital:
  - More refined highest educational level achieved (six groups)
  - Work experience in years
- Household location:
  - Degree of urbanization[12]: densely populated, intermediate area, sparsely populated
  - Regional breakdown

Group Labeling
The resulting groups are then labeled according to the greatest proportional characteristics within groups that also aid in distinguishing among groups. Granted, a large number of characteristics describe these groups, and only a few are taken into account for the purpose of labeling. In part, some of these

characteristics may exhibit a large degree of heterogeneity and may thus not be relevant for defining a group. In addition, some characteristics may be more relevant for the purposes of policy design than others. In short, though the labeling of groups can be considered more an art than a science, when taken together with detailed descriptions of a group's most prominent characteristics, labeling can serve as an important starting point in the design and prioritization of activation policies.

The analysis relies on cross-sectional as well as panel data from the European Union Statistics of Income and Living Conditions (EU-SILC) surveys for 2008–11, which combine individual-level information with household characteristics. The first part of the note presents a cross-sectional analysis for the years 2008, 2009, 2010, and 2011. In particular, the latent class analysis on 2008 data shows the main characteristics of the out-of-work before the global economic crisis hit Romania, and thus highlight what could be considered more structural issues of the country's labor market. The 2011 latent class analysis will contrast this initial assessment with more recent developments. The second part of the note exploits longitudinal data between 2008 and 2010[13] to trace the prior labor market status of individuals observed last in 2010 in various classes, and will shed light on the relative persistence in the out-of-work status among different classes of individuals. The set of variables chosen for the cross-section and the longitudinal analysis are slightly different, due to minor differences in the set of variables recorded in each of the two types of data sets.

Main Findings

Out-of-Work Population: Group Profiles from Cross-Sectional Analysis

The latent class analysis supports the classification of the out-of-work into eight major groups, some of which have remained stable over time. The groups were named according to their most salient characteristics. Figure 8.5 shows the share of each of the eight classes identified for the year 2011 while table 8.2 presents their most salient characteristics.

The eight main clusters emerging from the LCA analysis in 2011 can be characterized as follows (for more detail, see Appendix A for a link to the online-only annexes):

- Cluster 1: *Retirees.* This group of retired individuals has represented between 21 and 27 percent of the out-of-work throughout the years analyzed. It is largely made up of females (58 percent), and as of 2009, it generally includes individuals who have hit retirement age (60–64 years).[14] They can be considered low- to mid-skilled, with 38 percent having less than an upper secondary education and half having upper or postsecondary education. On average, they have 33 years of work experience. Even though 62 percent do not have at least one working adult in their household they are at very low risk of poverty,[15] with only 8 percent living in the bottom income quintile. In part, this can be explained by the fact that they live in households without dependent children

Figure 8.5 Classes of Out-of-Work Individuals in Romania, 2011
percent

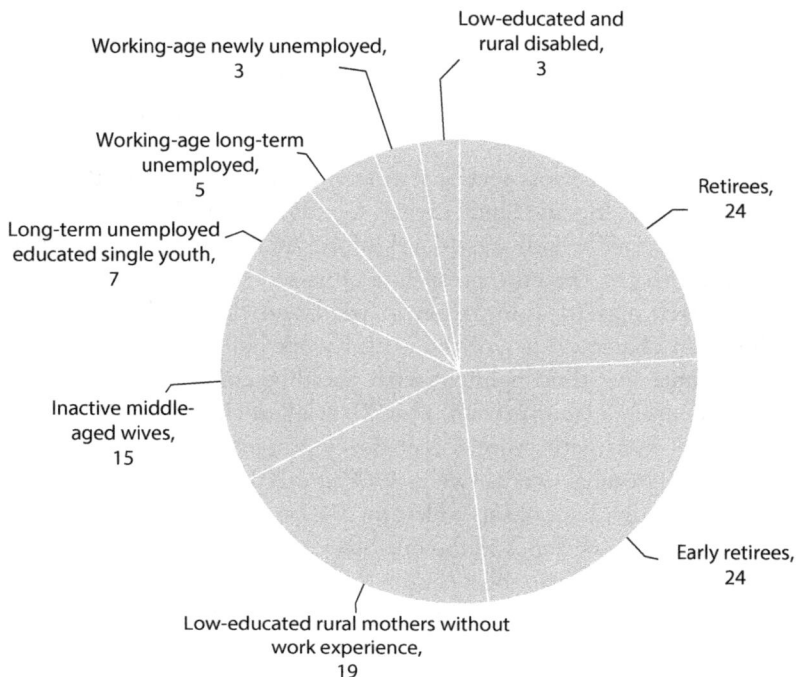

Source: World Bank staff analysis based on EU-SILC.

Table 8.2 Summary Characteristics of Latent Classes of Out-of-Work Population in Romania, 2011

1: Retirees (24%)	*2: Early retirees (24%)*
• 98% are retired	• 96% are retired
• 58% are female	• 59% are female
• 94% are 60–64 years old	• 91% are 45–59 years old
• 68% are married; 23% are widowed	• 77% are married; 11% are widowed
• 58% have a partner who is not working; 62% have no working adults in household	• 28% report strongly limited capacity to work
• Low-to-mid-skilled: 38% have not completed upper secondary education; 49% have completed upper or postsecondary	• 50% have a partner who is not working; 57% have at least one working adult in household
• 95% worked before, but less than 2 months in the previous year; 33 years of experience on average	• Mid-skilled: 73% have completed upper or postsecondary education
• 79% live in households without dependent children	• 95% worked before, but less than 2 months in the previous year; 27 years of experience on average
• Very low poverty risk: 8% are in poorest income quintile	• 64% live in households without dependent children
• 87% receive old-age benefits	• Low poverty risk: 12% are in poorest income quintile
	• 49% receive disability benefits; 42% receive old-age benefits

table continues next page

Table 8.2 Summary Characteristics of Latent Classes of Out-of-Work Population in Romania, 2011 *(continued)*

3: Low-educated rural mothers without work experience (19%)

- 97% are inactive
- 99% are female
- 84% are 20–44 years old
- 73% are married
- 67% have a working partner; 91% have at least one working adult in household
- Low-to-mid-skilled: 46% have not completed upper secondary education; 40% have completed upper or postsecondary
- Only 22% have worked before; 9 years of experience on average
- 83% live in households with dependent children; 46% in households with children younger than 6 years old
- 77% live in rural areas
- High poverty risk: 43% in poorest income quintile
- 76% receive family/child benefits

4: Inactive middle-aged wives (15%)

- 91% are inactive
- 100% are female
- 77% are 35–54 years old
- 85% are married
- 61% have a working partner; 78% have at least one working adult in household
- Low-to-mid-skilled: 37% have not completed upper secondary education; 54% have completed upper or postsecondary
- Only 40% have worked before; 16 years of experience on average
- 64% live in households with dependent children; 20% in households with children younger than 6 years old
- 69% live in rural areas
- High poverty risk: 39% in poorest income quintile
- 56% receive family/child benefits

5: Long-term unemployed educated single youth (7%)

- 55% are long-term unemployed; 33% are inactive
- 67% are male
- 76% are 20–29 years old
- 80% are single
- 77% have at least one working adult in household; 81% are living with parents
- Mid-to-high-skilled: 47% with complete upper or postsecondary education; 25% with complete tertiary
- Only 11% have worked before; 4 years of experience on average
- Very high poverty risk: 48% in poorest income quintile
- 51% receive family/child benefits; 32% social exclusion; only 8% receive unemployment benefits

6: Working-age long-term unemployed (5%)

- 74% are long-term unemployed
- 72% are male
- 93% are 25–54 years old
- 52% have at least one working adult in household
- 66% are married
- Mid-skilled: 66% have completed upper or post-secondary education
- 92% worked before, but less than 2 months in the previous year; 15 years of experience on average
- 56% live in households with dependent children
- Very high poverty risk: 46% in poorest income quintile
- 50% receive family/child benefits; 30% social exclusion; 21% receive unemployment benefits

7: Working-age newly unemployed (3%)

- 75% are unemployed
- 68% are male
- 72% are 25–54 years old
- 62% have at least one working adult in household
- 57% are married
- Mid-skilled: 66% have complete upper or post-secondary education
- 99% have worked 2 or more months in the previous year; 15 years of experience on average
- 66% live in households with dependent children; 33% in households with children younger than 6 years old
- 62% live in rural areas
- Low poverty risk: 18% in poorest income quintile
- 56% receive family/child benefits; 16% receive unemployment benefits

8: Low-educated and rural disabled (3%)

- 71% report their labor market status as disabled; 18% are retired
- 61% are male
- 70% are 20–44 years old
- 76% are without a partner
- 69% report strongly limited capacity to work
- 76% have at least one working adult in household
- Low-skilled: 45% have not completed upper secondary education; 33% have never studied before or are illiterate
- 100% have never worked before
- 57% live in households with dependent children
- 87% live in rural areas
- High poverty risk: 39% in poorest income quintile
- 67% receive disability benefits; 53% receive family/child benefits; 46% receive social exclusion benefits

Source: World Bank analysis based on EU-SILC.

Note: Percentages in parentheses following the group names refer to the share of the total out-of-work population. "Years of work experience" refers only to those individuals who have worked before. "Dependent children" include children younger than 18 years of age and household members ages 18–24 years who are economically inactive and living with at least one parent. "Working adult" refers to adults ages 25 years and older. For this report's purposes, we define the at-risk-of-poverty rate as the relative risk of being in the first quintile of the income distribution. The reference period for income reported in EU-SILC surveys is the year preceding the survey year.

(17 percent also live alone) and almost all receive old-age benefits. On average, benefits make up 77 percent of their total gross household income.

- Cluster 2: *Early retirees.* This class represents 24 percent of the out-of-work population in 2011, and its relative size has remained fairly stable over time.[16] Its members are almost exclusively early retirees between the ages of 45 and 59. Although less than one-third report strong limitations on capacity to work, one-half receive disability benefits; forty-two percent also report receiving old-age benefits. Like their retired counterparts, they are mostly female (59 percent) and, on average, have a similar number of years of work experience (27 years). However, they are somewhat more educated than the *retirees*, with 73 percent having completed upper or postsecondary school. Although more than half (57 percent) have at least one working adult in the household, benefits still represent most of total household gross income (61 percent). Their relatively small households may also explain why only 12 percent live in the bottom income quintile, putting them at a very low risk of poverty.

- Cluster 3: *Low-educated rural mothers without work experience.* Representing 19 percent of the out-of-work in 2011, this group makes up the larger of two groups of inactive women, the other being *inactive middle-aged wives.* What mainly sets this group's members apart from those of the smaller group is their relative youth (84 percent are between 20 and 44 years of age) and the fact that a great majority (83 percent) have children, with a large percentage (43 percent) having children younger than 6 years of age. They are largely concentrated in rural areas (77 percent), most have a working partner, and almost all (91 percent) have at least one working adult in their households. They are also more likely to have never worked before (78 percent), and a significant proportion of them (46 percent) have not completed upper secondary school. Finally, this group is characterized by very high benefit receipt: seventy-six percent receive family/child benefits. Nonetheless, on average benefits represent 28 percent of their total household income, the lowest percentage among all identified groups. Low benefit generosity, as well as their large families (4.7 members on average), in part explain why 43 percent are in the poorest income quintile.

- Cluster 4: *Inactive middle-aged wives.* This smaller group of inactive women made up 15 percent of the out-of-work in 2011, and represented as little as 8 percent of our sample in 2010. They are middle-aged (77 percent are between 35 and 54) married women who for the most part have children (64 percent), although only 20 percent have children younger than 6 years old. Most (60 percent) have not worked before, but they have more years of work experience than their younger counterparts and are also better educated, with over half having completed upper or postsecondary education. They are more likely to be married than their younger counterparts but also less likely to have a working adult within the household. They, too, are concentrated in rural areas, though less so than their younger counterparts. In terms of welfare, although they live in smaller households (4.0 members on average) than the *low-educated rural mothers without work experience*, they have slightly lower labor incomes on average, and a lower percentage (56 percent) receives family/child benefits. Overall, they have a similar income profile as the younger inactive women, with as many as 39 percent in the bottom income quintile.

- Cluster 5: *Long-term unemployed educated single youth.* Representing 7 percent of the out-of-work in 2010 and 2011, this group consists of mostly men (67 percent in 2011) between the ages of 20 and 29 and resembles the unemployed youth who have been particularly hard hit by the economic crisis across the EU. About 55 percent of them are long-term unemployed, and another third are out of the labor market. Some of them could be discouraged workers. In 2011, this group stood out as having the highest percentage of members with a tertiary education (24 percent). Their lack of work experience may thus explain their long-term unemployment status: almost 90 percent have never worked before. Aside from being young, the members of this group are for the most part single and still living at home with their parents. Even though they live in households where there is at least one working adult and just over half receive family/child benefits and one-third receive social exclusion benefits at the household level, a very high percentage of this group is still at a risk for poverty: 48 percent are in the poorest income quintile. In part, this is explained by the fact that they live in large households with 4.8 members on average.

- Cluster 6: *Working-age long-term unemployed.* This group only emerged in 2010 and represents 5 percent of the out-of-work. Its members are primarily men (72 percent) in their prime age (25–54) who have largely been unemployed for over 12 months (74 percent). The majority are married (66 percent) and a smaller majority (56 percent) live in households with dependent children. They are mid-skilled individuals (66 percent have completed upper secondary) and have previous work experience. Another characteristic of this group is its high dependence on benefits. Although just over half have a least one working adult in the household, benefits represent over half of their total household income (one-half of these receive family/child benefits, about a third receive social exclusion benefits, and one-fifth receive unemployment benefits). Despite high benefit receipt, a large percentage (46 percent) are in the bottom income quintile. Finally, it is notable that this group is relatively more urban, with 50 percent living in urban areas.

- Cluster 7: *Working-age newly unemployed.* This group, representing 3 percent of the out-of-work in 2011, closely mirrors the group of *working-age long-term unemployed.* What primarily sets them apart is the fact that they worked for at least two months during the last year, meaning that they have just recently lost their jobs. They have a similar education profile to their long-term unemployed counterparts and are primarily in their prime age, although they are somewhat younger (72 percent are in their prime age and 19 percent are younger than 25 years of age). Although they are somewhat less likely to be married, two-thirds live in households with dependent children. However, due to high labor income within their households, unlike their long-term unemployed counterparts they are at a relatively low risk for poverty, with only 18 percent in the bottom income quintile. A majority receive family/child benefits (56 percent) and one-fifth receive social exclusion benefits. Despite the fact that they are newly unemployed, only one-sixth receive unemployment benefits, in contrast to one-fifth of the long-term unemployed. Before 2010, the members of this group belonged to the *working-age newly unemployed or inactive*.

- Cluster 8: *Low-educated and rural disabled.* This group, representing from 3 to 5 percent of the out-of-work population, reports its labor market status as disabled (71 percent) or retired (18 percent), and has very low education levels. A majority (67 percent) also report strong limitations on work due to a health condition. In terms of benefit receipt, the most commonly received by this group are disability benefits (67 percent) and family/child benefits (46 percent). Benefit dependency is high, with benefits representing 54 percent of total household income. The members of this group are also characterized by the absence of a partner and live in households without a working adult. They are at high risk of falling in poverty, with 39 percent belonging to the poorest income quintile. The great majority live in rural areas.

Tables 8.3 and 8.4 present the main characteristics of each group in 2011. For the complete table, including inactive covariates, see Appendix A for a link to the online-only annexes.

The composition of the identified classes of out-of-work population has experienced considerable changes over the last few years. In figure 8.6 and table 8.5, clusters are compared over time between 2008 and 2011, both as a share of the total out-of-work population and in absolute numbers. From the graph, the first important observation is that the size of the out-of-work population has not increased—it has actually decreased by a bit more than 100,000 individuals, or 2.5 percent. Furthermore, the same clusters are not identified in all years, and some of the clusters identified in 2011 that were present in previous years underwent changes in relative size and also in composition. The fact that the composition of the groups changes over time is particularly important to keep in mind when interpreting changes in group size. For instance, significant increases (decreases) in group size are sometimes due to reassignments of individuals across groups, resulting in changes in group composition. Thus, although some groups may retain similar names across years due to their most salient characteristics, they may nonetheless vary in their composition across years. The evolution in terms of group size and group composition over the 2008–11 period can be summarized as follows:

- *One striking change is the increase in unemployment, especially in its nature, from short- to long-term unemployment.* The cluster of working-age long-term

Table 8.3 Latent Classes of Out-of-Work Population in Romania: Indicators, 2011

Indicators	All out-of-work	1. Retirees	2. Early retirees	3. Low-educated rural mothers without work experience	4. Inactive middle-aged wives	5. Long-term unemployed educated single youth	6. Working-age long-term unemployed	7. Working-age newly unemployed	8. Low-educated and rural disabled
Cluster size (%)	**100**	**24**	**24**	**19**	**15**	**7**	**5**	**3**	**3**
Population	**4,093,906**	**978,034**	**962,887**	**776,614**	**606,307**	**292,714**	**223,937**	**136,327**	**117,086**
Indicators (%)									
Labor market attachment									
Unemployed	4	0	0	0	0	8	9	75	0
Long-term unemployed	9	0	2	0	0	55	74	0	0
Retired	49	98	96	3	8	4	0	9	18
Disabled	2	0	1	0	1	0	0	0	71
Other inactive	36	1	0	97	91	33	17	16	12
At least one working adult in household									
No	37	62	43	9	23	23	48	38	31
Yes	63	38	57	91	78	77	52	62	69
Work experience									
Never worked	34	2	0	78	60	89	8	0	100
Less than 2 months in last year	58	95	95	8	39	11	92	1	0
2 or more months in last year	8	3	4	14	0	0	0	99	0
Self-assessed physical capacity									
Strongly limited	13	12	28	1	7	0	2	1	67
None/limited	87	88	72	99	93	100	98	99	33

Source: World Bank staff analysis based on EU-SILC.

Table 8.4 Latent Classes of Out-of-Work Population in Romania: Active Covariates, 2011

	All out-of-work	1. Retirees	2. Early retirees	3. Low-educated rural mothers without work experience	4. Inactive middle-aged wives	5. Long-term unemployed educated single youth	6. Working-age long-term unemployed	7. Working-age newly unemployed	8. Low-educated and rural disabled
Cluster size (%)	**100**	**24**	**24**	**19**	**15**	**7**	**5**	**3**	**3**
Population	**4,093,906**	**978,034**	**962,887**	**776,614**	**606,307**	**292,714**	**223,937**	**136,327**	**117,086**
Active covariates (%)									
Age groups (4)									
16–24 years	8	0	0	18	2	49	0	19	23
25–34 years	18	0	1	57	1	51	32	20	27
35–59 years	50	6	99	26	91	0	68	61	49
60–64 years	24	94	0	0	6	0	0	0	2
Gender									
Male	33	42	41	1	0	67	72	68	61
Female	67	58	59	99	100	33	28	32	39
Education (4)									
Primary	34	38	25	46	37	23	17	16	45
Secondary	54	49	73	40	54	47	66	66	18
Tertiary	7	12	0	8	1	24	11	11	0
Never studied before/illiterate/NA*	5	2	2	6	9	6	6	6	37
Urban or rural									
Urban	38	44	45	23	31	46	50	38	13
Rural	62	56	55	77	69	54	50	62	87

Source: World Bank staff analysis based on EU-SILC.

*NA = not available.

Figure 8.6 Classes of Out-of-Work Population in Romania, 2008–11
In thousands of individuals

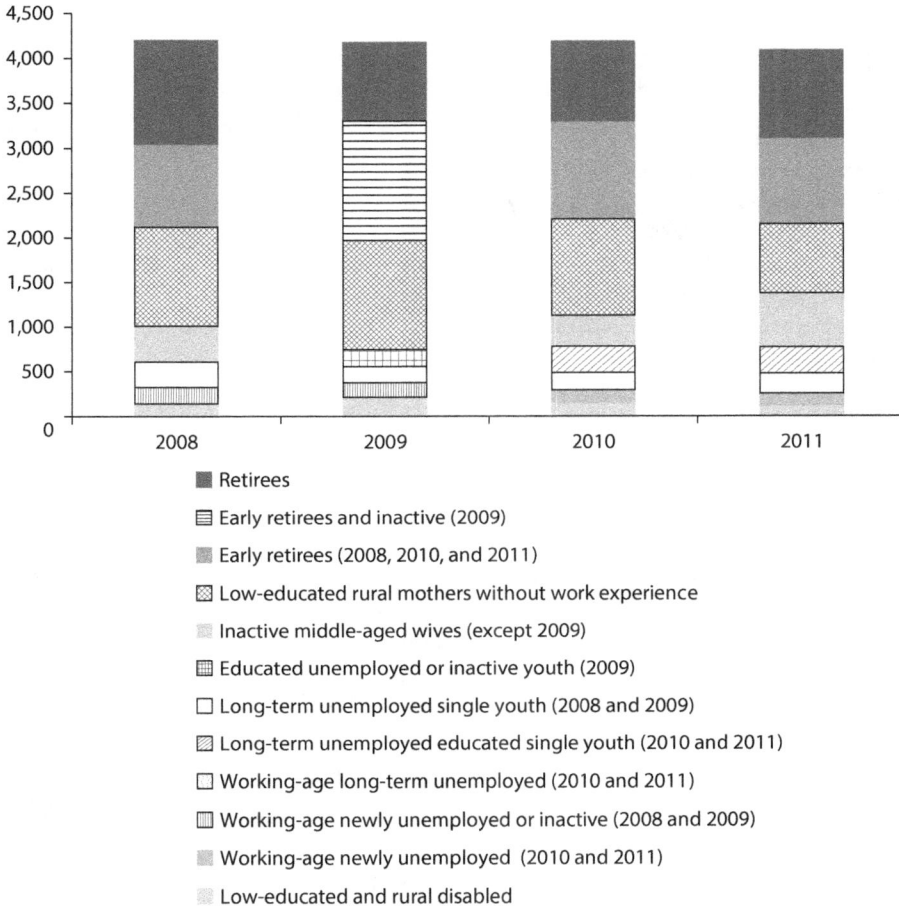

Retirees

Early retirees and inactive (2009)

Early retirees (2008, 2010, and 2011)

Low-educated rural mothers without work experience

Inactive middle-aged wives (except 2009)

Educated unemployed or inactive youth (2009)

Long-term unemployed single youth (2008 and 2009)

Long-term unemployed educated single youth (2010 and 2011)

Working-age long-term unemployed (2010 and 2011)

Working-age newly unemployed or inactive (2008 and 2009)

Working-age newly unemployed (2010 and 2011)

Low-educated and rural disabled

Source: World Bank staff analysis based on EU-SILC.

unemployed appears for the first time in 2010.[17] Its size is comparable to the existing cluster of unemployed men. Thus, when considering the two clusters of prime-aged unemployed (short- and long-term) together, the absolute number of unemployed in their prime age more than doubled in size between 2008 and 2010.

• *Another important change during the crisis period was the increase in the size of the youth cluster.* In 2009, a new group of out-of-work youth emerged (the group labeled as *educated unemployed or inactive youth*) alongside the already existing group of *long-term unemployed single youth*). The result was a 30 percent increase over 2008 in the absolute size of the out-of-work youth population identified in our analysis. This situation was reversed in the following two

Table 8.5 Classes of Out-of-Work Population in Romania as a Percentage of Total Out-of-Work Population, 2008–11

percent

Name of cluster	2008	2009	2010	2011
Retirees	27	21	21	24
Early retirees and inactive (2009)	n.a.	32	n.a.	n.a.
Early retirees (2008, 2010, and 2011)	22	n.a.	26	24
Low-educated rural mothers without work experience	26	29	26	19
Inactive middle-aged wives (except 2009)	10	n.a.	8	15
Educated unemployed or inactive youth (2009)	n.a.	5	n.a.	n.a.
Long-term unemployed single youth (2008 and 2009)	7	4	n.a.	n.a.
Long-term unemployed educated single youth (2010 and 2011)	n.a.	n.a.	7	7
Working-age newly unemployed or inactive (2008 and 2009)	4	4	n.a.	n.a.
Working-age long-term unemployed (2010 and 2011)	n.a.	n.a.	5	5
Working-age newly unemployed (2010 and 2011)	n.a.	n.a.	4	3
Low-educated and rural disabled	3	5	4	3

Source: World Bank staff analysis based on EU-SILC.
Note: n.a. = not applicable.

years, when once again only one youth cluster was identified; however, by 2011, the total number of out-of-work youth still remained about 4 percent higher than in 2008. Moreover, it is worth noting that the youth cluster identified in both 2010 and 2011 represented relatively educated youth. Specifically, in 2008, 72 percent of the *group of long-term unemployed single youth* was composed of individuals with upper secondary or postsecondary education, and only 2 percent of them had attained tertiary education. In 2009, this group was split along two lines: a more educated cluster *(educated) unemployed or inactive youth* (36 percent of which had tertiary level education), and a group of *long-term unemployed single youth*. In 2010 they appear together in one cluster again, but represent a more educated group: 15 percent have tertiary-level education.

- The cluster of *retirees* became smaller, probably due to an improvement in its differentiation from the other clusters. Between 2008 and 2011, the group of retirees became 15 percent smaller. However, in 2008, 68 percent of the individuals in this cluster were 60–64 years old, while 32 percent of them were between 35 and 59 years of age and had for the most part not reached retirement age.[18] In 2011, this cluster became composed of individuals who were likely to have reached retirement age, with 94 percent between the ages of 60 and 64 years.

- The cluster of *early retirees* has remained roughly comparable in absolute size to the *retirees* cluster itself; both represented around one million people. In 2008, 19 percent of the individuals in this cluster declared strong health-related limitations on their capacity to work; in 2011 this share increased to 28 percent. The percentage receiving disability benefits also increased during the period, rising from 41 percent to 49 percent. Another significant change occurred after 2008, when the share of males in this group fell from 60 percent to about 40 percent. Of note also is the fact that in 2009, the group of *retirees* incorporated a large number of "other inactive" individuals also between the ages of 45 and 54 years, constituting a separate group labeled as *retirees and inactive*.

- *The size of the combined groups of retired individuals fell between 2008 and 2011.* Together, the *early retirees* and the *retirees* made up about 2.1 million people in 2008. By 2011, this number had fallen by 7 percent, to 1.9 million individuals. Although the largest fall in numbers appears to be among the *retirees*, it is important to recall that, in 2008, the group of *retirees* incorporated a significant share of *early retirees*.

- The two groups of retirees (*retirees* and *early retirees*) demonstrate the lowest share of household poverty (members of the cluster in the poorest income quintile) with 8 and 12 percent, respectively. While the average old-age pension payment in Romania was below EUR 200 in 2013 (Government of Romania 2014), the relative small household sizes (2.8 and 3.4, respectively [the lowest among all the 8 groups]) and the regularity of the old-age payment contributed to the low poverty exposure experienced by this cluster compared to the other out-of-work clusters in this analysis. Partner labor income appears to play a minor role in the welfare condition of these households, as 90 percent of *retirees* and 72 percent of *early retirees* either have no partner or no working partner. This is reflected in the fact that the benefit share of household income among these two groups is the highest among all the 8 groups.

- Finally, the group of *inactive middle-aged wives* increased by 50 percent during the period, from 400,000 to 600,000 individuals in 2011. Not only has its size changed, but also its characteristics. In 2008, 85 percent were living in households with at least one working adult, 99 percent had worked before, and benefits represented 23 percent of the total household income. In 2011, 78 percent of them were living in households with a working adult, 60 percent had never worked before, and benefits represented one-third of their household income.

- On the other hand, there was a decrease in the size of the cluster of *low-educated rural mothers without work experience*, whose absolute number was reduced by 320,000 individuals—around 30 percent of its size in 2008. Some characteristics changed, since 91 percent had a working adult present in the household in 2011 compared to 77 percent in 2008, and the share receiving family/child benefits increased from 67 percent to 76 percent. Moreover, in 2008, 88 percent did not have prior work experience, compared to 78 percent in 2011. It is apparent that, across time, some reassignments took place between this group of stay-at-home women and the previously mentioned group, *inactive middle-aged wives*.

Structural Aspects and Emerging Trends in the Profiles of the Out-of-Work

The clusters identified in the out-of-work population for the period from 2008 to 2011 reflect both structural and cyclical aspects of the labor market. This section identifies some of the key structural aspects of the Romanian labor market and uses cross-sectional and longitudinal analysis of clusters of the out-of-work population to further examine the effects of the crisis.

Among youth, not only is unemployment high and employment low, youth labor force participation rates in Romania are among the lowest in the EU. Since 2008, Romania's NEET rate has increased by 5.6 percentage points, reaching 17.2 percent in 2013. Youth labor force participation rates, at only 30.8 percent in 2013, are well below the EU average of 42.2 percent (figure 8.7). In part, low labor force participation and employment rates among youth reflect a full-time work tradition in Romania. In many EU countries, youth have higher labor force participation rates because they are able combine their studies with part-time work. For example, as many as 75 and 40 percent of youth in the Netherlands and Slovenia, respectively, report working part time (Dimitrov and Duell 2013). In Romania, in 2013, only about 18 percent of youth (15–24 years old) reported working part-time (Eurostat).

Retired individuals make up almost half of the out-of-work population analyzed in this note, but about half of retirees have not reached retirement age. In the working-age sample used in this analysis, two main clusters of retirees emerge, representing almost half of the out-of-work population. This may in part reflect that a relatively high percentage of population between 15 and 64 years old has already reached retirement age. Retirement comes at a very young age in Romania, especially for women, who become eligible at age 59 (the male retirement age is 64 years). However, about half of those retired people are considered early

Figure 8.7 Labor Force Participation (Ages 15–24 Years), European Countries, 2013
percent

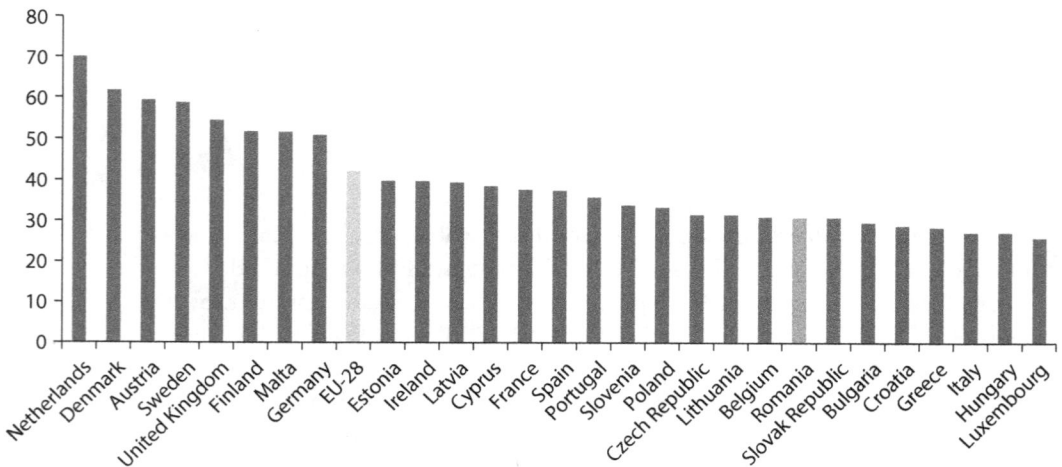

Source: Eurostat, EU-LFS.

Figure 8.8 Labor Force Participation (Ages 55–59 Years), European Countries, 2013
percent

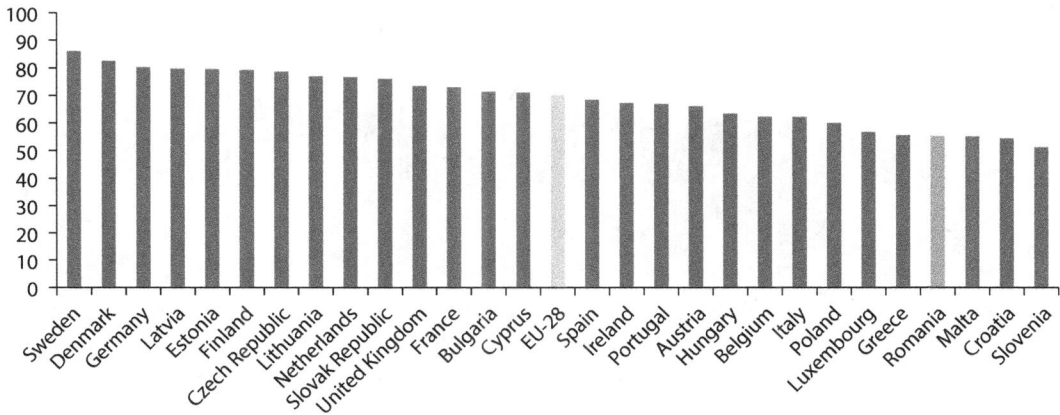

Source: Eurostat, EU-LFS.

Figure 8.9 Expenditures on Old-Age Benefits as a Share of GDP in Europe, 2008 and 2010
percent

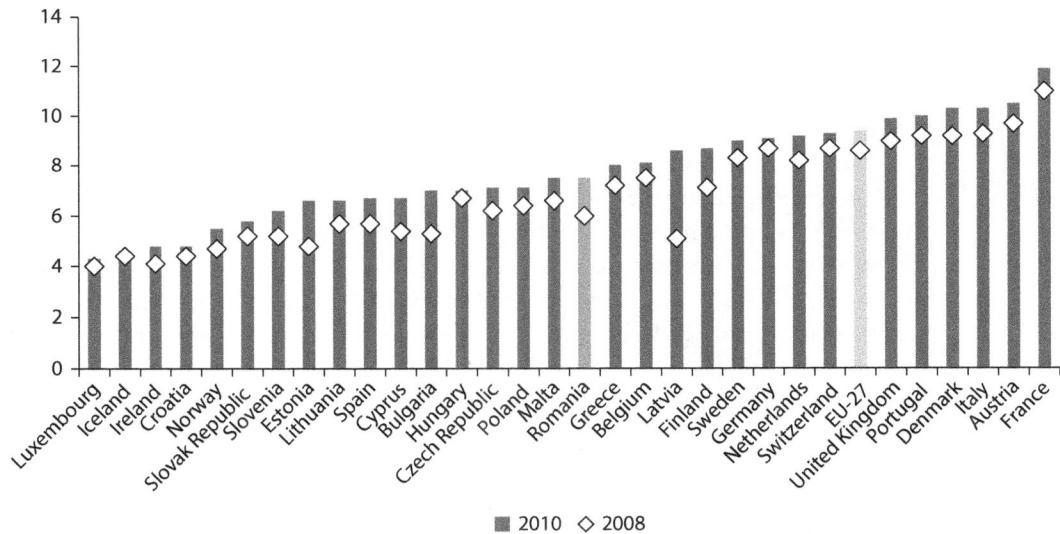

■ 2010 ◇ 2008

Source: Eurostat, EU-LFS.

retirees: among this group of early retirees, 35 percent are 45–54 years old and 57 percent are 55–59 years old. In fact, labor force participation rates for people between 55 and 59 years of age are among the lowest in the EU (see figure 8.8). In the case of individuals 55 and 64 years old, rates are 10 percentage points lower than the EU-27 average of 54.5 percent. Such low labor force participation rates are having an effect on old-age benefits. As shown in figure 8.9, between 2008 and 2010, expenditures on old-age benefits as a share of GDP increased

Figure 8.10 Labor Force Participation among Women Ages 25–54 Years, European Countries, 2013
percent

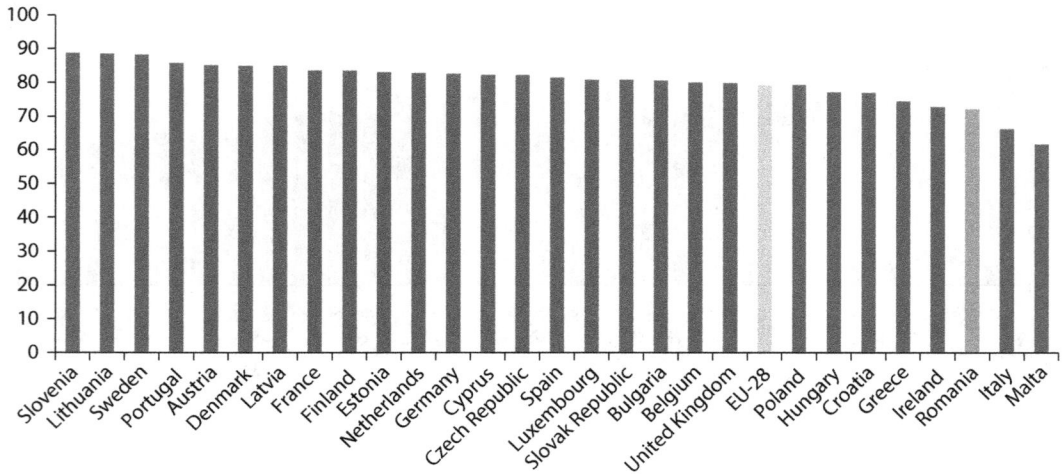

Source: Eurostat, EU-LFS.

by 1.5 percentage points (reaching 7.5 percent), which represents twice the growth for the EU-27 average in the same period. As the working-age population shrinks and life expectancy rises, raising the retirement age and increasing labor force participation among older individuals may prove vital to counteract a shrinking workforce and rising old-age benefit outlays.

Inactive women, many of whom are in their prime age, represent one-third of the out-of-work. Inactivity among women is a structural issue in Romania, as labor force participation rates for women of working age were around 55 percent even before the crisis. In comparison to other European women, Romanian women of prime age (25–54 years) are 7 percentage points less likely to participate in the labor market; only in Italy and Malta are labor force participation rates among women of prime age lower (figure 8.10). Data from Eurostat also show that among European countries, children in Romania are the least likely to be enrolled in formal child care. However, factors other than lack of available child care seem to be at play in the low labor force participation of Romanian women, as the percentage of women who report being inactive because of personal and family responsibilities is less than 10 percent, compared to an average of over 15 percent within the European Union (Eurostat, EU-LFS 2012). Women have important potential for increasing the labor force, especially as Romania, like other European countries, faces a shrinking population of working-age individuals.

Finally, with respect to the unemployed two main patterns emerged: an absolute increase in the number of individuals in unemployed groups, and the appearance of a cluster of long-term unemployed. One of the most concerning developments between 2008 and 2011 is the increase in the number of unemployed individuals in the out-of-work population. Consider that in 2008 only 57 percent of the 185,000 people in the *working-age newly unemployed or inactive* group were unemployed (that is, around 100,000 people in their prime age were unemployed). By 2011 this number had increased by almost three times. Long-term unemployment not only imposes a significant financial burden on households, but also affects the long-term health status of jobseekers, negatively impacts government finances, and results in a lower overall long-term level of skills among a country's workforce, with permanent negative effects on productivity (Katz 2010). Equally worrisome, many individuals who have been unemployed for extended periods become discouraged and drop out of the labor market altogether. In fact, a significant proportion of the groups labeled as unemployed are inactive: around one-sixth of the groups in their prime age and around one-third of the group of young men. It is possible that many of these individuals are discouraged workers. Addressing the plight of the long-term unemployed should be among the policy priorities for Romanian policy makers.

Another topic of immediate concern to policy makers in the government of Romania is the situation of the working poor. While this group is by design not the focus of this report on the out-of-work, some salient facts about them (working households that are in the bottom 20 percent of the income distribution, regardless of their inclusion in one of the clusters of this report) can help to illustrate their labor market and social situation. From the EU-SILC data, a picture emerges that shows a mainly prime-aged (83 percent between 25 and 59 years old), majority male (64 percent), very low-educated (more than 50 percent with only primary or lower secondary education), and almost fully rural (92 percent) population. Their household income is mainly derived from labor income (72 percent).

Out-of-Work Population: Group Profiles from Longitudinal Analysis

In order to better understand the dynamics within clusters and other labor market movements, LCA analysis was also applied to longitudinal EU-SILC data for the period 2008–10. The EU-SILC survey allows the tracking of individuals in both 2008 and 2010, albeit with a smaller sample size than that available in the cross-section surveys. The latent class analysis of the out-of-work population in 2010 yielded similar results in terms of clusters, although due to the reduced sample size, the number of clusters was also smaller. For a sample of around 900 observations, six classes were defined:

- *Low-educated rural inactive women without work experience* (34 percent)
- *Retirees* (24 percent)
- *Early retirees and inactive with previous work experience* (23 percent)
- *Low-educated and rural disabled or inactive* (8 percent)
- *Unemployed rural single youth* (7 percent)
- *Middle-aged low-educated unemployed* (5 percent)

Annex 3 (see Appendix A for a link to the online-only annexes) shows the full statistical description of the latent classes, while table 8.6 summarizes the key features of each cluster.

Table 8.6 Longitudinal Analysis: Summary Characteristics of Latent Classes of Out-of-Work Individuals in Romania, 2010

1: Low-educated rural inactive women without work experience (34%)

- 97% are inactive
- 95% are female
- 85% are 25–54 years old
- 69% are married; 25% are single
- 86% have at least one working adult in household
- Only 15% have worked before
- Mid to low-skilled: 48% have not completed upper secondary education; 46% have upper secondary
- 63% live in households with dependent children
- 78% live in rural areas
- High poverty risk: 38% in the poorest income quintile
- 64% receive family/child benefits

2: Retirees (24%)

- 91% are retired
- 58% are female
- 94% are 60–64 years old
- 11% report strongly limited capacity to work
- 73% are married; 20% are widowed
- 52% have at least one working adult in household
- 99% have worked before
- 53% live in urban areas
- Low poverty risk: 8% in poorest income quintile
- 82% receive old-age benefits

3: Early retirees and inactive with previous work experience (23%)

- 55% are inactive and another 45% are retired
- 66% are female
- 89% are 45–59 years old
- 22% report strongly limited capacity to work
- 77% are married; 12% are widowed
- 60% have at least one working adult in household
- 97% worked before, but less than 2 months in the previous year
- 65% live in rural areas
- Low poverty risk: 15% in poorest income quintile
- 38% receive disability benefits; 35% receive old-age benefits

4: Low-educated and rural disabled or inactive (8%)

- 58% are inactive and another 42% report their labor market status as disabled
- 56% are female
- 83% are 35–64 years old
- 66% report strongly limited capacity to work
- 54% have at least one working adult in household
- 40% live with at least one parent
- 60% have never worked
- Low-skilled: 59% have not completed upper secondary education
- 69% live in rural areas
- Moderate poverty risk: 31% in poorest income quintile
- 50% receive disability benefits

5: Unemployed rural single youth (7%)

- 88% are unemployed
- 74% are male
- 90% are 20–29 years old
- 87% live with their parent(s)
- 96% are without a partner
- 73% have at least one working adult in household
- 15% have worked before; 3 years of work experience on average
- 82% live in rural areas
- Very high poverty risk: 47% in poorest income quintile
- 56% receive family/child benefits

6: Middle-aged low-educated unemployed (5%)

- 81% are unemployed
- 86% are male
- 75% are 35–59 years old
- 48% have a partner who is not working; 25% do not have a partner
- Low to mid-skilled: 47% have not completed upper secondary education; 48% have completed upper secondary
- 49% live in households with dependent children
- 66% live in rural areas
- High poverty risk: 41% in poorest income quintile
- 57% receive family/child benefits; 28% receive unemployment benefits

Source: World Bank staff analysis based on EU-SILC.
Note: "Years of work experience" refers only to those individuals who have worked before. "Dependent children" include children younger than 18 years of age and household members ages 18–24 years who are economically inactive and living with at least one parent. "Working adult" refers to adults ages 24 years and older.

An advantage of the panel analysis is to provide information on the flow of individuals among clusters and in and out of employment. Table 8.7 shows the flow of individuals into each cluster of out-of-work population or into employment in 2010 according to their labor market status in 2008. Between 2008 and 2010, 94 percent of the employed remained at work. Indeed, there is

Table 8.7 Romania: Composition of 2010 Clusters Based on 2008 Labor Market Status (Column Percentages)

Cluster	Working-age population in 2010	Labor market status in 2008					
		Unemployed	Retired	Disabled	Other inactive	Employed	Total
1	Low-educated rural inactive women without work experience	6	1	31	45	1	9
2	Retirees	4	52	7	2	2	9
3	Early retirees and inactive with previous work experience	3	43	14	12	2	9
4	Low-educated and rural disabled or inactive	1	3	41	5	0	2
5	Unemployed rural single youth	19	0	0	4	0	1
6	Middle-aged low-educated unemployed	26	0	0	1	1	2
NC	Employed	42	2	7	32	94	68
	Total	100	100	100	100	100	100

Source: World Bank staff analysis based on EU-SILC.
Notes: Students ages 16–24 years who were inactive or unemployed are excluded from the sample. Numbers referred to in the text appear shaded in gray.

Table 8.8 Romania: Composition of 2010 Clusters Based on 2008 Labor Market Status (Row Percentages)

Cluster	Working-age population in 2010	Labor market status in 2008					
		Unemployed	Retired	Disabled	Other inactive	Employed	Total
1	Low-educated rural mothers without work experience	3	1	4	85	7	100
2	Retirees	2	81	1	3	13	100
3	Early retirees and inactive	1	63	2	20	14	100
4	Low-educated and rural disabled or inactive	2	21	26	45	6	100
5	Unemployed rural single youth	46	0	0	49	5	100
6	Middle-aged low-educated unemployed	59	0	0	7	34	100
NC	Employed	2	0	0	8	90	100
	Total	4	14	1	16	65	100

Source: World Bank staff analysis based on EU-SILC.
Notes: Students ages 16–24 years who were inactive or unemployed are excluded from the sample. Numbers referred to in the text appear shaded in gray.

also an interesting flow into employment among those who were unemployed or inactive. In 2010, 42 percent of those who were classified as unemployed and 32 percent who were classified as inactive in 2008 were found to be employed.

On the other hand, table 8.8 shows the labor market status in 2008 for each cluster and at-work population in 2010. Two main results emerge. First, for the cluster of *unemployed rural single youth*, 46 percent were already unemployed in 2008, which might reflect difficulties in entering the labor market for those starting professional careers. Second, the *middle-aged low-educated unemployed* were the most affected by employment losses, with 34 percent of them employed in 2008.

Box 8.1 Roma Population and Labor Market Exclusion in Romania

Labor market exclusion in Romania cannot be discussed without giving special consideration to the situation of the country's Roma population, a population that faces significant structural barriers. Because EU-SILC data do not include a differentiating indicator for Roma and non-Roma, the groups of out-of-work population identified in this latent class analysis exercise cannot directly be linked to a Roma/non-Roma pattern. A World Bank analysis titled *Diagnostics and Policy Advice for Supporting Roma Inclusion in Romania* (World Bank 2014) provides a more focused analysis of the current situation of Roma in Romania, including the employment dimension.

According to the most recent (2011) national census information, approximately 612,000 citizens declared themselves to be of Roma origin living in Romania (corresponding to 2.9 percent of the total population). This number reflects the lower bound of estimates, because many Roma choose to not report their ethnicity in surveys. A 2010 estimate from the Council of Europe put the number of Roma in Romania between 1.2 million and 2.5 million, corresponding to 5.7–11.9 percent of the population. However, an increasing share of new labor market entrants come from Roma families: depending on the estimates of the Roma population[19]; between 6–20 percent of labor market entrants in Romania today are Roma. As the working-age population in Romania is projected to fall by 30 percent by 2050, this share is expected to grow.

Members of the Roma minority are poor, vulnerable, and largely excluded from labor market opportunities in Romania. According to the UNDP/European Commission/World Bank regional Roma survey (2012), in 2011 the at-risk-of-poverty rate for Roma was 84 percent, in contrast with 31 percent among non-Roma families living nearby, and with a national at-risk-of-poverty rate of 22 percent. In the same year, the employment rate of the Roma stood at only 42 and 19 percent, against 66 and 53 percent (respectively) for men and women within the general population. Among the employed Roma, jobs are unstable and informality is abundant: the regional Roma survey (2012) shows that only about 36 percent of Roma employment[20] is formal (based on a written contract or legal business documents) and includes health and pension insurance. The survey also shows that unemployment rates are also disproportionately high among Roma, standing at 28 and 43 percent for Roma men and women, respectively. The high rates of joblessness and unstable employment do not reflect preferences: the vast majority of Roma express a desire for stable jobs, similar to the responses by non-Roma neighbors, with 74 percent of Roma men and 76 percent of women reporting a preference for "Secure employment but low paid" instead of "Having a higher income but insecure and irregular."

Unfavorable labor market outcomes among the Roma population can be in part explained by a significant education and skills gap between Roma and non-Roma, which starts early in life: in 2011, Roma enrollment in preschool education stood at 37 percent, compared to 63 percent for non-Roma children living nearby. Roma children's opportunities for skills development are further hindered by the high level of classroom-level segregation of Roma pupils, with nearly a quarter of Roma children currently attending basic education in classes where

box continues next page

Box 8.1 Roma Population and Labor Market Exclusion in Romania *(continued)*

most of the children are Roma. Not surprisingly, only 10 percent of Roma adults report having completed secondary education in 2011, compared to 58 percent of the non-Roma living nearby. In addition to the skills gap, discrimination and other barriers also hinder the employment of Roma: according to the Roma regional survey, among Roma who looked for work in the past five years, 30 percent report that they experienced discrimination because of their ethnicity, while only 11 percent of non-Roma living nearby report the same.

The number of identified Roma who participated in Active Labor Market Policies implemented by the Romanian Public Employment Service in 2013 stood at 72,000 (MLFSPE communication to EC DG EMPL, May 7, 2014). About 4,200 persons were placed in employment (60 percent in permanent and 40 percent in temporary contracts). Another 600 individuals were referred to training courses, counseling services, or wage-subsidy schemes. In 2013, two persons of Roma origin benefited from labor force mobility support, according to MLFSPE.

Roma inclusion is not only a moral imperative, but also smart economics for Romania. With an aging population, pension and health care costs are bound to increase in the near future. Equal labor market opportunities could enable faster *productivity growth*, and could contribute *fiscal benefits* through increased revenue from taxes and lower social assistance spending. According to a World Bank estimate on the basis of 2008 data (World Bank 2010), assuming an equal number of working-age Roma men and women, and that average wages in the economy remain unchanged, equalizing labor market earnings in Romania for Roma could result in potential economic benefits ranging between EUR 887 million and 2.9 billion annually, and fiscal benefits ranging between EUR 202 million and 675 million annually. In addition, the social and economic inclusion of Roma is essential for Romania to meet its EU2020 targets, as Roma are significantly poorer and more vulnerable than the non-Roma.

Source: World Bank 2010, 2013, 2014.

From Profiling to Activation

Activation and Inclusion Policies in Romania

Activation and inclusion policies in Romania operate on a very low level of spending and are mainly articulated around European programs. Policies for social inclusion include a whole range of social assistance benefits that are often categorical in nature (EC 2013) and are not well targeted to the poorest sections of the population (only 17 percent of the social assistance spending reached the poorest income quintile of the population in 2009) (ibid.). A guaranteed minimum income (GMI) program is better targeted but has relatively low coverage of the poor (ibid.). With the onset of the economic crisis and ensuing austerity measures, benefit levels and budget allocations have been reduced a number of times. Strategies for the coordination of social inclusion between policy areas are often formulated in strategic documents for EU funds but are "not visible in the implementation" (ibid.).

Labor market integration is (in theory) supported by activating design features of the GMI. The design of the GMI program in Romania in theory supports formal paid employment by anchoring the benefit well below a market wage rate and offering a simple working benefit component. In reality, this work incentive is probably not large enough to offset potential earnings from parallel informal employment (ibid.).

Nominally, the National Employment Agency (NEA) is tasked with delivering public employment services and activation policies. Functioning under the authority of the Ministry of Labor, Family and Social Protection, the agency operates 41 county offices and more than 150 local offices, as well as regional and national training centers. While a number of priorities for training and activation have been articulated, the number of participants in active labor market programs actually decreased after the start of the crisis (in line with falling budget allocations, see figures 8.11 and 8.12 (ibid.).

From the Annual Employment Action Plan of the NEA, a number of ALMPs can be derived; but measurement of effectiveness appears limited (EC 2013). With an overall beneficiary base of 1.4 million in 2011, among the measures listed by the NEA are the following (all placement data for 2011):

- *Job fairs.* About 360,000 jobseekers are reported to have found employment after attending one of the job fairs. Job fairs are organized for specific categories of jobseekers: young graduates, single professions, Roma, and so on.
- *General counseling and job orientation.* This form of service reportedly helped approximately 65,000 jobseekers into employment.
- *Training courses.* These were offered for 35,000 participants, of whom 14,000 are reported to have been subsequently placed in employment.
- *Job subsidies.* Different job subsidies are reported to have brought 27,000 participants into employment.

Figure 8.11 Labor Market Policy (LMP) Beneficiaries in Romania
Number of individuals

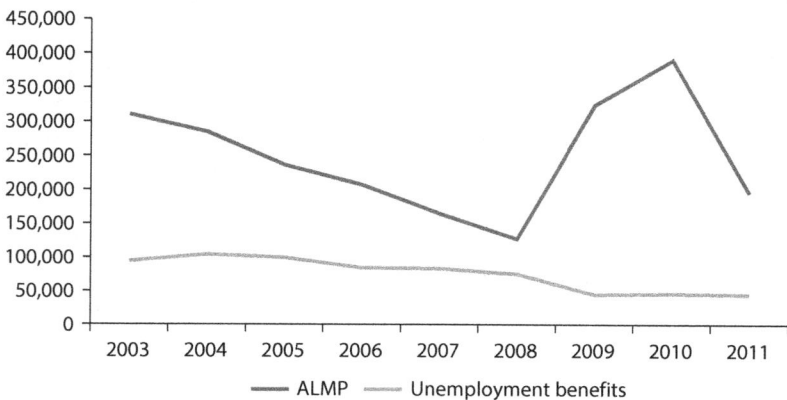

Source: Eurostat, OECD.

Figure 8.12 Composition of Spending on ALMPs in Romania, 2008 and 2011
Euro millions

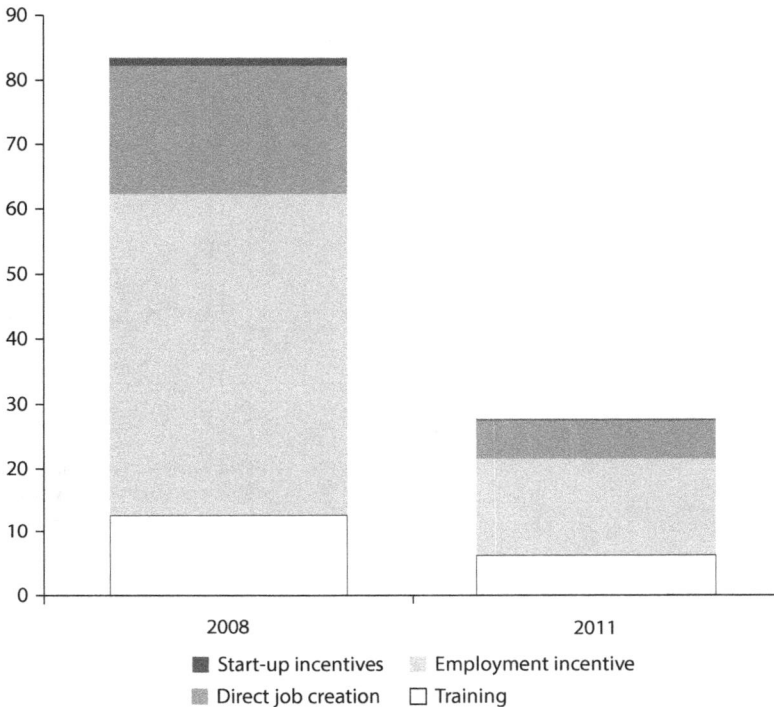

Source: Eurostat, OECD.

- *Various other measures.* These include mobility grants, incentives for graduate employment, and business start-up support; all were reported to have led to fewer than 5,000 employment placements.

Since spending on labor market policies is very low in Romania, passive policies make up the bulk of spending. The economic crisis of 2008 precipitated a downward trajectory in spending on ALMPs in Romania, which last stood at 0.029 percent of GDP, one of the lowest figures in the EU. Passive payments for unemployment benefits responded to the uptake in unemployment during the crisis starting in 2008. They have receded since, being subject to cuts in benefit levels and tightening of eligibility requirements (figure 8.13).

Activation Priority, Activation Type, and Benefit Receipt by Group
When further considering the approach toward labor market integration, an assessment of the priorities and potentials of the identified groups needs to be undertaken. Given the precarious low level of resources for activation programs in Romania, further prioritization of intervention is all the more important.

Figure 8.13 Labor Market Policy (LMP) Spending in Romania as a Share of GDP
percent

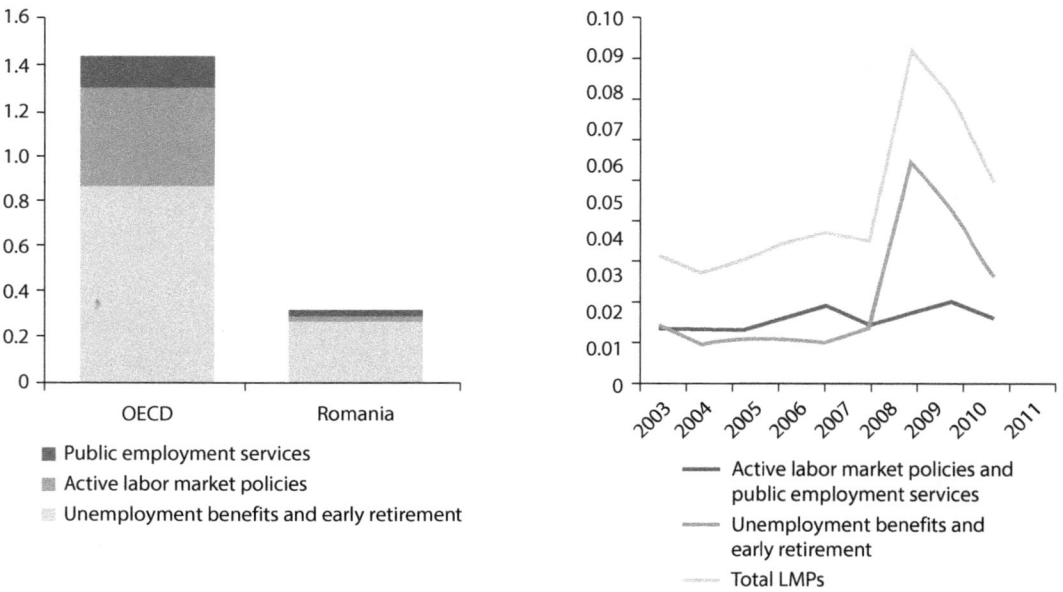

- ■ Public employment services
- ▦ Active labor market policies
- ▨ Unemployment benefits and early retirement

— Active labor market policies and public employment services
— Unemployment benefits and early retirement
···· Total LMPs

Source: Eurostat, OECD.

This prioritization does not alleviate any of the pressure to increase funding for a minimum set of intermediation and activation services in the country.

After a *first step* ("activation priority") of prioritizing the intervention along activation need and activation potential, a *second step* ("activation type") will attempt to classify the groups according to the kind of activation intervention needed, depending on social or labor market barriers to be overcome. Lastly, as a *third step*, information on *household income composition* of the different groups will be used to assess potential cross-dependencies of the benefit system with the labor market status and activation approaches.

Activation Priorities

Table 8.9 gives an overview of the identified inactive classes and their respective activation need and activation potential. The total number of persons estimated in these clusters was about 4.1 million in 2011, representing 31.2 percent of the working-age (16–64) population of Romania.

In the table, *activation need* refers to a group's level of need for inclusion in the labor market in order to achieve income and reduce or end poverty. This parameter is mainly driven by the poverty exposure of the household. *Activation potential* describes that group's ability or motivation to be included in the labor market. A high activation need could be driven by high poverty risk (as in the case of the *working-age long-term unemployed*) whereas a high activation potential could be driven by previous work experience or a relatively good educational

Table 8.9 Activation Need and Potential of Different Clusters in Romania

Share % (2011)	Cluster	Activation need	Activation potential	Priority for action
24	Retirees	Low	Low	Low
24	Early retirees	Low	Medium	Low
19	Low-educated rural mothers without work experience	High	Low	Medium
15	Inactive middle-aged wives	High	Medium	Medium
7	Long-term unemployed educated single youth	High	High	High
5	Working-age long-term unemployed	High	Medium	High
3	Working-age newly unemployed	Medium	High	Medium
3	Low-educated and rural disabled	Medium	Low	Low

Source: World Bank staff analysis and assessment 2014.

base (for example, the *long-term unemployed single youth*). Overall priority for action can also be supported by the size of the group. In the end, this matrix is a base for rationalizing a further policy discussion, and not an arithmetic exercise.

From this overview, a set of five priority groups arises: *low-educated rural mothers without work experience, inactive middle-aged wives, long-term unemployed educated single youth, working-age long-term unemployed,* and *working-age newly unemployed* are classified as high or medium priorities for activation. Their high priorities for activation stem mainly from high activation needs, as expressed by strong exposure to poverty. At the same time, they show (potential) labor market proximity by having acquired an education, by not having declared an inability to undertake daily activities, and by falling into the prime-age bracket (compared to the large groups of retirees and the small group of disabled). *Retirees, early retirees,* and *low-educated and rural disabled* are not prioritized for activation measures or policies due to their lower activation need (having reached official retirement age) and potential (many report strong limitations on capacity to work).

When reviewing the receipt of disability benefits among the identified groups, a problematic constellation can be identified for the *early retirees*. While only 1 percent of the group declares disability as their labor market status and 28 percent of the group report strong limitations in activities because of health problems, 49 percent of the group's members receive disability benefits. A review of the disability/retirement status of this group could be an additional discussion item when translating the findings from this analysis into possible policy action. While it might be difficult to activate some of the members of this group out of their disabled and prime working-age status (92 percent are between 35 and 59 years), special attention should be paid to not increasing the number of younger disability recipients beyond the absolute minimum necessary, and to tightly controlling inflow into this group.

Activation Type

As a second step, the relative severity of labor market or social obstacles to be overcome for labor market integration serves as an orientation for activation

Figure 8.14 Activation Types of Prioritized Clusters in Romania

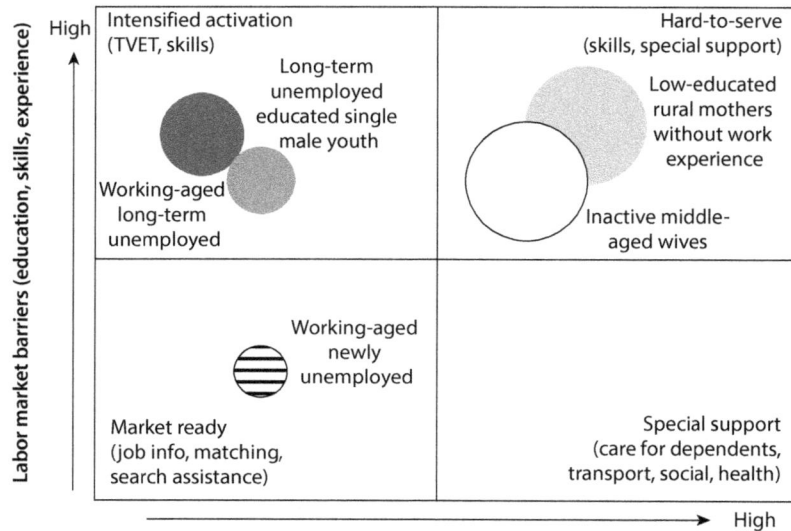

Source: World Bank staff analysis and assessment 2014.
Note: TVET = technical and vocational education and training.

approaches. Figure 8.14 depicts the prioritized clusters along the labor market and social barrier dimensions; the size of the bubbles corresponds to their relative group size.

When mapping the respective barriers for labor market integration faced by the five prioritized groups, we can see that most of them are quite removed from the labor market by virtue of their long inactivity, generally low qualifications, or lack of work experience. The two female groups face higher social barriers as to the availability of child care. Among the other three groups (which are more male-dominated), the *working-age newly unemployed* can (for now) be regarded as a more "market-ready" group. The two long-term unemployed groups mainly face labor market and mobility barriers.

Household Income Composition

When analyzing the 2011 household income of the prioritized groups, we can see that only a few groups show a benefit share of household income that could be an indication of excessive reliance on benefits: As already indicated, 49 percent of *early retirees* report receiving disability benefits while only 1 percent report their labor market status as disabled and only 28 percent report strong limitations activities because of health problems. Other groups (*working-age long-term unemployed* or *low-educated and rural disabled*) also have high benefit shares, but this can be seen as a correct function of the social safety net because of legitimate limitations on self-supporting work. However, the fact that the unemployed groups (*long-term unemployed educated single youth, working-age long-term unemployed*, and *working-age newly unemployed*) only receive an unemployment benefit in 8, 21, and 16 percent of cases, respectively, could be interpreted as a sign of a safety net or insurance dysfunction.

Given the overall picture of benefit receipt revealed by EU-SILC data, the greatest need for action emerges around a potential review of disability benefit allocation among early retirees and on the adequacy of the unemployment benefit, especially for the "market-ready" newly unemployed groups.

Suggestions for Activation Measures and Further Analysis

This section sets out a set of potential activation measures for each of the priority groups. Areas for further policy dialogue are also outlined. The suggestions below should be considered as a *starting point for further policy dialogue* between EC DG EMPL, the World Bank, and the Romanian authorities, bearing in mind that the groups identified still carry some heterogeneity that may affect the level and type of support required. Accordingly, these suggestions are also not meant to be an exhaustive set of possible activation measures.

It is important to keep in mind that the groups have been derived from the 2011 EU-SILC. Since that time, general economic development, policy actions by the government of Romania, and European Commission country-specific recommendations might have already reflected some of these policy suggestions or rendered them obsolete.

Low-educated rural mothers without work experience (19 percent, Priority: High). Owing to the relatively young age of this group, it received an A priority. This is the largest among the prioritized groups in Romania (776,000 members). It is almost exclusively female (99 percent) and 77 percent rural. No member of this prime-aged group declared herself as unemployed. Overall, there is little work experience in this group (78 percent of its members have never worked). Eighty-six percent of the group has at most a primary or secondary education.

- *Offer short "second chance" schooling with a focus on professional skills.* Given the fact that the secondary schooling of this group's members did not translate into an immediate job start (most probably owing to family formation and child-care responsibilities), and 75 percent of the group are between 16 and 34 years old, labor market activation could be based on linkage to simple, short, vocationally oriented school degrees. Ideally, these courses would be offered for about six months in local or regional schools or vocational schools. Child-care offerings would need to be provided in parallel to the courses. For older women, potential "second chance" training, schooling, or entrepreneurship offerings for this group will need to build on the "life experience" and skills already acquired by them.

- *Improve child-care offerings (partly through self-organization).* Improved availability of child-care and school after-care offerings would enable many of the women in this group to better participate in the labor market and to take part in professional training or entrepreneurship offerings. Some of the child care could be delivered via supported cooperatives from within the same group of women.

- *Provide short-term work placement combined with training offerings.* In proximity to urban or regional centers, potential beneficiaries from this group could be linked in short-term work placement programs.

Inactive middle-aged wives (15 percent, Priority: Medium). In terms of its makeup, this group is similar to the previous group, the *low-educated rural mothers without work experience.* The *inactive middle-aged wives* are also rural, are a bit older, have slightly more work experience and a slightly higher share of secondary education (54 percent). Their rate of marriage is also higher (85 percent) and they have slightly smaller households (an average of 4.0 members instead of 4.7). Households with children represent 64 percent of the cases, but the share of children younger than six years of age is only half of the previous group (20 vs. 43 percent). Owing to the great distance from the labor market of this group, any activation measure will have to start with very basic professional skills and will need to include self-organization and community approaches toward this group of women.

- *"Second chance" programs with focus on professional skills.* For this group of middle-aged women, potential "second chance" training, schooling, or entrepreneurship offerings will need to build on the "life experience" and skills already acquired instead of focusing on remedial school education.
- *Community-based social work and entrepreneurship education.* Given the structure of the local economy, self-employment, cooperative structures, and entrepreneurship approaches need to be an important part of any labor market integration approach. Potential beneficiaries from this group could be assisted in forming cooperatives for local (social) services with support for professionalization.
- *Social community self-organization and entrepreneurship.* Potential employment opportunities for women from this group can also be generated through new and regional-based forms of community self-organization and entrepreneurship. Groups of women could be assisted to form and operate cooperatives for local services (domestic, child care, elderly care, and so on).
- *Short-term work placement combined with training offerings.* In proximity to urban or regional centers, potential beneficiaries from this group could be linked to short-term work placement programs.

Long-term unemployed educated single youth (7 percent, Priority: High). This group is made up mainly of men (66 percent) younger than 35 years of age who have very little work experience (almost 90 percent have never worked). Despite a decent level of education (24 percent of the group has a tertiary degree), this group appears to have never taken root in the labor market in the first place. The rural/urban split is only about 50/50 but at least the urban portion of this group could be helped to better link to available employment in large cities and regional centers. Despite mostly living with their parents, this group represents the highest share of the lowest income quintile (48 percent). Potential activation measures for this group include, but should not be limited to, the following:

- *(Renewed) work placement in the field of study or specialization.* Building on any initial experience or exposure to a specific professional (in technical education) or academic field, the members of this group could be linked to the labor market again via subsidized work placement with companies for a limited amount of time.
- *Entrepreneurship support.* Given the fact that some of this group's members have relatively good formal and academic skills, the potential for self-employment and small firm creation should be supported.
- *Community activism support for inactive youth.* To prevent "scarring" and further distancing from the labor market or any other form of activity, some members of this group could benefit from community-based and publicly supported volunteering or community types of work.

Working-age long-term unemployed (5 percent, Priority: High). This group is between 25 and 59 years old and 72 percent male. Again, the rural/urban split is 50/50, potentially supporting integration and attachment to employment for those in urban or regional centers. Educational attainment is mainly upper secondary (61 percent), with some 11 percent having tertiary education. The members of this group have an average of 15 years of work experience prior to their current unemployment. Potential activation measures for this group include, but should not be limited to, the following:

- *Build on work experience for training and work placement.* Taking into account the years of work experience and potential industry or trade knowledge of the members of this group, training measures combined with temporary work placement in companies, nonprofits, or social enterprises could help to strengthen labor market attachment.
- *Support self-organization, entrepreneurship, and cooperatives.* As with some of the other groups, self-employment and entrepreneurship support can help some of this group's members to attain self-sufficient lives and improve their welfare.
- *Strengthen social and functional skills.* Building on any initial experience or exposure to a specific professional (in technical education) or academic field, the members of this group could be linked to the labor market via subsidized work placement with companies for a limited amount of time. In these placements, and the accompanying training, special emphasis should be placed on social and functional skills, foreign language, information and communications technology skills, and so on.

Working-age newly unemployed (3 percent, Priority: Medium). This small group registers the highest proportion of formally unemployed (75 percent), testimony to the recent beginning of their unemployment spell and a potential indicator of immediate interest in work. Men form the majority (68 percent) but women make up a third of the group. The group is majority rural and has mainly achieved a secondary education. With 15 years of work experience and recent attachment to formal employment, this group will mainly need to be supported with mainstream job-search and self-mobilization assistance. Potential activation measures for this group include, but should not be limited to, the following:

- *Job placement support via PES or private employment agencies.* Given the fact that this group of jobseekers is still quite close to the labor market because of the recent beginning of unemployment, initial support could be focused on skill certification, application support, and job-matching intermediation.

In general, further policy dialogue with the Romanian authorities ought to focus on the general level and setup of resources devoted to labor market integration and activation of the inactive and out-of-work. Within this discussion, a deeper conversation could be had around specific measures for specific groups. The following three items appear especially important:

- *Integration with employment demand generation.* While active labor market policies, activation, and job-matching support can help to smooth friction in the labor market, they will not lead to stable and sustainable employment. Demand for jobs comes from the economic activity of firms and from the social sector. Integration with regional economic development policy is especially important.
- *Bring "active" programs to scale.* Reviewing the distribution between active and passive labor market spending as well as the overall spending level on productive inclusion will be a necessary prerequisite for any of the measures described in this note.
- *Calibrate focus from "unemployment" to "inactivity."* While the headline unemployed stood at about 5–6 percent in Romania over the last few years, the identified inactive groups in this analysis represented over 30 percent of the working-age population.

In summary, Romania could benefit from improving its knowledge of the composition and socioeconomic situations of different groups of out-of-work citizens, especially with a unified view across traditional labor market categories (employed/unemployed) and social inclusion dimensions (poverty, living conditions, access to services), because the two are intrinsically linked, especially for the labor market's most marginalized participants.

Notes

1. Prior to the crisis, the labor force participation rate in 2008 was 62.9 percent. In 2013, it reached 64.6 percent.
2. In 2013 this rate was 82.4 percent.

3. Individuals ages 16–24 years who are out of work and enrolled in education are considered to be investing in their final stages of human capital formation and therefore not a particular target group for activation policies. In 2011, this population amounted to about 1,517,000 individuals, representing 58.5 percent of the total population ages 16–24 years and 27 percent of the total out-of-work population of working age.

4. For the latest developments on active inclusion in Romania, see EC (2013b).

5. This variable is constructed using the self-reported current work status in the EU-SILC survey that has four categories: at work, unemployed, retired, and inactive. The unemployed are further classified into short- and long-term based on how long they have been actively looking for a job. The inactive is combined with another question to separate this group into students, disabled, military, and other inactive.

6. To construct this variable, individuals 25 years of age or older are considered adults.

7. This is a binary variable that takes the value one if an individual answered "yes, strong limitations" to whether they had been hampered in their usual activities because of health problems for at least the last six months. The value is zero if the answer is "yes, limited" or "no, not limited."

8. The equivalized household income takes into account an equivalence factor to weight the number of household members used in the denominator when calculating household income per capita. The first adult 18 years of age or older has a weight of 1.0, children younger than 14 years old have a weight of 0.3, and other individuals 14 years of age and older have a weight of 0.5. The sum of the weights of all household members is equal to the equivalent household size.

9. Note that income reported in EU-SILC surveys is for the year preceding the survey year.

10. Total household gross income is defined as the sum of: (at the individual level) gross employee cash or near-cash income; company car, gross cash benefits or losses from self-employment (including royalties); unemployment benefits; old-age benefits; survivor benefits; sickness benefits; disability benefits; education allowances; and (at the household level) income from rental of property or land; family/children related allowances; social exclusion not elsewhere classified; housing allowances; regular inter-household cash transfers received; interests, dividends, profit from capital investments in unincorporated business; pensions from individual private plans; and income received by youth younger than 16 years of age. Total household net income, in turn, was calculated by subtracting from total household gross income regular taxes on wealth, taxes on income and social insurance contributions, and regular inter-household case transfers paid.

11. Social benefits are aggregated in eight branches using the European System of integrated Social PROtection Statistics (ESSPROS) definitions. For more information, see Eurostat (2011).

12. According to EU-SILC guidelines, dense areas have more than 500 inhabitants per square kilometer, where the total population for the set is at least 50,000 inhabitants. Intermediate areas have more than 100 inhabitants per square kilometer, and either a total population for the set of at least 50,000 inhabitants or a location adjacent to a dense area. The remaining areas are categorized as sparsely populated.

13. The EU-SILC longitudinal survey consists of a four-year rotating panel. In each year, approximately three-quarters of individuals present in the previous year are retained. The samples used in the latent class analysis include about 3,000 observations for each year in the cross-sectional analysis and 500 observations in the longitudinal analysis. The population is weighted with individual weights.

14. The retirement age in Romania is 59 for women and 64 for men.

15. Risk of poverty is here understood as the relative probability of living in the poorest income quintile. By definition, 20 percent of the population lives in this quintile; risk is thus gauged relative to a benchmark of 20 percent.

16. With the exception of 2009, when the early retirees were grouped together with a number of "other inactive" individuals and grew to represent 32 percent of the out of work. This group is thus labeled as *early retirees and inactive* in 2009.

17. Before 2010, the only group identified as long-term unemployed consisted of youth.

18. As previously mentioned, the current retirement age in Romania is 59 for women and 64 for men.

19. Estimates range from 535,140 (National Census in 2002) to [730,000–970,000], according to a Romanian Government and World Bank 2005 survey called "The Roma Communities Social Map," to 1,850,000, according to the EU Communication "An EU framework for National Roma Integration Strategies up to 2020," based on the data from of Council of Europe. Source: *Strategy of the Government of Romania for the Inclusion of the Romanian Citizens Belonging to Roma Minority; 2012–20.*

20. The employed are defined as those who declared that they worked at least one hour last week (only 36 percent of the working-age population).

References

Collins, L. M., and S. T. Lanza. 2010. *Latent Class and Latent Transition Analysis: With Applications in the Social, Behavioral, and Health Sciences.* Hoboken, NJ: Wiley.

Dimitrov, Y., and N. Duell. 2013. *Activating Vulnerable Groups in Bulgaria.* Washington, DC: World Bank.

EC (European Commission). 2013a. "EU Measures to Tackle Youth Unemployment." MEMO, Brussels.

———. 2013b. "Assessment of the Implementation of the European Commission Recommendation on Active Inclusion: A Study of National Policies: Country Report—Romania." DG Employment, Social Affairs & Inclusion, European Commission, Brussels.

Eurofound. 2012. *NEETs—Young People Not in Employment, Education or Training: Characteristics, Costs and Policy Responses in Europe.* Luxembourg: Publications Office of the European Union.

Eurostat. 2011. *ESSPROS Manual: The European System of Integrated Social Protection Statistics.* Luxembourg: European Union.

Government of Romania. 2014. Romania Pension System, Mimeo.

Katz, L. 2010. "Long-Term Unemployment in the Great Recession." Testimony for the Joint Economic Committee, U.S. Congress Hearing on "Long-Term Unemployment: Causes, Consequences and Solutions." April 29.

Kaufman, L., and P. J. Rousseeuw. 1990. *Finding Groups in Data.* New York: Wiley.

Magidson, J., and J. Vermunt. 2002. "Latent Class Modeling as a Probabilistic Extension of K-Means Clustering." Quirk's Marketing Research Review, March 20, 77–80. http://statisticalinnovations.com/technicalsupport/kmeans2a.htm.

UNDP and EU FRA (Fundamental Rights Agency). 2012. *The Situation of Roma in 11 EU Member States*. Survey Results of the UNDP, World Bank, and EC Regional Roma Survey at a Glance. Vienna: UNDP and EU FRA.

Vermunt, J. K., and J. Magidson. 2005. *Latent GOLD 4.0 User's Guide*. Belmont, MA: Statistical Innovations Inc.

World Bank. 2010. "Roma Inclusion: An Economic Opportunity for Bulgaria, Czech Republic, Romania, and Serbia." Policy Note Europe and Central Asia Region Human Development Sector Unit, Washington, DC.

———. 2013. *Gender at a Glance. Romania*. Washington, DC: Europe and Central Asia Region Poverty Reduction and Economic Management Sector Unit.

———. 2014. *Diagnostics and Policy Advice for Supporting Roma Inclusion in Romania*. Washington, DC: Europe and Central Asia Region, Human Development and Sustainable Development Sector Units.

CHAPTER 9

Proceedings of Workshop in Brussels

A results workshop on the Portraits of Labor Market Exclusion (PoLME) study was held in Brussels, Belgium, on May 26, 2014. The workshop's title was "From comprehensive profiles to tailored activation policies" and was jointly organized by the World Bank and the European Commission in order to present potential themes for discussion derived from the study and receive inputs from national delegations and policy experts.

The list of participants included government counterparts from the participant countries of Bulgaria, Estonia, Greece, Hungary, Lithuania, and Romania; policy experts and desk officers from DG Employment, Social Affairs and Inclusion; participants from other EC DG's and experts from the OECD, the Institute for the Study of Labor (IZA), and the Hungarian Academy of Sciences.

In their opening remarks to the workshop, Dr. Lieve Fransen (Director for Social Policy and Europe 2020 at the European Commission's DG Employment, Social Affairs and Inclusion) and Mamta Murthi (Country Director for Central Europe and the Baltic Countries at the World Bank) provided a setting for the day's discussion. In their remarks, they outlined the cooperative approach between the Member States, the Commission, and the World Bank in achieving the results of the "Portraits" analysis. Dr. Fransen highlighted that the workshop participants would have the dual possibility not only to understand and challenge the applied methodology, but also to exchange insights on approaches in social and labor market policy and national programming of European funds. Ms. Murthi framed the workshop's policy relevance by underlining the demographic challenges for most European countries and the importance of integrated competiveness, labor demand, and labor supply policies.

Following the introduction, the World Bank PoLME Project Team presented two sessions during the workshop. During the morning session, Ramya Sundaram discussed the methodology as well as some of the results and limitations of the study. In the afternoon session, Ulrich Hoerning presented the main findings of the cluster analysis and some policy ideas for activation, based on the clusters' needs, potentials, and priorities for activation.

Speakers from the national delegations also contributed presentations. They partly confirmed initial assessments from the joint country missions of the European Commission and World Bank, validating country-specific findings and methodology, while identifying greater needs for dialogue and analysis about potential policy responses and activation approaches for different profiles. The main points from each country presentation and the general plenary discussions are summarized as follows.

Greece

The Greek representative presented the country's national strategies to tackle youth unemployment. The focus of the presentation was on the group of highly educated youth that is not in employment, education, or training (NEETs).

As shown in figure 9.1, there are different programs to support youth employment, lifelong learning, and entrepreneurship in Greece. It was shown that the majority of the beneficiaries of the National Action Plan (NAP) receive guidance or job orientation, and another considerable share benefit from support in the transition from education to work and from vocational education to training.

Figure 9.1 Greece: Highly Educated Youth Not in Employment, Education, or Training

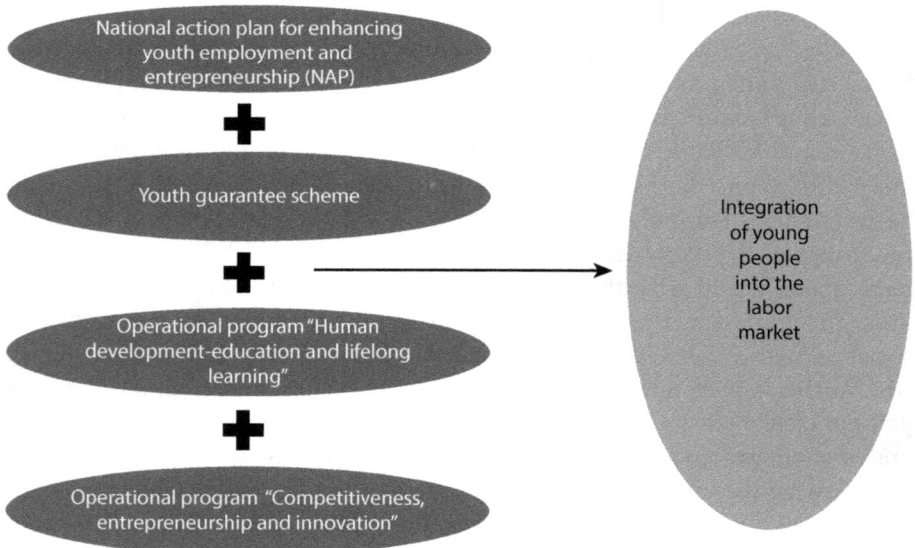

Source: Presentation of Greece at "Portraits of Labor Market Exclusion" workshop in Brussels, May 26, 2014.

For the period of 2014–20, NAP target groups will include young people not in employment, education, or training; unemployed 30- to 64-year-olds; long-term unemployed; unemployed individuals with low educational qualifications; jobless households; working mothers facing the risk of unemployment; and other vulnerable groups.

Lithuania

Officials from the government of Lithuania presented the country's experience with measures for reducing youth unemployment. As shown in figure 9.2, factors related to youth unemployment are lack of work experience, lack of motivation, and displacement, while some factors accounting for its reduction are skills matching, job creation, and increase in employability.

In Lithuania, youth unemployment has been decreasing, with youth participation in ALMPs almost doubling in size, from 16.2 percent in 2011 to 31.3 percent in 2013. In 2012, integrated solutions were implemented to reduce youth unemployment, such as vocational guidance (career planning) services, labor market services and labor market monitoring, analysis and evaluation. These initiatives involved different ministries: the Ministry of Education and Science, the Ministry of Social Security and Labor, and the Ministry of Economy. The success of these measures is reflected in the decreasing youth unemployment rate, from 35.7 percent in 2010 to 21.9 percent in 2013, according to the country presentation.

Figure 9.2 Lithuania: Youth Unemployment Reduction

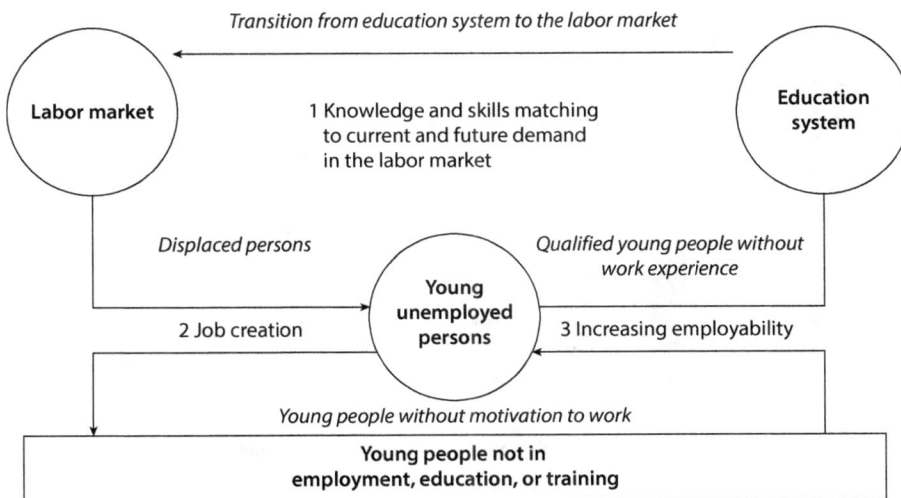

Source: Presentation of government of Lithuania at "Portraits of Labor Market Exclusion" workshop in Brussels, May 26, 2014.

Estonia

The Estonian representative discussed a reform in Estonia's incapacity for work scheme. Because individuals with some level of incapacity are willing to work and employers are ready to hire them, there was a discussion on how to provide a more individually oriented approach and adapt the work environment for such people. Another change Estonia has made is in the evaluation mechanism for applicants, which now focuses on a person's work ability and not their incapacity for work.

The graph shown in figure 9.3 depicts the number of persons with permanent incapacity and those in employment, disaggregated by the level of permanent incapacity. It was shown that disabled people will get improved attention, with one managing authority—the Unemployment Insurance Fund—being responsible for the evaluation of work capacity, benefit payments, and the delivery of labor market services, rehabilitation, and technical aid.

Romania

The Romanian delegation presented some details of the country's social assistance system reform. Two main points are highlighted in figure 9.4: the Modernization Project and a new benefit called "Minimum Insertion Income."

The idea behind the modernization of the social assistance system is to strengthen performance management, improve equity, improve administrative efficiency, and reduce error and fraud. The new system, which will combine three benefits into only one, is expected to start by January 2016.

Figure 9.3 Estonia: Reforming Incapacity for Work Scheme

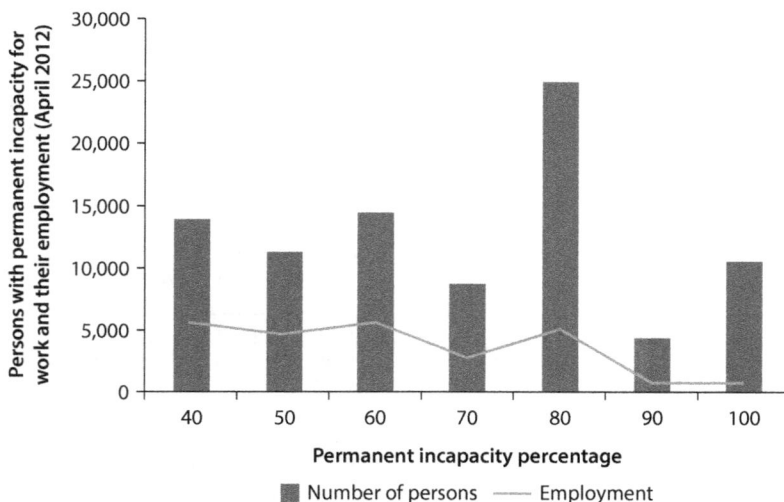

Source: Presentation of government of Estonia at "Portraits of Labor Market Exclusion" workshop in Brussels, May 26, 2014.

Figure 9.4 Romania: The Reform of the Romanian Social Assistance System

Social assistance system modernization project (SASMP)
• Focus on the main governmental programs for low-income households, persons with disabilities and families with children;   • Developed through a loan agreement between the government of Romania and the International Bank for Reconstruction and Development (IBRD or World bank);   • Implementation timeframe: April 2012–August 2016;   • Project value: 500 million euros-equally shared between 20 disbursement linked indicators (DLIs) of 25 million euros each;   • DLIs: reflect the tangible measures that have to be implemented;
New benefit
The minimum insertion income (MII) :   • Three benefits consolidated into one-guaranteed minimum income (GMI), family allowance (FA) and heating benefits (HB);   • Current number of beneficiaries: – GMI – 225,000 families;   – FA – 260,000 families;   – HB – 1,000,000 families;   • MII aims at targeting the poorest 30% of population;   • Following the legislative process, the new benefit will come into effect January 2016.

Source: Presentation of government of Romania at "Portraits of Labor Market Exclusion" workshop in Brussels, May 26, 2014.

Representatives of Romania also highlighted some activation incentives that have been attached to existing benefits: requirements related to school attendance, which is now compulsory for children in households receiving a family allowance (FA); an increase in the guaranteed minimum income (GMI) by 15 percent if one member of the household is in the labor market; and fiscal incentives for employers hiring elderly persons.

Hungary

The Hungarian representatives discussed the trends in their labor market indicators and highlighted gaps between their performance and the performance of the EU-28 countries (figure 9.5).

Despite lagging labor market performance, they pointed out that active labor market programs have been in the forefront since 2007. They presented the Social Renewal Operative Program 1.1.2, whose objective is to improve the employability of a number of disadvantaged groups with personalized,

Figure 9.5 Hungary: Active Labor Market Programs—Good Practices to Prevent Labor Market Exclusion

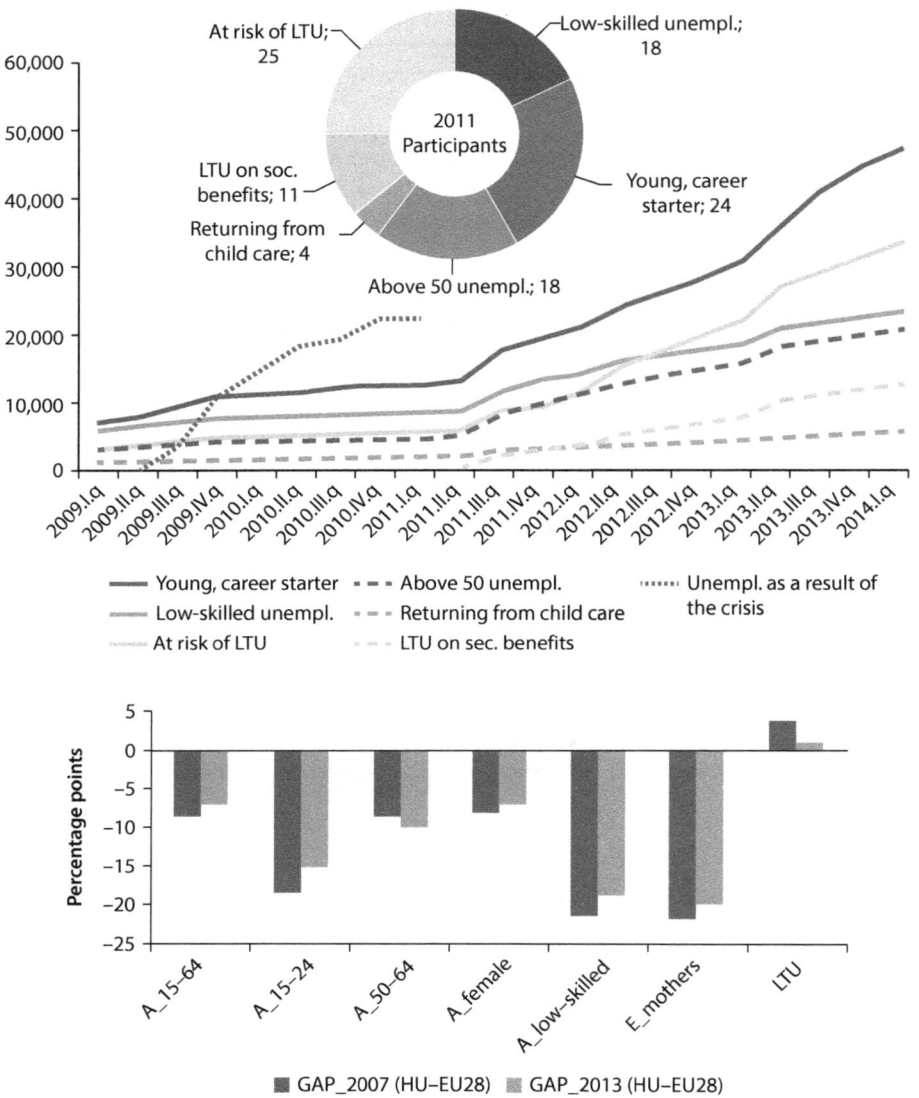

Source: Presentation of government of Hungary at "Portraits of Labor Market Exclusion" workshop in Brussels, May 26, 2014.
Note: Eurostat; A = Activity rate; Low-skilled = ISCED 0–2; E = Employment rate; Mothers are defined as females (age 15–64) with two children less than 6 years old; LTU= Share of long-term unemployment in total unemployment.

tailor-made, complex labor market programs: the low-skilled, young and career-starters, those over 50 years of age, those returning from child care, and those receiving social benefits.

Some of the main program elements are: wage subsidies, mobility support, training support, training cost subsidies, child care during training, and services such as counselling, orientation, information provision, mentoring, and entre-preneurship support. County labor offices have developed their own local program plans, matching the target groups' needs and reflecting local opportu-nities. Labor offices have developed individual, tailor-made program plans together with the participants, reflecting personal potentials and challenges. The program has a decentralized financial allocation mechanism, reflecting local labor market's employment situation.

For the second phase of the program, the expected result is the inclusion of a minimum of 110,000 participants, with a minimum of 16,500 Roma people; 32 percent of the participants will be young people. As of July 2014, 132,659 participants had already been included, of which 19,561 were Roma.

Bulgaria

The government of Bulgaria presented some measures that have been taken to increase activity rates. They showed trends in their inactive population, which represented a major challenge in the context of the economic crisis. In Bulgaria, the inactivity level was among the highest in the European Union in 2010.

Policies have focused on training. There are two main programs: the national program "Active Inactive Persons" (some details shown in figure 9.6) and the grant scheme "Take Your Life in Your Own Hands," which focuses on increasing the activity and integration of vulnerable, inactive, and discouraged people into the labor market.

Salient Points from the Plenary Discussions

Methodological questions focused on the urban/rural divide described in many country reports of the Portraits. Here participants were interested in the EU-SILC base data's ability to adequately measure the welfare of subsis-tence farming rural households. Other comments focused on the prevalence of "passive" benefits in many countries, benefits that do not carry an incentive for work uptake. Disincentives for (formal) work were further reported to be aggravated in many countries by the wide use of informal work arrangements. Another element of interest raised during the discussion was the phenome-non of the "in-work-poor" (which is a challenge for many Member States but was not captured by the current Portraits analysis because of a focus on the inactive and unemployed). All of the Member States presentations elicited a series of questions and comments from the participants. Discussions arose around the policy approaches to worker incapacity insurance. Strategies of identifying and reclassifying working incapacity benefit recipients were dis-cussed. Also, the role of employers in labor market integration of hard-to-place groups was a major point of interest. On the level of potential interventions, Member State experts underlined the need to link any labor supply side

Figure 9.6 Bulgaria: Measures for Integration of Inactive and Discouraged People

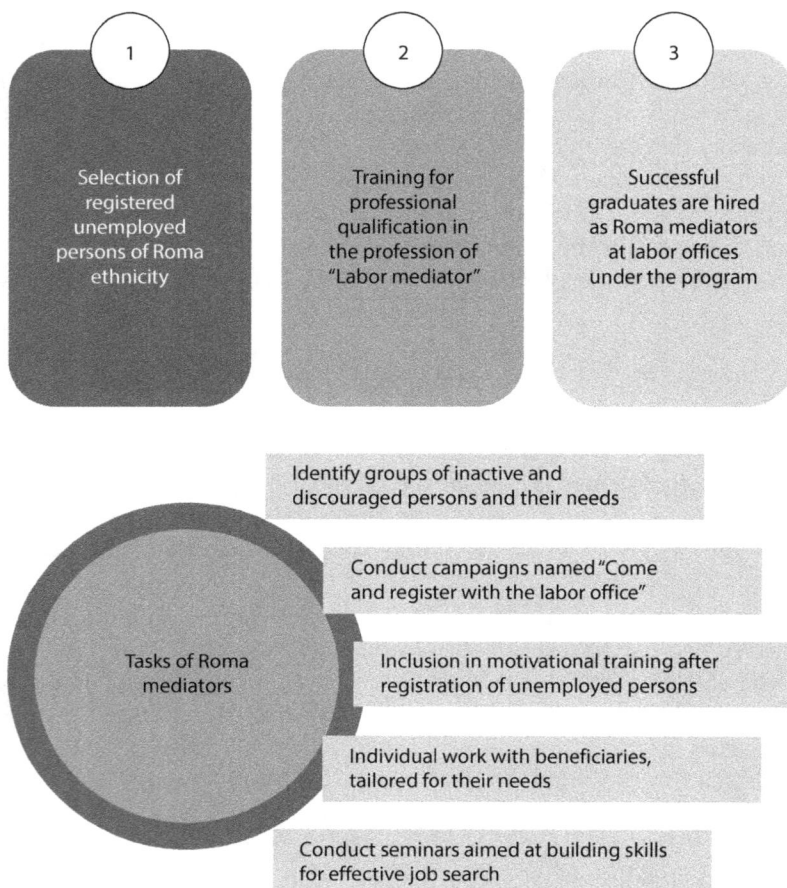

Source: Presentation of government of Bulgaria at "Portraits of Labor Market Exclusion" workshop in Brussels, May 26, 2014.

support with general economic development promotion policies and to focus entrepreneurship support on individual recipients who would show a chance to succeed in a competitive market. Also the need to enhance the positive interaction between various policies for successful labor market growth was underlined.

External Experts' Points of View

After the country presentations, academic experts commented on the findings, the methodology, limitations, and potential areas for further improvement. The first to speak was Prof. Werner Eichhorst, Director of Labor Policy Europe, IZA, followed by Dr. Zsombor Cseres-Gergely, from the Hungarian Academy of

Sciences, Center for Regional and Economic Studies, Institute of Economics. Among the salient points of comment were the following:

- Recognized the attractiveness of a holistic approach around social protection and labor policies;
- Underlined that heterogeneity still remains within the clusters, so deriving latent class analysis (LCA) profiles for policy planning does not substitute for individualized service provision to the citizen (in balance with fiscal afford-ability and administrative capacity);
- Stressed the importance of whole-economy/labor-demand side reforms to provide the economic dynamic to absorb the unemployed and inactive;
- Recommended application of a more extensive analytical approach to deriving policy recommendations from the descriptions of the profiling, underlining the need to address all levels of policy action: (a) whole-economy reforms, (b) program-level ALMP type interventions, and (c) benefits and services to individual citizens.

More specifically, Prof. Eichhorst commented that while the excluded out-of-work population has expected characteristics such as low skills, lack of work experience, health problems, age and gender, rural background, and so on, there are some new and interesting findings from the clusters, such as the urban/rural divide, the highly skilled unemployed in Greece, the new population of prime-aged unemployed in Lithuania, the increase in the number of disabled and early retirees. Yet, the high heterogeneity within clusters indicates that individual needs within each group may be quite different. Hence, he cautioned that there is a risk of neglecting relevant target groups or subgroups when using LCA-type clustering to identify activation potentials and priorities. In a social investment context, no individual should be left behind, he said. Therefore activation policies should consider all policy action levels, from overall structural policies to medium-level ALMPs-type interventions and tailor-made policies derived from individual assessments.

Prof. Eichhorst also emphasized that the analysis is based on data from 2011, and that more recent or ongoing changes may be relevant to setting policy. He concluded that structural issues seem to be more relevant than cyclical ones and that more attention should be paid to these general, structural policies and the policy recommendations derived from them. Many of the policy suggestions derived from the Portraits profiles are focused only on the program level, but structural policies have the potential to affect all the groups. Among the struc-tural policies he mentioned that should receive more emphasis: the importance of stimulating labor demand and its flexibility; removing disincentives to work, particularly for second earners and benefit recipients; and measures that tackle early retirement and urban mobility, among others.

Dr. Zsombor Cseres-Gergely pointed out that LCA is more comprehensive than "ordinary" analysis. Nevertheless, it is a very complex method, intuitive only at a very basic level, and carries with it values and theory implicit in the choices of indicators, active and passive variables, and number of groups. Despite its limitations and complexity, Dr. Cseres-Gergely recognized that the analysis is a pragmatic way of looking at individuals through the lenses of both poverty/welfare status and labor market indicators. He concluded that there is an important connection between these fields. He also remarked that the analysis could be repeated locally, and might be initiated by building capacity for regular, high-quality, in-depth analysis.

In closing remarks, Andrew Mason (Manager for Social Protection in Europe & Central Asia at the World Bank) and Dr. Lieve Fransen (Director at the European Commission's Directorate General for Employment, Social Affairs and Inclusion) highlighted several points that emerged from the discussion. Speaking in broader terms of the World Bank's analytical and policy dialogue work in countries in and beyond the European Union, Mr. Mason strongly appreciated the feedback received from the Member State delegations and academic experts. Fitting into the Bank's work on efficient and equitable social safety nets across the region, a further development of the Portraits approach would need to reflect an improved analysis of individual life and benefit situations as well as a broader range of possible policy recommendations.

In her final remarks, Dr. Fransen mentioned the general quality of the analytical tool and its embedding into the dialogue between the Member States and EC, as well as the quality of the discussion with Member States throughout the project, was appreciated. While there is still the need to derive a more differentiated set of policy responses and not settle for simplistic policy prescriptions for certain demographics, she remarked on the usefulness of the Portraits methodology. Portraits-type analysis is a tool that could be used in the future for "social investment" choices in Member States, and it also has the potential to be used in performance monitoring for ESF activities between the European Commission and Member States, she said.

Appendix A: Link to Online-Only Annexes

Online-only appendixes appear on the World Bank's Open Knowledge Repository:

https://openknowledge.worldbank.org/bitstream/handle/10986/21632/PLMEannexes.pdf

green
press
INITIATIVE

www.ingramcontent.com/pod-product-compliance
Lightning Source LLC
Chambersburg PA
CBHW080415270326
41929CB00018B/3029